FRENCH EXPLORERS
IN THE PACIFIC

FRENCH EXPLORERS
IN THE PACIFIC

BY

JOHN DUNMORE

II

The Nineteenth Century

OXFORD
AT THE CLARENDON PRESS
1969

Oxford University Press, Ely House, London W. 1

GLASGOW NEW YORK TORONTO MELBOURNE WELLINGTON
CAPE TOWN SALISBURY IBADAN NAIROBI LUSAKA ADDIS ABABA
BOMBAY CALCUTTA MADRAS KARACHI LAHORE DACCA
KUALA LUMPUR SINGAPORE HONG KONG TOKYO

PRINTED IN GREAT BRITAIN

CONTENTS

LIST OF MAPS

THE NAPOLEONIC ERA

THE CHANGING SCENE

MARCHAND had been unfortunate in returning to France as the main shock-waves of the Revolution and Counter-Revolution broke over the provinces. By the middle of 1794, however, Robespierre had fallen, and internal troubles were soon over-shadowed by the successes of French armies along the north-eastern frontier, leading to the conquest of Holland and the establishment of the Batavian Republic. The power of the old revolutionaries waned as Napoleon's star began to rise: the Convention was dis-solved in 1795; Napoleon conquered Italy in 1796. This is not to say that improvements in the internal condition of France kept in step with the changing fortunes of her armies abroad. Victories in Holland and Italy were costly, in spite of Napoleon's efforts to live off the conquered lands, and the weight of taxation and the spiral of inflation continued to disfigure the economy. Little wonder then that, rejoicing at the stability the recent victories seemed to promise, the citizens voted into power in 1797 a right-wing majority committed to curbing the army. But if criticism of the generals could be permitted at all—and Napoleon soon showed it could not—right-wingers, associated in the minds of many with reaction and a yearning for a monarchical system, were the last who could be allowed to voice it. The parliamentary majority was overthrown, and Napoleon went on to distract attention by his Egyptian campaign. When this, in spite of some brilliant initial successes, turned into a failure, he returned to France to quieten nascent discontent by a judicious mixture of reforms and firmness. The *coup d'État* of 1799 ended ten years of chronic instability. France's destiny was to remain linked with his for the next fifteen years.

One consequence was to direct attention to colonial matters and to the East—not because of any settled or coherent colonial policy —but as a way of weakening Britain's trade or increasing her isolation. France's own colonies had anyhow drawn attention to themselves during the Revolutionary period. The colonists in particular had welcomed the possibility of constitutional changes. They had sent deputies from the Indian settlements to the Constituent Assembly as early as 1790; two came from the Île de France in February 1791. What the Revolution appeared to promise was the establishment of local councils and some measure of local autonomy. A constitution was in fact adopted in the Île de France in April 1792, giving power to the assembly to levy taxes, and accepted by the new governor, Malartic. A similar development followed in India, a local assembly being set up in Pondicherry, while elsewhere, by formal agreement or in practice, the powers of the governors became subordinated to the decisions of the municipalities.

Since economic and cultural considerations made a complete break with Paris undesirable, the situation might have continued quite happily had it not been for the question of the franchise. The Constituent Assembly's main concern was not a radical measure such as the abolition of slavery, but the granting of voting rights to coloured freemen. This moderate proposal met with strong opposition in the colonies and was soon set aside; but in the rich island of Santo Domingo 50,000 negro slaves rose against their masters in a bloody uprising lasting from August 1791 to February 1793. This disquieting piece of news led the Assembly in Paris to restore its earlier decree granting the vote to coloured freemen. It solved nothing, for by now pressure was building up for the complete abolition of slavery.[1] Leaving aside the problem of compensation—and a sweeping abolitionist decree in February 1794 made no provision for this at all—it was a proposition totally unacceptable to the white colonists, for with the granting of universal franchise it would simply have put the emancipated slaves in power. The deputies for the Indian Ocean islands were successful in getting the application of the decree delayed, but in Santo Domingo French colonists appealed to the British, who promptly landed troops on the island, setting in motion a long and bloody sequence of war, repression, and

[1] Out of 300 books written on colonial problems between 1789 and 1800 250 are concerned with slavery. Gaffarel, *La Politique coloniale en France*, p. 9. '

devastation, which ended ten years later with the total overthrow of French rule and the creation of the first independent negro republic.

In the Indian Ocean a quite different situation developed. The French India Company had been revived in 1785, but had made little headway. Quarrels on precedence divided the settlements of Chandernagore and Pondicherry. The question was soon decided by the British, who captured Pondicherry in August 1793 and the other towns shortly after. French adventurers retained some degree of influence at a number of native courts, but only for a limited period. The Mahratta Confederation obtained the services of Benoit Leborgne, later Comte de Boine, a soldier of fortune who had served in Russian and British forces as well as in the Île de France; he raised an army for the Mahratta leader Sindiah and defeated the Rajah of Jaipur in 1792; an able administrator as well as a good military leader, he was shrewd enough to retire in 1796, taking his fortune with him. Another Frenchman, one Raymond, commanded a force in French uniforms for the Nizam of Hyderabad. Tipu Sahib at Seringapatam encouraged refugees from Pondicherry to settle in his capital and form a Jacobin club; acting on their advice, he asked for French assistance against the British and the Mahrattas, and Bonaparte drew up plans for the dispatch of 15,000 men from Suez; but Tipu's death in May 1799 ended France's hope of regaining a military foothold on the Indian continent. Only in distant and troubled Cochin-China did the future hold any distant promise: there a politically minded missionary, Pigneau de Behaine, adviser to Emperor Gia-Long, was laying the foundations of French Indo-China.

Thus the focus of French policy in the East could only be the Île de France and its sister isle of Bourbon, both of which remained loyal until their eventual capture by the British in 1810. The degree of local autonomy which the unsettled situation in France made possible perfectly suited the colonists. When a troublesome decree, such as the one abolishing slavery, was received from Paris, it was simply ignored; the negroes were not told, and no trouble resulted. Indeed, slaves here do not appear to have been badly treated by comparison with their less fortunate fellows in other colonial territories. Arago, who visited Port Louis in 1818 after similar stays in Rio and the Cape commented of Mauritius: 'Had I seen slaves only in this place, I would have believed their condition good enough to wish it on most of our workers.'[1] The cause of moderation was further helped by the fall of Robespierre. The local republican group, which had gone so far as to set up a guillotine at Port Louis, was overthrown, and the colonists, led by the moderate Malartic, breathed more freely. When representatives of the Directory arrived in 1796, they were prevented from landing and unceremoniously sent home. However, Malartic stifled a number of tentative moves towards greater autonomy and even independence; their appeal anyhow was limited as the islands were enjoying considerable prosperity, a good part of it the result of raids on British shipping. After the fall of Pondicherry, Cornwallis and his squadron had returned to Europe, leaving only one sloop to protect shipping, so that, until the end of 1794, French raiders from Port Louis could roam at will through the Indian Ocean, inflicting heavy losses on English Indiamen. Even with the arrival of a new squadron and the fitting out of a number of India Company ships as cruisers, the French were able to continue their profitable raids: they could by then refit in the Dutch colonies. But Malartic died in 1800; his successor Decaen, who arrived in 1803, returned the islands to the control of the metropolis, and a consequently greater challenge to British colonial interests then thrust the islands into a dangerous limelight.

While circumstances virtually kept France away from the Pacific, other nations were continuing their efforts there. Spain's tenuous claims to the North-West Coast had suffered through the Nootka incident, but the Russians began a gradual descent along the Alaskan coast. Baranof founded Novorosiisk in Yakutat Bay in 1796. A settlement at Sitka followed in 1799; destroyed by the Indians, it was restored in 1804. This period of Russian expansion also witnessed the voyages of Bellingshausen, Kruzenstern, and Lisianski. Spain did send out Bustamente and Malaspina in 1791, and Caamaño in 1792, but her position in the Pacific was being

[1] *Promenade autour du monde*, vol. i, p.195.

constantly eroded. Trade between Acapulco and Manila languished; the Philippines remained undeveloped—so much so that the French planned at one time to open negotiations for the cession of the islands. Her place was being filled more and more by the United States, whose merchants became active in the Pacific from the 1790s, seeking furs and trading with China and Hawaii, while Lewis and Clark were to set out for the Rockies and the Pacific coast in 1804, preparing the way for an eventual challenge to Russian expansion.

At the same time, the British were strengthening their hold in Asian waters. They had occupied Penang in 1786, and seized Dutch Malacca in 1795. The weakness of the Dutch East India Company opened new possibilities for trade and expansion. French intervention prevented further encroachments by the British, but the Dutch proved resentful and, with some justification, suspicious of proferred military aid. Sercey in 1796–7 and Linois in 1803–4 were received with ill grace; the Twelfth Battalion, sent from the Île de France and stationed in Java from 1797 to 1802, fared little better. In Canton, most of the trade was controlled by the British—China's best customers. A suggestion made to Napoleon for a French embassy to Peking, to get the British excluded from the China trade, came to nothing. Meanwhile, the British settlement in New South Wales was making slow but sure progress: by 1800 the population—not all of it real settlers, it is true—had reached the 6,000 mark. In the Pacific itself, the evangelical London Missionary Society sent its first missionaries to Tahiti in 1795, and soon after the Anglican Church Missionary Society began to establish its own missions. There was very little that France, embroiled in the European struggle, could do either here or in the Far East.

The key was naval power: good bases, good ships, and well-trained, well-disciplined men. These the French did not have. The Revolution had resulted in the loss, by desertion or dismissal, of many good officers, while attempts to develop a classless democracy on board the ships had simply created chaos. Even after the fall of Robespierre the situation improved but slowly. In Toulon, in 1795, local riots broke out as soon as it was proposed that the fleet should sail and leave the town relatively unprotected. The seamen themselves, in no hurry to leave their sheltered position for the dangers of the open sea, joined the mob and threatened to march on Marseilles. Order was restored, but by then large numbers of sailors had deserted. It was little consolation to the naval chiefs of staff to learn in the following year that the British Navy was having similar problems. The abortive expedition to Ireland failed in large part because the French Navy was poorly organized: 'such as the French navy had become, through the loss of its heads and the vagaries of the legislature, such it sailed on the expedition to Ireland'.[1] The improvements that followed the gradual return to normality and the rise of Napoleon had little effect on the Navy. By 1798 all French ports were being blockaded and, while this could hardly prove fully effective, it was enough to cripple maritime trade. All that was left was privateering. But this indeed flourished:

From St. Malo to the Texel, a distance of over three hundred miles, the whole coast became a nest of privateers of all kinds and sizes— from row-boats armed only with musketry and manned by a dozen men, or even less, up to vessels carrying from ten to twenty guns and having crews of one hundred and fifty. In the principal Channel ports of France alone, independent of Belgium and Holland, there were at one time in the winter of 1800 eighty-seven privateers, mounting from fourteen to twenty-eight guns, besides numerous row-boats.[2]

Under these circumstances, it is not surprising that France could only organize and equip one expedition to the Pacific between the fall of Robespierre and the end of the First Empire; nor was it likely that such an expedition could escape from the troubles and disorders so prevalent in the metropolis.

[1] Mahan, *The Influence of Sea Power*, vol. i, p. 350.
[2] Ibid., vol. i, p. 207.

BAUDIN

THE true motives behind the Baudin expedition have remained a matter of controversy. Baudin sailed at a time when mistrust and suspicion poisoned all fields of human endeavour, and when the most obvious activities were interpreted as subtle diplomatic moves. His voyage can easily be ascribed to a desire for scientific and geographical discoveries at a time when Napoleon wanted to impress Europe with his interest in non-military questions—the cultural offensive is a familiar feature of authoritarian governments. At the same time, this motive can in turn lead to confusion and over-simplification. It is somewhat misleading, for instance, to state, as some have done, that the expedition sailed under the patronage of the Emperor, since Napoleon did not assume that title until two months after the expedition had returned to France; although, in view of the power held by Bonaparte in 1800, when it sailed, there is no denying that Baudin could never have left without his personal approval.

What must be borne in mind is that the expedition was Baudin's own idea, a 'projet de voyage' for exploration of part of the South Sea having been drawn up by him and forwarded to the Minister of the Navy as early as 1798, when Napoleon was in Egypt. Although the times were still unstable and consideration of the plan was delayed by financial difficulties, the Institut National, to which the proposal had been referred, set up a committee to examine it; among its members were Fleurieu—who probably played his usual major part in drawing up the instructions,[1] Bougainville, and the scientist Lacépède. In April 1800 the committee had drawn up its own 'plan de voyage', stressing that it was along the Australian coast that the greatest expanse of uncharted territory lay.[2]

[1] See E. Scott, 'Baudin's Voyage of Exploration to Australia', *English Historical Review*, Apr. 1913, p. 343.

[2] The sequence is as follows: the Committee examined Baudin's suggestion in March 1800, and a delegation called on Napoleon on 1 April; Napoleon gave

The proposed expedition, considered the Institute, would be 'most interesting for the sciences as well as for politics. It is important for France to become well acquainted with the two straits which divide New Holland—from Van Diemen's Land in the south, and from New Guinea in the north. This consideration alone would be a sufficient motive to decide on this expedition'.[1]

Was the delay between Baudin's original proposal of 1798 and its eventual acceptance in a modified form two years later due to the normal processes of the administration under the Directory, to economic difficulties, to the war—or to an indifference that was not banished until Napoleon came on the scene and realized the political advantages that could derive from the exploration of an unknown tract of land in an enormous continent? The British had begun to settle in the eastern regions, but it was not too late to forestall them in the comparatively unknown south and west. To the British this last motive seemed the more likely one; their belief was strengthened by the publication of the first volume of the official account by François Péron in 1807, with an English translation in 1809. In it Péron, for purely personal reasons, never mentions Baudin by name; he does not ascribe the original conception of the voyage to the Institute. To the British, locked in a great struggle with the French Empire, the expedition appeared to have been planned, not by a scientifically minded sailor at a time when Napoleon was only a successful general, but by an ambitious head of state. The instructions themselves, reprinted by Péron, revealed the hope held at the time that Australia might be not one continent, but two: '[We were] to visit the part of the continent masked by these islands [St. Peter and St. Francis] where it was supposed that a Strait existed communicating from this point with the bottom of the Gulf of Carpentaria, which, in consequence, would have cut New Holland in two great islands of practically equal size.'[2]

his approval in principle six days later (Faivre, *Expansion française*, p. 104). The Institute then drew up detailed plans at the end of April, and these were approved by the Minister of the Navy, and, one presumes, by Napoleon himself, soon after.

[1] E. Scott, op. cit., p. 343.
[2] Péron, *Voyage de découvertes*, vol. i, p. 5. Péron himself had no doubts about

The natural inference was that the French hoped to found a settlement on the western island and even expel the British who had settled at Port Jackson. The exploration of the south coast and of Bass Strait was thus of interest not solely to the sciences but also, as the Institute had pointed out in the hope of attracting Napoleon's favour, to politics. It was also a survey of the quickest route from Pondicherry or the Île de France to Port Jackson, a near-indefensible settlement isolated from Europe and embarrassed by large numbers of convicts who could be expected to side with France if an attack eventuated.[1]

Whether all these considerations entered Napoleon's head when he approved the proposal is uncertain. The question must be kept in perspective, and viewed against the wider background of European politics. As we have seen, long before Napoleon there were Frenchmen interested in the economic and strategic possibilities of settlements and outposts in or near the Pacific, but it is easy to overestimate their influence. Certainly, Napoleon, aware of the impending struggle with England, had no objection to a project that could advance science, shed some glory on his administration, embarrass his enemies, and bring back reliable information about British plans in the Western Pacific. It is unwise to read more into Baudin's expedition than this; the voyage belongs to the tradition of scientific travel that went back to Bougainville; it is the last of the great adventures. What is certain is that, if the French were sent as spies, then never has a spy ring been so carefully camouflaged by layers of scientists, and never has a band of spies squabbled more, or been less efficient in the execution of its secret orders.

It is hard to say how much of the disruption which soon showed itself on board was due to Baudin's character, how much to the independent and quarrelsome spirit of the scientists, and how

the political basis of the expedition. 'Always vigilant in regard to whatever may humiliate the eternal rival of our nation,' he wrote, 'the First Consul, soon after the Revolution of 9 November 1799, decided upon our expedition.' Péron to Decaen, 11 Dec. 1803, quoted in H. M. Cooper, *French Exploration in South Australia*, pp. 193–4. Péron's reliability is limited to scientific subjects.

[1] For a study of the political possibilities, see Faivre, *Expansion française*, pp. 109–13.

much to the social upheaval of the time. Baudin was no Kerguelen
—he was driven by the determination to carry out his task at all
costs, even of his life. 'An old sea dog, hard towards himself and
towards others, a slave of duty, insistent on the strict observation
of the time-table—something which is difficult to work in with
the requirements of scientific work—heavy-handed towards the
younger men who were themselves unruly, disrespectful to the
point of insolence, certainly restless and determined to have their
own way',[1] he was nevertheless deeply interested in scientific
research, and thus all the more impatient of the younger scientists
—the most troublesome, François Péron, was only 25[2]—who in
turn despised him. Yet Baudin had already distinguished himself
on three botanical voyages when in the service of Joseph II,[3] and
led a scientific expedition to the West Indies from 1796 to 1798.

The success of this last voyage, during which he first evolved
his plan to explore the Australian coast, earned him the rank of
captain and the friendship of the scientists who had gone with
him—some like Mauger and Riedlé willingly accepting his
invitation to accompany him a second time.[4] His energy and
enthusiasm on the Australian voyage revealed once more his
ability, and his capacity for work over and above the ordinary
duties of a captain at sea: 'His journal', wrote Bory de St.-Vincent,
the zoologist, 'was an enormous bound volume opened out on
his table . . . This journal contained a multitude of drawings of
molluscs, fishes, and other items of natural history, painted with
a perfection and a lifelikeness that nothing can approach.'[5]

And yet Hamelin, who commanded the second ship of the
expedition, the *Naturaliste*, had far less trouble; there was a
difference in the atmosphere of the ships that cannot entirely be

---

[1] Bouvier and Maynial, *Une Aventure dans les mers australes*, p. 36.

[2] Baudin was 46. Péron, who had served in the Revolutionary Army in his
teens, had lost an eye in battle and had been taken prisoner before his nineteenth
birthday. His primary interest was anthropology.

[3] In 1786-9 and 1792. He was not an *émigré* but, having joined Joseph II's
service before the Revolution, he remained abroad until 1795.

[4] *Voyage aux Îles Ténérife, la Trinité, Saint-Thomas, Sainte-Croix et Porto Rico*,
by A.-P. Le Dru, was published in 1810 as a defence against Péron's implied
accusations. It praised Baudin's ability and courage on his earlier voyage.

[5] Bouvier and Maynial, *Une Aventure*, p. 83.

explained by the lesser responsibility borne by Hamelin. In addition, a high proportion of those who sailed with Baudin achieved high honour in later life, whereas Kerguelen's trouble-makers had relapsed into obscurity. A proportion of blame must fall on Baudin's shoulders, and the cause is probably his ill health—the pulmonary tuberculosis from which he died, and which made rapid progress in the cramped conditions of the ship. His task was not made any easier by the twenty-two savants—botanists, zoologists, mineralogists, painters, draughtsmen, and gardeners—who had been added to the expedition as a result of the enthusiasm of the Institute, or of their own string-pulling. The scientific equipment—including even a sextant once used by Cook—the additional personal luggage and extra stores created an *encombrement* that was a constant worry to him. When, in the later stage of the voyage, food became scarce, it did not relieve the pressure on space, for room then had to be found for the growing collections of natural-history specimens.

Apart from Baudin himself, the most important man on the voyage was Jacques-Félix-Emmanuel Hamelin, who was then 32 years old. He had, as frigate captain, taken part in the abortive French attempt to assist the Irish in 1796, and had led a number of brief cruises off the French coast, before requesting to join the Baudin expedition. He was eventually to reach the rank of rear-admiral, and to head the Dépôt des cartes et plans. Baudin's own second-in-command in the *Géographe* was Le Bas de Sainte-Croix, also a frigate captain; his astonomer was Pierre-François Bernier, a brilliant young mathematician from the École Polytechnique. Also in the *Géographe* was Pierre Gicquel des Touches—La Billardière's worthy 'citizen Gicquel', whose presence of mind and sharp eyes had saved d'Entrecasteaux's ships off New Britain in 1793, and whose name as a result appeared on French charts—now no longer a mere ensign, but a lieutenant. Two brothers served as ensigns—one to each ship, as was the custom—Henri de Freycinet and his younger brother Louis who was to be the later and somewhat partial historian of the expedition. To these must be added the name of Hyacinthe de Bougainville, who was one day, like his more illustrious father, to lead his own expedition

into the Pacific,[1] and of the ensign Cricq of the *Naturaliste*, a
nephew of Admiral Mazarredo y Salazar, the Spanish ambassador
to Paris and later Minister of the Navy under Joseph Bonaparte.
Among the scientists, Bory de St-Vincent and Leschenault de
la Tour were to achieve later fame; the latter, who spent three
years studying the flora of Java, was to undertake with the
blessing and protection of Sir Joseph Banks an epic six-year
voyage through India and Ceylon. Alexander von Humboldt,
already on his travels in South America, had hoped to join
Baudin's expedition, but circumstances were against it.

The two ships—the *Géographe*, 350 tons and 30 guns, formerly
named the *Galatée*, and the *Naturaliste* of a slightly smaller tonnage
and 20 guns, formerly the *Menaçante*—were copper-sheathed.
The smaller ship was also much slower, something which was to
be a source of constant irritation. They were both ready to sail in
October 1800, and on the 19th of that month, after a ceremonial
send-off, they sailed from Le Havre. Outside, the *Proselyte*, a British
frigate, stopped them to examine the passport which the British
Government had previously issued in their favour.[2] They proceeded to the Canaries, where trouble started; Baudin blamed the
scientists, 'whose knowledge is not so extensive as their numbers
would lead one to think'. The painter Lebrun came to blows on
the mole with the surgeon, while Henri de Freycinet, 'one of my
officers, and much too young to be one',[3] fell into bad company;
the departure from the port 'was not without its difficulties,
because all the scientists, wanting to know what was going on
on board or on the pier, were mixed in with all the manœuvres,
and impeded us infinitely'.[4] Already weary of the squabbling
youths, Baudin made up his mind to leave at the Île de France
those he considered the ringleaders. Unfortunately, at this stage,

---

[1] His father had lent him his journal of the first voyage to the Falkland Islands
to use as a model for his own. Note of H. de Bougainville, dated Aug. 1815, in
B.N., N.A.F. 9407–26.

[2] The passport had been granted 'without a moment's hesitation', wrote
Sir Joseph Banks to A. L. de Jussieu on 10 Aug. 1796. See Gavin de Beer, 'The
Relations between Fellows . . .', *Notes and Records of the Royal Society*, 1952, p. 257.

[3] Henri was 23, Louis 21.

[4] Baudin, Journal, 23 brumaire, an 9 (15 Nov. 1800).

he made an error of judgement that brought into question his ability as a sailor and helped to undermine his authority, so that only by being severe to the point of harshness could he retrieve it. He first of all sailed too close to the African coast, and found himself plagued by calms and contrary winds; then, hoping to make up for lost time, he sailed down to the thirty-sixth degree of southern latitude, where he hoped to find a southerly wind that would take him speedily to the Île de France; he found instead weak breezes and a strong north-westerly current. These setbacks resulted in the expedition taking five months, instead of the customary three, to reach Port Louis, arriving there on 15 March 1801. This unfortunate start had far-reaching consequences: too much food had been used during this passage, and little was obtainable in wartime from the Île de France; the health and the morale of the sailors were low, so that desertions were numerous; and, finally, the proposed itinerary had to be abandoned. According to the original instructions,[1] Baudin was to obtain a third ship at the Île de France,[2] and sail straight to d'Entrecasteaux Channel in Tasmania, there to survey in detail the various rivers seen by the French in 1792 and 1793 but not thoroughly examined at the time; he was then to sail around the north-east coast of the island to Bass Strait, which had been discovered in 1798. From there he was to begin sailing in a westward direction, completing the exploration of the entire length of the south coast of Australia as far as Cape Leeuwin, and thence, along the west coast, north to Timor. From this island he was to sail down the south-west and south coasts of New Guinea as far as Endeavour Strait, and return to Port Louis direct from the coast of Carpentaria.

As we shall see, the alteration of this plan, which was forced on Baudin by the delay incurred in the Atlantic, was to cost him the honour of being the first discoverer of many features of the coast of South Australia. And the third ship was quite out of the

---

[1] As published by Péron, *Voyage de découvertes*, vol. i, pp. 5–7.

[2] 'For the safety and success of captain Baudin's expedition, it would be advantageous if he had at his disposal a light vessel. . . .' Unsigned draft of a letter to the administrators of the Île de France, 30 Sept. 1800, B.N., Marine BB4–995.

question. The French in the Île de France had no intention of depleting their limited supplies by helping a scientific expedition which could bring them no relief or profit. Nor had they any respect for orders from France signed by ministers who, for all they knew, had already met their fate on the guillotine. The new arrivals insisted that General Bonaparte was bringing stability to the administration of France, but it was the sort of tale the colonists had heard before. There certainly did not appear to be much stability about the Baudin expedition: twenty officers and scientists were leaving it, some at the captain's request, others at their own; and, encouraged by local privateers, forty sailors deserted. Baudin's relations with the Intendant became so strained that they finally refused to meet, and resorted to communicating by letter. Eventually, Baudin realized that the local authorities had no intention of helping him; quite the opposite: they were trying to retain his ships and his crews for their own ends.

Unable to obtain funds from the French, Baudin finally succeeded in borrowing 10,000 piastres through a Danish captain, though at a rate of $33\frac{1}{3}$ per cent. To force the Intendant to bring back some at least of the deserters, he kept thirty negro slaves on board, knowing fully that the local authorities made a good income by renting their services to shipowners.

The two ships finally sailed on 25 April 1801, making east-south-east. Some of the weaker elements had been left behind, and there was, at any rate, more room to move about. In the expectancy of reaching a land where they would be able to engage in research, the scientists spent the following weeks in relative peace; it almost seemed as if the men left behind had been the sole cause of the dissensions. Australia was first sighted on 17 May in 34° 20′ of latitude,[1] which is practically that of Cape Leeuwin. After clearing up the question of the existence of the so-called St. Allouarn islands, Baudin followed the coast in a northerly direction—gone was the plan to sail to Tasmania; what now mattered was to get supplies from Timor. So impatient were the scientists to begin their work that they dredged the sea bottom, bringing up a variety of weeds, sponges, and corals;

[1] Freycinet, *Voyage de découvertes aux terres australes*, p. 4.

it was an excitement which Baudin, as keen on natural history as any of them, enthusiastically shared. On 30 May 1801 the ships anchored in what is now Géographe Bay, in latitude 33° 30′ east, not far from the present town of Busselton. Henri de Freycinet, the gardener Riedlé, and the mineralogist Depuch were the first to step ashore. A stay of well over a week was contemplated, and there would be opportunities to do some valuable work. Enthusiasm and impatience led to a tragedy. A lake or river had been seen inside Géographe Bay; it might provide entry into the hinterland. The longboat was sent, but a high wind prevented its return to the ship and it grounded. Lebas de Ste-Croix, Baudin's second-in-command, who was in charge, delayed his return in the forlorn hope of saving the boat, while Baudin sent him impatient signals. All that happened was that some of the materials sent to repair the craft had to be jettisoned, as did the plants and specimens collected by the naturalists; and, in attempting to load some of these, a sailor named Vasse was drowned.[1]

Baudin intended to survey the west coast of Australia on his way to Timor, and two meeting-places had been decided upon in case of separation—Rottnest Island off the mouth of the Swan River, and Dampier's Shark Bay further north. When, as Baudin had expected, the high wind developed into a gale, and the two ships were driven out of sight of each other, the *Naturaliste* sailed for Rottnest, where she arrived on 14 June. While waiting for Baudin, Hamelin dispatched one of the boats to explore the Swan River, while another travelled for fifty miles up-river from the estuary;[2] a survey was also made of Rottnest and of the nearby islands, which Freycinet was to name 'Îles Louis-Napoléon'.[3] The *Géographe* appeared on 18 June to the south-west of the anchorage, but the weather was bad and Baudin apparently failed to see the *Naturaliste*. Hamelin, realizing that Baudin had gone to Shark

[1] His name remains today in the Vasse river, and in the town of the same name, five miles south-west of Busselton—a greater honour to his memory than has been accorded to Baudin himself. There is, however, a tradition, told to local settlers by aborigines, that Vasse survived and lived in the area for some years. *Australian Encyclopedia*, vol. 2, p. 222.

[2] Freycinet, *Voyage*, p. 5.   [3] Ibid., p. 169.

Bay, promptly set sail, but by the time he arrived Baudin had already left for Timor. This series of errors did not end until the two ships eventually rejoined company at Timor, though neither vessel had wasted the intervening period. Baudin had reached Dirk Hartog Island on 23 June 1801; he entered the bay four days later by way of Géographe Channel and explored it, although no landing was effected on the 'Middle Island', which was not an island but a peninsula—Péron Peninsula. Some time was spent visiting the 'Sterile Islands' at the entrance to the bay—Dorré and Bernier islands—where the officers hunted the kangaroo and the naturalists gathered specimens. The inevitable clash occurred between Baudin and Péron, who, led by his usual enthusiasm, got lost ashore and caused the captain to waste a day waiting for him. On 14 July the *Géographe* sailed out, going north and north-east towards 'Witts' Land', which Baudin's instructions required him to survey. This work took nearly a month, from 20 July to 10 August 1801. A number of islands and features were discovered and named: Montebello Islands, Legendre Island, Thévenard Island, Cape Dupuy, Cape Lambert, Point Thouin, these names remaining today. Deprived of her consort and with too great a draught, the *Géographe* could not hazard herself too far between these small islands, for there was no one to come to her assistance if she should become grounded on a shoal or strike a hidden reef. Nor was the coast attractive: it was the low arid line of Eighty Mile Beach, with the great desert behind it. Shortly after this the *Géographe* reached the group of islands still known as Bonaparte Archipelago; on 14 August the expedition was off Cassini Island, near Admiralty Gulf: Cape Bougainville lay ahead, after which the coast would begin to run to the east. The choice was now between continuing the exploration to Arnhem Land and sailing north to Timor. 'At this time, the shortage of food and, especially, of drinking water made a respite imperative. The weariness of the crew, their exhaustion, the sickness that was already developing, were pressing reasons for forsaking an inhospitable coast. These considerations persuaded the commander to sail for Timor, where, moreover, he had hopes of meeting his consort.'[1]

[1] Freycinet, *Voyage*, p. 5.

Kupang was reached on 22 August 1801. The Dutch were co-operative—they were glad to see a friendly ship, as they had been attacked by the English during the previous year and were in fact so short of gunpowder that the Governor sent a message to

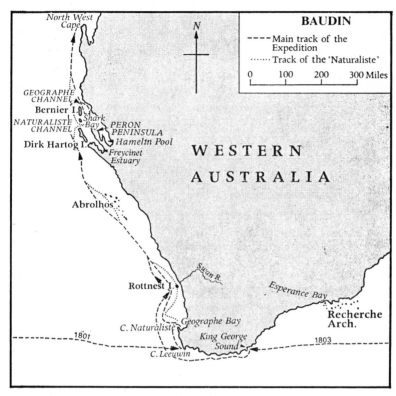

North West Cape

N

GEOGRAPHE CHANNEL
Bernier I.
NATURALISTE CHANNEL
Dirk Hartog I.
Shark Bay
PERON PENINSULA
Hamelin Pool
Freycinet Estuary

Abrolhos

Rottnest I.
C. Naturaliste
Geographe Bay
C. Leeuwin
Swan R.
King George Sound
Esperance Bay
Recherche Arch.

WESTERN AUSTRALIA

1801

1803

BAUDIN

- - - - Main track of the Expedition
· · · · · · · Track of the 'Naturaliste'

0   100   200   300 Miles

Map 1. Baudin: Western Australia

the French requesting them to omit the customary salute. The island was another rich hunting-ground for the naturalists, but it was also unhealthy—dysentery struck Baudin himself, Riedlé, and many others.

Meanwhile, Hamelin had been charting Shark Bay. The *Naturaliste* had arrived there on 16 July—only two days after Baudin's departure. Hamelin might just have caught up with the *Géographe* had he not delayed on the way to carry out a brief examination of Houtman's Abrolhos. The *Naturaliste* entered the bay by the channel north of Dirk Hartog Island—Naturaliste Channel. An observatory was established on Péron Peninsula, and boat and walking parties carried out a very thorough exploration of the large bay and its extremely indented coastline: a host of French names now commemorate their work—the main ones being Hamelin Pool to the east, which is separated by the sixty-mile-long Péron Peninsula from Henri-Freycinet Estuary. As Bouvier and Maynial point out in their history of the voyage, the two harbours should have been called Baudin and Hamelin, after the two captains;[1] it might be argued that Baudin did little work here and that it is fair that the name of Freycinet should be remembered since it was a Freycinet who was responsible for some of the best charting carried out in the bay, but Henri, whose name the estuary bears, was on board Baudin's ship—so that this is just another instance of the many slights done to the captain by his officers.

Having found and restored an inscription left by Vlamingh on Dirk Hartog Island, commemorating the arrival of the *Eendracht* in 1616, the French added a mention of their own visit. The *Naturaliste* had now spent over six weeks in the bay. On 4 September Hamelin sailed for Timor, and anchored in Kupang on 21 September, a month after Baudin's arrival.

Troubled by sickness and what amounted to a near-mutiny among his officers, Baudin sailed with both ships from Kupang on 13 November 1801. The southern summer was now approaching and it was time to go south. Forced out towards the west, the ships sailed in a wide arc down the Indian Ocean and towards Tasmania. Le Villain, the zoologist, and Sautier, the second gardener, both died during this passage. Concerned lest these sad events should further depress the other scientists affected by illness, Baudin endeavoured as best he could to keep the deaths from them. Van Diemen's Land was sighted on 13 January 1802; the ships first anchored in d'Entrecasteaux Channel, then sailed to Oyster Bay on the east coast on 17 February, remaining there until the 27th of the same month. The new longboat, which the

[1] *Une Aventure*, p. 115.

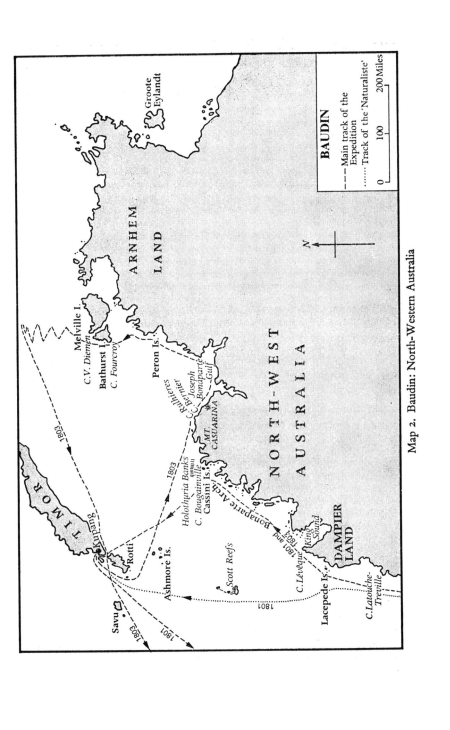

Map 2. Baudin: North-Western Australia

French had begun building at Timor and completed at sea, was
sent to examine the neighbouring bays to see if the British had
established a settlement at any point. None was found: Tasmania
was still uninhabited, except for roaming bands of friendly
aborigines.[1] Faure, the hydrographer in the *Naturaliste*, solved the
problem of Tasman Island by proving that it was in fact a peninsula; it was the only matter of importance d'Entrecasteaux
had left for them. Hunting was popular, but it grew to such proportions that Baudin and Hamelin were compelled to issue orders
that no one was to go ashore with guns—whereupon Bailly, the
mineralogist, killed a wallaby by hurling his geological hammer
at it. Tension had begun to develop on board the *Naturaliste*, and
Hamelin, perturbed by this, requested Baudin to take his young
second lieutenant, Millius, into the *Géographe*, but Baudin declined—he had quite enough trouble of his own.

  While in Oyster Bay, Faure discovered Géographe Strait
between Schouten Island and the mainland, and the headland
which forms the bay was carefully charted and named Freycinet
Peninsula, a name it still retains. It was here, too, that Baudin lost
his old friend Mauger, who was buried on Maria Island on
21 February.

  Baudin wanted a complete chart of the east coast of Van Diemen's Land, which d'Entrecasteaux had not been able to examine;
it had been seen by Furneaux in 1773, and by Bass and Flinders in
1799, but there was still a great deal to be surveyed, especially as
the French had only imperfect knowledge of the 1799 expedition.
On 6 March Baudin dispatched the longboat under Maurouard,
to enable the hydrographer Boulanger to draw plans of the coast,
'as he is short-sighted, and can take bearings only when he has his
nose against the land'. Maurouard had instructions to keep within
sight of the ships and return before nightfall. Either because the
ships had drifted too far, or because Maurouard neglected his
instructions until it was too dark, the longboat was lost to sight;

[1] 'Péron was the first trained anthropologist to enter into personal relations
with Tasmania's vanished race' (L. A. Triebel, 'Péron in Australia', *Australian
Quarterly*, vol. xxi, no. 1, Mar. 1949, p. 103). Anthropology at the time, however,
had hardly begun, and it would be rash to regard Péron as trained in the modern
sense.

there was no sign of it the next morning. While the two ships were manœuvring under shortened sail to find the longboat, the *Naturaliste* collided with the *Géographe*, inflicting, fortunately, only slight damage.[1] To complicate matters, Baudin fell ill and was forced to hand over command to Henri de Freycinet; soon after this, contact with the *Naturaliste* was lost in the rising wind. The *Géographe* spent four days sailing slowly along the coast in a northerly direction, hoping to find the longboat; then, at a meeting of officers and scientists, it was decided to return to the south, as it seemed clear it could not be so far to the north. There were, however, some English whalers about: the *Géographe* met one on 10 March, and at nearly the same time Hamelin was speaking to the captain of the *Harrington*, an English brig, who had found the longboat and its occupants, and now transferred them to the *Naturaliste*.

Freycinet, his search still fruitless, decided to sail to Waterhouse Island, the appointed rendezvous, to await the *Naturaliste*, but once again the two ships missed each other. While Hamelin sailed south to look for the *Géographe*, Baudin decided to undertake alone the exploration of the south coast of Australia. It was a difficult decision, but supplies were short, and Baudin could not spend an indefinite period cruising off Tasmania in the hope of rescuing the longboat: that task he left to the *Naturaliste*. As it turned out, he was right; but there is, on the debit side, the strong probability that Baudin was not sorry to get rid of the slower vessel.

When the *Naturaliste* entered Bass Strait on 1 April, Baudin was already off the Australian coast; Hamelin put in at Port Dalrymple on 5 and 6 April and at Port Western on the 9th to 17th; then, thinking that the *Géographe*, which was in a bad way, had been forced to go to Port Jackson, he sailed to the British settlement, arriving on 25 April. There was no news of her. Indefatigably, Hamelin sailed out again on 18 May, as soon as he had taken in a few supplies. He was becoming increasingly worried about the other ship, which he now firmly believed to be in real trouble somewhere along the Tasmanian coast, but his

[1] Baudin, Journal, 15 ventôse, an X.

further voyage to the south yielded no results and, when a violent storm endangered his own vessel, he returned to Port Jackson. There, on 28 June, he found the *Géographe* at anchor. The efforts made by Hamelin to find Baudin deserve the greatest praise; it was unfortunate that they were unnecessary, but this in no way detracts from the honour due to him.

Baudin had begun his survey of the Australian coast on 28 March from Wilson's Promontory[1] at the entrance to Bass Strait, and sailed towards Port Philip Bay, where modern Melbourne now stands, but he did not see the concealed entry into this fine harbour.[2] The charts the French drew of the Victorian coast are not always reliable, justifying the complaints made by Baudin about his officers, who were anxious to have the work over and done with before the supplies ran out.[3] They made for the uncharted coast of Australia and, after sailing from Lacépède Bay towards a great gulf to the north-east, they sighted a ship in the distance, coming towards them. 'We thought at first it was the *Naturaliste*, because we were far from believing that there were other Europeans in these waters and in that season of the year.'[4] It was, however, an English vessel, the *Investigator*, under the command of Matthew Flinders.

The English had left Europe after Baudin, and there is little doubt that they hoped to forestall the French. The time taken by Baudin to reach Mauritius, his difficulties on the island, and his consequent decision to go from Western Australia to Timor, had destroyed any hopes the French might have had of making prior discoveries in the Australian Bight, because Flinders himself had come straight from Cape Leeuwin. This meant that the strip of southern coastline where the French could claim original discoveries stretched only from Cape Banks, which Grant and

[1] The western cape of this peninsula he named Cap des Représentations, because his officers had made certain complaints to him on that day. Freycinet altered this to Cap Marengo.

[2] Péron claims the harbour was sighted from the topmasts, but Baudin does not mention this in his journal. What Baudin does claim to have seen is Western Port. See E. Scott, *Terre Napoléon*, ch. iii; Baudin, Journal, 8 to 10 germinal, an X.

[3] Cooper, *French Exploration*, p. 185.

[4] Baudin, Journal, 18 germinal, an X.

Murray in the *Lady Nelson* had reached not many years before, to the place of their meeting with Flinders, now called Encounter Bay; to this strip can be added the southern and western sides of Kangaroo Island—which Flinders had not seen, since he had sailed north of it through Investigator Strait. It is in this area that the French names remain as memorials to Baudin's voyage— Rivoli Bay, Guichen Bay, Lacépède Bay, d'Estrée Bay, Cape Gantheaume, Maupertuis Bay, Cape Borda. Had Baudin been able to carry out his original instructions, he would have had an advantage of nine months over the Englishman.

The two captains discussed their respective discoveries. Baudin betrayed no trace of disappointment—although he expresses some surprise in his journal. Yet the likelihood of meeting a British vessel off a continent where there was already a growing and well-established settlement must have been present in his mind. Off Tasmania he had already encountered a whaler from Port Jackson and, as we have seen, Boulanger was rescued by another English ship. Flinders, who had at first taken the *Géographe* for a privateer from the Île de France, was rather more reserved than Baudin. 'The English captain . . . congratulated himself on this pleasant meeting, but was very reserved on other matters', wrote Baudin,[1] but Flinders knew what he was about, whereas the Frenchman certainly did not realize the extent of Flinders's mission until the second day of their meeting.[2] Even then Baudin, who had as little English as Flinders had French, did not get a very clear picture of the work done by the *Investigator*. 'Baudin sometimes became confused by Flinders's explanations obtained through an interpreter.'[3] For instance, Baudin thought the Englishman had lost a sister ship, whereas Flinders was talking about a cutter. Although it is possible that Baudin did discover

---

[1] Baudin, Journal, 17–18 germinal, an X. E. Scott, *Terre Napoléon*, p. 46, believed that 'there was no need for reserve, and none was shown'. This applied only to Baudin.

[2] 'It somewhat surprised me that Captain Baudin made no enquiries concerning my business upon this unknown coast, but as he seemed more desirous of communicating information, I was happy to receive it' (Flinders, *A Voyage to Terra Australis*, vol. i, pp. 189–90).

[3] Faivre, *Expansion française*, p. 144.

more when he finally called at Port Jackson, it is fairly clear, especially in respect of the names given by Flinders to his discoveries, that Baudin learned very little. This is of some importance, because, when Péron and Freycinet published their account, during and after the Napoleonic Wars, French names were given to many features discovered by the Englishman. Since Flinders was later imprisoned for some years in the Île de France with his charts, the inference is that the French appropriated some of his discoveries and claimed them as their own, publishing the result of their work while their rival was in their power. This claim will be considered later; what concerns us at this stage is whether Baudin was himself a party to it, and how much he really knew of Flinders's voyage.

Baudin stands convicted at least of having altered Flinders's appellation of Kangaroo Island to Borda Island; he did so knowingly, but he justified his action in a letter to the Minister of the Navy, dated 29 May 1803:[1] 'Although the English discovered it several days before me, they have only seen a very small part, whereas I have examined it entirely and the dangers attached to it. I consider myself sufficiently authorised to change the name they had given to it.'[2] He was thus prepared to alter a name given by Flinders only because he felt that he had a good claim to do so. Now, if Flinders was 'very reserved', as Baudin states and Flinders himself confirms, it would indicate that the Englishman did not go into details about his discoveries, or show charts to the Frenchman—in which case Baudin would have no alternative but to use French names as he continued his survey westwards. That Péron and Freycinet later altered for political reasons almost the entire nomenclature adopted by Baudin is a rather sordid episode that need not concern us at this point.

Baudin and Flinders parted after two days. Flinders continued eastwards towards Bass Strait and, in giving a line of breakers near Cape Jaffa the name of Baudin's Rocks, paid the Frenchman

[1] Quoted by Cooper, *French Exploration*, p. 89.
[2] These reasons are much the same as those put forward by James Cook to explain his altering to New Hebrides the name Grandes Cyclades given to those islands by Bougainville. See *The Voyage of the* Resolution *and* Adventure, p. 521.

the only tribute ever accorded to him in Australia. His name appears nowhere else in Australian geography.

Baudin, for his part, sailed on towards Recherche Archipelago, where he would be able to complete the French survey of the entire south coast, and perhaps add some features which Flinders might have overlooked. The mighty opening of Spencer Gulf he left for later detailed examination, realizing that scurvy and the growing shortage of supplies would prevent a protracted stay at sea. 'The biscuit we were using was not very good, and for a long time had been crumbling, riddled by worms and eaten by moths.'¹ It was an understatement—the famished sailors were throwing the maggoty food overboard rather than eat it.² Firewood had completely run out, and they resorted to using broken planks and barrels to heat the stoves. By early May westerly winds were beating the ship back, and Baudin was compelled to alter course for Tasmania; he intended to return after obtaining refreshments, and considered his initial survey sufficient. He had reached the appropriately named Cap Adieu. But the unhappy French sailors, in their weakened condition and with unfavourable weather, found themselves unable to enter d'Entrecasteaux Channel; they anchored instead in Adventure Bay, off the west coast of Bruny Island, on 10 May. The halt was very welcome, but southern Tasmania did not then provide satisfactory supplies for a European ship—no more in fact than a plentiful supply of fish and a few varieties of greens. No one, not even Baudin, could doubt that only at Port Jackson would help be found, but when they weighed anchor on the 22nd he still did not hasten to New South Wales, but hugged the coast, completing the survey left unfinished on his previous visit. 'At this time the westerlies were blowing fiercely; the atmosphere, continually clouded and humid, the sky laden with dark clouds, hampered the completion of our geographical work, and were harmful to the health of the crew which was reduced to the utmost distress. Scurvy indeed had, for a long time, been causing fearful ravages.³

¹ Baudin, Journal, 16–17 floreal, an X.
² Péron, Voyage, vol. i, p. 331.   ³ Freycinet, Voyage, pp. 11–12.

Yet the French remained on the east coast of Tasmania 'for thirteen days, vainly endeavouring to verify a few geographical positions already fixed by our previous work'.[1] Baudin ignored complaints and sarcasms. It was a combination of blind determination and of a desire to punish the officers, with whom he was now so much at loggerheads.

The officers, like the naturalists and the scientists, were annoyed at my not taking advantage of the favourable wind to sail [to Port Jackson]. That was not really a matter of concern to me, since I had made up my mind and wanted to delay a little longer before leaving, rather than have to return a third time to this coast which, through their fault, had not been completed at a time when, unfortunately, I was ill, on account of their having not taken advantage of so favourable an opportunity.[2]

Baudin, however, was not at war with his men, who if anything suffered more than the officers. Lharidon de Créménec, the surgeon, drew up a list of the sick, and submitted it to the captain to encourage him to make promptly for the British settlement. Frightening as this list was, it was no exaggeration, for soon, on 4 June 1802, there were only four sailors fit enough to work.[4] Baudin still hesitated, but Nature, in the form of a gale, took a hand and punished yet further the wallowing ship. The captain persisted in his task, defying equally the rolling seas, the approach of midwinter, and the illness that was killing him; but it was no use, and he had to make for Port Jackson. Even this was now beyond the strength of the crew; the *Géographe* was unable to pass through the Heads unaided, and it was a relief crew of English sailors who helped the French to drop anchor at Port Jackson on 20 June 1802.

So weak were the crews, such was the condition of the ships, that the expedition had to remain five months in Port Jackson— until 18 November. Death had so affected the rolls that it was

[1] Freycinet, *Voyage*, p. 12.

[3] Baudin, Journal, 7 to 11 prairial, an X. The officers replied that they had not surveyed the coast while looking for Boulanger since that was his work and they did not want to compete with him.

[4] Freycinet, *Voyage*, p. 12.

decided to send the *Naturaliste* back to France; in her would sail
those who were not strong enough to withstand the hardships of
further exploration; Hamelin was also to take back the naturalists'
collections, thus making room in the *Géographe* for further
specimens. Getting rid of the slow and cumbersome *Naturaliste*
was a welcome move: for all Hamelin's goodwill and seamanship,
she had been more trouble than she was worth. Baudin purchased
instead a small ship for close investigation of the coastline, the
Casuarina, so called because it was built of that timber, twenty-
nine feet long, and of very shallow draught. Louis de Freycinet
was placed in command.

The stay in New South Wales provided opportunities for
scientific expeditions in the environs of the settlement, social
functions, and an evaluation of the first part of the voyage.[1] The
presence of Flinders and the opportunity this provided for an
assessment of French discoveries along the south coast of New
Holland removed whatever illusions the French may have
cherished: it left them the uncontested discoverers of not more
than 400 miles of coastline. Henri de Freycinet is reputed to have
admitted this in a toast to Flinders. 'Captain,' he said, 'if we had
not been delayed so long picking up shells and catching butterflies
in Van Diemen's Land, you would not have discovered the South
Coast before us.'[2] It is the kind of remark that sounds true, and
it may have been an indirect gibe at Péron, who was a great and
often indiscriminate collector—Freycinet, the sailor, would have
little patience for such landlubbers—but it was less then fair: it
was rather the lengthy crossing from France to Port Louis, and
the shortage of supplies at the Île de France, which had enabled
Flinders to catch up and precede Baudin.

The three ships sailed on 18 November 1802, making for King
Island, at the western extremity of Bass Strait. They anchored
there, in Elephant Bay, on 6 December; three days later Hamelin
sailed for France: he was to reach Port Louis on 2 February 1803,
and was later to be captured in the Channel, taken to Portsmouth,

[1] Péron's account of Port Jackson and its environs will be found in his *Voyage*,
vol. i, pp. 368–90.
[2] Flinders, *A Voyage to Terra Australis*, vol. i, p. 103.

and only released through the immediate good offices of Sir Joseph Banks, finally arriving at Le Havre on 7 June.

On the day the *Naturaliste* sailed, an English ship, the *Cumberland*, arrived at King Island. She had been dispatched there by the anxious British governor. Baudin had never concealed from the British his intention to examine the northern coast of Tasmania and, in particular, King Island. The strategic importance of this uninhabited island, commanding as it did Bass Strait and the direct route from Europe to Port Jackson, was not being overlooked by the British, and the fear of a French settlement there had prompted Governor King to dispatch the *Cumberland* to take formal possession of it. The French, it is true, had established a camp on it but purely for scientific purposes, and Baudin was understandably surprised when, with a minimum of tact, the British flag was raised over the tents.[1] The situation was not without its absurd side, for the *Cumberland* had left in such a hurry that she lacked supplies and even enough gunpowder to fire a musket; the French, glad to repay in some way the hospitality shown to them earlier by the British, gave them food and other supplies, including twelve pounds of gunpowder, whereupon the newcomers proceeded to salute the British flag by firing rifles loaded with French gunpowder.[2]

Though not acrimonious, the correspondence which passed between King and Baudin as a result of this action was couched in stiff terms. King explained that he had received advice that the French intended to establish a settlement somewhere in Tasmania. 'My informant adds that such are the orders that you have received from the Republic; that is what Colonel Paterson told me after your departure, having learned of it himself from a person in your ship.'[3] Although Baudin did not recognize any primary British right to Tasmania, he had no instructions to leave a settlement behind at King Island or anywhere else, whatever

---

[1] He tersely comments that he thought the Union Jack hanging limply from the branch of a tree was someone's washing left out to dry (Journal, 23 frimaire, an X).

[2] Ibid., 18–21 frimaire, an XI.

[3] Ibid., 18 frimaire, an XI (10 Dec. 1802). Paterson was Lieutenant-Governor of New South Wales.

ultimate possibilities might derive from his discoveries. 'All your work', the Navy Minister had written to Baudin, 'must aim at the advancement of science; you must observe the strictest neutrality, avoid raising the slightest doubt about your correctness in keeping within the object of your mission, such as is mentioned in the passports that have been handed to you.'[1]

Once again, the guilty party was Péron, although Baudin apparently remained unaware of it. In a letter to Decaen, Governor of the Île de France, the young scientist boasted that 'the commander of the troops in New South Wales, M. Paterson, a member of the Royal Society of London, always treated me with particular regard. I was received in his house, one might say, as a son.'[2] This, there can be little doubt, was Paterson's 'person in your ship' King was referring to in his letter to Baudin. Thus, Péron was responsible for the incident and, in the long run, for hastening the British settlement of Tasmania.

Although it was an annoyance and a humiliation, Baudin submitted to the British officer's silent supervision, contenting himself with sending a firm protest to the Governor. More important were repairs to the *Casuarina*, which had been damaged in a storm and was making three inches of water an hour[3]—not the last trouble he was to have with this vessel. He also organized a careful survey of King Island itself, under the charge of Faure, who was probably the first man to circumnavigate it; finally, when the *Casuarina* had been repaired, he dispatched Freycinet to the north-west coast of Tasmania and to Hunter Islands.

At the end of December, Baudin sailed to Kangaroo Island, which he wanted to survey in greater detail. The western point of the island was sighted on 2 January 1803; the *Géographe* then sailed to Nepean Bay, and anchored off Cape Delambre, its eastern headland. Surveys were made in the *Casuarina* and in the ship's boats, and a new longboat was built of local timber to replace one which had been lost off King Island. The coast of

---

[1] Letter of 29 Sept. 1800 quoted in E. Scott, 'Baudin's Voyage of Exploration to Australia', p. 345. See also Scott's *Terre Napoléon*, pp. 208-9.
[2] Letter of 11 Dec. 1803, quoted in Cooper, *French Exploration*, p. 194.
[3] Freycinet, *Voyage*, p. 16.

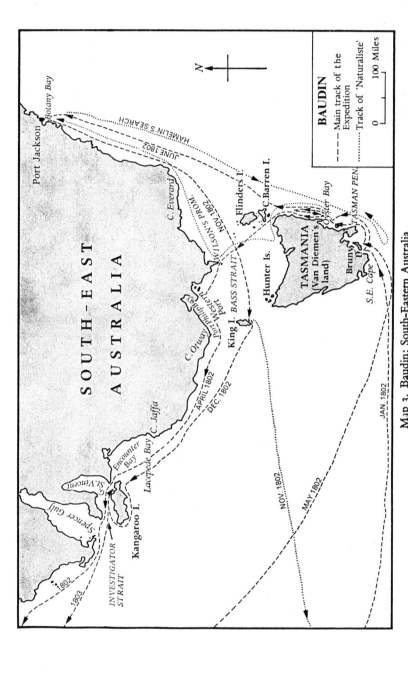

Map 3. Baudin: South-Eastern Australia

Kangaroo Island was charted in a few days. 'On 14 Nivôse [5 Jan. 1803] we finished our geographical work on the whole of the island named Kangaroo,[1] so that, if the English have over us the advantage of having arrived a few days earlier, we have over them the one of having completely circumnavigated it, and of having determined its geographical position in a manner that leaves nothing to be desired for the safety of navigation.'[2] But there remained the problem of the theoretical channel that might divide Australia into two land masses.

Flinders had reported the existence of two large gulfs biting deep into the land—Spencer and St. Vincent. Baudin had instructed Louis de Freycinet to explore the two gulfs, but to return within twenty days, as water was short. Freycinet, delayed by contrary winds, just failed to keep the rendezvous, and there resulted a new series of misunderstandings, for which Baudin's impatience must bear the blame: on 2 February 1803 the *Casuarina* was sighted from the *Géographe*, and seen to be sailing eastwards; Baudin shortened sail to await Freycinet, but the latter continued on his course, and eventually sailed right out of sight.[3] The *Géographe* went on her way slowly, awaiting the *Casuarina* in case she should veer back—something which Baudin doubted, as he suspected Freycinet of planning to return to Port Jackson. Freycinet, for his part, accuses Baudin of sailing westwards without making any effort to allow the slower *Casuarina* to catch up,[4] although his smaller ship altered course almost as soon as the *Géographe* was in sight. The mystery remains unsolved—unless we are to suspect that Baudin, angry at the return of the *Casuarina* one day later than had been arranged, had decided to abandon Freycinet to his fate. It is even possible, as Bouvier and Maynial have suggested,[5] that he welcomed the opportunity of losing the small vessel, whose slowness was setting back his plans.

[1] This is one of the rare occasions when he uses Flinders's designation instead of his own Borda Island.

[2] Baudin, Journal, 13–14 nivôse, an XI.

[3] 'It is difficult to explain this manœuvre on the part of citizen Freycinet, and no doubt he will make it clear to us at the first opportunity' (ibid., 12 pluviôse, an XI). When the two met again they simply blamed each other.

[4] *Voyage*, vol. i, pp. 12–20.   [5] *Une Aventure*, p. 191.

Whatever the reason—and it might have been nothing more than unknown currents, unstable winds, and muddled manœuvres —Baudin now sailed to the St. Francis Islands, and then due west to King George Sound on the south coast of Western Australia. There, on 18 February, the *Casuarina* rejoined him. The expedition stayed eleven days, examining the coast in detail and replenishing stocks of water. In a bay near by, the French found an American ship whose crew was hunting for seals. No more reserved than he had been with Flinders, Baudin supplied the American captain with charts and details of the entire south coast of Australia, including therefore his own discoveries.[1] Once again, this was not the action of a man on a secret political mission.

On 1 March 1803 the *Géographe* and the *Casuarina* sailed from King George Sound. Baudin had given Freycinet sealed orders to be opened in case they should become separated. The *Casuarina* in such an eventuality was to proceed to the Île de France. On 6 March the *Casuarina*, sent to survey an opening in the coast, was hidden in a bank of fog; this gave Baudin an excuse to complain that Freycinet would no doubt seize the opportunity to sail for home. But he underestimated his officer's reliability and courage, for Freycinet did not consider the two ships finally separated and sailed to Rottnest Island, where he rejoined the other vessel. On his way there Baudin had visited Port Leschenault Inlet to the north of Bunbury in Géographe Bay.

Baudin and Freycinet left Rottnest Island practically at once, and proceeded to Shark Bay, where they anchored on the evening of 16 March. Freycinet was sent to sound the northern waters of the bay, around the mouth of the Gascoyne river,[2] while Péron went ashore, collecting shells and endeavouring to contact the unfriendly natives, and once more getting lost.

The expedition then weighed anchor, and from North-West Cape began anew the exploration of the northern coast of Western Australia. The *Casuarina* this time enabled the French to explore the labyrinth of islands and passes, which had proved too dangerous in 1801, and to get near an inhospitable shore which no navigator had so far been able to chart with any

---

[1] Faivre, *Expansion française*, p. 168.   [2] Freycinet, *Voyage*, p. 23.

semblance of accuracy.[1] This work was not achieved without danger: on 2 April the *Géographe* nearly grounded on Banc des Antiphones, north of Condon Creek—the second near-disaster in the space of a week.[2] On 24 April, off Cassini Island, her boat was dispatched to explore this island, which had never been properly surveyed before; near by she found twenty-six Malay boats fishing for trepang off Holothuria Banks.[3] It was from here that Baudin had sailed for Timor in 1801; he decided to do so once more, before undertaking his final task—the exploration of the Arnhem Land coast and the Gulf of Carpentaria. The *Géographe* and the *Casuarina* sailed from Australia on the last day of April, reaching Kupang six days later.

The French stayed nearly a month in the Dutch port, where, so they learned, Flinders, still in the *Investigator*, had spent some time during the previous month.[4] On 14 May a sail was seen outside the harbour, and the slow and pointless manœuvres of the ship showed she was in trouble; the French rowed out to her aid, and found the *Hunter*, an American trading vessel, with her crew so weakened by dysentery that only three men could still stand. Kupang was really no place for sick men, and the *Hunter* was later abandoned. Nor was Baudin particularly desirous himself of prolonging his stay here, for many of his men were weak after nearly three years of hardship and bad food. Six had already deserted; four had been recovered, but Baudin left the other two to their fate, unwilling to waste any more time. Leschenault, the botanist, was too weak to sail, and he too had to be left behind; the astronomer Bernier did sail, but died soon after.

The two ships sailed from Kupang on the morning of 3 June; the Australian coast—the northernmost shores of Western Australia—was sighted on 12 June. Winds in this region made progress difficult, and to many the task seemed impossible, but Baudin refused to give up; he drove his wasting body as hard as he drove his men. He remained fixed in his earlier determination: 'I decided, upon leaving Timor, to take up again the

---

[1] Faivre, *Expansion française*, p. 169.
[2] Péron, *Voyage*, vol. ii, pp. 233, 236-7.
[3] Freycinet, *Voyage*, p. 24.   [4] Péron, *Voyage*, vol. ii, p. 256.

work on the north coast of New Holland, although several sailors I had consulted were persuaded that it would be impossible to travel eastwards in the face of the south-east monsoon.'¹

Painfully, the ships worked their way into Joseph Bonaparte Gulf. It was not possible, however, to carry out a thorough survey, although a number of points were fixed, namely Cape Rulhières, Mount Casuarina, Lacrosse Island, and Péron Island. Clarence Strait was not explored, and the French sailed north to Cape Fourcroy, which is the south-west point of Bathurst Island; Baudin then veered east towards the northern coast of Arnhem Land, but the monsoon proved too much of an obstacle. Having reached Cape Van Diemen on Melville Island, he decided to give up his attempt to fight the winds, and sailed for Cape Valsch in New Guinea, intending to go from there in a south-easterly direction back to Arnhem Land. It was 28 June, the sea was rough, and the small *Casuarina* forced the *Géographe* to slow down considerably. Nine days later, on 7 July, the two vessels were still 175 miles from New Guinea. There were practically no medical stores left to help the increasing number of sick; there was only a month's supply of biscuit, providing the small ration of ten ounces a day was maintained; there was water for only two months and some of it was going bad already. This water shortage was made more acute by the presence on board of precious live animals for French zoos, among them emus, kangaroos, and cassowaries; and of many rare plants and shrubs. Above all, the crew was weakened and emaciated to such an extent that the handling of the ship was becoming impossible. Baudin himself had suffered a haemorrhage. On 7 July he gave up, and issued instructions to turn back. When the rumour spread that he had set a course for the Île de France, and that they were going home, the men were so incredulous they came up on to the bridge throughout the night to check the reading.²

Baudin's journal, taken up again after his recovery from his

---

¹ Baudin, Journal, 14 prairial, an XI; see also Péron, *Voyage*, vol. ii, p. 252.

² Faivre, *Expansion française*, p. 173. 'On the journey home, Baudin was no more than the shadow of a captain on a ghost ship' (Bouvier and Maynial, *Une Aventure*, p. 210).

earlier illness, ends abruptly on 5 August 1803. Two days later the *Géographe* reached the Île de France. The *Casuarina* arrived on 12 August; the crew was paid off on the 29th and transferred to the *Géographe*. On 16 September Baudin died. Millius, the former second-in-command of the *Naturaliste*, who had been left behind on account of ill health, rejoined the expedition, and took over command of the *Géographe* for the return passage to France, where she arrived on 24 March 1804 after an absence of nearly three and a half years. Of the original sixty officers and *savants* who had sailed from Le Havre in 1800, only thirty-two completed the voyage as far as Mauritius—and two of these, Baudin and the mineralogist Depuch, died on the island. Péron himself was to outlive them by only a few years.

Without doubt Baudin died a disappointed and embittered man, for so much of his time had been wasted in disputes and petty vexations. Illness and the shortage of supplies had prevented him from completing his work with the thoroughness he would have wished. That Flinders had preceded him on the southern coast of Australia must have added to his disappointment, although he does not say so in so many words in his journal. Yet, because of the difficulties under which he laboured, his achievements deserve the highest praise: he rejected all the excuses—unchallengeable, most of them—that offered themselves to him; and he continued his voyage in spite of everything, driven by his inexorable will. But, even with Flinders ahead of him, his expedition brought back a wealth of geographical details—the newly charted bays and capes, and the carefully surveyed islands. In addition, because Flinders was kept prisoner in Mauritius, the French were able to give the world, in 1807, the first detailed and complete map of the Australian continent. To this must be added the anthropological work of Péron, the drawings and reports of the botanists and zoologists, and the truly astonishing cargo brought back by the *Naturaliste* and the *Géographe*.

Apart from a multitude of cases of minerals, dried plants, shells, fishes, reptiles, and zoophytes preserved in alcohol, of quadrupeds and birds stuffed or dissected, we still had seventy great cases full of plants in their natural state, comprising nearly two hundred different species of useful plants, approximately six hundred types of seeds contained in several thousand small bags and, finally, about a hundred living animals, rare or absolutely new.[1]

The animals included two kangaroos which were presented to the Empress, together with a mass of artefacts now lost;[2] the plants included over two hundred trees, most of which found their way to the botanical gardens. It was the most important collection of zoological and botanical specimens ever received by the administrators of the Museum.[3]

The importance of the expedition was recognized—its value was perhaps a little over-stressed on account of its political usefulness—and membership of it became a valuable reference. Possibly sheer survival indicated in those who came back an innate resistance and an easy adaptability to difficult conditions. Millius, Henri de Freycinet, and the young *aspirant* Duval d'Ailly all achieved in time the governorship of the island of Bourbon, the main French possession in the Mascareignes after the loss of the Île de France; two other *aspirants*, Peureux de Meslay and Brue, became governors respectively of Pondicherry and of St. Pierre and Miquelon; Charles Baudin—no relation of the captain's—ended his career as an admiral, and Bougainville the younger, who had served as an *aspirant* in the *Géographe*, soon obtained his own command.

But, to the dead, fate was less kind. Péron was entrusted with the task of writing the official account of the expedition, a mission he carried out in a spirit of partisanship which only his death, and his supercession by Freycinet, tempered when the second volume appeared. This, and the Franco-British bitterness which resulted from the claims made by Péron and Freycinet, covered Baudin's memory with an opprobrium which has only been lifted in the last half-century.[4]

---

[1] Péron, *Voyage*, vol. ii, p. 313.
[2] Faivre, *Expansion française*, p. 176.   [3] Ibid., p. 175.
[4] In the mid nineteenth century it was still possible for a biographer of Péron, in a volume that is admittedly hagiographic, to write that the expedition faced 'privations which the sordid avarice of Captain Baudin was to inflict on brave men who remained faithful to their mission' (L. Audiat, *François Péron*, p. 34).

When Péron's volume appeared, the south coast of Australia—
Terre Napoléon—showed a purely French nomenclature, based
to a large extent on the names of scientists and of the imperial
family. Flinders's Kangaroo Island was no longer even Borda
Island—in itself a questionable appellation—but bore the name of
Decrès, Minister of the Navy from 1801; Spencer Gulf had become
Bonaparte Gulf, and St. Vincent's was Josephine Gulf. Yet, since
the French had spent five months at Port Jackson, they were fully
aware of the British contribution to the knowledge of the coastline. Rivalry and patriotism, at a time when the two nations were
at war, account in part for the erasure of names given by Flinders
and Grant; a lesser excuse is the desire on the part of Péron and
Freycinet to ingratiate themselves further into the favour of the
Emperor, who, by that time, was no longer immune to the
grosser forms of flattery; but this eventually redounded to Freycinet's disadvantage when he continued the publication of the
account under the Restoration: 'I should have liked to change a
nomenclature, which the present political and moral situation of
France and Europe now rejects, but the first volume had already
been in the trade for some years.'[1]
     To the British this specious excuse soothed no wounds, for
Flinders had been imprisoned in Mauritius from 1803 to 1810;
his journals had been in French possession, and the inference
could too easily be made that the Baudin expedition had really
discovered very little, and that the information appearing in the
French volumes came from Flinders's manuscripts. The publication of Flinders's *A Voyage to Terra Australis* in 1814 strengthened
this belief and discredited Péron—and therefore Baudin—in the
eyes of non-French geographers. The task of rehabilitation was
a slow one, and it was due to a growing interest on the part of the
Australians themselves in their early history. Scott, in 1910,
expressed doubt that Péron and Freycinet had had access to any
of Flinders's journals—Baudin, of course, had died before Flinders's
arrival at the Île de France—and there is no real evidence that

[1] Freycinet, *Voyage*, Introduction, p. viii. It should be remembered that the
Napoleonic names given to Australian features replaced Baudin's names as well
as Flinders's.

Decaen had ever communicated information obtained from Flinders to the two compilers. 'The third log book was the only document pertaining to Flinders' discoveries that Decaen ever had in his possession. It was never returned. The rightful owner never saw it again. It has never been produced.'[1]

But this log-book did not concern the period of French exploration in Australia, and therefore could not have been of much use to Péron. When Baudin's journals came to light, the achievements of the French and of Flinders were put into proper perspective, and the political gloss of the Napoleonic nomenclature stood revealed.

It was an episode discreditable to those who were responsible for it, and one which, unfortunately, has assumed too much importance. It has obscured for far too long the true achievements of the Baudin expedition.

Thus, with Baudin, in misery and acrimony, ended a chapter of French Pacific adventures. Baudin's voyage was the last in a series of tragic, often glorious, and sometimes incompetent expeditions. With the nineteenth century, exploration was to become subordinate to the new aims of territorial expansion, political influence, and trade.

---

[1] Scott, *Terre Napoléon*, p. 69. However, Decrès wrote to Admiral Rosily on 10 Jan. 1814; 'Here is a journal of Capt. Flinders, which had remained in the hands of General de Caen, and which has just been handed to me, after having been several times asked for by the English. I should be obliged if, before sending it, you would examine it, and extract everything that might be of interest. It might be advisable to transmit it to Captain Freycinet' (S.H.M. Cn. 102–35).

THE NEW CENTURY

THE BACKGROUND

LOCKED in a continental struggle with Britain, Napoleon had nevertheless not lost sight of the French colonies, nor of the advantages that might be gained from weakening Britain's overseas empire. His plans for the reorganization of the French administrative framework had taken into account the Navy and colonies: maritime prefects in each main port from Toulon to Antwerp, captains-general and colonial prefects in the colonies, were to ensure, if not the supercession, at least the stream-lining, of the old system of administration. The Peace of Amiens provided an opportunity for action. The most urgent task was the reoccupation of lost territories; the instructions to the Minister of Marine and Colonies were thorough and peremptory:

> We must take possession of the Indies, Citizen Minister, within six months of ratification of the treaty at the latest, that is before I Brumaire, Year XI. The colonial prefect or some other agent, with a few junior employees and engineer and artillery officers, must be sent straight to Pondicherry by corvette as soon as possible. General Montigny might be sent. This commissioner should arrive before the end of Thermidor, so as to make all arrangements for the resumption of possession and to send us news of the situation in India.
>
> The expedition we shall have to send has two parts: first to take possession of Mauritius; second, to take possession of India. I wish each to consist of at least two battleships.
>
> It seems that to occupy Mauritius will need 2,000 men. I wish them to be ready to leave Toulon before the end of Floréal. I wish the second expedition to be ready a month later.
>
> The first must carry the Captain-General of India. Send me a report on all these matters.[1]

These plans were to be put into effect by Decaen, who was dispatched 'to make preparations for driving the English out of

[1] Napoleon to Decrès, 15 Apr. 1802, in Howard, *Letters and Documents of Napoleon*, vol. i, p. 520.

the peninsula, by setting up, in contrast to the British tyranny, a regime of "sweetness, dissimulation and simplicity". But, as England shilly-shallied about restoring the posts, Decaen never got beyond the Île de France (1803) and had to be content with reorganizing the military government there'.[1] Decaen indeed deserves credit for his work in the Île de France, which under his administration was prosperous and well defended, with a good network of roads. Agriculture flourished, unaffected by the decree for the restoration of slavery, since the earlier one abolishing it had never been put into effect. But slavery, as we have seen, had not been oppressive; nor did Decaen's rule tend to make it so; it was not difficult to buy one's freedom, and freemen were recognized as equal citizens. Hospitals were built, as were a number of primary schools and a *lycée*—Decaen has some claim to be called the founder of Mauritian public education. At the same time a post was established in Madagascar under Sylvain Roux to ensure regular supplies for the islands. The Mascareignes thus became a strong naval base, actively waging war against the British. The end came in 1810, when, each in turn, Rodriguez, Bourbon, the Île de France, and the Madagascar settlement fell to the British, who could tolerate no longer these painful thorns in their side.

The renewal of hostilities in 1803 did not turn Napoleon from his original plans. Still firmly held by the lure of India, he had toyed with the idea of invading it through Persia and Afghanistan with a Franco-Russian force under Masséna; he now examined a proposal by Decaen for a landing with 4,000 men on the coast between Goa and Bombay; he decided instead on a combined Franco-Spanish force of 40,000 men sailing direct from France—until Decrès persuaded him this was not feasible. Napoleon then returned to his first plan of a thrust through Persia. An agreement was signed in May 1807 with the Shah's envoy, guaranteeing free passage and assistance to French troops in exchange for the recognition of Persia's interests in Georgia. The Treaty of Tilsit led France to switch sides in the Georgian dispute, whereupon Napoleon suggested to the Tsar the overland invasion of India

[1] Priestley, *France Overseas through the Old Regime*, p. 348.

by a joint force 50,000 strong, supported by a landing of 15,000 men from the Île de France. The situation in Spain, and eventually the capture of the Mascareignes, put an end to these schemes. While Spain remained within the French sphere of influence, the Philippines had presented very real possibilities. In 1805 Decaen dispatched Paul Ducamper as adviser to the governor of Manila, who was already being assisted by Renouard de Sainte-Croix, an officer who had gone to the Philippines after the fall of Pondicherry. Ducamper sailed in the *Sémillante*, Captain Motard, in March 1805, by way of the Straits of Sunda and Gaspar, reaching Manila in June. The Governor was aware of the declaration of war between Spain and Britain, and his resources were extremely meagre. Motard agreed to carry out a protective cruise before sailing back to Port Louis, and, indeed, in August he met and drove off two British vessels in San Jacinto Bay. He then sailed out through San Bernardino Strait and south off the east coasts of Samar and Mindanao into the Molucca Sea, to Timor, and home to the Île de France, which he reached on 30 October 1805. It was the first time since the outbreak of war that a French ship had entered Pacific waters.

Captain Motard has made a large number of observations and notes of value to geography and navigation. His longitudes based on lunar readings as well as on his chronometer differ very little from those based on the more numerous observations made by the d'Entrecasteaux expedition when more time was available. Throughout this voyage, Captain Motard appears to have given new evidence of his ability, bravery and devotion, and has acquired a knowledge of [East] Indian waters that may prove most valuable in the future.[1]

A year later Decaen instructed Joseph-César de Bourayne, captain of the *Canonnière*, to proceed to Manila. Bourayne sailed first to Ceylon, seeking a likely prize, then to Sunda Straits. He reached Manila on 30 September 1806, where he received a warm welcome. The Governor was in need of funds, as the galleons no longer considered it safe to cross the Pacific. Bourayne agreed to help and, after carrying out much-needed repairs on his ship,

[1] Decrès to Napoleon, quoted in Faivre, *Expansion française*, p. 189.

which had been battered in earlier engagements with the British, sailed for Mexico on 19 April 1807. South-easterlies drove him towards Japan; on 8 May he sighted an uncharted low island, to which he gave the name of Île de la Canonnière. Judging from the position he gives, this was probably Okino-Oagari, one of the Daito group, south-east of the Ryukyus. He sailed now almost due east to the north of the Hawaiian Islands, and anchored in Acapulco on 21 July. His was the first French ship to cross the Pacific in over sixteen years. The *Canonnière* remained in Acapulco until 23 October, then sailed back to the Philippines by a route that took her south of Hawaii and through the Marianas. Successfully avoiding three British frigates lying in wait for him along this route, Bourayne dropped anchor without loss in Manila Bay on Christmas Eve. Refusing any recompense for his voyage, which saved the colony from financial collapse, he remained in the Philippines until late March 1808, and reached the Île de France in July with three prizes captured off the coast of Sumatra.

The Philippines might easily have played a key role in French plans, and men like Ducamper and Bourayne certainly worked hard to gain the goodwill of the authorities. But the occasional ship which Decaen could spare could do little more than show the flag, and the alliance between France and Spain was short-lived. Perroud, in the *Curieux*, which arrived in Manila in September 1808 after ten months in the China Seas, met with a cool reception. Soon after this Ducamper was asked to leave. The crew of the *Mouche*, which entered Manila Bay in 1809, were taken prisoner and only released after strong protests. To all intents and purposes, the Philippines had passed over to the enemy. The changed situation nullified Decaen's efforts in the East, and made nonsense of such plans as Malte-Lebrun's 1809 proposal for a settlement on Formosa.[1]

Similarly, France's tenuous foothold in the Dutch East Indies was soon lost. To Decaen, and to some of the Dutch, a link between the Mascareignes and the East Indies had seemed essential; it would keep open the route to China, be a step nearer the

[1] Gaffarel, *La Politique coloniale en France*, p. 477.

British settlement at Port Jackson, and, in the wider context of a Franco-Spanish alliance, open the way to Spanish possessions in America as well as in the East. Strategic considerations aside, the Dutch colony could supply the Île de France with rice, oil, timber, and ropes. Here again, the changing pattern of European alliances had its effect: Spain was slipping from Napoleon's grasp, but, in 1810, Holland entered the French orbit. Java at once assumed greater importance. The *Méduse*, the *Sapho*, and the *Nymphe* sailed from France in December 1810, carrying supplies and men, including the new governor, Janssens. On 13 April 1811 the Australian coast was sighted in 22° 35' north—probably North-West Cape. Sailing north-east, the French discovered Méduse Shoals and Sapho Reef, reached the island of Sumba on 20 April, and arrived in Surabaya not long after. Whatever hope the French may have had of using Java as a base was short-lived, for Britain had already decided on its capture and occupation. Even as the French ships were making their way from North-West Cape to the Sunda group, an armada of a hundred ships was sailing from Madras. The Dutch possessions fell to the English within a matter of months. And by the end of 1811 Janssens and the French ships were back in France, the Mascareignes were under British occupation, and France had finally been banished from the eastern seas.

The curtain was to remain down until the end of the war. One isolated plan, drawn up in 1812 by Charles Baudin, who had sailed with the *Géographe* expedition, envisaged raids on ships and whalers around Cape Horn and in New Zealand waters, the destruction of the North American fur trade, and the eventual isolation and ruin of the Australian settlements.[1] As might be expected, this came to nothing, and the British were left in peaceful occupation of the Pacific, troubled only by an occasional American raid after the outbreak of war with the United States in 1812.

Britain agreed to return a number of French possessions even before Waterloo. The Treaty of Paris of 30 May 1814 provided

[1] 'Projet d'expédition militaire autour du monde pour détruire le commerce anglais dans la Mer du Sud . . .', quoted in Faivre, *Expansion française*, p. 182.

for the transfer of all the former French colonies, except St. Lucia, Tobago, the Île de France, Rodriguez, and the Seychelles. Renewed hostilities, following Napoleon's return from Elba, did little more than delay its fulfilment. Bourbon, however, had already been reoccupied by the French. Louis XVIII owed a debt to Athanase Bouvet de Lozier, the son of the explorer, a rabid royalist and émigré who had risked his life for the King's cause; he promptly appointed him Governor of Bourbon, a position his father had held before him. Bouvet arrived in the island in April 1815. He decided to ignore the Hundred Days, and accordingly refused to take any notice of an attempt by Farquhar, the Governor of Mauritius, to take over the island. The island was blockaded for a time, but was saved by the Peace of Vienna. With a mediocre harbour and poorly equipped, it presented no real threat to the surrounding British-held islands. Bouvet's administration proved too expensive, and he was recalled in 1816 and replaced by Millius, one of Baudin's officers. Formerly known as Île Bonaparte and eventually to be renamed La Réunion, Bourbon was now able to take the first steps towards self-sufficiency, which in time might help to cushion its economy against the effects of the eventual abolition of slavery. Its value as a naval base remained slight; it served as a port of call for a number of Pacific-bound expeditions, although such an unsatisfactory one that some commanders preferred British Mauritius. In Madagascar the trading post established by Sylvain Roux, which the French had been compelled to abandon, was not at first recognized by Farquhar as coming under the provisions of the peace treaty. It took three firm protests from Paris before he complied and allowed the French to reoccupy the posts. The Indian settlements, five in number, came under a special clause of the Treaty of Vienna, which delayed the return of colonial territories still in the hands of the British until the settlement of certain debts. They were finally handed over in April 1817, in spite of a dispute over the actual boundaries of Mahé, which dragged on until 1853. The most important consideration affecting India was a clause requiring full French recognition of British rights over the rest of the continent. The five towns thus lost all political significance: the French could engage in trade, but not interfere in Indian politics. Britain at last had a free hand on the continent and could create an empire without fear of any foreign interference.

Whereas France's few bases in the Indian Ocean were thus further reduced or neutralized, her rivals in the Pacific had strengthened their position. Australia was developing apace; Tasmania had been settled in 1803; New Zealand was slowly but surely being dragged into the British orbit; what amounted to British missionary rule had been established in Tahiti; trading vessels and whalers could be found in Fiji, Tonga, or Hawaii. The Dutch and the Spanish had retained their colonial possessions. Russia, with Kotzebue's voyage of 1815-18, was displaying a greatly increased interest in the Pacific. Russian traders, 600 in number, were active from the Gulf of Alaska to San Francisco and Hawaii. A hint that trade and exploration might be a prelude to colonization came in 1816, when a group of Russians made an abortive attempt to set up a protectorate over Kauai. They were thus reaching not merely into nominally held Spanish possessions —which the South American authorities were powerless to defend—but into regions where Britain and particularly the United States were developing their own strong claims. The latter, in particular, were gaining influence. By 1819 Spain had recognized American rights on the Pacific coast. Meanwhile, bold and independent-minded traders, mostly from Massachusetts, were sailing to the North-West Coast for furs, to the Sandwich Islands for sandalwood, and to Canton for tea. An attempt by the American, Porter, to annex Nukuhiva was more typical of Yankee audacity than of a settled policy, but it did show how much the emergent States had to be reckoned with in the new post-war Pacific.

This then was the situation facing France after the Napoleonic Wars. With their ports in ruins, their maritime trade almost at a complete standstill, the French had little opportunity of organizing or financing a major voyage of exploration, at least during the first years of the new reign. Nevertheless, the carefully hoarded plans of scientists and geographers were promptly dusted and sent to the appropriate ministries. The impulse given by the great voyages of the eighteenth century had grown into a tradition now strengthened by economic resurgence and new national ambitions. For a quarter of a century France had led Europe, firstly with advanced political reforms which contained the seeds of innumerable other revolutions, later as a conqueror on a hitherto unparalleled scale; national pride called for activities, now inevitably of a peaceful nature, that would help to retain France's position as a great European power. A number of circumstances were to imbue these activities with a strong commercial spirit. Chief among them was the composition of the new government, which numbered among its most influential members and supporters men from the Bordeaux region. Richelieu and Decazes, Louis XVIII's Prime Ministers, both had strong links with the Gironde; Lainé, Minister of the Interior from 1816, and Baron Portal, in charge of the colonies from 1815 and of the Navy from 1818, were both from Bordeaux. From this port, the richest in France in the Restoration period, ships soon left for the West Indies, the United States, and South America, taking wine, cloth, and manufactured goods. The mercantile spirit of the age was reflected in the protectionist policy of 1816, under which a system of preferential trade was fostered between the metropolis and the colonies, to the detriment of foreign merchants. It was accompanied by the promotion of new trading posts and commercial ventures. Sylvain Roux was back in Paris, pressing for a new expansionist policy in Madagascar; foundations were laid in 1818 for fortified trading posts in Senegal; the appointment of a French consul at Canton was under active consideration; Catineau-Laroche, a government official and a strong advocate of colonization, drew up a plan for a large-scale private settlement of French Guiana; another would-be colonizer, Ruthye, attempted to direct the Government's attention to South America, in the hope that intervention among the former Spanish possessions might open the way for French trading interests. Conditions were therefore favourable for a resumption of voyages of exploration, but with a strong bias towards discoveries useful more to trade and colonization than to geography; and, as the Government's resources were inadequate, so soon after the war, to equip an official expedition, it was logical that the first moves would come from a trading concern and equally to be expected that this concern should have its office in Bordeaux.

Probably the most important, and certainly the most adventurous, among Bordeaux shipowners at the time of the Restoration were the two Balgueries—Balguerie-Stuttenberg, whose particular concern was the resumption of relations with Cochin-China, and his cousin Etienne, known as Balguerie Junior, the President of the Bordeaux Chamber of Commerce. The latter decided to test the possibilities of trade in Pacific and China waters; for this he fitted out a ship of 200 tons, the *Bordelais*, which had sailed on privateering raids during the wars, and appointed to command her a naval lieutenant on leave, Camille de Roquefeuil.

The aim was to buy in the Pacific and on the North-West Coast 'goods in demand in China, whose proceeds were to be used to obtain consumer goods for France, and which could thus be supplied to our markets without loss of currency and by putting to good use the products of our soil and of French industry'.

The *Bordelais*, a three-masted vessel, of 200 tons burden, was fitted out in the summer [of 1816] . . . She was provided with spare stores for two years; with a long boat, as large as could be put on board, two whale boats, one in pieces, and a jolly boat; she had two cannons (four pounders), six carronades (eight pounders), a sufficient quantity of arms, of all kinds, for the crew and for the boats. Besides the usual nautical instruments, we had an excellent chronometer by Breguet. Vice-admiral Rosily had the kindness to send me several maps and books, among which were the chart of the north-west coast of America, and Vancouver's *Voyage*. Our crew consisted of thirty-four men, including the officers, who were Messrs Foucault, lieutenant in the navy, Briole, and Salis, and the surgeon, M. Vimont.[1]

The Government was thus sympathetic towards Balguerie's plans. At exactly the same time, it was considering Louis de Freycinet's plan for a circumnavigation, which it was shortly after to approve, very nearly *in toto*. This in no way prevented the authorities from unofficially endorsing a sound, well-planned

---

[1] Roquefeuil, *A Voyage round the World*, p. 4.

project put forward by a respected shipowner for an expedition which could only 'improve our knowledge of navigation and make some new discoveries'. It was the Navy's Dépot des Cartes et Plans which, at the request of Rosily, himself once a Pacific explorer, provided Roquefeuil with the required charts and reports.

The *Bordelais* sailed from the port of Bordeaux on 11 October 1816, and anchored off Pauillac, a small town some miles up the Gironde estuary, taking on further stores; on the 19th she finally sailed into the Atlantic. The crossing was uneventful; after sighting the Canaries and Fernando de Noronha, Roquefeuil reached Tierra del Fuego on 3 January 1817, entered Le Maire's Strait, and turned Cape Horn without much difficulty, in spite of several patches of rough weather. 'The weather became more favourable as we proceeded towards the north, and we were able to open the hatchways and dry the ship.' The coast of Chile hove in sight on the first day of February; the French anchored in Valparaiso on the 5th, and were received 'in a most handsome manner' by the local governor, although courtesy was not unmotivated by interest.

I had occasion to perceive in the course of my visits, that the spirit of revolutions had not forgotten this country. . . . I was dining with M. de Villegas [the Governor] at the house of a merchant, when he received a packet, the reading of which sensibly affected him. A corps of troops had passed the Andes, and obtained some successes, which, without being decisive, greatly alarmed the company which consisted of European Spaniards. . . . On the 17th, a Spanish transport arrived at Chili with recruits. The governor obliged me to deliver to him the muskets which were on board the *Bordelais*; however, I delivered to him only the half, and I had the strongest assurances from him that those which he took should be either restored or replaced, if the resources of the arsenal of Saint Jago permitted it; otherwise they were to be paid for at any advantageous price.[1]

Roquefeuil was witnessing the final stage of a struggle for independence which had begun in 1808 with Napoleon's intervention in Spain and had first emerged in the open in 1810 with

[1] *A Voyage round the World*, pp. 8–9.

the setting up of a junta at Santiago. The defeated revolutionaries had been gathering an army at Mendoza in the Argentine under the leadership of José de San Martin; it was this force which crossed the Andes soon after Roquefeuil's arrival in Valparaiso. The Spanish governor, thrown back on his own meagre resources, was obviously eager to make what use he could of the presence of a well-equipped French vessel. Roquefeuil was determined to proceed with caution. A victorious Spanish administration might show a great deal of gratitude to those who had helped it, but victory was far from assured. Indeed, the low morale of the local officials was obvious: 'The passage of the mountains had not been known twenty-four hours, and they were preparing for flight. The officers of the Government were the first to embark their property, with a scandalous haste.' On 12 February San Martin crushed the royalists at Chacabuco and appointed the Chilean patriot, Bernado O'Higgins, 'Supreme Director'. The next day, disorganized bands of soldiers began to arrive in Valparaiso, 'the officers generally preceding their soldiers'. The townspeople now rose, spiked the guns of the batteries defending the city, and prepared to welcome O'Higgins. There was no attempt on their part to attack the fleeing soldiery, but Roquefeuil could not ignore the possibility of the Governor issuing orders to fire on the populace and provoking a full-scale riot. The *Bordelais* was a merchantman; his orders were to open up new channels for French manufactures: whatever possibilities for lucrative trade might offer themselves later, this was not the right time. He sailed on the evening of the 14th, and made for Callao.

Roquefeuil reached Callao on the 26th, and a few days later went to Lima. It was urgent to capitalize on the goodwill of the royalist authorities before the spreading rebellion overthrew them. The Viceroy was indeed friendly, and readily authorized Roquefeuil to sell a part of his cargo. But the time was hardly propitious: competition and the bad news from Chile so depressed prices that the small profit was swallowed up by 'expenses, charges, and enormous duties'. The Viceroy was reluctant to replace the muskets Roquefeuil had handed over in Valparaiso; after some argument the French obtained a total of thirty from the local

arsenal, the balance being paid for at a satisfactory price. Roquefeuil reinvested the proceeds of his various operations in trade
goods for California and the North-West Coast, and copper for
China. It was also his intention to buy sandalwood from the
Marquesas—he had learned from his conversations with whalers
and from the journal of Captain Porter of the *Essex* that there was
a good market in China for this commodity—and he laid in a
supply of whale teeth, as a suitable article of trade in the islands.
All this took time, and the commercial practice then current in
Peru of allowing debtors two months in which to pay for goods
purchased was no help. Roquefeuil filled the time with excursions
around the capital, making a number of wry comments in his
diary. Half-way to Callao he noted 'a small church and a public
house, both objects of regard to the postillions, who never fail
to make the sign of the cross before the one, and to stop at the
second'.[1] His stay coincided with Holy Week and Easter cele-
brations, and he witnessed the colourful scenes in and around the
churches, which dramatized penance, sorrow, and resurrection.
A visit to the theatre left him unmoved. 'I cannot say much in
favour of the performance, or of the performers . . . as soon as the
curtain is let down, the noise of flint and steel is heard on all sides,
and every mouth, even the most delicate, is furnished with a
segar [sic], and the theatre is filled with a cloud of smoke, so that
you cannot see from one side to the other.'[2] A bullfight attended
by a crowd of 10,000 was more straightforward and more pro-
fessional. Visits to other captains proved useful: a Captain Hagemeister, in charge of two Russian vessels, gave him a letter of
introduction to the Governor of the Russian American Company,
Baranof. But French inexperience in the Pacific after the long
wars was making itself felt: trade along the Coast as in China had
changed very considerably since the days of Marchand. 'What he
told me of those countries led me to expect but little success in
that quarter, on account of the bad selection of our goods intended for exchange, but this was the principal object of our
expedition, from which I was not at liberty to depart.'[3]

---

[1] *A Voyage round the World*, p. 13.   [2] Ibid., p. 19.
[3] Ibid., p. 20.

The *Bordelais* sailed from Callao on the morning of 29 May. Salis, one of the officers, who was ill, was left behind, as was a sailor wounded 'when discharging a cannon, at an entertainment which I gave on board the ship'. Five others had deserted. They might have believed that the possibility of a republican Peru was more promising than the certainty of a return to royalist France. To Roquefeuil, a conservative by birth and nature, Peru's future was bleak: he had as little faith in the Creoles' ability to rule themselves as he had in the royalist chances of preventing a revolution. He sailed south and west of the Galapagos. His hope was to avoid the calms that are frequently to be found between them and the mainland, but he was not altogether able to avoid changeable and contrary winds. The coast of California was not sighted until 5 August. Late that day, he anchored in San Francisco Bay, near Goat Island. A pleasant reception awaited him, the officials being understandably astonished to see a French ship. Water and food were taken on board, and there was time for a quick visit to the near-by mission before the *Bordelais* sailed again on the 14th, making for the North-West Coast.

On 1 September Roquefeuil was a few miles north of Nootka, seeking an opportunity to enter the sound; calms and fog held him up for four days. Large numbers of Indians came alongside and trade began: the first day yielded some fish and four otter skins. The natives were helpful, friendly relations were maintained with their chiefs, and Roquefeuil was able to land and explore in safety. But there was little left in the way of furs so late in the season. A month of trading yielded only twenty furs. Other attempts further along the coast were even more fruitless. The French sailed for the Russian settlement at Bodega, but found the port obstructed by a bar and learned that the Governor, whom Roquefeuil had come to see, was away in California. There seemed no point in further delay; the men were weary and sickness was spreading. Roquefeuil returned to San Francisco, where he arrived on 16 October. The Californian sunshine helped to dispel a growing feeling of disaffection among the men, of which Roquefeuil remained unaware until the 21st, when two men deserted.

It was now that I had the first information of a plot, formed during our stay at Nitinat, to carry off the ship, after getting rid of the officers. Ostein, one of the two deserters, had been the author of it, but found so few of the men wicked enough to commit such a dreadful crime that he was obliged to give up his project. Circumstances not permitting me to investigate this affair, without injury to my employers, I thought it best to dissemble, and retain for the success of the expedition men who had no claim to mercy.[1]

The sick recovered slowly, causing the stay to be twice as long as had originally been intended. One death occurred, that of the boatswain Renom, 'universally regretted'. The length of the stay proved unfortunate for the deserters, who were caught and put in irons two days before the *Bordelais* was due to sail. Ostein, however, still had sympathizers on board: Roquefeuil unmoored late on 19 November and Ostein disappeared during the night. The *Bordelais* sailed without him. Roquefeuil had made no attempt to get him back, for he cannot have been too certain how far the feelings of mutiny had spread, and life in the ship would be safer without at least one leading troublemaker.

The easternmost of the Marquesas Islands was sighted on 22 December. 'In Comptroller Bay, we sailed along the coast, at a distance of a mile . . . we perceived at the farthest part of this fine anchoring place a three-masted vessel, which immediately hoisted the American colours.' The French anchored close to; the American was the *Resource*, from New York, and her captain, Sowle, promply came on board. He had been in the Marquesas for some time and was due to sail for China shortly after Christmas; he had therefore useful information to impart to Roquefeuil, some of it already too late.

While I conversed with Captain Sowle, who explained the reasons which had induced him to exclude the women from his ship, one of my people came to inform me that about fifty of them had got on board my vessel, having swum to it, and entered by means of ropes hanging down. Notwithstanding the prudent advice of Mr. Sowle, I did not think fit to drive them away; and, besides, I should not have

---

[1] *A Voyage round the World*, p. 40.

known what means to adopt to expel such an enemy, who was already in possession of the deck.[1]

A few days later, Roquefeuil sailed to Hiva Oa, and was again surrounded by natives; but, as he had been warned that a boat from the merchant vessel *Flying Ship* had been attacked three months earlier, he considered it more prudent to seek the safer waters of Atuona. There he obtained close on half a ton of sandalwood. This promising beginning was due to the advice of another American, Ross, who had been sent to the Marquesas by the American consul in Canton in order to assist white traders, the majority of whom came from the United States. Ross had become accepted by the Marquesans and understood the importance of fair trading and of maintaining friendly relations by all means possible. 'In order to keep up a good understanding, it had been necessary to admit some young girls, who had expressed a desire to become acquainted with our people.'[2] By 25 February Roquefeuil had collected eighty tons of sandalwood, so that some of it had to be stored on deck; in addition he had bought hogs and vegetables. The whale's teeth had proved valuable, each one being worth 200 lb. of timber, but muskets sold for 500 lb., this higher value being explained by the current native wars. When Roquefeuil sailed on the 28th, Siepki, his third officer, who was ill, was left behind at his own request.

Roquefeuil made for the Russian settlement of New Arkhangelsk in Sitka Sound. Hagemeister was now in charge, and his earlier acquaintance with Roquefeuil led the two of them to organize a joint otter-hunting expedition. The agreement may have been weighted in favour of the Russian company, or Hagemeister may simply have wished to protect the local Indians, for whom he felt responsible. Whatever the true reasons, Roquefeuil agreed to pay an indemnity in respect of any Indian killed or wounded and to pay a proportion of his takings to the company. He sailed across the Gulf of Alaska to Kodiak Island, arriving on 12 May. He recruited the desired number of Kodiak Indians and sailed back again, anchoring at Prince of Wales

[1] Ibid., p. 41.   [2] Ibid., p. 43.

Island on 7 June. The first results were mediocre: a total of less than thirty skins. It soon became apparent that Hagemeister's concern for the Kodiaks was based on sound common sense. It was obvious that local Indians would view with great disfavour the arrival of what amounted to an expedition of poachers. The Kodiaks had set up a camp on shore, as was their custom; the local Indians attacked them in a matter of days. Of the forty-seven Kodiaks in the camp, twenty were killed, two were missing, and of the twenty-five who managed to escape twelve were wounded and one subsequently died. The survivors, understandably enough, could not be persuaded to return ashore. The *Bordelais* made for New Arkhangelsk, where the wounded could be cared for, but Roquefeuil now owed the Russians a considerable sum. Hagemeister invited him to join another expedition, which was about to sail. Roquefeuil agreed, believing that all he had to do was to persuade the surviving Kodiaks to agree to go with him once more. It was the French crew, however, which objected. The dangerous but necessary task of protecting the Indians was not work covered by a sailor's normal terms of engagement, and any disablement resulting from wounds suffered in any such actions would not entitle one to compensation. Roquefeuil was hardly in a position to offer, on behalf of Balguerie, the kind of protection on which Hagemeister had insisted for his Kodiaks. He argued with the men, pointing out that natives were far less likely to attack groups of well-armed Europeans, but this proved unconvincing in view of the fact that two Russians had recently been killed within sight of the fortified Russian settlement. All that could be attempted was trade with the would-be aggressors themselves. The *Bordelais* sailed for Admiralty Island on 6 July. Three ships were already there, whose captains reported only mediocre results. Roquefeuil was soon able to prove these claims for himself; he then decided to make for Chatham Strait. Now at last he met with some success. He bought forty-five skins in two days—more than he had obtained on the unlucky voyage to Prince of Wales Island—but his lack of suitable trade goods was a serious drawback. The Indians were not interested in French woollen goods—the quality was not remarkable—nor

were they interested in muskets of Spanish manufacture. If buying were to continue on the basis of French muskets and
powder, Roquefeuil would be able to buy only another 200 skins.
He tried his luck in Cross Sound, but the pilot misdirected him in
the fog, and he found himself tacking to little purpose in a labyrinth of channels. A group of Indians did come out in a canoe,
including an old woman to whom he presented 'a grey blanket
and a small looking-glass, which had to reflect the most hideous
countenance ever worn by a human creature'. Shortly after this,
he met the *Brutus*, Captain Nye, of Boston. The two men agreed
to co-operate and share their purchases equally; but there was
very little to share, and they soon parted, Roquefeuil taking two
Sandwich Islanders from the *Brutus* to strengthen his crew now
affected by sickness. He continued on his way, stopping at
various points to pick up a few furs. On 18 August he was back
in Sitka Sound.

Captain Robson of H.M.S. *Columbia*, newly arrived from
Europe, gave him news of 'the departure of the *Uranie* for a
voyage of discovery, without being able to tell me the name of
the commander'. Of greater importance at the moment was
raising funds to settle the debt to Hagemeister. Roquefeuil sailed
to Queen Charlotte Island, where, so he was told, it was not too
late to find furs. There, venturing too close inshore, the *Bordelais*
ran aground. Fortunately the sea was fairly calm, and she was
refloated. Roquefeuil, however, was heartily sick of these un-
profitable manœuvres: he decided to head for San Francisco,
which he reached on 20 September. His intention was to collect
the proceeds of goods he had left behind on his earlier visit, and
buy fruit and vegetables for his crossing of the Pacific; the
Russians had furthermore agreed to purchase any grain Roquefeuil could bring back from California. These plans were jeopar-
dized when news came that the *Bordelais*, as a trading vessel, was
subject to a recently promulgated set of prohibitions affecting
foreign shipping: Roquefeuil would be allowed to stay in port
only for as long as was necessary to take in urgently needed
supplies; he was forbidden to communicate with local residents
for any other purpose, and then only at the beach. He wrote at

once to the Governor, asking for permission to remain in the bay for two weeks, to land his sick, and to make such arrangements as were necessary to meet Hagemeister's claims. The Governor was sympathetic but had no wish to be accused of neglecting his instructions. His reply was 'conceived in very polite, but vague terms. I thought it tolerably satisfactory'. Even more satisfactory was the permission granted to the Franciscan mission to sell him corn—ostensibly as urgently needed supplies. The two weeks' grace lengthened into three, then nearly four. The *Bordelais* sailed on 18 October, leaving two sick men behind; the others had sufficiently recovered. Sitka was reached late on 9 November, after a severe storm which caused considerable damage. The corn was unloaded, the ship repaired, the sandalwood—which had been stored ashore, both for convenience and, from the Russian point of view, as a guarantee of payment—was taken on board, a cable and anchor, spars, cordage, and sail-cloth were bought, and the French were ready to sail. It was 13 December 1818. 'We finally quitted the North-West Coast of America, which we had explored during ten months, with more danger and fatigue than I had ever endured at sea.'[1]

On 9 January 1819 the *Bordelais* anchored 'off the village where Ta mea mea resided'. This was Kailua on the west coast of Hawaii. Roquefeuil was impressed by the pleasant climate and the apparent fertility of the soil. There were few subtropical crops, he noted, that would not do well in the islands, and already a considerable sea trade was developing. The Hawaiians would soon hear more of the French. Roquefeuil next sailed to Oahu, where he purchased food and some sandalwood. He left on 26 January, steering south to latitude 18° north, which he followed until 24 February, when he sighted Asunción and Agrihan Islands in the Marianas. It had been an uneventful crossing, and remained one as he sailed into the Philippine Sea and north of the Batan Islands to Macao, where he arrived on 11 March. He now discovered to his dismay that the demand for imported goods had fallen, while Chinese products were dearer. He applied for a reduction of customs charges, on the grounds that his vessel was

[1] *A Voyage round the World*, p. 110.

much smaller than the normal Indiaman, but to no avail. He
sailed from China on 27 April, in company with the *Indienne*
from Nantes. The voyage home was slow. He did not leave
Mauritius until 17 July as his ship had developed a leak. He
reached the Cape of Good Hope on 13 August, then was delayed
by unfavourable winds in the Atlantic, so that before he was in
sight of the Azores he was 'obliged to ask a supply of provisions
from three different vessels and did not make the coast of Oleron
till 19 November'. Two days later, the *Bordelais* entered the river
Gironde 'and thus completed her voyage round the World in
37 months and two days, having been 22 months and 6 days
under sail'. It was obvious that the voyage would not show a
profit. The French had been too long away from the Pacific; their
information was too scant and unreliable for them to reap any
benefit in a trade where competition had been making itself felt
for years. On the other hand, viewed purely as a reconnaissance,
the expedition had been well worth while: France now had an
up-to-date report on conditions on the west coast of America
from California to the Aleutians, on Hawaii and the Marquesas,
and on the prospects of trade in each of these areas. If Roquefeuil
was not followed by other trading captains, it was because he had
shown that an isolated merchantman, without prearranged contacts, with little or no support from his government, was not
likely to succeed. This may not have been a very positive result,
but it was nevertheless useful. A minor, temporary advantage
was gained by the Balgueries, who obtained a reduction of 50 per
cent on the duty payable on most of the *Bordelais*'s cargo: it was
now up to them and other shipowners to use this as a precedent
for further concessions—a question which promptly generated
a bitter political struggle, the outcome of which was likely to
affect France's entire overseas trade.

French merchants preferred to turn their attention to the East.
Balguerie-Stuttenberg had already dispatched the *Paix* to Annam
in 1817, which was at once followed by the *Henry*. But here the
attitude of local rulers called for some caution. The same could
be said of South America, where the political upheavals, while
providing pickings for the lucky few, brought in their wake

certain dangers, not the least being ill-disguised piracy. Most traders preferred to wait for the Government to give them support, something French whaling firms also required. Jurien de la Gravière, now an admiral, sailed on a flag-showing mission to South America in 1820, and two more such expeditions, led by Captain de Mackau and Captain Roussin respectively, left at intervals during 1821. Kergariou, in the *Cybèle*, had been sent to Cochin-China in 1817, and de la Ville-Hélio, in the *Cléopâtre*, made a second attempt in 1821.[1] It was clear to all that the French Government would do all it could to assist traders, while observing the restraints imposed by its international obligations and the requirements of diplomacy. In the interim, interest would centre once more on expeditions of a scientific nature, the first of which —as Roquefeuil had learned in North America—was already on its way.

[1] See on these voyages the chapter on Bougainville, *infra*.

FREYCINET

LOUIS DE FREYCINET had, by 1816, completed the account of the Baudin expedition. The ending of hostilities offered at last an opportunity for a new voyage of exploration which he himself might hope to command. He drew up a plan, and sought the support of the Minister of the Interior, Lainé, who came from Bordeaux, and of du Bouchage, Minister of Marine. Such help was necessary, as Parliament was in a mood for economies and was in fact to reduce the combined naval-colonial vote in 1817. Louis XVIII, however, was ready to support the proposal, which was accepted very nearly in its entirety. The emphasis was not on discovery—for there was not much left to discover—not on close hydrographic surveys, but rather on scientific work. The Academy of Sciences outlined some of the research Freycinet might undertake, while admitting that there would not be time for everything. The measurement of the globe's southern hemisphere, the observation of magnetic and meteorologic phenomena, and experiments related to air pressure and the temperature of the sea at various depths were to be the expedition's main preoccupations, while reports would be expected on natural history, and on the customs, products, and languages of native peoples. The special commemorative medal struck for the expedition emphasizes these aims: one side shows the King encircled by the words 'Louis XVIII, Roi de France et de Navarre', the other has 'La Corvette l'*Uranie*, Mr Ls. de Freycinet commandt, S.A.R. le duc d'Angoulême Amiral de France, Mr le Vte du Bouchage Ministre de la Marine 1817', surrounded by the words 'Hémisphère austral. Physique. Astronomie.'

It may be surprising, therefore, that no scientists were invited to join the expedition; but Freycinet had learned from his experiences with Baudin that a group of scientists is likely to be a source of trouble, and he preferred to have the scientific work carried out by naval officers, whom he could easily control. He

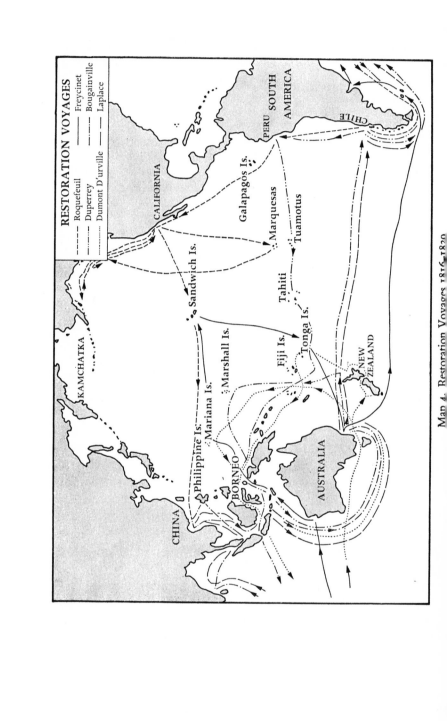

RESTORATION VOYAGES

- —————— Roquefeuil
- ·············· Duperrey
- —·—·—·— Dumont D'urville
- —————— Freycinet
- —··—··— Bougainville
- ———— Laplace

KAMCHATKA

CALIFORNIA

CHINA

Philippine Is.
Mariana Is.
Marshall Is.

BORNEO

Sandwich Is.

Fiji Is.
Tonga Is.

Galapagos Is.
Marquesas
Tuamotus
Tahiti

PERU SOUTH
AMERICA

CHILE

AUSTRALIA

NEW
ZEALAND

MAP 4. Restoration Voyages 1816–1820

was fortunate in his choice of men. His first officer was Lamarche, a Norman, promoted frigate-captain at the end of the voyage. Labiche, a nephew of Blondela, who had sailed to his death with La Pérouse, was to die in the East Indies; Louis-Isidore Duperrey was soon to lead his own expedition into the Pacific; the two surgeons, Quoy and Gaimard, were able naturalists; the pharmacist, Charles Gaudichaud, had a wide knowledge of botany. The scientific work could also be shared by the ten *élèves* or *aspirants*, all of whom were promoted during the voyage or shortly after. The draughtsman was Jacques Arago, brother of the famous savant: he had volunteered for the post, was accepted at a salary of 600 francs a year (about which he often complained), and subsequently wrote several accounts of the voyage. The King suggested as chaplain Quélen de la Villeglée, a canon of the royal chapter of St. Denis. The total complement was 125, including a company of six soldiers from the Seventh Battalion Naval Artillery who were to desert to a man in South America. Most of the seamen, but only a few of the officers, were southerners. Freycinet had taken care to engage sailors who could also boast of a trade—carpenters, sailmakers, ropemakers, blacksmiths— something which was to stand him in good stead after the ship was wrecked in the Falklands. The *Uranie* was a corvette of 350 tons, carrying 20 guns, formerly known as the *Ciotat*. The Government had been generous with supplies: there were large quantities of d'Appert tins, iron barrels for fresh water—an innovation in the French Navy—enough spare sails for two years, and every anti-scurvy remedy suggested by Keraudren, the Navy's Inspector-General of Health. Most of Freycinet's requests for scientific apparatus and books were met without hesitation.

The ship was ready by September 1817. The instructions, to which Freycinet adhered fairly closely—after all, the plan was largely his—provided for entry into the Pacific from the west, allowing for a return to Baudin's Shark Bay; the *Uranie* was then to sail to Timor or Amboina, thence to Waigeo, along the north coast of New Guinea to Guam and Hawaii, to Tahiti or the Marquesas, to Dusky Sound in New Zealand to rest and refit, then across the Southern Pacific to Cape Horn and Bouvet Island.

The expedition sailed from Toulon on 17 September 1817. Contrary winds held it back for over three weeks. After tacking hopelessly off the south-east coast of Spain, Freycinet sailed into Gibraltar on 11 October. His was the first French war vessel to visit the fortress since 1793. The Lieutenant-Governor, General Don, received his visitors with great courtesy; formerly Lieutenant-Governor of Jersey, he spoke French with fair fluency. He did, however, excuse himself from entertaining his visitors further, on the grounds that his cook was away at his country house. This excuse sounded specious, for, Gibraltar being a small place, the cook could hardly have been even an hour's travelling away. Was the general unwilling to receive other than formally a former enemy? This is hardly likely, even though the date was still only 1817, for Freycinet was in the service of Louis XVIII, whom the British were anxious to please, and the *Uranie* was flying the Bourbon flag they had pledged themselves to restore. Rumours spread at the time, later being confirmed by Arago, that Don had been shocked by the presence, and, above all, by the unconventional attire, of Freycinet's wife.

The presence on board of Rose de Freycinet had been discovered two days after the *Uranie* had left Toulon. She had been smuggled on board during the night of the 16th, and had remained hidden in the captain's cabin until the vessel was well out of sight of the French coast. Then the commandant had brought the whole thing into the open by inviting officers, chaplain, and artist to an informal tea. Rose, so it appeared, had been so unwilling to be separated from her husband that she had prevailed on him to accept her as an illegal passenger. The reason was given as Louis's delicate health, which needed special care. It may be unchivalrous to note that he was to survive an epidemic of cholera, which proved fatal to her, and reach the relatively ripe age of 63. The risk he was taking was obvious: his action was clearly contrary to naval regulations, and her presence on board was bound to cause eyebrows to rise in ports wherever they called. The first of these was Gibraltar. The Freycinets had agreed that Rose should wear masculine clothes—a long blue frock-coat and trousers to match—and this, so Arago reports, upset the Lieutenant-Governor.

It was even reported in Paris that her uniform had been that of
a naval ensign, but this was untrue. The Minister in Paris, who
would have been entitled to order Freycinet to leave his wife
behind at some suitable port, decided to ignore the matter.
Rose, for her part, abandoned her male disguise, and there
was no further coolness shown by any host for the rest of the
voyage.

The *Uranie* sailed on the 14th. The complement was already two
short: a young ensign, Pratt-Bernon, had concealed a feverish
condition when he embarked in Toulon and had died at sea; and
a gunner was left behind in Gibraltar on account of home-sickness, which at first sight reveals a rare generosity on the part of
Freycinet, until one remembers that the majority of explorers
were anxious that those who sailed with them should do so 'de
bonne volonté'. The *Uranie* now made up some of the time lost
in the Mediterranean. Tenerife was reached in a week, and after
a brief call to take in stores Freycinet made for Rio, where he
anchored on 6 December. Rose was a good sailor, who enjoyed
life at sea, in spite of the absence of female company.

As she stepped on to the deck, the officers deferentially withdrew;
for a while the men on the lower deck, to whom she was clearly
visible, showed their respect by ceasing their usual oaths and ribald
songs, a tribute that their captain's wife would acknowledge with a
pleasant smile. But soon their normal curses and ditties would inevitably
break forth; then, Mme de Freycinet, turning troubled eyes on the
waves, would appear to be listening to the soft swishing of the water,
to be oblivious of the furious noises in the forepart of the ship. It was
highly embarrassing to everybody, says Arago, but also amusing, as
good as a play: the Commandant was not in a position to show resent-
ment, for Madame, strictly speaking, was not on board; the officers,
suddenly absorbed in their tasks ignored what was going on under
their noses; the hilarious sailors spoke just loud enough to make certain
that their jokes were audible, while the boatswain's violent signs commanded silence in vain. In the end, Mme de Freycinet would return
to her quarters, vowing to emerge as seldom as possible for movement
and a change of air.[1]

[1] M. Bassett, *Realms and Islands*, p. 17.

Rose's presence on board was not altogether an advantage. There were rumours of dissension among the officers, and there must have been caustic and angry comments on occasions. Gabriel Lafond, who visited the Marianas not long after the *Uranie*'s visit, states that, according to reports:

she was also an apple of discord, thrown not just to three goddesses but to a crowd of young men whose jealousies and passions could not fail to be aroused. Always of dignified, becoming and discreet behaviour, never herself giving cause for a single derogatory comment by her mere existence, young Mme de Freycinet furnished a topic of conversation likely to disturb the good harmony, even the discipline, essential in a naval ship.[1]

Yet she was not always so discreet and staid: she was only 22, lively and vivacious, not to say excitable. She described herself as 'the gay, the thoughtless madcap Rose',[2] and friends who met her upon her return commented on the steadying effect of the voyage, finding her subdued where she had been impetuous and excited. This is hardly to be wondered at, after the hardships and near-tragedies of the campaign. But, however unsettling her presence may have been, her obvious charm and constant solicitude and devotion to her husband must have more than compensated for it.

The arrival at Rio provided a pleasant respite, although it was marred by the death of one of the gunners, killed while the ship was saluting the town. The French consular representative lacked efficiency, and over a week elapsed before Freycinet found a house where the observatory could be set up; when he was about to move in it was discovered that the house had been let to someone else. Not all this time was wasted: there were opportunities for excursions and visits, one of them to be received by the King, another to meet a Bonapartist refugee, General Hogendorp, now living in poverty in Brazil. By and large, the French were bored. In Rio harbour, stated Arago, are several islands, 'Rat Island, Snakes Island, Governor's Island, which take their name from the different animals that live on them'.[3] Arago tends to be

---

[1] Quoted in Bassett, *Realms and Islands*, p. 148.   [2] Ibid., p. 244.
[3] *Promenade autour du monde*, vol. i, p. 83.

sweeping in his judgements and his books are full of generaliza-
tions, but his caustic wit often expresses the feelings of his fellow
voyagers. When the *Uranie* sailed out of Rio on 29 January 1818,
few aboard her felt any regret. Freycinet had already experienced
some of the troubles that were to plague him throughout the
voyage: 'We left Rio on 29 January, after renewing a part of our
crew. I am not trying to discover the reasons for our sailors deserting; I am afraid I might guess right.'[1] Indeed, thirty-one men had
to be left behind, twenty-three of them deserters; eleven replacements were taken on.

In February a second officer died. On the evening of the 14th,
Laborde, a young ensign, strained his voice while giving out a
command and spat out some blood. He was apparently tubercular:
a violent haemorrhage laid him low the next day, and he died
early on the 23rd. His death cast a feeling of gloom over the ship,
which was not dispelled until the *Uranie* dropped anchor in Table
Bay on 7 March. Freycinet paid the usual visit to the Governor,
Lord Charles Somerset, and to Kotzebue, who, in the Prussian
ship *Rurick*, was completing a circumnavigation which had taken
him around the Horn and as far north as the Bering Sea. Supplies
were taken in, and the French left the Cape on 5 April, making
for Mauritius, or, as Freycinet still called it, the Île de France.
Here on 7 May he was reunited with 'a brother, from whom I
had been separated for twenty years and who, I had just learnt,
was about to leave for Bengal on business. I was, alas, never to
see him again.' This was Charles, his youngest brother, who was
in business, and had recently been acting as private secretary to
George Smith, the island's chief magistrate.

Mauritius was now a British colony, but retained all its French
features: the language in daily use was French, the place-names
were French, and for those, like Freycinet, who had been in the
island before 1810 there were sad memories at every step. Arago,
in his usual style, declared: 'Ask a question today of any citizen of
Mauritius, and the first maxim you will get from his reply will
be hatred! Hatred of the English!!! Misfortune has a long
memory.'[2]

---

[1] Ibid., vol. i, p. 155.   [2] Ibid., vol. ii, p. 268.

But Freycinet was most courteously and hospitably treated. George Smith offered him his town house, with rooms for him and his wife, for his secretary, for the abbé Quélen, and for the two officers in charge of the observatory. Smith's generosity may have been motivated out of friendship for Charles, but it may also have reflected a desire to conciliate the island French. Governor Farquhar's firm rule cannot have endeared him too much to them during his first years—if Arago is to be even half-believed; he was away on leave in Britain when Freycinet arrived, and the acting-Governor, General Hall, was a stern disciplinarian who had spent seven years as a prisoner of the French during the war. Hall was polite but cool when Freycinet called on him. Smith may thus have been seizing an opportunity, in Farquhar's absence, to smooth a situation which was in danger of becoming tense. From Mme de Freycinet's point of view especially, Smith's hospitality was a blessing, as the *Uranie*'s copper sheathing was found to be seriously damaged, so that the ship had to be careened, and not until 16 July could the French, all repairs completed, all supplies loaded, sail from Port Louis. The intervening weeks were spent on excursions and social functions. The Anglo-Saxons organized horse races which the French found particularly dull: 'The races we attended are, to my mind, truly the most insipid and petty thing in the world. Three or four horses ridden by men dressed as harlequins are the champions that compete for the prize.'[1]

Rose found these occasions less dreary: she had a woman's interest in clothes, and a keen observing eye for customs. In the morning, she consigned her thoughts to her journal,[2] or commented in lively style in letters to a friend on the events of the previous day. There was a visit to Pamplemousses, where the heroine of Bernardin de Saint-Pierre's *Paul et Virginie* was reported to be buried; a day trip to the Governor's country house, *Le Réduit*; and balls, of course, including one given by Hall at Government House. This she decided not to attend—the cost of having a suitable gown made for this single occasion was not

---

[1] Freycinet, *Voyage*, vol. i, p. 362, quoting the *élève* Pellion.
[2] Printed in Paris in 1927.

warranted, she declared. But a refusal, coming from Judge Smith's guest, was bound to be regarded as having political undertones. 'Mme Hall attributed my absence to the advice of Mr. Smith, then at open war with the General.' This was not surprising, as Smith was holding that same evening a dinner-party for sixty guests! Discretion was called for: Rose complained of a migraine, and excused herself from the dinner as well. The presence of the British naval vessel *Magicienne*, Captain Purvis, provided another opportunity for an exchange of visits, and also for a pointed comment in Freycinet's book: 'Mrs. Purvis, who was travelling with her husband, was our hostess.' Louis was probably not sorry to find another case of a naval captain sailing on an official mission accompanied by his wife, although, as Purvis was attached to the India station, the two cases were not quite similar. Rose, on the other hand, was delighted.

His wife, who is very young, travels with him. But what a difference between Louis' mission and his! He sails the Indian seas to protect the merchants from pirates; at all the stations he finds a house, furnished, and with servants to wait on them. Sometimes he makes short cruises without his wife, so as not to tire her with too much voyaging. She gave birth to a pretty little boy soon after the frigate arrived at the Île de France for repairs. She is a charming little woman, very well brought up; the resemblance between our situations brought us together.[1]

After their departure from Mauritius, the French called briefly at Bourbon, the neighbouring island which the British had returned to the French crown. Bourbon was far less prosperous, but quieter and less bitter in its internal political struggles. The Freycinets threaded their way with caution through the inevitable petty rivalries and jealousies of Restoration colonial society, paying formal visits to the leading Créole and French families. There were a few supplies to be taken in, vegetables, chickens, and refreshments for the sick and the officers, and Freycinet was ready to sail.

At the same moment that we arrived on board, *La Cybèle*, a French frigate coming from China, anchored a few cables from us, but she

[1] From Rose's Journal, translated M. Bassett in *Realms and Islands*, pp. 68–9.

manœuvred so badly that she struck us and broke an anchor that we have on that side, and did other damage that forced us to stay until next day to have it repaired. . . . Seeing that nobody in the frigate was co-operating in the movements necessary to free the vessels from one another, Louis went on board the *Cybèle* to find the captain to urge him to give the appropriate orders; what was his astonishment, instead of finding him on the bridge seeing to the safety of his ship, he saw him in the midst of ladies and gentlemen, passengers in the frigate from Mauritius to Bourbon, drinking, laughing and singing, etc: his first word to Louis was to invite him to sit down and have a drink, but Louis refused, saying he had to attend to his ship; perhaps from the state the captain was in (having drunk a little too much) or from an inconceivable indifference, he said it was the Harbour Master's responsibility to attach a cable to his frigate. Louis, concluding that the captain was not capable of doing anything, came to an understanding with the frigate's officers and in a short time the ships were safe.[1]

The *Cybèle*'s captain was Achille de Kergariou, who was on his way home from a mission to Cochin-China. Kergariou, by no means irresponsible in the normal course of events, had no doubt fallen a victim to Créole light-heartedness and to a feeling of relief at the end of a voyage. Freycinet, impatient to begin his scientific work, was naturally less sympathetic. He sailed without regrets, making at last for the coast of Australia. Shark Bay was reached late on 12 September. His intention was to anchor north of Péron Peninsula, but first he sent a boat to Dirck Hartog Island to fetch the commemorative pewter plate which had been discovered and restored by Baudin in 1801. The thought of the plate left on a pole in a deserted island at the mercy of the weather and of any irresponsible sailor or aborigine who might be visiting the island had nagged at him for years. The almost incredible chain of circumstances which had led to its discovery, half buried in the sand, after nearly two hundred years, might never be repeated.

Believing that such a rare plate might again be swallowed up by the sands, or else run the risk of being taken away and destroyed by some careless sailor, I felt that its correct place was in one of these

[1] Bassett, *Realms and Islands*, p. 81.

great scientific depositories which offer to the historian such rich and precious documents. I planned, therefore, to place it in the collections of the Académie royale des inscriptions et belles-lettres de l'Institut de France, and this I had the honour of doing . . . on 23 March 1821.[1]

This concern was sound and reasonable, but it nearly led to the final loss of the Vlamingh plate. In 1897, in reply to an inquiry from Australia, the French had to admit the plate was lost. They suggested that Freycinet might have borrowed it when writing the account of his voyage and neglected to return it. In view of Freycinet's concern for the safety of the plate and his obvious pride at having placed it in what he believed would be the right place for it, the explanation sounded unconvincing. It was clear that, when Freycinet had returned it, its importance had been overlooked and it had not been put back in the appropriate room. In 1938 the Historical Society of Victoria wrote to the Académie des Inscriptions et Belles Lettres asking for a further search to be made. Then, in 1940, it was discovered in a cupboard 'on the lowest shelf, jumbled up with the copper-plates that had been used for illustrating old memoirs, in the dark little room filled entirely with shelves where old reports are kept'. This was not to be the end of its travels. It was sent to Australia in 1947 as a gift from the French Government, which the Commonwealth Government reciprocated by sending a collection of aboriginal artefacts to the Paris Museum. The plate was now nearly 250 years old, and extremely frail. It was accordingly sent to London to be restored by a group of experts, and, when returned, was placed on view in Canberra in 1950. Its final resting-place was then the subject of controversy, some believing it should remain in the national capital, others that its rightful place was Western Australia. It clearly could not return to the still desolate shores of Dirck Hartog Island. The compromise was for replicas to be made and distributed to institutions in various states, while the original was transferred to Perth.

While a party searched for the Vlamingh plate, an observatory was being set up on Péron Peninsula. It was also necessary to set up a distilling machine, as water was running short and the bay

[1] *Voyage*, vol. i, p. 449.

offered little except the brackish waters of low-lying ponds and sluggish tidal creeks. Pellion was put in charge of the small camp, and was joined by Gaudichaud, who planned to start botanizing at once. Aborigines appeared, nine in number, who stood some distance from the Frenchmen, gesticulating and shouting rhythmically: 'ïou . . . cana . . . anana, words fairly regularly articulated by them, were clearly instructing us to withdraw.' Pellion had no intention of so doing, but was equally reluctant to use force to drive them away. French words, spoken in a soothing voice, had no effect. Pellion, noticing the apparent rhythmic nature of the natives' speech, started his men singing and dancing. This at once proved effective, and the Australians accepted, though cautiously, a number of small gifts. Others joined them, appearing fearfully from between the sand dunes, until their number grew to fifteen. Each new arrival was greeted by a French dance. In this way incidents were avoided and the French were able to return to their own work. Pellion wanted to establish some more satisfactory form of contact with his visitors who were now chanting and beating rhythmically on their spears. Arago arrived and was at once accepted when he began to play on his castanets. A print of the scene shows him performing in this way, while Pellion or Gaudichaud is offering small gifts which a native is gingerly accepting on the end of a spear. At sunset the aborigines dispersed, indicating by signs that they would return. Freycinet and Rose did indeed see them the next day—'a troupe of savages, quite naked and armed with assegais and spears', as Rose told her friend Caroline de Nanteuil in a letter—then unaccountably they disappeared and were seen no more.

What had they said to their strange French visitors? Nothing is more difficult than trying to identify the few words, or fragments of words, which the French were able to catch and set down phonetically in their journal. It is impossible even to hazard a guess at *ïou*, and *cana* could mean several things, but *anana* could well be *wanja*, meaning 'to leave', a rendition confirmed to some extent by the gestures which the aborigines are reported to have made towards the ship or the open sea, and by the tendency of tribesmen in the district north of the Swan River to lengthen words with an additional syllable. Another possibility is *djangaka*, meaning 'the dead'. This term was used to denote Europeans, who were believed to be dead people seeking their way back to their tribe. Arago is of little help: although he devotes nearly fifty pages to a South Sea vocabulary, it includes only one word from Australia—*ayerkade*, which he interprets as 'go away'. It is clear that, by shouts and gestures, the aborigines were endeavouring to persuade the French to leave their tribal grounds, but they correctly interpreted the sailors' dances and Arago's castanets as attempts to express friendship, and, having satisfied themselves on this point, left the immediate neighbourhood of the camp, although no doubt keeping careful watch on the activities of the French.

The group which had been sent to Dirck Hartog Island was now overdue. Freycinet sent a boat with Pellion in charge and a carpenter in case the party had been wrecked on the island. All that had happened was that a high wind had marooned them on the island. Everyone returned none the worse for the adventure. It was soon the turn of Gaimard to give rise to anxiety. He had gone out with Freycinet's secretary, Gabert, Raillard, the young ensign from the Bordeaux region, and the boatswain Bonnet. Gaimard's hope was to meet the aborigines and try to prove his theory that they could drink sea-water. He could not conceive any other possibility in such a dry and desolate spot. But no natives came within sight, even though some might have been observing the four men as they stumbled through scrub-covered hillocks and dried salt-pans. Gaimard stopped with Gabert to examine natural-history specimens, leaving the others to go on for a short while. It would not have been too difficult for him to catch them up, even taking into account the broken nature of the landscape, but Gaimard had no sense of direction. They blundered from one dune to another, unable to catch a glimpse of the sea. When night fell it soon became so cold that they were unable to sleep and had to start walking again. On the 20th Freycinet sent Bonnet, with Arago and the *élève* Ferrand, to see what traces they might find. The lost men, however, were on their way back. Gabert had worked out their position in relation to Dirck Hartog

Island and the camp, and led his companion back. From then on, botanizing and scientific observations were carried out close to the anchorage. An exception was made in the case of Duperrey, who went to Hamelin Pool to make a number of observations and surveys left undone by the *Naturaliste*. Freycinet was also desirous of completing Baudin's hydrographic work around the chain of islands which defend Shark Bay on the seaward side. On the morning of 26 September he weighed anchor and sailed slowly towards Bernier Island. A number of soundings were taken, the weather being calm and the sea smooth. Suddenly, at 6 p.m., the *Uranie* grounded on a sandbank. Fortunately the tide was not yet high, and the weather remained favourable. As the sea rose, the ship floated and was towed off. Freycinet anchored for the night; he had come to realize that the bay still concealed many dangers which only a regular survey with the ship's boats would reveal. For this he had no time. He sailed cautiously out of Shark Bay in the morning, and made for the Dutch colony of Timor.

On the evening of the 27th the coast of Endracht Land disappeared into the dusk. The crossing was uneventful. Roti and its off-shore islands were sighted on 7 October, offering a restful picture of greenery and cool waterways after the bareness of Australia; the *Uranie* then sailed along the coast of Semau on the 8th and entered Kupang harbour early the next morning. The French found the colony in a state of war, the Rajah of Amanubang having rebelled against his Dutch overlords. The Governor was away with his troops in the interior, leaving the colony in charge of the government secretary, Tielman. The settlement was in fact in a parlous state. There were few provisions available, and Freycinet granted Tielman's request to omit the customary exchange of salutes between the town batteries and the ship. The reason given was that the Governor had taken the keys of the powder store with him, an implausible excuse which Freycinet neither believed nor queried. Tielman and his wife did their best to entertain their visitors. There were soirées: slaves played recognizable European airs on violin and flute, a small native girl performed excellently on a harp, Mrs. Tielman herself entertained at the piano. The scene, dark complexions aside, was little different from what one might have expected in a small French provincial town. A Chinese religious festival was more exotic and colourful. Candles and burning sandalwood in the moonlit air, the strangeness of the various ceremonies, fascinated Rose, and at the same time saddened the believer in her. 'Poor people! How I pity them! . . . In the midst of these idolators my heart was filled with thankfulness that I was Christian.'

On 23 October the *Uranie* left Kupang. The oppressive heat, the lack of supplies, and the dangers to health ever present in the East Indies far outweighed the advantages of resting the crew for a few days longer. There were already five cases of dysentery on board.[1] Freycinet's intention was to sail along the northern coast of Timor and proceed without further stop through the Moluccas to Waigeo, off the north-western tip of New Guinea. But his hopes dimmed as calms, contrary winds, and currents held back the *Uranie* for twenty-four days in the Straits of Ombai between Portuguese Timor and the small island of Alor; the French had to contain their impatience. A small party landed on the island of Ombai itself. The islanders had a bad reputation, which their fierce appearance seemed to confirm. But Arago once more brought out his castanets, did a few conjuring tricks, and sketched a quick portrait of one of the warriors. No one could resist such overtures; the French returned safely, having exchanged glass beads and knives for a chicken, some fruit, and bows and arrows. The *Uranie* was not the only ship in difficulties. An English whaler, the *Ocean*, whose captain, Benjamin Hammat, came on board to dine and invite Freycinet to visit him, had been cruising in the Molucca seas and was bound for London, which he hoped to reach within six months. A fortnight later, yet a third vessel appeared, the *Thomas Scattergood* of Philadelphia, making for Canton. But luck played an important role in the days of sailing ships: in the night a strong westerly breeze came up, and they were all soon on their way.

It was now 16 November. Freycinet had not been able to buy sufficient supplies in Kupang, very little had been obtained from

[1] Dr. Quoy, in his report, states that there were six (Freycinet, *Voyage*, vol. i, p. 600).

Ombai; with an increasing number of sick he could not risk sailing
at once to New Guinea. He made instead for Dili, the chief
settlement of Portuguese Timor. He was received with more
formality than at Kupang—perhaps this was only to be expected
from a governor with the resounding name of Dom José Pinto
Alcoforado d'Azevado e Souza. Salutes were exchanged, and
each commandant sent one of his officers to pay his respects
to the other. Freycinet then landed with his entire *état-major*;
Azevado, learning of Rose's presence on board, sent her gifts
of fruit and freshly baked bread, and invited her to meet the
ladies of the colony. She came the next afternoon, to the accompaniment of a six-gun salute, the local ladies displaying
an obvious interest in the French woman's Paris clothes, and
genteelly deprecating their own.

A magnificent dinner of about 40 covers was served, partly in the
Portuguese manner and partly in the English *mode*. A great profusion
of meats and stews composed the various services; these were succeeded by a very fine dessert of various pastries, Chinese preserves,
and fruits, which are superb in Timor. Faithful to my word, I ate only
mangoes and some of the exquisite pineapple. The china and glass,
which covered the table, were worthy of the rest; there was an air of
grandeur about everything, the slaves of both sexes were numerous
and served us very well. The healths of the kings and princes of France
and Portugal were drunk in Madeira wine; at each toast the cannon
was fired, and musicians played almost throughout the meal. After
dinner, the Governor who is amiable and extremely gay, proposed
dancing: the ladies seemed to like the suggestion, and I accepted the
hand of don José and we danced an English measure, but the heat
seemed to me so intolerable that I begged to be allowed to rest.[1]

But it was not to be the last such function, although Freycinet
was anxious to leave. He was buying large quantities of supplies—
300 fowls, several buffaloes, maize, rice, and tobacco. The
Governor issued an invitation to another dinner, as did his second-
in-command, Captain Mor Francisco de Assis Monteiro. The
festivities did not end until midnight on the eve of the *Uranie*'s
departure. Azevado offered Freycinet a gift of four young slaves,

---

[1] Bassett, *Realms and Islands*, pp. 104-5.

which Freycinet, taken aback, declined. Azevado put this refusal down to the formalities of politeness and insisted. To avoid giving offence, Freycinet was forced to accept one, a small boy, who was taken on board and baptized Joseph Antonio. He was to die in Paris at the age of 16 'of a scrofulous disease'.

The *Uranie* sailed from the heat-oppressed shores of Timor on 22 November. There was a great deal of sickness and exhaustion on board: six men were seriously attacked by dysentery, and new cases were reported daily; those included Labiche, the second lieutenant, and possibly the chaplain, Quélen, who was thin and weakened. Within a week three men had died, including the young sailor Bernard, 'whom an excess of zeal led to conceal his illness and carry on with his work'.[1] Labiche himself was to die in Rawak, New Guinea. For many the illness dragged on until the French reached the Marianas, five months later. This was the only cloud over the expedition as it made its way towards Buru Strait. The steady breeze not only favoured the ship, but at last cooled the previously intolerable temperature. Islands, covered with luxuriant and restful green vegetation came into view at frequent intervals, spice trees turning the air gently fragrant. Amboina was sighted on the 29th; wasting no time Freycinet sailed through Buru Strait and entered the Serang Sea. The breeze weakened as the *Uranie* made her way north and north-east towards Pisang Island, and the straits between Halmahera and New Guinea. Native craft circled the ship, causing Freycinet to order the gunners to their posts, for neither appearance nor reputation inspired confidence in the islanders who frequented these waters. On 7 December, off Pisang, two large native vessels —'corocores'—sailed up, each mounted by approximately fifty men. They came from Gebe, the island north of Pisang, between Halmahera and Waigeo. Their leader, Abdalaga, was persuaded to come aboard, and his mien and personality impressed all the French, several of whom have left a description of him:

This chief . . . seems to be in his early forties. He wears a turban which covers his head down to his eyebrows; his eyes are lively and full of

---

[1] Quoy's report (*Voyage*, vol. i, p. 601).

expression, his nose somewhat heavy and squat, his mouth very large, his chin cleft and covered with long sparse hair; he is five foot three tall, his complexion is yellow, his teeth very black . . . he smiles, and his smile seems to lack sincerity; he aims to be persuasive, and inspires only fear; he promises much but asks more. His sudden appearance in the middle of this Moluccan archipelago, his three or four sailing craft, distant more than five leagues from each other, the agility of their crews, their look of independence, or rather of superiority, their equipment, everything seemed to indicate at first glance one of these daring pirates.[1]

Rose, of course, described the scene in her diary, but is more kindly and sympathetic than Arago:

Not only was he well received, but Louis invited him to lunch—and he needed no second invitation. Soon he made it plain that his fancy was taken by one of our chairs, which was at once given to him; to prove his pleasure he could think of nothing better than to remove his hat and to put it on Louis' head. It seemed to me a very amusing hat, a sort of straw parasol of very fine workmanship with a pointed crown, rather like the lid of one of our *casseroles*. The name of this singular personage is Abdalaga-Fourou. The captains of the other *corocores* arrived to join us and like him stayed to dine with us. The Kimalaha, better dressed than the others, had trousers and a sort of open dressing-gown of striped Indian cloth with red flowers on it, and under his hat a little red turban with a crown of fine straw. His skin is copper-coloured, his face lively and intelligent. These men chew betel-nut and lime, which they carry packed in pretty little boxes of fine straw, dyed in various colours.[2]

The Kimalaha's friendship was useful, less in respect of trade for the French had little the Gebeans wanted, than for the information he gave them on the neighbouring islands and their people. One of the aims of the expedition, it will be remembered, was to obtain information on the inhabitants and economic resources of the countries it visited. Freycinet was thus able to write at length on the appearance, the dress, and the customs of Abdalaga's people. But more, the chief was literate, and he gave Freycinet a brief document in a mixture of Malay, Gebean, and

---

[1] Arago, *Promenade*, vol. i, pp. 361–2.   [2] *Realms and Islands*, p. 112.

Portuguese, which was both a note of thanks and a passport, 'I, Abdalaga, chief and commander, leader of a fleet of three vessels, have met a French ship commanded by Captain Freycinet: a generous man whose kind heart gave me a chair, to whom I gave a hat as a souvenir of Gueby. Freycinet also gave me delicate dishes. End.'

In the night a breeze sprang up which enabled the corocores to sail away, but it was hardly strong enough for the *Uranie*. Still off Pisang, Freycinet sent a group to explore the island. Quoy and Gaudichaud, accompanied by Arago, and protected by a group of men under the two young ensigns, Raillard and Bérard, spent a fruitful but tiring day on the shores of the small islands. Colourful birds darted overhead, filling the hot calm air with the shrillness of their cries, and there were botanical specimens, exciting new varieties for the naturalists' boxes, although uncertainty about the natives kept them from wandering too far in the forest.

On the 9th the breeze firmed enough for the *Uranie* to continue on her way; three days later she entered Djailolo Strait between Gebe and the small island of Muor. Now veering east, Freycinet encountered a number of islands which he named after his officers and naturalists: Laborde, Quélen, Stéphanie, Pellion, Quoy, Labiche, Gaimard, Gabert, Héclars, Requin, Gaudichaud. There was little justification for this action, none of the islands being new discoveries and simply forming the Wajag group. Later generations and political changes have eliminated from modern maps all traces of Freycinet's work in this area. The ship was now proceeding towards Waigeo through 'Passage de l'Uranie', between the Wajag islands and Rouib, now known as Kawe. Finally, on 16 December, the *Uranie* dropped anchor in Rawak harbour. The coast seemed uninhabited: a few derelict huts along the shore enabled the French to set up some sort of a camp and store the equipment they were reluctant to leave in tents. The presence of tombs a little further on was taken as evidence of the unhealthy nature of the district—but even a healthy community must have somewhere to bury its dead. The French, anyhow, were not left alone for long; canoes soon appeared from various small coves and from behind the headland, cautiously making their way towards the strange ship. Trading began in a desultory manner, the Papuans being more interested in the white men's strange behaviour. Freycinet especially puzzled them by watching the oscillations of the pendulum. What was he doing? There were no words adequate to translate this for the primitive minds. 'This question was very natural and it was later put to me by other chiefs of this country; but what could I reply? How could I tell them that I was measuring the earth? Would they not have thought me mad?'

In time novelty wore off, and a market developed to which the islanders brought daily supplies of fruit, fish, pigs, and occasionally turtles, receiving in exchange knives, trinkets, and lengths of cloth. While the sailors gathered firewood and refilled the water-casks, Quoy and Duperrey went to Boni to 'see if any traces of d'Entrecasteaux's stay still remained', but nothing could be seen but the river, winding its way through the jungle. Duperrey discovered a new variety of dove, which he named colombe Pinon, this being Mme de Freycinet's maiden name. Duperrey paid further compliments to the captain's wife, giving the names Pointe Rose and Anse Rose to two features on his map of Waigeo, ephemeral tributes to her charm and continuing high spirits.

On 1 January the Gebean chief Abdalaga kept a promise he had made to meet the French in Waigeo. He brought with him nine members of his family, among them his elder brother Abas, who remembered a visit by French ships over forty years earlier. These were not Bougainville's, who had indeed sailed here in 1768, but Coëtivy's, who had left the Île de France in June 1771, reached Luzon in September, and sailed down to Mindoro and Panay in December. The ships had then separated, one going to Jolo, and rejoined at Zamboanga in western Mindanao in February; proceeding very cautiously they sailed east and south-east in a wide arc, keeping well clear of Halmahera, until on the 20th they arrived at an island which the careful narrator does not name, but which clearly was Gebe. The reason for caution, and for avoiding the Dutch settlements, is obvious: Coëtivy had been sent by Pierre Poivre to find spices and similar plants which could be acclimatized in the Île de France and Bourbon. This was simply poaching in the Dutch possessions, and there was no doubt in anyone's mind that the Dutch would have impounded the ships and arrested the entire crews. Even the published report could have led to protests and possibly to some kind of reprisals. But, from local rulers in islands distant enough from Dutch posts, there was very little to fear.[1]

It would seem that the ships had stopped briefly at Gebe, where they were seen by Abas, then a youth accompanying the chief, and sailed on to Pulo Pisang, where they were able to buy supplies, including nutmeg plants. They then continued south to Timor, passing through the Strait on 28 April, and reaching the Île de France on 4 June. Abas easily recognized the white French flag, which had impressed him in his youth as quite different from the Dutch emblem. His enthusiasm and loquacity when meeting Frenchmen again made him something of a nuisance on board the *Uranie*. Indeed, all the new arrivals had to be tactfully but firmly asked to return later, as they had arrived on the first day of the year, which Freycinet had already set aside as a day of rest and an evening of restrained celebration. The visitors went ashore, and the French were left to enjoy their dinner in peace, but Abdalaga was back in the morning, still in high spirits. Freycinet found it impossible to continue his work in the face of constant questions and requests for gifts. Another drawback was that the Papuans, who had formerly brought supplies daily, disappeared as soon as the Gebeans entered the bay. Yet Abdalaga and Abas were genuinely pleased to see the French; they obviously had more time to spare than at Pisang and had arranged their expedition to Waigeo with a view to instruction, profit, and enjoyment. Without offending them, Freycinet succeeded in getting rid of his importunate visitors by explaining he was now preparing to sail. The Gebeans departed on the morning of the 4th, shouting many protestations of friendship. Late on the 5th Freycinet prepared to weigh anchor.

Sickness was spreading through the ship. Rose de Freycinet ate

[1] See Sonnerat, *An Account of a Voyage to the Spice-Islands and New Guinea*.

some fruit which caused a bout of vomiting and severe stomach cramps. Dysentery was affecting an increasing number of men—Labiche died of it. On the same day malaria broke out. 'At first five men, then thirty, including four *élèves*, fell sick. As soon as the first group recovered, others took their place below, so that it can be estimated that forty men were affected.'[1] Two died, both men just entering their fifties, 'worn out by long campaigns'. The others, younger and fitter men, recovered, but now another scourge—scurvy—was making its appearance:

We soon ran out of fresh food; everything from our private stores was used up for the sick, and still their condition worsened. . . . The humidity, the heat, and boredom whose effect is always debilitating after a time, were responsible for the outbreak of scurvy which affected four men, including our chaplain, the worthy abbé Quélen. We used hot sand baths for this secondary affection, but less fortunate than other navigators we met with no success.[2]

Slow and painful navigation eastwards along the Equator brought the *Uranie* in sight of Bougainville's Hermit Island on 12 February. The next day, the Admiralty group hove into sight. The French had no inclination or time for a survey: on the 25th Freycinet changed to a northerly course. His first landfall in the Carolines was Pulusuk, which had been discovered in 1799 by the Spanish captain Juan Ibargoitia. Twelve canoes came out to the *Uranie*, which took several in tow, a number of natives climbing on board. There was lively trading to the accompaniment of much laughter, dancing, and shouting. Three days later, on 15 March, more islands, Puluwat and Pulap atolls, came into sight. Freycinet sailed slowly between them, surrounded by canoes, buying fish, coconuts, and artefacts from the clamorous natives. But the sick were too numerous, and their condition was too serious, for any delay. The western Carolines, anyhow, were not unknown. Pulap had been discovered by Alonso de Arellano as far back as 1565.[3] Further investigation could be left to later voyagers. The *Uranie* arrived at Guam on 17 March, and dropped anchor in

[1] Freycinet, *Voyage*, vol. ii, p. 67.
[2] Ibid., p. 69.
[3] Sharp, *The Discovery of the Pacific Islands*, p. 35.

Umatac Bay. The Spanish sent refreshments at once. 'The
Israelites in the desert did not welcome the manna with more joy
and thankfulness.'

On the 18th ship and shore exchanged a twenty-one-gun salute.
This ceremony 'was the cause of a great misfortune to two soldiers
of the garrison who, no doubt unused to handling guns, were so
badly burned that concern was felt for their lives'.[1] The Governor,
Don Medinilla y Pineda, came on board shortly after and promised every assistance. Bananas, figs, milk, and greens followed
his announcement. The sick, numbering twenty,[2] were sent
ashore and quartered in a disused religious building. The abbé
Quélen was taken into the Governor's own home. Having thus
disposed of the most pressing matters, Don Medinilla proceeded
to enjoy himself. Life on Guam was seldom exciting, and the
presence of a French warship was a rare occasion for celebration.
Freycinet and his officers went to return his call, and were offered
what they took to be a buffet lunch. Reflecting that the meagre
fare possibly denoted a local day of fast, they decided to make the
best of what seemed to be a thin meal, only to discover that the
pastries and fruit were merely the hors-d'œuvre, locally termed
refresco, and simply a prelude to a substantial dinner. It did not
take long for the French to realize the Spanish ate well. The
Spanish ship *La Paz* was about to sail for Acapulco; the Governor
gave a farewell dinner for her officers and passengers, to which
the French and island notabilities were invited. 'Someone had
counted forty-four plates of food at each service, of which there
were three complete ones. The same observer said the dinner cost
the lives of two bullocks and three large pigs, to say nothing of
the smaller inhabitants of the forest, the farmyard, and the sea.'[3]

The next day, being the Governor's birthday, provided yet
another occasion for a celebration, including a concert by violins
and basses, and a children's choir. It seemed to have mattered little
that this was Lent: no doubt the presence of the French was

[1] Arago, *Promenade*, vol. i, p. 373.
[2] Bougainville considers this to be an understatement. He writes of the
Uranie: 'Cette corvette y relâcha manquant de tout et comptant sur les cadres plus
de quarante hommes en danger de la vie' (*Journal de la navigation*, vol. i, p. 165).
[3] Freycinet, *Voyage*, vol. ii, p. 138.

excuse enough to waive the rules of abstinence. Easter week was
marked by processions, cockfights, and dances:

Last Thursday, which was Holy Thursday, there were great ceremonies. The Governor took Easter communion. At the end of mass
and after the sacred emblem was placed on the tomb, the priest placed
round Louis' neck a plaited gold ribbon to which the key of the
tabernacle was attached. It was an honour that Don Medinilla relin-
quished to the Commandant, and that was not without its drawbacks,
for with it went the obligation to carry a cross at the head of the procession making a tour of the town, and the heat was great. So the good
Governor felt obliged to make many excuses to Louis for the trouble
he had caused him in ceding to him thus the honours of the position.
The staff of the *Uranie* followed the procession with much decorum.
This morning, High Mass and another procession, but Louis carried
nothing but his grave and thoughtful bearing, which I find such a
good example. He has given our doctor strict orders to keep M. the
abbé de Quélen at home: he cannot yet drag himself along without
the help of a stick: they hold out hope to him that he will be able to
go to church next Sunday.[1]

Don Medinilla's courtesy and generosity remained constant
during their stay, and when the French prepared to leave he
refused all payment for the stores he had put at their disposal.
All Freycinet could do was to recommend him to Louis XVIII,
who bestowed on the kind Spaniard the decoration of the Legion
of Honour. The long series of festivities had not altogether halted
the expedition's scientific work. The *Uranie* had sailed from Umatac on 28 March and anchored in Apra Harbour, a safer anchorage
and closer to the capital, Agaña. The usual observatory was set
up on shore. Bérard, Gaudichaud, and Arago set off in canoes on
a scientific expedition to the neighbouring islands of Rota and
Tinian, where they remained for eleven days. Rose contented
herself with an excursion to the nearby shrine of the Jesuit martyr
Fr. Sanvitores. Finally, on 6 June, after a stay of eleven weeks, the
French sailed from Guam.

The aim was now to cross the Pacific to Hawaii. After a few
days exploring the northern waters off Guam, Freycinet set his

---

[1] Bassett, *Realms and Islands*, p. 133.

ship on an easterly course. The crossing was not eventful. The weather cooled rapidly; the French encountered heavy damp fogs and in mid July a particularly cold snap, but apart from colds the health of the crew remained good. There was one exception, a sailor named Rio, who had already drawn attention to himself by his fondness for wine; he celebrated his feast day too well and fell head first from the quarter-deck to the orlop deck and was killed instantly. The death of this rather intemperate but popular and efficient sailor, as Freycinet comments, cast a gloom which was not dispelled for some days.

Hawaii was sighted on 5 August. The natives were accustomed to Europeans and promptly came out in canoes to trade fish and fruit for knives. The press of boats and gesticulating natives became so great that the *Uranie*, now becalmed, was completely surrounded. Only chiefs were allowed on board, the first of these, Pui, being invited with his wife to stay for a meal. The guests had none of the restrained bearing of some of the important chiefs the French were to meet later:

It did not take me long to convince myself that my guests were true beggars; they cast covetous glances on everything. And so, in order to remain good friends, we had to give them the glass, the plate, the bottle and the very napkin they had used; even then these presents, far from satisfying them, merely made them harder to please. Pui decided to buy my uniform from me and to offer in exchange four coconuts. He wanted a musket and some powder; he wanted some cloth; he wanted everything he saw, and appeared ill-tempered every time I refused him something. In order to check this flood of absurd requests, I told him I would give him nothing more unless he brought me some pigs, which I needed for the provisioning of my ship. He promised to send me some on the morrow, but did no such thing, and I never saw him again.[1]

On 8 August the wind rose sufficiently to allow the French to anchor in Kealakekua Bay. Freycinet received the visit of Kuakini, also known as John Adams, who was in time to achieve prominence as Governor of Hawaii. The chief showed a degree

[1] Freycinet, *Voyage*, vol. ii, p. 520.

of intelligence and education which the Frenchman had not expected from a native:

Having learnt that I had been sailing on a voyage of discovery, he asked me in fairly good French if I had reached the Sandwich Islands by way of Cape Horn, or whether I had first gone to the Cape of Good Hope. He also asked for news of Buonaparte and wanted to know whether, as someone had assured him, the island of St. Helena had been submerged and swallowed up with everyone on it. I do not know who was the author of this fable, but it was so widely believed in the Sandwich Islands that I had to answer the same question on several occasions.[1]

Both Kuakini and his wife were very tall and heavy. The chief himself was at least six foot three and, like most of the Hawaiian notabilities, extremely fat. His wife was built on similar proportions, 'a big woman, much overweight, displaying without any ado her robust naked charms to our astonished eyes'. But he was also friendly and helpful. He had brought a gift of fruit with him, receiving in exchange a scarlet cloak. He placed two near-by huts at Freycinet's disposal to be used as an observatory. And he sent a message to the new king, Liholiho, apprising him of the *Uranie*'s arrival. Freycinet had reached the island at a time of great political ferment. The great king Kamehameha I, who had known Cook, had died in May after a long reign. Liholiho, who had assumed the name of Kamehameha II, had not established himself, and the islands, united by his father, now faced the possibility of civil war. The opportune arrival of a French expedition, likely to recognize without hesitation the supremacy of the King, was to be used by Liholiho in the political manœuvres so necessary to the preservation of his crown. A messenger was sent at once, inviting the French to Kawaihae, further north along the coast, where the King was in residence. To assist them, he also sent a pilot, an excellent man, whose only weakness was a tendency to blow his nose in his table napkin. With his assistance the *Uranie* made her way north and on 12 August 1819 dropped anchor opposite Liholiho's headquarters. It was, as Rose remarked, a

[1] Freycinet, *Voyage*, vol. ii, p. 522.

singular court, a mixture of old and new, in which the crumbling
of the old order was as apparent as the pressure of European ideas
and interests.

Liholiho, dressed in a British naval uniform, met Freycinet on
the beach; around him were lesser chiefs and advisers, including
a Frenchman, Jean Rives; further off stood the King's wives.
Freycinet was given a seven-gun salute, whereupon the party
proceeded to Liholiho's house, where discussions began on the
question of provisions. The King made no difficulty, and the
meeting ended with a glass of wine and an exchange of gifts,
Freycinet receiving an artistically fashioned lance in exchange for
his sword, which Liholiho had greatly admired. The next duty
was a visit to the old queens, widows of Kamehameha I. The
French were still not accustomed to the traditional corpulence of
the Hawaiian nobility:

It was truly a strange spectacle to see in a small apartment eight or
ten great human bodies, semi-naked, the least of which weighed at
least three hundred pounds, lying down flat on their stomachs. Not
without difficulty we found a place where we too could lie down so as
to conform to custom. . . . Most of these female colossi, which one
could say seemed to exist merely to eat and sleep, stared at us in a dull-
witted manner.[1]

Finally a visit was paid to John Young, the English sailor who
had acted for many years as adviser to the old king. And now the
political manœuvres began. A key role was played by Rives, who
was Liholiho's confidant and was later to accompany him to
England. As is the case with most of the Europeans who had settled
in the Pacific, Rives's background is shrouded in mystery. He
would seem to have been born in Bordeaux in 1793, and arrived
in the Sandwich Islands in an American ship as early as 1805.
He apparently gained the confidence of Kamehameha I through
displaying some knowledge of European medicine, and was given
a grant of land. At some stage, he appears to have sailed to China
on behalf of the King. His chance came, however, when Liholiho
came to the throne. He assumed the title of Secretary to the King.

[1] Quoy's account in Freycinet, *Voyage*, vol. ii, pp. 531–2.

It is clear that he was simply an adventurer, whose plans for enrichment only coincidentally corresponded with the interests of France. Freycinet, to whom he attached himself, had certain reservations about him: 'He spoke French with a certain amount of difficulty and moreover did not strike me as a man who had been well educated.'[1] Arago frankly disliked him:

The first time he came to present his respects to our commandant, he was dressed in so grotesque a manner that we thought at first he was a native.... A silk coat, far too long, flapped against his legs, which were enclosed in a fairly well-made pair of riding boots; his trousers and his waistcoat were quite clean, but to adjust them to his size he had to resort to the use of pins and lace.[2]

But Arago had petty grievances against Rives, who he felt had slighted him and prevented him from remaining alone with the wife of Kalanimoku, Liholiho's prime minister, 'the most attractive person I had yet seen on the island'. Arago failed to realize that Rives was probably endeavouring to avoid some awkward incident. Rives, in fact, has been much maligned, especially as a result of the failure of the later expedition of Duhaut-Cilly. It seems evident that the little Frenchman rapidly got out of his depth after Liholiho's death in 1824, and had tried to grasp opportunities which were bound to elude him in the rapidly changing situation.

With the *Uranie* in the bay, Rives attempted to establish his position as official interpreter and adviser with the aim of strengthening his influence at court. Indeed, anything Freycinet did to assert French influence would redound to Rives's advantage; the converse may also have been true, but of that Freycinet needed to be convinced. It is clear, however, that Europeans in Hawaii saw in the arrival of the French warship a way of containing, at least temporarily, Liholiho's enemies, and delaying, perhaps for good, the feared outbreak of civil war. John Young pointed this out to Freycinet, while Rives also urged the commandant to throw his prestige on the side of the young king. Freycinet agreed

[1] Freycinet, *Voyage*, vol. ii, p. 528.
[2] *Promenade*, vol. ii, p. 153.

to address the council of chiefs, in the presence of Liholiho and the Dowager Queen, Kaahumanu.

Mr. Rives, who spoke the Sandwichian language fluently, acted as interpreter. I began by reminding the island chiefs of the kind of treaty which had been drawn up in the past, through the agency of Captain Vancouver, between King Tamehameha and the King of England; I then declared that, as commandant of a warship belonging to the King of France, who was himself an ally of Great Britain, I was very glad to make known my interest in Riorio, and how desirous I was that peace and order should reign in his dominions; that should civil war, by some misfortune, break out in the Sandwich Islands, the merchant ships that had been calling for reasons of trade for so long would refuse to stop there, and vessels belonging to sovereigns friendly to their King, anxious to preserve his power, would not fail to take severe steps against anyone who had ignored his authority. I adjured them accordingly to range themselves in good faith around a ruler whose only aim was the prosperity and well-being of their country; finally I dwelt on the happiness that is born of tranquillity, commerce, and the progress of civilization.

This speech seemed to produce the impression we had hoped for; however, Queen Kaahoumanou took the floor, and said the lively interest I was showing in the King made her fear that his enemies would believe the rumour, which had already been spread by evil tongues, that not only I had asked for the cession of the Sandwich Islands to the King of France, but that this had already taken place; something which would not fail to vex the English and throw doubt on the Sandwichians' good faith. Struck by this comment, I hastened to deny with vigour these malicious tales, declaring that, if Riorio himself, of his own freewill, had wanted to place his country under the protection of France, I would have neither wanted nor been able to lend myself to such a transaction.[1]

Arago's account is less flowery and rather more to the point. Freycinet, he states, declared that Liholiho's claim to the throne was quite unchallengeable, and that any attempt to overthrow him would lead to intervention by the united powers of Europe. But here again he deprecates Rives's part: 'Mr Rives tried to translate . . . and either because his memory proved of little

[1] Freycinet, *Voyage*, vol. ii. pp. 534–6.

assistance or because the Sandwichian language is speedier than ours, he finished his task in four words, and no doubt his lack of skill is responsible for the small effect of this Catiline oration.'[1]

It is not easy to judge of the effectiveness of Freycinet's intervention. Liholiho's main opponent, Kekuaokalani, had refused to attend the meeting, and Arago reports that another chief, 'Ooro', walked out, whistling loudly, just as Freycinet prepared to speak.[2] Nevertheless, the presence and attitude of the French must have given food for thought to some waverers. As far as French influence was concerned, the speech was worth very little: Freycinet merely stressed the alliance between France and Britain, and endorsed by implication the treaty which Vancouver had promoted between Britain and Kamehameha I. France had in fact no interest in the Sandwich Islands: it was to be aroused later, but as a result less of an expansionist policy than of a need to protect French missionaries.

Strangely enough it was in the field of religion that the French left a tangible mark of their passage. So far only Protestant missionaries had settled in the islands, yet one of the chiefs approached Freycinet with a view to being baptized by the Roman Catholic chaplain. The man in question was Kalanimoku, the Prime Minister, whose adopted name was William Pitt. He paid a visit to the French shortly before the *Uranie* sailed to Maui for supplies. Pitt told Freycinet that he had long wished to become a Christian and that his mother had been baptized on her deathbed and had made him promise to do so as soon as the opportunity should arise. The mystery remains of who, if anyone, had received Pitt's mother into the Catholic Church. The likely candidate for this honour is Don Francisco de Paula Marin, a Spanish trader who had lived in the Sandwich Islands since the days of Kamehameha I, and by all accounts was an upright and religious man. Alternatively, it may have been the Reverend Howell, an Anglican clergyman who may have been remembered as belonging to a different group or denomination from the American missionaries.[3] Whatever the prime cause, Quélen could

---

[1] *Promenade*, vol. ii, pp. 185–6.   [2] Ibid.
[3] See Yzendoorn, *History of the Catholic Mission in the Hawaiian Islands*, p. 19.

not but feel delighted at the request. A ceremony was arranged, which Liholiho decided to attend, with the five Queens and Liholiho's young brother, Kauikeaouli, who was destined to become Kamehameha III, the last independent King of the Sandwich Islands. Liholiho arrived dressed in a blue hussar's uniform with gold braid, and accompanied by five personal attendants, one of whom was in charge of the King's pipe and kept it lit for him by regular but discreet puffing. Pitt was sponsored by Freycinet and received the appropriate baptismal name of Louis. Liholiho expressed regret that political considerations prevented him from undergoing a similar ceremony, but consoled himself with the collation which followed, during which the guests ate and drank enough to feed ten people for a month.[1] Pitt's allegiance to the Church of Rome succumbed in 1825, when he was received into a Protestant denomination.

Late on 15 August the *Uranie* sailed for Maui, anchoring off Lahaina at midday on the 16th. Supplies were reputedly more plentiful there, but Freycinet was disappointed. Rives, who claimed to own land on the island, had given him a letter asking his agent there to provide the French with all the pigs, poultry, and other refreshments that could be spared. The man in question was duly found, but he denied being Rives's agent or having ever heard of land or cattle belonging to the Frenchman. This did little to raise Rives in anyone's esteem. Freycinet then asked a passenger, Keeaumoku, to help him obtain the pigs which Liholiho had assured him were available at Maui. Keeaumoku, who appears to have been Governor of Maui at the time, argued that the King had promised ten pigs, not twenty, and brought to the ship's side hogs of a very inferior quality. The prices he asked were quite unreasonable, and Freycinet told him he preferred to seek supplies in Oahu. Seeing the ship about to leave, Keeaumoku lowered his prices and finally provided a total of twenty-five pigs, so that, laying the blame on an English interpreter, they parted on good terms. Nevertheless, Freycinet sailed without any regrets on the 25th and dropped anchor off Honolulu the next day. There he met the Governor, Boki, who was Kalanimoku's

---

[1] Freycinet, *Voyage*, vol. ii, p. 540.

brother; an American trader, Captain William Henry Davis; and the elderly Spaniard, Don Francisco de Paula Marin. Whether again as a result of the latter's influence, or more simply because of a wish to imitate his brother, Boki asked to be baptized by Quélen. The ceremony was performed on 27 August, again on board but without the pomp which had surrounded Kalanimoku's baptism. Although Freycinet believed that keeping up with his brother, rather than faith, was the motive for this conversion, Boki was to prove himself a better friend of the Church of Rome. Quélen was already pleased with him because he had only one wife; later missionaries were to look upon him as the protector of the Catholics against the persecution of Kaahumanu, the widow of Kamehameha I, who became regent after the departure and death of Liholiho in 1824.[1] Boki's stand against the old Queen's religious intransigence was not wholly due to his earlier admission into the Church; he was far more shrewd than Freycinet, unimpressed by his great bulk and lethargic appearance, had believed him to be. Freycinet had been put out by his lackadaisical attitude: the natives of Oahu seemed more interested in sport than in supplying the French with much-needed firewood. Finally, by 'a judicious mixture of vigour and patience, Louis succeeded in extracting all the wood and some more provisions'. On 30 August the *Uranie* set sail for Australia.

From Honolulu, Freycinet sailed almost due south to pass between the Samoan and the Cook Islands, and later veered south-west to Port Jackson. The passage was largely uneventful. He entered the southern hemisphere on 7 October, sighting Danger Islands in the northern Cooks on 19 October. Arago and others on board hoped they might call at Tahiti, but this was not to be. 'It must have been that the commandant was not required to go there, since we did not make for it although we were so close to it.'[2] Had the French gone to Tahiti, they would have found the island profoundly changed by the influence of English missionaries and the Tahitian mirage dissolved under the effect of the evangelical mind. Two days later, on 21 October, what was

[1] Kuykendall, *The Hawaiian Kingdom 1778–1854*, pp. 141–2.
[2] Arago, *Promenade*, vol. ii, p. 251 n.

thought to be a new discovery broke the monotony of shipboard life: '. . . being east of the Navigators Islands, we discovered an islet which was not shown on our maps, and which I named Rose Island, from the name of someone who is extremely dear to me.'[1]

Mme de Freycinet was understandably elated. 'Now it is done, behold my name attached to a little point on the globe; very small, certainly, for the envious might perhaps call it only an islet . . .'[2] But new discovery it was not. Roggeveen had sighted it in June 1722 on his way to the Samoas, and named it Vuyle Eyland or Bird Island.[3] The latitude given of 14½° south corresponds with Freycinet's observation of 14° 32′ 47″ south. The *Uranie* sailed two miles off the east side of Rose Island, which is a small triangular-shaped atoll. Freycinet, and indeed most people,[4] seemed to have remained unaware of Roggeveen's prior discovery, which may be one of the reasons why, although so many European names have disappeared from the map of the Pacific, Freycinet's homage to his wife still remains today.

Shortly after passing Rose Island, the French sailed east and south of the Tonga group, fixing the position of Pylstart, or Ata Island, and of Howe Island. The coast of New South Wales was sighted on 13 November, but a succession of storms and calms delayed them until the evening of the 18th. 'At last!' exclaimed Rose as the *Uranie* dropped anchor in Neutral Bay. Freycinet, who remembered the town from his stay of 1802, was astonished at the growth of this 'European city prospering in the middle of what is still a nearly wild country'. Arago, to whom all this was new, waxed lyrical:

I cannot describe the city I have just visited; I am in a realm of enchantment, and I prefer to let my admiration rest. Magnificent homes, majestic castles, houses extraordinary by their taste and elegance, fountains adorned by sculptures worthy of the chisel of our

[1] Freycinet, *Voyage*, vol. ii, pp. 623–4.
[2] Basset, *Realms and Islands*, p. 175.
[3] Sharp, *The Discovery of the Pacific Islands*, p. 99.
[4] Faivre stresses it as 'la seule découverte de l'expédition' (*Expansion française*, p. 266).

best artists, spacious and lofty apartments, expensive furniture, most stylish carriages, horses and gigs, immense stores: could one expect to find all this four thousand leagues from Europe?[1]

Former acquaintances, the first of them being Piper, the port captain, came on board to renew old friendships. A house was rented on Bunker's Hill for Freycinet and the scientific instruments, conveniently close to the Sydney observatory. Supplies were obtained at first from Governor Macquarie and later from local merchants, although here again Macquarie had to help, for Sydney traders were unwilling to accept bills drawn by Freycinet on the French treasury, and he had to authorize the Deputy Commissary General to cash them for him. The botanists set forth on various expeditions: Gaimard went to Botany Bay, where he also visited a factory owned by Piper and the guard-post near La Pérouse's Jardin des Français; Quoy, Pellion, and Gaudichaud undertook a more arduous journey to the Blue Mountains, reaching the newly discovered Bathurst Plains. For Louis and Rose, however, the stay was one long series of social events, most welcome after the monotony of the recent months. Local society rapidly succumbed to the charm and vivacity of the commandant's lady—'a very genteel amiable woman'.[2] Governor Macquarie invited Freycinet, Quélen, and several officers to visit his country residence at Parramatta, and sent the regimental band to serenade them as they sailed up the harbour.

We landed a mile from the *château*, near some old barracks, where an *aide-de-camp* to H.E. awaited us with a small and very light carriage, in which Louis and I mounted. After a few minutes with the Governor, who received us marvellously, we were given an equal welcome by Mme Macquarie; this lady, they say, has much merit; she paid me many civil attentions that at once put me at my ease with her.[3]

Macquarie had been embarrassed by a misfortune which had struck the French almost as soon as they arrived in Sydney. During the night of 23 November, Freycinet's silverware, part of

---

[1] *Promenade*, vol. ii, p. 265.
[2] *Historical Records of Australia*, I, vol. x, p. 284. The comment is Macquarie's.
[3] *Realms and Islands*, p. 183.

the table linen, and a quantity of other personal effects which had
been sent ashore were stolen. Freycinet took the loss philosophic-
ally, bearing in mind the number of thieves who had been landed
on 'roguery's classic shore' since the foundation of the colony
thirty years earlier. But Macquarie was less pleased that his guests
should have been reminded so soon and so forcibly of New South
Wales's reputation. The thief was caught, but the goods were
not recovered. The Governor wanted to make good the loss;
Freycinet would accept neither cash nor new silverware, replying
that he had only himself to blame and should have known better.
To efface this bad impression, the Governor and his wife overwhelmed the French with courtesies, and sent on board a number
of useful gifts: a milch cow and her calf, two goats, a dozen sheep,
and six barrels of lime juice. Captain MacArthur, the father of
the Australian wool industry, and by now a less controversial
character than he had been at the turn of the century, added
a pair of merino sheep, which he hoped might do well in France.

   Of all those who entertained the French, the wealthiest and
the most hospitable were John Wylde, Judge-Advocate of New
South Wales and later Chief Justice of Cape Colony, and John
Piper. Wylde gave two spectacular balls, inviting on each occasion all the local notables. Piper entertained Freycinet in the lavish
manner for which he had become famous and which was soon
to cause his bankruptcy. As port captain he was in charge of the
customs and the harbour police and, under the rather peculiar
system in force at the time, was entitled to five per cent of all
duties collected. By 1819 his income was close to £4,000 a year,
most of it spent on racehorses and receptions. All this entertainment
tired both Rose, who began to complain of migraines, and Louis,
whose time was increasingly taken up by social functions. Neither
truly regretted it when the time came to leave Sydney, particularly
as this was to mark the beginning of the final lap. The *Uranie*
sailed through the Heads on Christmas Day 1819. Freycinet,
having been warned about the likelihood of stowaways, had his
ship searched and was able to send one wretched convict away
with the pilot. The next day ten more crept out of their hiding-
places. The French were now too far from the coast and the wind

was too unfavourable to return them to Sydney. Although not in
the least anxious to retain these men, who had no knowledge of
the sea and no skill as sailors, Freycinet was compelled to keep
them.

As the *Uranie* made her way south-south-east in order to pass
well to the south of New Zealand, Freycinet and his officers
turned to the voluminous notes they had gathered on Australian
history, geography, political organization, and trade. There was
enough, eventually, to take up 558 pages of the *Voyage*, not
counting the specialized volumes on zoology, botany, and hydrography. But within a few days Freycinet was called from his work
to examine a leak: 'The wind, which was blowing wildly, was
responsible for a leak close to the water-line . . . we examined the
damage and found it was not serious, for the ship only made three
inches of water an hour when the sea was rough and much less
when the wind was not strong.'[1]

Yet this does raise the question of the *Uranie*'s condition as she
sailed across the Southern Pacific. Was the leak, admittedly a
minor one, an isolated instance of trouble, or a symptom of a more
general weakness? She had been at sea for over two years without
any major overhaul, through dangerous seas and in all climates.
The small, troublesome leak may have been a warning of misfortune ahead, and may help to explain why, in the Falklands, she
was holed so fatally when she struck a submerged rock.

On 4 January 1820 the *Uranie* was approaching the longitude
of Puysegur Point, the south-westernmost cape of New Zealand,
but far to the south and out of sight of any land. Three days later,
the dark peaks of Campbell Island were discerned nestling under
an overcast sky. There was nothing to stop for at this lonely and
bleak outpost, although one of the English convicts insisted that
it was inhabited.

One of the English convicts we had on board, who claimed to have
spent several months seal-fishing on this island, assured us there was
on the south-east side a fairly good anchorage on a clay bottom. We
did indeed notice a low and very long headland in the eastern part of

---

[1] Freycinet, *Voyage*, vol. ii, pp. 1209-10.

the island but, as this same man told us obviously absurd tales of natives who live there and of a kind of tiger found there, his lies made us doubt his whole account.[1]

And, indeed, unless the man had been frightened by another party of sealers, or lain awake listening to the roar of the sea elephants, he must be dismissed as a mere spinner of tales. In such latitudes there are few land animals and fewer men. The black swans, the parrots, the cassowaries, and the opossums gave melancholy proof of this as they died one by one in the high latitudes. On 21 January the first iceberg appeared, eighty to a hundred feet high, looming up through the sleet and hail. The temperature was now down to 37° Fahrenheit, although it was midsummer and the *Uranie* never went further south than 58° 30'. The sun rose bleakly shortly after 3 a.m. and set after 8 p.m. 'Insomnia was almost general, caused by what amounted to perpetual daylight.' However, a strong westerly was driving the *Uranie* towards Cape Horn. On 5 February, less than six weeks after leaving Port Jackson, the French sighted Cape Desolation through sheets of rain and melting snow. The rain cleared the next day, enabling the corvette to turn Cape Horn under a cloudless sky. 'It treated us as friends and everyone said it was not as black as it was painted', wrote Rose.[2] The picture presented by the coast of Tierra del Fuego—dark-green forests between headlands of bare rocks under a blue sky—was deceptive: a brief attempt to anchor and land was foiled by a sudden squall which threatened to drive the ship on to the near-by rocks. The French made for Le Maire Strait; the squall had blown up into a storm which split the main-topsail from top to bottom 'as if it had been made of gauze'. Rain and low clouds hid the coastline, causing one of the convicts to cry out in terror that there was land ahead. But soon the *Uranie* was through the strait and in the Atlantic. The storm died down on the 9th and, except for occasional patches of fog, the weather remained fine.

Freycinet's plan was to sail to the Falklands, where he could repair his ship and refresh his men. The islands were sighted on 12 February, half hidden in the fog. Two days were spent, sailing

[1] Ibid., p. 1211.   [2] *Realms and Islands*, p. 198.

cautiously off shore, looking for French Bay, where Bougainville had once attempted to establish a settlement. On 14 February the fog disappeared, the sky was clear, and the sea only slightly choppy. It is ironical that disaster struck under such favourable circumstances:

We had reached the entrance of French Bay; the day was clear, the sea calm, and a pleasant breeze drove us along at five knots; look-outs at the head of the masts and in the bow could see nothing which might give rise to any anxiety; we were constantly sounding from the main chain-wales; and the entire crew were at their stations ready to cast anchor. At 5.45 p.m., the lead, which so far had not found bottom at 20 fathoms, gave indications of the presence of rocks at that depth and shortly after at 18 fathoms; we were then only half a league from land. Out of caution, I thought it advisable to bear off a little, and therefore bore away two points, a precautionary move which was to prove fatal! It was indeed at the very moment when everything seemed to be proceeding as we wanted that the corvette suddenly found herself holed, with a sudden shock, by a submerged rock! . . . The sounding-line at that moment was registering 15 fathoms to starboard and 12 on the port-side, so that the fatal reef we had just struck was not so wide as the corvette: it was like the top of a steeple.[1]

Manœuvring the *Uranie* off the rock presented little difficulty, but the presence of broken pieces of wood floating close to the ship was an indication of serious trouble. Water was reported to be pouring in through the hole, and all hands, officers included, were put to the pumps. Even so, the water continued to rise. A wide pad was sewn out of sails to fill the gap and reduce the rush of water. But it was clear the *Uranie* was doomed unless she could be beached quickly. Freycinet began to tack towards the nearest stretch of sand just inside French Bay, but at 11 p.m., on an outward tack, the breeze failed, and the anchor had to be lowered. The ship was still a mile from its objective. The water was now up to the orlop deck. While pumping continued, Duperrey went in the yawl to examine the beach. At 1.30 a.m. on the 15th a light breeze rose, sufficient to fill the sails. Helped by the rising tide, the *Uranie* slowly made her way towards the beach. Darkness and

[1] Freycinet, *Voyage*, vol. ii, p. 1232.

the weakness of the breeze prevented her from striking the beach exactly where Duperrey hoped, and she did not ground squarely. She settled with a list of twenty degrees. It was 3 a.m. The pumps continued working for another hour, then the exhausted men were allowed to take some rest.

When dawn rose the full extent of the disaster became plain. All around them not a tree or a shrub to relieve the dismal monotony of sandhill, rock, and stiff sparse grass; nothing but a watery sun in a dull grey sky, and the lonely screeching of sea-birds. After a *Te Deum* of thankfulness that they had been spared this far, the French began to examine their stricken ship and to bring out what stores could be saved: the logs, journals, and notes were salvaged, but many of the natural-history specimens were lost or stained; Gaudichaud's herbarium, in particular, had suffered, as had Arago's sketch-books. Most of the arms and powder were intact, and John MacArthur's two merino sheep were safely brought ashore. But stocks of biscuits and salted meat were low and, with the melancholy thought that rescue might be months away, the French prepared to live as much as possible off the island's meagre resources.

I know that with powder, ingenuity, and *Robinson Crusoe*, one seldom dies of starvation, even in a desert; but as soon as the sun rose on the morning after the shipwreck and showed us the bare stony mountains which dominate the country, and our saddened eyes were able to see the dry plains and the sand dunes around us, we felt the need to call that philosophical attitude of mind to our rescue.[1]

Tents were set up, for the sick at first, then for the officers and men, and another for the powder and stores. To maintain discipline by keeping the men legally under his control, Freycinet announced that they would continue to be paid—it was normal for pay to be stopped after a shipwreck—so that any attempt at independent action by anyone could be treated as mutiny. There was in fact very little trouble, apart from a few minor thefts, most of them by the Port Jackson convicts: the majority of the men realized that discipline had to be maintained for the common

[1] Arago, *Promenade*, vol. ii, p. 406.

good. The situation did not look too hopeless. There was no shortage of water; there were penguins and sea-elephants for food, and even, as was discovered a few days later, herds of wild horses whose meat, particularly to Frenchmen, was most palatable. 'This was great news.' Bougainville's settlement near by, on the other hand, was of little use: a few walls subsisted here and there, providing shelter from the wind but not from the cold or the rain. 'There merely remain today of this settlement eight or nine ruined buildings and two ovens, one of which is still in good condition and more than six foot high.'[1]

The *Uranie* was carefully examined and declared to be beyond repair. Bad weather in late February caused further damage and silenced even the most sanguine. On 28 February it was unanimously agreed that the only possible course was 'to deck our longboat, and send it to Montevideo with a small number of hand-picked resolute sailors'. Work began the next day, and here the tradesmen among the crew proved invaluable. The longboat, on which so much depended, was to be named the *Espérance*, and to be placed under the command of Duperrey, for Louis's continued presence in the Falklands was essential if discipline was not to suffer. Freycinet would anyhow have been unable to stand the rigours of the voyage, for his health was giving way under the strain. But by mid March the work was nearing completion. Rose now felt that deliverance was in sight:

It is very fine today and my husband decided to take a walk to the ship-yard; we found the *chaloupe* very advanced and ready to be launched in two or three days; her masts and gear are all ready. Yesterday they salvaged something very precious from on board, something particularly precious for the *chaloupe*, that is, a barrel of pitch. Also a barrel containing 66 cheeses in good condition. Today the pork was distributed. Each table had its share, very small certainly, but it seemed delicious to us, so long is it since we have eaten something so unlike our usual fare.[2]

She had written this on 18 March. The very next day a sloop was seen at the entrance to the bay. When it came within hailing distance, Freycinet learned that it was named the *Penguin* and

[1] Arago, *Promenade*, vol. ii, p. 414 n.   [2] *Realms and Islands*, p. 212.

attached to the sealing vessel *General Knox* from Salem, Massachusetts. Young Dubaut was sent in the *Penguin* to begin negotiations with the master of the *General Knox* for the rescue of the French party. As the days went by, Freycinet became increasingly concerned. The officer in charge of the *Penguin* had shown a great deal of reluctance, and it was by no means certain that Captain Orne[1] of the *General Knox* would be prepared to interrupt his sealing campaign to take the French to South America. Louis's health was still poor and the men were naturally impatient. He decided that, if the *Penguin* returned without Captain Orne or with only empty promises, he would seize the sloop and sail it himself to seek help. But such extreme measures were unnecessary. On 28 March a three-master appeared in the bay—not indeed the *General Knox*, but the *Mercury*, Captain Galvin, a ship of 280 tons from Buenos Aires, flying the flag of the Argentine rebels and on her way to Valparaiso with cannon and cannon-balls for the Chilean rebels. The *Mercury* was putting in for repairs at the Falkland Islands, enabling Freycinet to court the captain's goodwill by at once offering his men to repair the leak in exchange for a passage to Rio. Galvin agreed to a proposition which 'seemed reasonable to him, and he expressed his gratitude at my haste to render him service'. But while the work was still in progress Captain Orne arrived.

Freycinet was now faced with two would-be rescuers, both of whom were motivated by a desire for gain, if not by sheer rapaciousness. Dubaut had been faced with a request for 51,000 piastres, well over a quarter of a million francs, which Orne finally reduced by half. It was still a very large sum for a voyage of less than a month, including the time required to sail back to the sealing grounds. However, Freycinet was by now committed to sail with Galvin and in no further need of Orne's service. He made up for the time the latter had wasted over the negotiations by giving him a number of items salvaged from the corvette, and they parted amicably enough. The trouble had been less with Orne than with his officers and men, who had realized that most of the passage money would have gone to the owners, whereas

[1] Or, more probably, Horn.

they themselves would have lost all chances of bonus payments
while the sealing was suspended. Galvin now asked Freycinet for
14,000 piastres before sailing the shipwrecked party to Buenos
Aires. Louis really wanted to go to Rio, where there was a French
consul and greater resources available. Buenos Aires, in a state of
revolt, was far less satisfactory. Galvin agreed to sail to Rio for
18,000 piastres, with an escape clause providing for a payment of
10,000 should the French agree or be forced to disembark at
Buenos Aires. The *Mercury* was ready to sail on 27 April. It was
then discovered that James Weddell, the future Antarctic explorer,
was at Port Egmont aboard the brig *Jane*, and that the officers of
the *General Knox* had been careful to conceal from him the presence of the French. He did learn about them in time, and was
able to call on Freycinet and express regret that it was now too
late to do anything other than wish him God-speed.

Now no longer in command of a ship, Freycinet devoted his
time to scientific work. But the *Mercury* was far too crowded and
most uncomfortable. And her captain seemed very uneasy. The
passengers who had been on their way to Valparaiso were
naturally incensed at the delay, but they were also concerned at
the thought of going to Rio, as Portugal was at war with the
Buenos Aires insurgents. They were accordingly applying pressure on Galvin, which he was finding all the more difficult to
resist in that he was visualizing the impounding of his ship and his
own imprisonment if he should sail into Rio harbour. He had
hoped to persuade Freycinet to put into Buenos Aires, but as the
Mercury made her way north it became increasingly clear to him
that Freycinet could not be persuaded. Finally, a formula was
found: Galvin agreed to sell his ship for the sum of 18,000 piastres
previously stipulated as passage money for Rio, and in return
Freycinet would sail to Montevideo and allow Galvin and his crew
and passengers to disembark. Thus, on 8 May, Freycinet was able
to take over command of the *Mercury*, which he renamed the
Physicienne, and sail under French colours into Montevideo
harbour.

Life seems rapidly to have returned to normal. The overcrowd-
ing was reduced by paying off all those who wished to leave the

expedition, thus bringing the complement down to seventy-nine. The local inhabitants showed a great deal of sympathy for the French, who, after their seventy-three days on the bleak Falklands, looked wan and exhausted. Supplies were easily available, hospitality was widespread. There were dinners, a ball, visits to the theatre, an excursion into the country. After just under a month, Freycinet was ready to sail:

> On the morning of the 7th [June], the weather was fine and the breeze fair; we made haste to weigh anchor, letting out all the canvas and saluting the town with the customary salvoes; one of the forts returned this salute, but as it did not return the same number of shots I hove to and sent a message with my just complaints to the Governor. He apologized for the fact that his instructions had not been carried out to the letter, and informed me that the salute was to begin again with a number equal to mine, which was duly carried out.[1]

Before the *Physicienne* reached Rio, on 20 June, she was to meet with more trials. A storm struck her almost as soon as she veered north, carrying away the bowsprit and a boat in which hay for the last surviving merino was stored. Then, as she neared Rio, calms held her prisoner overnight. And, as she finally sailed into the harbour, her appearance misled the customs officers, who 'came up alongside, thinking they were dealing with a merchant ship, in spite of the war pennant at the masthead'. But, apart from this initial misunderstanding, the French had no cause for complaint. The Royal Arsenal was made available for anything Freycinet might need for a complete overhaul of the ship. There was the usual round of official visits, balls, dinners. The abbé Quélen celebrated a requiem mass for the duc de Berry, assassinated, by a coincidence which impressed Freycinet, on the very day the *Uranie* had struck. On 18 August a French squadron arrived, commanded by Jurien de la Gravière, who had sailed with d'Entrecasteaux and had recently been promoted to rearadmiral, and Claude du Campe de Rosamel, also an admiral and later to be Minister of Marine. Able to report on his misfortunes and the progress of the repairs, Freycinet was also happy to meet

---

[1] Freycinet, *Voyage*, vol. ii, p. 1327.

his colleagues and exchange reminiscences about Shark Bay and Port Jackson.

He sailed on the morning of 13 September; it was nearly three years now since the expedition had left Toulon. There could be no one on board who did not feel a desire for a quick passage home. 'As if the winds themselves wished to satisfy our impatience, they became more favourable than they had ever been, blowing freshly and in vigorous gusts.' In less than a month the *Physicienne* was across the line, passing in sight of the Azores on 27 October. Freycinet was once again indisposed, yet forced to drag himself on deck to supervise manœuvres in the fog which came down as soon as the ship entered the English Channel. He anchored briefly in Cherbourg, long enough to take on a pilot to guide the *Physicienne* to Le Havre, and to dispatch Lamarche to Paris with letters for the Minister. Arago and Quélen, unaffected by naval discipline, disembarked here too to return to their families. Two days later, on 13 November, after a voyage lasting three years and fifty-seven days and covering 18,622 leagues, the expedition reached Le Havre.

But all was not over. A court-martial was necessary to examine the circumstances under which the *Uranie* had been wrecked. The terms of reference did not include the question of Rose de Freycinet, whose illegal presence on board it had long since been decided to ignore. The court, presided over by Captain Delamarre de la Mellerie, met in Paris on 16 December 1820. It took only an hour and a half to reach its verdict:

The naval court-martial has declared by unanimous decision that frigate-captain Desaulses de Freycinet is honourably acquitted in con-nexion with the beaching and loss of the corvette l'*Uranie*, the com-mand of which had been entrusted to him by His Majesty; his sword has accordingly been returned to him by the president, who, on behalf of the court, has praised him for his conduct during the shipwreck and in the circumstances which followed.

What had Freycinet achieved? There were, as we have seen, no new discoveries, so that from the point of view of hydro-graphy we are in his debt only for surveys of already—though

imperfectly—known coasts. This work will be found in the large
volume, *Hydrographie*, which forms part of his five-volume
account of the expedition, and is reflected in the accompanying
Atlas, much of it the work of Duperrey. The scientific work,
especially the study of terrestrial magnetism and weather observations, is far from negligible and deserves the praise which the
Académie des Sciences bestowed on it in its report of 7 May 1821.
In the field of botany and zoology, the expedition's successes were
noteworthy, for, with a thoroughness inherited from Baudin,
Freycinet collected a formidable array of specimens. Although
18 cases had been lost in the Falklands, and the live animals—
including the 2 merinos—had died or disappeared, there still
remained 25 mammals, 313 birds, 45 reptiles, 164 fish, innumerable shells, and 30 skeletons—even one of a male Papuan. There
were 1,300 insects, 40 of them species unknown to entomologists,
and 3,000 botanical specimens of which nearly 500 were new to
the Natural History Museum's collection and 20 totally unknown
to science. Rock samples numbered 900, and the drawings of
Arago and of the officers, after allowing for those lost in the
wreck, totalled 500. All this, soon known and appreciated by
savants, was publicized by the accounts of the voyage which
appeared between 1824 and 1839. Although Freycinet was subject
to flights of rhetorical fancy and unfortunate purple patches,[1] his
reports are as valuable as they are exhaustive: his account of
Brazil fills 300 pages, of Timor 200, of the Marianas 350, of
Australia 558. They served to remind France of the importance of
Pacific exploration at a time when the French were still suffering
the traumatic after-effects of the collapse of the Napoleonic
empire, and encouraged the Government to dispatch Duperrey in
the *Coquille* in 1822. For historians and anthropologists, they had
a lasting value.[2] And for the general public there was Arago's racy
account of 1822, which English readers were able to buy in
translation within twelve months. Rose had to remain more

[1] e.g. 'How many unhappy travellers, roaming like blind men over an unknown element, exposed without protection to all the fury of the storms, became
victims of their inexperience and their daring, and paid with an obscure death
their first attempts!'
[2] See, for instance, Kuydendall, *The Hawaiian Kingdom*, p. 65.

discreet: there would have been a wide public for her *Journal du voyage*, but it was not to appear for more than a century. This is not to say that her escapade was not known, for Freycinet's voyage as a whole made a deep impression and was widely discussed—and this very fact counts as one of the expedition's most important results.

DUPERREY

FREYCINET returned to France to find people and Government largely apathetic about the Pacific. The problems of reconstruction, above all of restoring France's influence in the concert of Europe, had taken up all the Government's attention, leaving very little time for questions revolving around a distant ocean with little apparent political or economic value. Even the Catholic Church, more concerned with rechristianizing areas of France where its influence had waned during the Revolution and Empire, made no attempt to send missionaries to the distant islands of the Pacific and left the field clear for the London and Church Missionary societies. The few ships which had sailed to the threshold of the South Seas were more interested in trade or in the renewal of trade relations. This had been the case with the *Bordelais*; others were the *Golo*, commanded by Damblart de Lansmastre, which sailed for India in 1817; the *Cybêle*, which left later that year in an attempt to re-establish the links that had existed between France and Cochin-China; the *Normande* and the *Durance*, both under the command of Captain Philibert, which went to Java and Manila in 1819 in an unsuccessful attempt to obtain labour for plantations in French Guiana; the *Cléopâtre*, under Captain Courson, which sailed to China and Indo-China in 1821.

A great deal of this reflected the mercantilist policy of Portal and the Bordeaux lobby, which left only naval officers looking for promotion, together with members of the Académie des Sciences, as proponents of schemes of exploration. With Freycinet's success and the fall of Portal in 1821, the naval officers were to receive an increasingly sympathetic hearing. The new Prime Minister, Villèle, had been a naval officer in pre-revolutionary days, and his wife was the sister of a wealthy Bourbon colonist. Under his Minister of Marine, Aimé, comte de Clermont-Tonnerre, colonial administration was centralized, and the influence of the commercial interests reduced. Both were strong conservatives, hostile to the social and mercantile ambitions of colonialists and traders. The new Government's main concern was the preservation of existing colonial possessions and their defence against possible aggression. Greater powers were given to the local colonial governors, who were put in command of all available troops to defend their territories both from outside attacks and from local subversion. Nevertheless it is to be noted that in 1822 the Government expressed a desire to have 'in the islands of Polynesia and Australia a few places where French ships could transplant civilization and its benefits.'[1] By this time, however, Duperrey was well on his way. It was, indeed, Portal who had first authorized the expedition which the new Government later approved, neither Villèle nor Clermont-Tonnerre considering there was anything undesirable about a plan which, merely repeating what had been done under Louis XVI, involved no new commitments.

Duperrey had drawn his plan 'jointly with our colleague Mr. d'Urville',[2] almost as soon as the *Physicienne* docked in Le Havre. No doubt the idea had matured in his mind during his earlier voyage. Dumont d'Urville's part in this is not so clear: he had asked to join Freycinet's expedition, but his request had been turned down. He had then gone on a voyage to the Aegean and been promoted *lieutenant de vaisseau* not long after Duperrey's return. This promotion now enabled him to hope for higher things, although not as yet for the command of a major expedition. Did he cultivate Duperrey as someone likely to help him to achieve his aim of sailing into the Pacific? He had known him for some years, although they lost touch after the war, and it is clear that they held a number of meetings during 1821 and that d'Urville assisted Duperrey with the plan which was finally presented to Portal in October 1821. The purpose of the proposed expedition was scientific research rather than exploration: Duperrey was to report on natural history, meteorology, and magnetism; his hydrographic work was to tend towards perfect-

---

[1] Julien, *La Politique coloniale de la France* ..., p. 118, quoting the *Moniteur* of 9 May 1822.
[2] Duperrey, *Voyage autour du monde*, vol. i, p. 5.

ing existing maps rather than preparing charts of unknown areas. Political or strategic considerations were once again largely ignored. The most that Duperrey was enjoined to do by his instructions was to report on the possibility of establishing a settlement in Western Australia, which was not yet recognized as a British possession. The French Government's main concern here was the need for a convict settlement similar to the British establishment in Port Jackson. When the expedition returned in 1825, d'Urville and Lesson gave the Minister of Marine a report 'on two colonies to be established by France for the transportation of convicts, one in Port St. George [King George Sound] in New Holland, the other in New Zealand. Our memoirs were no doubt thrown away, but the English made haste to occupy both these places.'[1] It was not until after Duperrey's departure, following the outbreak of war with Spain, that the Government became fully aware of France's strategic weakness in Pacific waters and began to send naval commanders on political missions.

Portal's approval, in November, followed his earlier rejection of a proposal put forward by Philibert. The failure of Philibert's earlier voyage to Indonesia, China, and the Philippines may have predisposed the Minister against him. Yet Philibert, who was born in Bourbon and had sailed to Java with the French expedition of 1811, failed in 1819 only because he was unable to persuade the Chinese to allow him to recruit coolie labour for French Guiana. His reputation as an officer and navigator was not in question. He wanted now to explore the coast of New Guinea and the other Melanesian islands—from the Bismarck archipelago to the New Hebrides—an area where there was still a great deal of work to do. His proposed route along the coast of Western Australia would have fitted in with the still shadowy French plans for a convict settlement somewhere on this coast. The Solomon Islands and the Louisiade archipelago had never been surveyed in detail and reliable information on their peoples and products was still lacking. Philibert's plan of 1821 would have enabled France to fill in the last blanks in the map of the Pacific and initiate the systematic exploration of Melanesia, where a wide field of

[1] Lesson, *Notice historique sur Dumont d'Urville*, p. 120 n.

exploration continues, even today, to attract ethnologists.[1] His proposal may indeed have appeared too ambitious and too expensive, with few commercial possibilities, for Philibert was asking Portal to sanction an expedition lasting at least three years. Duperrey's character and past achievements were more likely to ensure his success with Portal. He was 35, had entered the Navy in 1803 at the age of 17, serving first as a novice in the *Vulcain*, which was then escorting convoys along the Brittany coast, then as *aspirant* in the *Républicain* in Brest. In 1809, promoted *enseigne*, he transferred to the Mediterranean fleet, sailing in May of that year to Tuscany with a hydrographic mission, which accomplished its object in spite of prowling British naval units and the hostility of the Tuscans. After two years in the *Suffren*, he was given command of the schooner *le Feu*, engaged in convoy work between the ports of Provence.

In 1815 he served as second-in-command in the *Rose*, then in the brig *Abeille*. This was followed by the voyage of the *Uranie*. His later career was devoted largely to preparing an account of his own voyage, and to scientific work—he was elected a member of the Académie des Sciences in 1842.[2] Dumont d'Urville's support no doubt strengthened Duperrey's case. Younger by four years, d'Urville had followed a career similar in many respects to Duperrey's. He was born in Normandy in 1790, being christened Jules-Sébastien-César. His father died in 1797, leaving the boy to be brought up by his mother and her brother, the abbé de Croisilles. This upbringing and the stern character of his mother may have been responsible for his somewhat austere and proud manner, not infrequently marked by a touch of pomposity. He undeniably showed himself to be a gifted and ambitious youth who resented failures and setbacks. This may explain why, after studying at the *lycée* at Caen for the entrance examination to the École Polytechnique and securing a bare pass, he decided to give up his studies and join the Navy. A less reliable tradition claims that this decision was the result of his imagination being fired by accounts of the voyages of Cook, Anson, and Bougainville, all of which were available in the *lycée* library. He joined the *Aquilon*

---

[1] Faivre, *Expansion française*, p. 242.   [2] He died in 1865.

as novice in November 1807, passed as *aspirant* to the *Amazone* in February 1809 and transferred to the Mediterranean fleet in November 1810—to the same *Suffren* in fact in which Duperrey served from 1811 to 1813. Enforced inactivity in the blockaded ports irked his active nature: as Duperrey specialized in hydrography, so he studied botany, acquiring among his fellow midshipmen a reputation as a rather withdrawn, bookish officer.

The parallel nature of the two men's careers was maintained when Dumont d'Urville, now an *enseigne*, sailed to Palermo in the *Ville de Paris*; Duperrey, it will be remembered, having sailed to Tuscany. Then, while Duperrey sailed with Freycinet to the Pacific, d'Urville went in the *Chevrette* to the Aegean sea. The publicity which surrounded the Freycinet expedition on its return was paralleled by the notoriety which enveloped d'Urville, who had, if not discovered, at least been instrumental in the recovery and purchase by the French of the statue of Venus in the island of Milo. This earned him the Legion of Honour and the sympathy and support of the Académie des Sciences. In August 1821 he was promoted *lieutenant de vaisseau*.

The joint plan provided for the exploration of the coast of New Guinea, the Micronesian group as far as the Marianas, the Society Islands, Easter Island, and the South Shetlands—this last foreshadowing d'Urville's later interest in the Antarctic. The proposal, widely discussed in the daily press and at meetings of the Académie des Sciences,[1] was accepted with a few modifications, such as the omission of Easter Island and of the exploration of the South Shetlands. Its acceptance may well have been eased by the moderate outlay which was scarcely to exceed the cost of an ordinary voyage,[2] a factor not without importance, but one which Philibert had overlooked. The ship allocated for the expedition was a sturdy corvette of 380 tons, the *Coquille*, carrying 12 guns, which Freycinet had declined, but which was to reveal such sterling qualities that Dumont d'Urville later returned with her to the Pacific. 'Forewarned by the disaster which had overtaken Mr. de Freycinet's expedition', the authorities had the

[1] Vergniol, *Dumont d'Urville*, p. 78.
[2] Faivre, *Expansion française*, pp. 243 and 263.

ship strengthened by an outer keel and completely overhauled. Indeed, once in dry dock, the *Coquille* was found to be in a much worse condition than had been expected, so that the date of departure had to be changed. Nevertheless, work proceeded 'with all possible speed without any interruption even for holidays'.[1] The Académie des Sciences, Rossel, and Beautemps-Beaupré helped with advice; the Inspector-General of Naval Health Services once again drew up instructions on hygiene and cleanliness. Five chronometers were supplied; there was fifteen to eighteen months' food, water for eight months, stored in iron casks, plus a distilling machine for sea water. Stocks of spare sails, ropes, and other equipment were estimated to last two years.

Dumont d'Urville, 'our intimate friend, was naturally invited to share with us all the risks of this honourable undertaking'. He arrived in Toulon in May 1822 and began to supervise the preparations and repairs, which were not finally completed until August. Whether or not he had hoped to be placed in command of the expedition is not clear: as the junior man, with no experience of eastern or Pacific waters, he can hardly have expected to be appointed over Duperrey. His later criticisms of the commander's actions, which are often caustic in the extreme, can be blamed more on his temperament than on a feeling of disappointment.[2] He was joined by six officers; two surgeons, Garnot and Lesson, both with qualifications in natural history; the ship's clerk and interpreter, whose secondary task was to prepare reports on trade and manufactures in the countries visited; and an artist, Lejeune. The crew was to consist of only fifty men, but this figure was increased to fifty-eight by order of the Minister, bringing the complement up to a total of seventy. Only three were over the age of 30: Duperrey, d'Urville, and one of the officers, Lesage, who was 37. Most, indeed, were very young: 'The small number of sailors available in port did not permit us to be very strict in the case of several of them, and we were forced

[1] Lottin, *Journal*, p. 1.

[2] Aware of the risks of friction, Duperrey had carefully divided the various duties between them, 'dès avant le départ'. He was to concentrate on hydrography, d'Urville on botany. See Duperrey, *Mémoire*, p. 4.

to accept a fair number of young apprentices who were barely twenty.'[1] This was not to prove a real disadvantage. Duperrey, like many other commanders, had to start by training his crew, and youth had its compensations: Lesson reports that during the crossing to Tenerife 'the sailors were bubbling over with high spirits'.[2]

Most of the officers were personally selected by Duperrey and d'Urville. Charles-Hector Jacquinot (1796–1879), whose duties included astronomical observations, was also to be taken on as first lieutenant by the latter for his *Astrolabe* expedition of 1826–9, and end a distinguished career with the rank of admiral. Bérard, who had sailed as *élève* with Freycinet, was to be placed in command of the New Zealand naval station after 1840. Jules Poret de Blosseville (1802–33) had already sailed to the West Indies and French Guiana; he was to go on a voyage of exploration to India and China in 1827 and take part in the siege of Algiers in 1830. Three years later he was granted permission to sail to the Arctic to carry out various observations on magnetism, and given command of the gunboat *la Lilloise*; he reached eastern Greenland, and was last seen by a group of fishermen on 15 August 1833; search parties sent out in 1834–6 found no trace of either ship or crew. Blosseville was a keen observer and indefatigable note-taker; some of his observations were incorporated in a history of the Australian penal settlements written by his brother, the Marquis de Blosseville. Garnot, the senior surgeon, developed dysentery in South America and had to be repatriated from Port Jackson. Much of the medical work thus fell on the shoulders of the second surgeon, Lesson, a man of talent and great energy, who has left a most readable account of the expedition.[3] Finally, Victor Lottin was to be invited by d'Urville to return under him to the Pacific in 1826.

On 6 August the *Coquille* was nearly ready. 'The crew were given the clothes they had bought against their pay, and in addition a heavy watch-coat, a waterproof jacket, a full set of

[1] Lesson, *Voyage médical*, p. iv.   [2] Lesson, *Voyage*, p. 7.
[3] *Voyage autour du monde* . . . in addition to his more specialized *Voyage médical autour du monde*.

flannel clothes, a red woollen shirt, and two pairs of shoes, given to them by the Government in view of the nature of the voyage.' Thus equipped, they prepared to sail. By 7 p.m. on the 10th everyone was aboard, with the exception of a missing apprentice, and early the next morning, with a good breeze and a cloudless sky, the *Coquille* sailed out of Toulon harbour. Gibraltar was reached on the 20th, and Tenerife on the 28th, but the men were unable to land, for the authorities, concerned about a recent outbreak of yellow fever in the western Mediterranean, imposed a week's quarantine. Duperrey had no intention of waiting so long, and sailed as soon as he obtained fresh water and some supplies. As the ship sailed into the tropics, the weather became increasingly oppressive, and the two surgeons, mindful of the young crew's well-being, set up a number of bathing-tubs on deck; the crossing of the line gave rise to more 'folle gaieté', including, as Lesson records in an undeniable pun, the ducking of 'un jeune dessinateur', who must have been the young artist, Lejeune.

The islands of Martin Vaz and Trinidad were sighted on 6 October. Duperrey had planned to make directly for the Falklands, but some of the cross-trees' timbers having snapped he decided to put in at Santa Catarina, in Brazil. It was not a propitious moment. No flag appeared at the fort masthead when the French dropped anchor. They were told this was because there was none: Brazil had declared its independence from Portugal a few days earlier. Very naturally, a certain tension reigned and the French ship was viewed with suspicion. 'Our ship appeared to many people an emissary spying on coastal defence', comments Lesson. As a result, they deemed it prudent to eschew all hydrographic and geographic work, and even held in check their interest in natural history. They obtained wood and water, purchased fresh food, and carried out repairs. Two men deserted and were not recaptured, their belongings being sold by auction, as was the custom, after the ship had sailed.

The *Coquille* left on 30 October. Almost at once she was assailed by a fierce *pampero* storm. A fortnight later, on 17 November, the Falkland Islands were sighted to the south-east, some thirty miles

off. That same afternoon Blosseville saw 'the sea break over the
rock that was so fatal to the corvette *Uranie*. As it is covered by
several feet of water, you can see only the water whitening at long
intervals'.[1] Shortly after, they anchored in the bay. It was a
melancholy place: 'When we arrived at the beach where the
Uranie had been abandoned, we found still there her keel, a few
carronades buried in the sand, iron casks and all kinds of debris.
The waves, lashed into fury by the storms that arise during the
bitter winters common in these high latitudes, had lifted her
broken carcass over a small chain of rocks.'[2]

Nevertheless, it was the first place of call where—there being
no humans about—they were not unwelcome. D'Urville was
able to go botanizing; Duperrey set up an observatory; the
younger men went hunting. The first foray yielded a horse and
twenty-three geese; but one of the sailors manning the boat got
himself lost and two parties had to be sent out to look for him,
the second group being successful and bringing him back to the
ship, clutching with determination the two geese he had trapped.
An ox weighing 350 lb. was killed a few days later, so that at no
time was there any shortage of fresh meat. These activities, as
well as repairs to the ship, took up most of the last week of
November and the first fortnight of December, and were carried
out in spite of frequent squalls and persistent cold rain. On 18
December the *Coquille* made her way out of the bay and headed
south. Staten Land was sighted to the south-south-east on the
28th. Three days later the French turned Cape Horn, being then
in 57° 54° south, and continued as far south as 59°, the highest
latitude they were to reach, before turning north towards Concepción. On 2 January, 'at midnight, people were reading on
deck, it was so light'. On the 15th a heavy south-westerly storm
arose, which battered the *Coquille* for several hours. The corvette
stood the test well, suffering as before only superficial damage:
Duperrey had every reason to be satisfied with her.

During the afternoon of 20 January the *Coquille* anchored off
Talcahuano, near Concepción. Poverty was visible everywhere,
the country, so recently freed from Spanish rule, now being in

[1] Blosseville, Journal, 17 Nov. 1822.   [2] Lesson, *Voyage*, vol. i, p. 46.

the throes of civil war. General Freire was about to challenge
O'Higgins, and Duperrey, using all his tact, obtained an assurance
from the authorities that the food supplies he needed would be
forthcoming. The corvette *Independencia's* arrival on the 26th
with nearly 400 soldiers made this a little less certain, and the
appearance of the schooner *Nuestra Señora de Mercedes*, with more
men, all of whom had to be fed and provided for, increased
Duperrey's anxiety. Fortunately, the new arrivals were commanded by a Frenchman, Colonel Beauchef, who had once
served with Napoleon's imperial guards and was now in Freire's
service. Beauchef was as helpful as Freire, and the imminence of
the fall of the Santiago Government made it likely that the soldiers
would not have to fight a protracted campaign, if indeed they
were needed at all. On 2 February news came that O'Higgins
had resigned. The fort and the ships celebrated the event with a
twenty-one-gun salute, and Duperrey entertained Freire and
Beauchef to dinner. He could now proceed with the loading of
supplies, which the events of the last few days had interrupted,
but food was still scarce and expensive. A short ride to Concepción
revealed the extent of Chile's poverty.

As soon as we came upon the plain in which the city of Concepción
is situated, our hearts were overwhelmed by pity and horror. The
baneful effects of the civil disorders impressed themselves on us at every
instant: the fields were devastated, the houses in ruins, the rural population covered in rags and very small in numbers . . . In many of the
streets of Concepción, which each side in turn had set on fire as victory
came to it, weeds were growing and flowering, even in the sacred
square outside the cathedral where the crowds once used to gather.[1]

This did not prevent four men from deserting, two sneaking
ashore in the jolly-boat, the others failing to return from shore
leave. The men knew the *Coquille* was about to sail and that the
local authorities would not make any real efforts to get them
back. After the customary ball and dinner given on board to
thank all those who had assisted the French, Duperrey sailed on
13 February. He took away with him one rather moving memory:
an old man had come to him who remembered La Pérouse.

[1] Duperrey, *Voyage*, vol. i, pp. 140–1.

He could remember, with great enthusiasm, the main events which had marked the stay of that famous navigator in happier days; he could remember particularly well the great dinner La Pérouse had given to his crew, which had been attended by all the officers, and he showed me, with some emotion, the building still standing, where this gathering had taken place. But this venerable old man . . . was quite unaware of what had happened later . . . tears came into his eyes when he learned suddenly that the expedition, dogged by misfortune, had been wrecked on some unknown shore.[1]

Duperrey's published account of his voyage ends with his stay in Chile. So unfinished is his *Voyage autour du monde*, so unexpected was his inability to continue publication, that his first and only volume breaks off, not simply in the middle of a sentence, but in the middle of a word.[2] Publication was interrupted by the Revolution of 1830 and never resumed. The main printed account is Lesson's *Voyage autour du monde*, in two volumes, published in 1838–9. Duperrey did complete a succinct *Mémoire sur les opérations géographiques*, which appeared in 1827, but the thought of his unfinished larger account must have remained with him for many years.

The *Coquille* reached Callao on 26 January. The French were 'courteously received by the authorities'. The port was as prosperous as Concepción had been poverty-stricken. Blosseville counted seventy sails in the roads, including six French merchantmen. One of the latter, the *Antique*, was about to sail for home, and her captain, Doutet, offered to take letters with him. Duperrey had already been able to send mail to France from Talcahuano through the good offices of the English whaler *Sarah Ann*. But, in spite of appearances, Peru was no less unstable than Chile: Duperrey on a short visit to Lima witnessed the installation of Aguerro as first President of Peru, but foresaw further political trouble ahead. The *Coquille* was ready to sail on 4 March, when it was discovered that three men had deserted during the night, escaping as their fellows had done in Talcahuano by stealing the

[1] Ibid., p. 134.
[2] The book ends on page 202 with the words 'Tous les habitants ont déclaré solennelle-'.

jolly-boat. There was no time to begin a search—all three deserters were 'mauvais sujets reconnus'—and as soon as the boat had been found, abandoned on a near-by beach, Duperrey sailed for Payta. D'Urville himself was not sorry to leave, for his interest in botany had nearly proved fatal. Collecting plants with Bérard in the hills around Lima, they had been taken for Spanish spies and pursued by a detachment of national guards, the lieutenant in charge succeeding only with difficulty in preventing his men from shooting them on the spot. Even arrest was unpleasant, as the captors, on the way back to Lima, had tried to steal the unlucky pair's money and watches. Payta, where the *Coquille* arrived on 10 March, was less likely to be inhospitable to foreign naval officers, for there was still much sympathy in this northern port for the royalist cause, both the port captain and the pilot expressing their violent opposition to the new government. But Duperrey had in fact little to do here and was eager to leave the former Spanish colony. Fresh water and supplies were taken on, and on the 22nd he was ready to sail. One deserter, a sailor assigned to unpopular kitchen duties, was replaced by a Mexican from Vera Cruz. Now that the expedition was leaving the European settlements, the problem of desertions which had plagued it for so long and was so bad for morale was about to disappear.

Duperrey had begun his work of exploration with a fruitless search 'for the rock seen by the ship *Hercule* in 1792 . . . the Spanish pilots I have consulted about it since have all assured me that it did not exist'.[1] Leaving Payta, he sailed south-west to seek 'le Trépied, a small group of islands placed on our old charts in 18° south and 100° west [of Paris]. On 1 April we were on this parallel and forty leagues to windward of the Trépied, standing west and heaving to at night for fear of missing the land. We maintained this course far beyond the position assigned to it, without sighting anything.'[2] His conclusion was that this group, which was reported to cover an area of thirty miles and appeared on the chart of the Dépôt des Cartes of 1818, should be erased. Soon the *Coquille* was nearing the north-eastern edge of the

---

[1] Duperrey, *Mémoire*, pp. 19–20.
[2] Ibid., pp. 20–1.

Tuamotus. On 13 April Duperrey gave instructions to reduce sail every evening and placed an extra man on look-out duty. Nothing but an occasional whale broke the surface of the ocean, 'which indeed deserved the name of Pacific', but on the 15th a sail appeared—the *Charles*, a whaler from Nantucket. Her captain came on board the French ship and expressed surprise that the *Coquille* should be sailing into such dangerous waters. He himself was on his way from the Galapagos to Pitcairn Island, where he hoped to refresh some scurvy cases, but he had no intention of entering the reef-strewn archipelago which most ships wisely avoid by keeping well to the south. 'We knew all this perfectly well, but we could hardly add to geographical knowledge by following the tracks of our predecessors.'[1] This policy was to be justified within a week:

On the 22nd [April 1823], the weather being fine, we were sailing through an area of sea that was completely open, when at three in the morning Mr d'Urville thought he could hear the dull roar of waves breaking over reefs; we hove to and at dawn found ourselves less than half a league from a low island scarcely rising above the water, whose gently sloping shores consisted of a white sand which reflected the light far out to sea, and whose centre was covered with green masses of pandanus and coconut trees. The inhabitants made their presence known by lighting a great fire, but when they saw that we did not respond to this signal they promptly sent a small outrigger canoe with three men, whom we could not persuade to come up to the *Coquille* ... losing patience at our inability to overcome their obstinacy or their suspicious caution, we sailed and continued our exploration. This is the island the captain of the *Coquille* named Clermont-Tonnerre, and which is found on the maps in 18° 28' south and 138° 46' west.[2]

This island was Reao, on the eastern fringe of the Tuamotus, and a new discovery. Blosseville confirms Lesson's account, adding:

At about 7.15 a.m. we saw several natives on the western point and a canoe leaving the shore and making for us. At 7.45 it was a cable's length away. We hove to. This canoe had three men on board each with paddles, naked to the waist, not very tall but well built and

[1] Lottin, Journal, p. 36.   [2] Lesson, *Voyage*, vol. i, pp. 227–8.

vigorous-looking with no visible tattooings. They kept a short distance
from us, saying a great deal and very loudly, and inviting us to land,
but they were never willing to come any closer, in spite of our friendly
gestures.[1]

Duperrey himself adds that he would have sent a boat to the
island, had it not been for the heavy seas hurling themselves at
the shore. He contented himself with sailing slowly along the
northern coast, continuing on a north-westerly course. Shortly
before 3 p.m. on the same day, land was sighted bearing west-
south-west. This proved to be Serle's Island or Puka Ruha, which
had been discovered by James Wilson of the *Duff* in 1797. Keeping to his north-westerly course in order to seek Boenechea's San
Narciso, Duperrey sailed to the north of Puka Ruha in splendid
weather and, at five on the evening of the 23rd, sighted more land,
bearing west-north-west, some twelve miles distant. This was
indeed Boenechea's island, whose native name is Tatakoto. In the
morning five canoes came out to the ship, which was sailing
slowly four or five miles off-shore while Lottin was taking
bearings. The *Coquille* hove to, but the natives could not be persuaded to approach.

Being now in the latitude of Tahiti, Duperrey altered course
to west and west-south-west. Hopes were high that unknown
islands might be discovered, for only three years earlier Bellingshausen in the *Vostok* had made several new discoveries or redis-
coveries in the archipelago. Indeed, Lottin, Lesson, Blosseville,
and Duperrey all eagerly set down in their journals claims to
'nouvelles découvertes', even though some, like Lesson, were
prepared to admit others might have already sighted, however
briefly, atolls they now considered 'comme notre propriété'.

On the 25th, in the evening, we saw land bearing west-north-west,
but as night was falling we put off exploring it until the next day. On
26th April at 7 a.m. the look-out saw it stretching along the horizon to
the south; we were then sixteen miles from it; at 10.15 we were two
miles off and proceeded along the coast at that distance. This island, D,
is very low, covered with greenery and fine trees, including coconut
trees. It is similar to the previous ones, with a vast lagoon inside and

[1] Journal, 22 Apr. 1823.

the south-westerly swell beating along the whole southern side. We saw no inhabitants, but nevertheless could make out a hut made of branches, which was in bad repair and seemed to be abandoned. We thought at first that this island D was Bougainville's Harp Island, but at one o'clock the look-out sighted more land to the south, and towards three o'clock we saw it clearly and there was no doubt that this was the north of Harp Island, so that island D is a new discovery.[1]

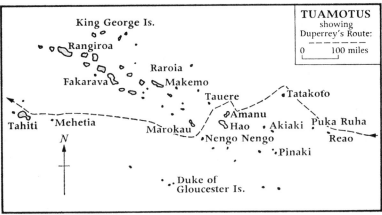

Map 5. Tuamotu archipelago

It was not a new discovery, but Amanu, discovered by Quiros in 1606 and later sighted by Joseph Andia in the *Jupiter* in 1774. The *Coquille*, having sailed north of Amanu and Hao, continued to bear south-west, but ran into rain during the night so that there were no sightings on the 27th. The weather cleared the next day, and on the morning of the 28th another island hove into sight 'which I named Lostange, in honour of the flag-officer of that name'.[2] Blosseville, who calls it 'île Toui-toui ou Lostange', describes it as wooded and very low, and, in common with Duperrey, places it in 18° 43' south and 144° 30' west of Paris. He does, however, add that Toui-toui is also known as 'Prince Henry Island', which confirms that the island in question is Nengo Nengo, discovered by Wallis in 1767 and named by him Prince William Henry's Island, its position being 18° 46' south and 144° 10' west of Paris.

[1] Lottin, Journal, p. 39.   [2] Duperrey, *Mémoire*, p. 23.

The French left the neighbourhood of Nengo Nengo under a canopy of storm clouds which soon hid the horizon. The next two days were stifling: 'Below decks it was a real furnace, and sweat poured off anyone who remained there for a few short moments.' Late on 1 May a lonely green cone was sighted—it was Mehetia. After being becalmed for a while, the *Coquille* sailed slowly north of it, making for Tahiti through yet another curtain of tropical showers. The horizon cleared a little the following morning, revealing the coast of Tahiti to the south-west. At 4 p.m. Duperrey dropped anchor in Matavai Bay. Expecting the kind of tumultuous welcome Bougainville had received, the French were surprised to see no activity along the shore, no canoes coming out to meet them: they had arrived on the Sabbath in an island where life had been totally transformed by English missionaries.

Largely unaware of the changes which had taken place in Tahiti, we were most surprised not to have seen a single canoe when we arrived in the bay; [we] had anchored for some minutes before the natives, running down the beach, came to dispel the thought that the island was deserted and that the houses were uninhabited. Another spectacle had already met our eyes when we sighted Point Venus—a red flag floating on the headland. We had at first taken it for the English ensign, without being surprised by this, but later we saw simply a white star.[1]

Natives who came aboard later told them that the flag they had seen was Tahiti's own, and their behaviour made it plain that Bougainville's Tahitian paradise was no more. 'We arrived in Tahiti, enthusiastic at the thought of what we would find there, but alas our imaginary happiness was short-lived, and after spending a few hours on this island we were close to wishing we could leave, to avoid discovering in greater detail the shameful condition to which fanatics from Europe have reduced these real children of nature.'[2] De Blois's annoyance is understandable. As Lesson says: 'During the first few days, those who were plagued by sensual visions were sorely disappointed. Bougainville's stories

[1] Blosseville, 'Notes, Île de Tahiti — événements, mœurs, descriptions, et usages', p. 1.
[2] De Blois, Journal, May 1823.

had given rise to such hopes that it was hard to see them fade away.'[1] He does, however, add that the puritanism imposed on the Tahitians by the missionaries was only skin-deep, and that some, true daughters of Eve, found ways and means to escape for a few hours.

Duperrey's first visitors were the two Tahitians who brought a letter from the missionaries, asking for details of the *Coquille*'s voyage and offering their services; and Captain Charlton, of the brig *Active*, who was engaged in pearl-fishing in the Tuamotus and was anchored a few miles away. It was Charlton who first explained to the French the changes that had taken place in Tahiti. He returned the next morning with Charles Wilson, of the London Missionary Society, who had first arrived in Tahiti in 1801 and had been in charge of Matavai Station since 1818. Wilson came to invite the French to land and meet his colleagues and members of the reigning family. It was now Monday, and since dawn a multitude of canoes had been surrounding the ship. Licentious behaviour apart, the islanders were as friendly as Bougainville had reported them to be. Upwards of two hundred of them clambered aboard, bringing fruit and artefacts to exchange for pieces of cloth and handkerchiefs. The noise, comments Lesson, reminded him of a provincial market town on a fair day. Duperrey, d'Urville, and Lesson went ashore at 10 a.m. They were met first by Henry Nott, who had sailed for Tahiti in the *Duff* in 1796, and was now possibly the most influential missionary in the island. He led the French to Pomare Norohai, the King's brother-in-law, who made them presents of a pig and some fruit. Lesson was unimpressed by the corpulent youth, who was only 16 and, like most Pomares, extremely heavy, and whom he considered dim-witted. The King himself, Pomare III, was to pay a visit to the *Coquille* a few days later, on the 8th, and to be given a wooden doll, which pleased him greatly, for this king was not yet 3 years of age, nor yet even crowned, being too young to keep still long enough for the ceremonies the missionaries had in mind. At Matavai, Lesson also met two visiting missionaries, Bennett and Tyerman, who subsequently paid several visits to Duperrey

[1] Lesson, *Voyage*, vol. i, p. 250.

and were later to quote him as praising the work of the London Missionary Society in the islands.[1]

Duperrey and Blosseville accepted Charlton's invitation to accompany him to Papeete, visiting on the way the tomb of Pomare II, the powerful king whom Nott had converted and who had died eighteen months earlier. The two Frenchmen were welcomed by the Papeete missionary, William Crook, who invited them to his house, an attractive structure, 'but greater was our astonishment when, going inside, we thought ourselves suddenly transported as by some magic back to Europe. Several ladies were gathered in an attractive and well-furnished drawing-room, and we scarcely expected to find such a gathering in the middle of the great Ocean, in an island 1,200 leagues away from any continent.'[2] The illusion was maintained by the tea which followed, 'with Tahitian milk supplied by cows from New South Wales'—for Crook had joined the mission in 1818 from Sydney. They returned the same evening to Matavai. The rest of the week was occupied in buying supplies from the natives, repairing the ship, and carrying out a number of observations on Point Venus, where Nott and Wilson had put a hut at their disposal not far from the headland where flew the Tahitian emblem. Pomare Norohai came on board, as did the rather formidable regent, Pomare Vahine, and later the two inspectors of the missions, Bennett and Tyerman. The repeated salutes these visits necessitated irritated Lesson, who considered it 'a custom it is time to do away with on these voyages; the least inconvenience they cause is to burn up powder without reason, while they also frequently endanger the smooth functioning of our chronometers'.[3]

As the first week ended, the Tahitians felt confident enough, one evening, to 'perform traditional dances which they are no longer allowed to indulge in and which they regret so much'. But on the 10th the French officers, in full uniform, went ashore to attend Sunday service at Wilson's request. Duperrey had no

[1] Lesson, *Voyage*, p. 255. Duperrey was certainly impressed by the Tahiti mission, but the widely held view that this was because he was himself a Protestant is now discredited. See on this Jore, *L'Océan Pacifique*, vol. i, p. 184.

[2] Blosseville, 'Notes, Île de Tahiti', pp. 5–6.

[3] Lesson, *Voyage*, vol. i, p. 290.

intention of providing the missionaries with an excuse to tell their
flock the French were an irreligious nation. Already, it had been
reported to him that, at a previous service, the preacher had
described France as a small, impoverished, and unimportant
nation. The appearance of the officers for the first time in their
colourful regalia caused a sensation which, so they believed, discomfited the English.

There was soon to be another opportunity to display their naval
uniforms. On the 11th the mission schooner *Endeavour*[1] arrived
in Papeete, bringing missionaries from outlying islands for the
annual general assembly due to be held on the 13th. Bennett and
Tyerman, as representatives of the London Missionary Society,
had naturally an important role to play in the meetings, but
Blosseville's opinion of them was not high:

M. Tyerman, who is a minister, has taken upon himself to do the
drawings and has already filled several books with sketches and plans
all badly drawn and ill-proportioned. M. Bennett, gentleman, has
a large fortune in England and travels without pay. His knowledge is
very superficial and it is more through ignorance than discretion that
he refrained from giving details on the places he has visited. He used
to know French but has forgotten it, and nothing was stranger than
his conversation, which consisted of a mixture of French, Tahitian
and English words.[2]

Most of the officers attended the meeting:

The famous annual meeting of all the ministers in the Archipelago
and of the greater part of the inhabitants took place on the thirteenth.
The purpose of this well-known convocation is to collect taxes and
prepare the annual report which has to be printed and sent to Europe.
It includes numerous ceremonies and, in particular, unusual services
at the residence of the Kings of Tahiti, in the great royal chapel of Pari,
established in 1818. The ceremony of this annual jubilee was too
interesting not to arouse the curiosity of an observer, and so I hastened
to join Messrs. d'Urville, Jacquinot, Bérard and Blosseville, so as to

[1] The *Endeavour* had been purchased by the Revd. John Williams of Raiatea,
although Blosseville claims it belonged to Tamatoa, king of Raiatea. It provided
an inter-island service as well as a link with Port Jackson.
[2] Blosseville, 'Notes, Île de Tahiti', pp. 19–20.

lose nothing of the stimulating scene all this promised. Mr. Duperrey
had told us to wear our uniforms, and Messrs. Bennett and Wilson
came to ask us to take them in our boat.[1]

The ceremonies were lengthy, beginning with prayers, hymns,
and a sermon in Tahitian on St. John's Gospel, which lasted an
hour and must have seemed truly interminable to the French,
who knew little English and far less Tahitian. D'Urville estimated
the attendance at 3,000 and the duration of the service at over two
hours. But it was only the start. Lunch, offered by the Queen,
followed, and at 2 p.m. the assembly returned to the chapel.
Lesson and Blosseville, having had their fill of services, seized the
opportunity to visit the neighbourhood, leaving d'Urville and
Jacquinot to follow as best they could a long argument on
taxation in which Tati, chief of Papara, was obviously the leading
spokesman for the anti-missionary side. This the French duly
noted, and it was no coincidence that Tati later became the main
advocate of a French protectorate and a most loyal collaborator
when it was finally established.

A small episode helps to shed some incidental light on the
character of Dumont d'Urville and his relationship with Blosseville. Soon after the start of the afternoon meeting, it began to
rain heavily; Lesson, unable to take a stroll as he had intended,
went instead to visit two sick sailors from the *Endeavour*. He then
returned with Blosseville to meet d'Urville, only to be curtly
told by the latter that he had offered two missionaries a passage
back to Matavai. Lesson and Blosseville were thus forced to make
their way to their ship through rain and mud, a journey which
took them an hour and a half.

I have seldom seen Mr. de Blosseville, a young man of a good and
even temper, in an angry state, but on that occasion the bitterness of
his comments was evident, and from that moment dates the strong
dislike he never ceased to feel for Mr. d'Urville, who anyhow, when
on board, was too frequently brusque (to use a polite term) for this
not to be inherent in his character.[2]

[1] Lesson, *Voyage*, vol. i, pp. 290–1.
[2] Ibid., pp. 301–3.

Blosseville foresaw clearly the coming clash over Tahiti. On the one hand, British influence was increasing daily and the time was fast approaching when 'a garrison will arrive to take possession of the country';[1] but, on the other hand, the strict evangelicalism of the missionaries held little appeal for the naturally carefree islanders.

The forms of the Protestant religion are too simple to hold the attention. Novelty alone can arouse curiosity, but this soon palls. Hymn books have served their purpose better, for their verses are often on the lips of the natives. The Catholic religion is more suitable for the islands of the South Seas. The colourful ceremonies, our religious practices our continual chants, the brilliant clothes of our churchmen, the decorations of our temples, and our processions, would have captured the admiration of natives who are usually attracted by what is colourful.[2]

At the same time, he admits that the bans on tattooing, flute playing, traditional songs and dances, and the wearing of flowers had improved morals. The ever-present contrast for the French was between the reports of the Bougainville expedition and what they now saw of the appearance and behaviour of the Tahitian women. D'Urville voiced the opinion of everyone on board when he wrote, 'Yesterday we had an opportunity to examine at our leisure the fair sex of Tahiti and I am in a position to affirm that it in no way corresponds to the alluring descriptions of the first navigators.'[3]

Duperrey was less critical. He could appreciate the civilizing aims of the missionaries while regretting their narrow-mindedness. He accepted with pleasure the Reverend Orsmond's invitation to visit neighbouring Borabora. John Orsmond had been in the Society Islands since 1817, working successively in Moorea and Raiatea before settling in Borabora in 1820. He was later to become a supporter of the French protectorate, an attitude which led to his dismissal from the London Missionary Society, but earned him an official appointment as 'Government Pastor' of the Protestant mission church at Papeete. He spoke fluent Tahitian

[1] Blosseville, 'Notes, Île de Tahiti', p. 58.   [2] Ibid., p. 9.
[3] Journal, 6 May 1823.

and John Davies's Tahitian-English dictionary is largely Orsmond's work.[1] The French found him a stern but able ruler, the
local chief Mai being little more than a puppet. The *Coquille*
sailed from Matavai Bay early on 22 May with Orsmond aboard
and five English and American sailors who had signed on for
Port Jackson. A large group of islanders gathered on the shore to
welcome the French; and an even larger crowd later collected in
and around the chapel to meet them officially and hear Orsmond's report and instructions. Indeed, wherever they went, the
French seem to have been accompanied by numbers of gaping
natives. The size of the warship and the colourful uniforms were
naturally enough objects of curiosity. Duperrey called on Mrs.
Orsmond, whom the missionary had married in Sydney in 1820,
and was impressed by her efficiency and the comfortable European-style home she had created in this isolated place. An observatory was set up on land the next morning and survey work
began at once. Bérard and Lottin went in one of the boats to
circumnavigate and chart the island, while Blosseville sailed to
Maupiti for the same purpose. These operations lasted a week.
Meanwhile those left on board had to face a serious and unexpected
danger. The *Coquille* was anchored very close inshore, so near indeed that the French were plagued by swarms of flies. But on
31 May a sudden wild squall arose, the cable chain snapped, and
mountainous seas began to drive the ship towards the reef. It was
a Sunday, a day which Orsmond had asked the French to keep
free from work, requesting them even to refrain from hunting and
fishing, so as not to cause scandal among the islanders on whom
he had successfully impressed the sanctity of the Sabbath. Here,
however, was a real emergency. Orsmond and Mai themselves
came down to the shore in the driving rain, leading a group of
300 natives who seized ropes and began to help. By evening,
although the thunder still rumbled in the lowering sky, the
Coquille was once more securely at anchor. Orsmond and his
islanders had played a major part in saving the vessel and, from
that moment, relations which had been friendly but cool became

---

[1] His granddaughter, Teuira Henry, used his notes for her *Ancient Tahiti*.
See Bibliography.

truly cordial. Most of the French realized that Orsmond, far from being suspicious and bigoted as most of his colleagues had appeared to be in Tahiti, was merely anxious to preserve the natives from too much contact with the rougher elements among the sailors. It was for his people's own protection and peace of mind that he set up an official market on land, which he could supervise, and banned private trading; that he asked the French not to offer liquor to the natives, for this infringed his own regulations and tended to frighten those who were thus being tempted to break the law; and that he tried to get the French, so accustomed to a continental Sunday, not to violate the Sabbath. Lottin voiced the opinion of most of his colleagues when he wrote:

> The natives have every confidence in Mr. Orsmond; his return to Borabora was like a father's homecoming. He is young, full of drive, and the only missionary in this small island; he is in a far more pleasant situation than are his colleagues in Tahiti. He is so to speak the real chief of the island. The natives around him, who are not numerous, zealously meet his wishes and have made it easy for him to bring civilization to them. Their restricted intercourse with outsiders has helped to give them stricter morals. Each individual is constantly under the eyes of the others, and the conduct of the women is generally speaking above reproach.[1]

On 9th July, after a farewell dinner at which, exceptionally, rum was served, the French sailed from Borabora, taking with them three English sailors who were later left, at their request, on various Pacific islands. The route lay to the south-west, north of the Cook group, towards the Tongas. On the 17th they sighted Niue, bearing south-south-west, twenty miles away. They approached to within three miles, then continued on their south-westerly course. The weather had cleared and the wind was fair. At eleven on the morning of the 19th, Eua hove into sight, bearing north-west, 'a considerable distance away; by four o'clock it was no longer visible', and dark storm clouds soon hid the horizon. Nothing more was seen for nearly a week, when Pylstart Island, or Ata, appeared in the north-east. The weather, which had been alternately fine and squally during the previous

---

[1] Journal, p. 53.

week, began rapidly to deteriorate. Except for a brief spell on
13 and 14 July, the wind endlessly screamed through the rigging,
accompanied by driving rain and heavy seas which battered the
ship and on one occasion nearly succeeded in carrying away the
helmsman. 'Our oldest sailors declared that they had never seen
such a frightful sea.' The *Coquille* was making no progress;
Duperrey, giving up hope of reaching Port Jackson, began to
think of seeking refuge in Vavau, but d'Urville pointed out that
supplies would not enable them to undertake any prolonged
exploration and that a call at a main supply port could not be
avoided. Duperrey accordingly decided to battle his way down
to New Holland.[1] A few days later, in the face of almost constant
south-westerlies, he changed his mind. 'M. Duperrey, having
decided to put into the Bay of Islands in New Zealand, in order
to await the fine weather, altered course to south by east.'[2] He
held to this for only three days, then, faced by a return of the
southerly storms, accompanied by wild rain and mountainous
seas, abandoned this new plan and turned north. Land was finally
sighted on 2 August, bearing north-north-east. 'We recognized
Edgecombe and Ourry Islands; at ten o'clock we saw a third
island, hardly visible: it was Recherche Island. The great distance
concealed its low-lying parts and clouds prevented us from seeing
the high lands. We thought we could see Santa Cruz, but were
certain of it only at one thirty . . . At night, we lost sight of all
this land.'[3]

The *Coquille* was now sailing north-west off the south coast of
Vanikoro—d'Entrecasteaux's Île de la Recherche—and west of
Utupua—Carteret's Edgecombe and Ourry. Santa Cruz, or Udeni,
lies to the north-west of Utupua and remained visible far longer
as the French continued on their way to the Solomon Islands.
The weather was much improved and far warmer, but soon
tropical downpours and strong gales were back, hiding San
Cristóbal and the rest of the Solomons until the 9th, when, the
sky having cleared, Duperrey caught sight of the highlands of
Bougainville. He sailed along the north-east coast at a distance of

[1] D'Urville, Journal, 13 July 1823.   [2] Ibid., 16 July 1823.
[3] Blosseville, Journal, 2 Aug. 1823.

twenty miles, then made for the north-easterly head of Buka. At
two in the afternoon, the ship was sailing slowly three miles from
the shore. Large numbers of natives had gathered along the beach,
and a canoe came out with eight islanders in it, some of whom
exchanged their weapons for a handkerchief and pieces of iron.
'At about four o'clock, we sailed W¼NW and soon we saw
ahead Sir Charles Hardy's Island, very low on the horizon and
hardly visible from the deck.' This was Nissan, the largest of the
Green Islands, to the north of Buka. A storm on the following
day hid most of New Ireland; when it abated it was possible to
see the coast of New Britain running south-west. The 11th was
the anniversary of the expedition's departure from Toulon. The
heat was stifling, supplies were very low, there was a growing
number of sick men. All Duperrey could do to mark the occasion
was to order punch for all hands. The next morning, he dropped
anchor in Port Praslin. It was not a day too soon: the weeks of
arduous battling and back-tracking in the empty stretch of ocean
south-east of the Fiji group had strained both ship and men. New
Ireland was far from an ideal place of refreshment, but it did
provide water 'from Bougainville's stream', firewood, a little
fish, and some fresh fruit. Fifty or sixty natives came down to the
ship with coconuts, pigs, and bananas. They were most friendly,
in spite of their rather wild appearance: 'Their black and oily skin,
their unkempt hair covered with red ochre dissolved in fish oil
forming a thick putty-like cover over their head, truly gave a
strange touch to their complete nudity; add to this a small stick
thrust crosswise into their nose, and white bars on the face con-
trasting with red dust on their cheekbones.'[1] Lesson, who observed
them at close quarters while collecting natural-history specimens,
was offered a fried lizard by one, but declined as courteously as he
could an offering which seemed particularly unappetizing. When,
however, he tried to find the village, the islanders showed signs of
disquiet, which caused him to desist. In return for their gifts of
food, the sailors gave them pieces of cloth, iron, or small knives,
and set up a small barber's shop: 'Their beard is thin and they like
to get rid of it. They kept on bothering the sailors on this point,

[1] Lesson, *Voyage*, vol. ii, p. 14.

and the latter never missed an opportunity of playing pranks on them, using their pocket knives to scrape those black chins well covered with a soapy lather.'[1]

The weather was fine and it did not take long for the sick to recover. Duperrey had taken care to keep the ship clean and dry below decks; he had been particularly careful to exempt from heavy duties anyone the surgeon reported as unwell, and, although this policy may have given rise to some abuses on the part of skilful malingerers, by and large it had paid good dividends: on 21 August the *Coquille* was able to sail with nearly all her men in good health. She proceeded towards the Bismarck Sea, keeping four to five miles off the coast of New Ireland, which the officers began to chart. On the 22nd, in spite of a choppy sea, a brisk trade began with natives of the Duke of York group, who came out in canoes to barter food for pieces of iron. A few days later, having had the benefit of a good north-easterly breeze, the French were in sight of the Schouten Islands in western New Guinea. These having no individual names apart from their native ones, Duperrey proceeded to repair the omission: they became Île Lesson, Île Jacquinot, Île d'Urville, Île Blosseville—all ephemeral names which have left no trace on modern maps. But at no time did he put into any of the bays here or elsewhere along the coast, contenting himself with sailing a good distance from the land— seldom, in fact, less than nine miles from the shore—so that the haze, or occasional downpours, often hid its main features. D'Urville, chafing as second-in-command, was later to criticize Duperrey for what he felt was excessive caution.

Numbers of dead tree-trunks were seen floating past the ship. On 31st August the French saw in the distance what they took to be a small decked boat seemingly mounted by men in distress. The whaleboat was sent to investigate, but found simply a large uprooted tree with a great number of sea-birds perched on its branches. Three days later, however, a real ship hove into sight, the first they had seen since Tahiti, flying an English flag. Duperrey altered course towards it, hoping to get news of Europe, but it promptly put out more canvas and disappeared, causing

[1] Lottin, Journal, p. 66.

him to suspect that she was engaged in contraband along the edge
of the Dutch empire. On 5th September he sighted Waigeo and
made for Rawak. Held up by calms and uncertain breezes, he
finally anchored in Offak Bay[1] on the 6th. Trade had already
begun with natives in canoes, but there seemed to be no one on
shore. Blosseville, sent to survey the western side of the bay,
found only a deserted hut; he left three knives in the doorway to
see if the inhabitants had truly departed or were hiding in the
jungle. When he returned the next day, he was faced with 'a
pyramid of coconuts, topped by one of the knives we had given
the day before, so as to show for whom they were meant'. The
officers sent to the eastern side of the bay found it similarly
empty, but natives did put out to the ship in canoes, one bringing
two very fine birds of paradise, others bringing small artefacts
or gifts of food. It seems likely that many had fled when the
Coquille sailed into the bay, afraid that the French might be about
to attack them or carry them off into slavery. As fear receded,
more appeared, until a large and picturesque market developed
around the ship.

I climbed down into one of the canoes, the last to arrive, and found
a crowd of objects we had not yet seen. There were large ivory brace-
lets or rings of shells, all carefully polished, red fruit they called maka
which seem to come from some palm tree, large grapefruits, fish
smoked in leaves, and especially numerous doughy cakes made of
sago flour, which they proudly called Papuan sagoes. Iron-tipped
spears, shields adorned with mother of pearl or shell ornaments, straw
baskets woven with great skill . . . found a ready market.[2]

The survey work took six days. The bay was explored and
charted, the coast surveyed for eight miles. 'It was important for
geography to verify the existence of a bay to the south, separated
from Offak by a very narrow isthmus. The peregrinations of
Messrs. d'Urville and de Blosseville thoroughly attained these
ends. I am giving the name of *Crousol* to this bay in honour of

[1] 'M. Duperrey had chosen the known harbour of Rawak, which had been
visited by the corvette *l'Uranie*. It is fortunate that the weather led us to anchor
in the fine port of Offak' (Blosseville, 'Notes, Île de Waigiou', p. 22).
[2] Lesson, *Voyage*, vol. ii, p. 78.

His Excellency, the Minister of Marine, under whose auspices the account of our voyage is being published.'[1] Once this work had been completed, water taken on, and the men rested, the *Coquille* was ready to sail. On 16 September she made her way west-north-west to the north of Sayang, then turned south towards Gebe and Pulau Pisang, passing to the east of the latter and south of Lowin and Kekik towards Buru. On the 23rd a weak breeze drove her towards the entrance to Caieli Bay; Duperrey fired two guns to call a pilot, but none came. Slowly the *Coquille* nosed her way in and anchored. The anchor was scarcely down when the Dutch Resident sent a French copy of the Governor-General's order which forbade him to allow any foreign vessels to enter the harbour. 'We had anchored, there was no wind, night was approaching'; the French were in no mood to worry about a prohibition couched in general terms. They had a letter from the King of Holland, allowing the expedition to call anywhere in his dominions, and this, plus the *fait accompli*, overcame, though not without difficulty, the Resident's objections:

After dinner [on the 23rd] the captain paid him a visit with some of his officers, but the Governor persisted in his attitude, pretending he did not understand, saying the island could not supply our needs, and continually interrupting the conversation to offer some Bordeaux wine, some gin, some palm wine and prevailing on us to follow his example. Two or three days went by in this way; we were obtaining very little from the natives, a fine herd of cattle was grazing near the fort, and we were living in want in the midst of plenty, when at last the Resident, becoming more aware of his own interests, asked the captain to outline in writing his reasons for coming here and his requirements, and offered to sell rice and some of his herd.[2]

Duperrey sailed from Buru on 1 October, leaving behind, at his request, one of the English sailors from Borabora. At Amboina, where he arrived three days later, Duperrey received a twenty-one-gun salute from the Governor, who dismissed the hesitations of the Caieli Resident as ridiculously pusillanimous—overlooking the fact that Amboina was one of the few Dutch ports open to

[1] Duperrey, *Mémoire*, p. 33.
[2] Blosseville, 'Notes, Île de Waigiou', pp. 39–40.

foreigners. Nevertheless he had little to offer in the way of supplies, so that, although the French remained in port until 28 October, the stay was not advantageous.

Our stay in Amboina is our longest so far; at the same time it has been of very little value to our mission and this long sojourn has exposed our crew to the ravages of that deadly illness, Asiatic cholera, which was still causing havoc in the colony. We were lucky indeed to lose nothing more than a great deal of time. During the twenty-eight [*sic*] days we spent at anchor our crew did little work; after the enormous efforts needed to bring the corvette to her moorings, they were only used to replace our water and finish some repairs to the rigging. . . . They were sent ashore on leave and would have enjoyed this privilege more often if the death of two of the English sailors we had just landed had not shown the dangers of excessive freedom.[1]

The unfortunate Englishmen were the remainder of those who had signed on in the Society Islands for Port Jackson and had ill-advisedly elected to remain in the Dutch East Indies. They had proved quite satisfactory, and Duperrey had given them all certificates of discharge and to one of them a commemorative medal; the latter was the first to die, on 12 October. In spite of this, four men disappeared on the 27th. 'As they are rather a bad lot, we have reasons to fear they are attempting to desert. The authorities at Amboina have undertaken to make every effort to make them rejoin their ship.'[2] They did indeed return the next day just in time to sail and receive twenty lashes each. The *Coquille* was now making for Timor, passing south of the small island of Ambelau and in spite of occasional calms proceeding almost due south across the Banda Sea towards Wetar and the Straits of Ombai. Duperrey had planned to put in for supplies at Dili, but his experiences at Caieli and Amboina had persuaded him that this would only waste more time. He preferred to let Bérard chart these ill-known waters while he made as quickly as he could for higher and healthier latitudes. It seemed clear now that cholera would not strike the ship, but there were two cases of dysentery on board, as well as other discomforts.

[1] Blosseville, Journal, 4–28 Oct. 1823.
[2] D'Urville, Journal, 27 Oct. 1823.

All we had left in the way of food were pieces of old salted pork, half tainted; some biscuits, full of worms; and to drink, ferruginous water which you could use to make an evil-tasting toddy by adding rice wine to it. Add to this thick fogs, angry seas, a continual pitching and tossing, the sudden change from a tropical to a southern climate, and you will realise by what sufferings we had to pay for our improvidence. A few sacks of rice which we had taken in at Amboina would have been our salvation if they had not been infested by mice dirt and cockroaches. The latter disgusting insects had multiplied so much through the ship that they turned our narrow cabins into torture chambers. Spreading in their thousands, they fouled the food, soiled the water and disturbed our sleep. They attacked everything, not overlooking the inkwells which they emptied without leaving a single drop, and even leather succumbed to their appetite. . . . Mr. d'Urville and I gave up our cabins and for more than ten months, for as long as our voyage lasted, we slept on a native mat stretched out on the deck from which even the rain could not drive us away.[1]

In mid November the *Coquille* sailed north of Sawu and south into the Indian Ocean. On the 23rd a brig was seen in the distance, flying the United States colours, and on 1 December, in 13° south and 110° west of Paris, a three-master hove into sight and made for the corvette. It was the *Melantho*, a whaler of 370 tons, Captain Folger, from London. Blosseville and Bérard went over to it, returning with letters for Port Jackson and news of French intervention in Spain. The two ships then went their separate ways, the *Coquille* sailing south-west. The weather remained fine until just before Christmas, when light rain heralded a fortnight of cloud and gales. On 1 January 1824 Blosseville opened his last two d'Appert tins—chicken and beans which he found to be in good condition in spite of their being three years old. Generally speaking, the tinned meats were proving satisfactory, although there was not enough of them for regular use and rust did spoil a proportion of them. On 11 January, south of Tasmania, the weather cleared and remained fine until the 17th, when the *Coquille* dropped anchor in Port Jackson.

After an exchange of twenty-one-gun salutes, the French landed to pay their respects to the authorities: Duperrey, in full uniform,

[1] Lesson, *Voyage*, vol. ii, pp. 225-6.

calling on Governor Brisbane, who was to extend every facility and help to the visitors. Others merely ambled though the streets of the growing city; some went to renew acquaintances with old friends, such as Captain Debs of the Tahitian *Endeavour*. While the men repaired the ship and went on carefully supervised walks ashore—escaping now and then for a quick roistering in a back-street grog-shop—the officers organized excursions to outlying districts, d'Urville going with Lesson to Bathurst, and with a larger group of young officers to Botany Bay on a pilgrimage to the spot where La Pérouse wrote his last message. A few rows of vegetables still survived in Frenchman's Garden, grown by the soldiers from the near-by fort, but the fruit trees were no more, killed off by the storms which lash this exposed spot. They went on to Father Receveur's grave. The copper plate Governor Phillip had had affixed to a tree close by had disappeared, so they carved in the tree itself, an old eucalyptus, the words 'Near this tree lie the remains of Father Receveur, visited in 1824.'[1]

In late February, Duperrey sent two officers on their way back to France in the *Forbes Castle*. They were Garnot, the senior ship's surgeon, who had caught dysentery while in Payta and had never really recovered, and Lesage, who had suffered a nervous break-down which left him unfit for service. It was time too to think of filling some of the gaps in the crew with local men. There was no shortage of willing recruits, especially among freed convicts who were yearning to return to Europe, but the New South Wales authorities were not willing to take chances: the law re-quired the names of men wishing to leave the colony to be published a fortnight before departure to give time to cull ticket-of-leave men and, indeed, convicts from bona-fide sailors. Du-perrey was not informed of this until quite late, so to save time he appealed to Governor Brisbane, who agreed to extend to the French the privileges of a British man-of-war, thus waiving this requirement. This did not deter the local police from carrying out a thorough search of the vessel, to which Duperrey raised no objection as he had no wish to take any convicts away with him. None was found and the *Coquille* started on her way to the Heads,

[1] H. de Bougainville, *Journal*, vol. i, p. 528.

having on board the harbour pilot and Captain Nicholson, who
was in charge of the inner harbour; as the ship neared the open
sea, she was greeted by a full salute from the guns placed around
the estate of Captain Piper. It was 8 a.m. on a fine morning, the
date being 20 March 1824. The French farewelled their English
hosts and, refreshed and in high spirits, entered the Tasman Sea.

They took with them five passengers, including two Maoris
returning home and a missionary, George Clarke, accompanied
by his wife and year-old son. Clarke had been offered a passage
at the request of the Port Jackson chaplain, Samuel Marsden, who
had been organizing a mission in New Zealand. Clarke was to be
stationed at Kerikeri for a time, then at Waimate, being appointed
protector of the aborigines by Governor Hobson in 1841. The
two Maoris had also been staying with Marsden, who ran a school
for New Zealanders—though not, it was noted, for the Australian
aborigines. All these passengers were soon ill in the storms which
promptly blew up. Even on 2 April, when the coast of New
Zealand was sighted, the weather was overcast, with an intermittent drizzle obscuring most of the features—as far as Duperrey
could see, he was close to Doubtless Bay and had a brief sight of
what he took to be Knuckle Point, the northernmost head of that
wide bay. On the morning of the 3rd they were in sight of the
entrance of the Bay of Islands:

The New Zealanders Taifana and Hapai whom we brought with us
from Port Jackson recognized the entrance of the great Bay of Islands,
so we veered a little distance of Point Pocock, near which Sentry Rock
may be seen. At one o'clock three whalers came out of the bay; one
of them, an English three-master, *The Sisters*, from London; a second,
an American, the *Boston*, from Nantucket; and the third, the brig
Mercury from Port Jackson. As the westerly winds were against us, we
had to tack between the islands and the north shore. . . . We dropped
anchor by Motu Rua, in twelve fathoms, fine sand and mud.[1]

Almost as soon as the anchor touched bottom, Maoris swarmed
over the ship, climbing the rigging, pouring into the galley and
the between-deck. D'Urville looked on this invasion with the

[1] Blosseville, Journal, 3 Apr. 1824.

eye of tolerance, for they were not really troublesome; but Lesson was shocked by their noise and greed and by the behaviour of the women—they were, he surmised, slaves captured in wars and now sent on board by their captors. More noble in appearance and restrained in behaviour were the chiefs, Hongi, Te Tuhi, and Pomare, who arrived the next day and were honoured with a five-gun salute. Hongi, the great warrior, once the guest of George IV, and now the disdainful protector of the uneasy English missionaries, did not impress Lesson, who realized that like the other chiefs all he wanted was muskets and powder to continue his raids deeper into the territory of his enemies. Te Tuhi—younger brother of Korokoro, who was believed to have been implicated in the death of Marion du Fresne but had recently died—had also visited England; the French considered him rather more attractive: 'he is dressed in European clothes and his manners indicate that he is a man accustomed to our courtesies . . . he is generally speaking serious-minded, keen to learn and never troublesome'.[1] He was, however, no less warlike than the others and was to be killed in battle six months later. Pomare, the Ngapuhi chief and personal protector of the missionary Kendall, was also soon to die in the almost constant wars of this period, which had become particularly costly of lives since the introduction of firearms and the development of European-style wars of conquest. Pomare like the others had been affected by dreams of royal power—originally called Whetoi, he had changed his name to Pomare out of admiration for the royal family of Tahiti. After a spirited 'haka', the Maoris began to trade with all the guile and experience of natives accustomed to European visitors. The French bought three pigs, some fish, and vegetables, while Lesson purchased a greenstone tiki and a preserved tattooed head, paying—reluctantly—in gunpowder. Meanwhile, an observatory was being set up ashore in the centre of Tangatu Beach, 'on the precise spot where Captain Marion had been murdered in 1772'. Bérard, who had gone sounding early that morning, found a more sheltered anchorage, to which the ship was moved the same day, in Manawaora Bay.

[1] Duperrey, *Mémoire*, p. 41.

On 5 April Kendall himself came on board to pay his respects
to the visitors and supervise the unloading of the Clarkes' luggage.
Duperrey and other officers, Lesson among them, went ashore and
visited the Maori village. It was here that Lesson was given a
version of the alleged incident which led to the murder of Marion
du Fresne: 'The sailors who had been sent to collect firewood had
sat down in a circle to have their evening meal when a high chief
entered the circle and, without permission, put his hand in the
bowl and took some food. A sailor got up at once and struck
him; as the angry chief was drawing his patu-patu to revenge
himself, a sentry shot him dead.'[1]

In the evening rain began which lasted until the 7th, when
Bérard and de Blois were able to start work on a survey of the
bay and the Maoris returned for further trade. On the 9th, the
weather remaining fine, Blosseville set off with Gabert, Lejeune,
and the gunner Rolland on a two-day trip to the northern shore
to buy supplies and visit the missionary establishments. They
rowed across the bay to the east point of Motu Roa, avoiding the
dangerous Black Rocks, and entered Mangonui and Kerikeri
inlets. There was little available in the way of provisions—they
obtained only five or six pigs for all their trouble—but they were
able to meet a number of missionaries: King and Hall, 'New
Zealand's first colonists; nine years' residence has not discouraged
them, although they have met with no success in respect of their
evangelical work and their agricultural enterprises have not been
so encouraging as is reported';[2] Kemp and Clarke, now settling
in, with whom they spent the night; and the Reverend White,
a missionary from Whangaroa, due to return to his station three
days later, who offered to take Blosseville with him and undertook to provide him with guides for the return journey, 'but
unfortunately this proposal which appealed so much to me did not
meet with the Captain's approval'.

They returned just in time: the wind rose in the late afternoon,
developing into a violent storm which lasted four days. There
was no trade, no opportunity for further excursions, merely a

[1] Lesson, *Voyage*, vol. ii, p. 329. See also *supra*, vol. i, p. 188.
[2] Blosseville, 'Notes, Rapport d'une visite aux villages', p. 1.

few hurried and uncomfortable trips for the sailors sent to obtain wood and water from the nearest land. On the 15th, however, the weather improved and Blosseville was able to go south to Paihia and Kororareka:

I arrived at Paihia where lives Mr. Williams, the head of the mission. His welcome was very gracious. He seemed to me full of zeal and particularly fond of the natives. His house, somewhat hastily constructed, is situated in a rather attractive plain called Marsden Vale, but he is about to erect a substantial building with thick walls, not a difficult task as the building material is available on the spot. The natives seemed to be numerous and were not troublesome. Nevertheless, Mr. Williams is compelled to barricade himself like his colleagues from Mangonui and Kerikeri. . . . North of Paihia is found Matauhi Bay, where lives Mr. Kendall, whom I was sorry not to find at home. . . . Mr. Kendall has shown greater tolerance and skill than the other missionaries: he has respected the natives' beliefs without displaying any feeling of disgust towards their customs and he owes to this conciliatory attitude the consideration and freedom he enjoys, for he is not forced to keep on his guard and there are no walls or palisades around his home.[1]

Kendall had in fact gone on board the *Coquille* while Blosseville was at Paihia. It was his only chance to meet Duperrey, for the next day, 'Good Friday, we flew the flag and pennants at half-mast', the observatory was dismantled, and final preparations were made for an early-morning sailing. The stay was being cut short because the season was now well advanced and the Bay of Islands had proved disappointing as a place of refreshment: even in exchange for good quantities of gunpowder the French had only been able to obtain some twenty pigs.[2] At a quarter to eight on 17 April, on a warm morning with a light breeze, the *Coquille* moved slowly out of the bay and sailed north. Cape Brett sank below the horizon at 2.30 p.m. and, shortly after, 'an Englishman named Burns'—according to d'Urville, but in fact an Irishman named O'Brien—was discovered hidden on board and allowed to remain as a passenger.

The weather remained fine as the French made their way

[1] Ibid., p. 6.   [2] De Blois, Journal, 17 Apr. 1824.

north-east and north-west, well to the west of the Fiji group. Late
on the afternoon of the 30th land was sighted to the north-west
it was the lonely island of Rotuma. The next day, there being
almost no wind, the *Coquille* was surrounded by canoes—Duperrey
counted twenty-three of them, each with five to ten men—
bearing fruit and various artefacts. Although Duperrey found
them likeable and in every respect deserving the praise bestowed
on them by Edwards of the *Pandora* and Wilson of the *Duff*, they
were, in the unanimous opinion of d'Urville, Lesson, and Blosseville, most tiresome thieves. As each theft was detected, the culprit
was driven off by sailors swinging rope-ends, but the others were
not in the least deterred and made off with whatever they could
lay their hands on, nails, rags, and even books. However, their
friendliness and high spirits contrasted favourably with the more
severe and warlike Maoris who had already been spoilt by frequent contact with Europeans.

The natives, coming up to us, asked whether the ship was taboo and,
on being told it was not, climbed about fifty of them onto the deck,
touching our hands, caressing us and repeating a hundred times . . . 'Rotuma very good', and encouraging us to make for their island, but the
calm prevented us. Our hearts, still frozen by the memory of the fierce
Zealanders, warmed up among these kind islanders. The contrast was
striking, none of the sailors failed to notice it: here, the native, trustful,
happy, clean, lightly clad, was bartering his surplus vegetables for our
shining trinkets; there the ferocious man, disfigured by a cruel tattooing, carrying the head of his fellow-man in his hand, had asked for
powder and arms to indulge in further killings.[1]

Eight Englishmen, deserters from the *Rochester*, were living on
the island, dressed in native style, well treated and happy. One of
them, however, asked for a passage back to Europe. Duperrey
agreed, to the distress of the Rotumans, who had only recently
elected him a sub-chief; but they were consoled by two of the
English sailors taken on at Port Jackson who now wished to
remain and were carried off in triumph to their new home. At
about five in the afternoon, a light breeze enabled the *Coquille* to

[1] Lottin, Journal, pp. 123–4.

sail on her way, leaving the singing and waving Rotumans behind
in their canoes. The French continued on their northerly course
in developing rain; when the weather improved on the 9th, they
sighted land which they identified as Maurelle's Cocal Island.
They were reaching the western edge of the Ellice group and this
was the small atoll of Nanumanga. Another island was seen the
next day: Nanumea, which lies about thirty-seven miles to the
north-north-west of Nanumanga. A week later they started to
make their way past the western Gilberts—Simpson's Drummond
and Sydenham Islands were seen on 15 and 16 May and can be
identified as Tabiteuea, a long, narrow sandy island whence a
canoe managed to reach the ship and sell some fish, and Nonuti,
a long cluster of small islands: 'as we advanced, new islands appeared'. An attempt was made to communicate with the natives,
but their language seemed to have little in common with any
of the vocabularies on board. The following day the *Coquille*
approached Arakuna and Kuria, described as twin islands separated by a channel approximately five miles wide, but it is
unlikely that Abemama was clearly distinguished, as the sky was
overcast. Nevertheless, Maiana was seen on the 18th and then the
next day three islands identified as Tarawa, Abaiang, and Marakei,
the latter being, in all probability, a new discovery.[1] Veering
further west, Duperrey missed Butaritari and saw nothing more
for nearly a week,[2] until he sighted the southern Marshall Islands,
probably Mili and, on the 28th, in storm and rain, Jaluit.

Much of this area had been little known until recent years.
Following their original discovery by Gilbert and Marshall in
1788, a few ships had passed through the islands, such as the
Royal Admiral, Captain Bond, in 1792; the *Britannia*, Captain
Dennet, in 1797; the *Nautilus*, Captain Bishop, in 1799; the
Elizabeth, Captain Patterson, in 1809; and the Russian expedition
of Kotzebue in 1815. Duperrey was thus verifying a number of
discoveries made during the long period of the European wars
when France had been banned from Pacific waters. That the
area was no longer isolated was shown by the appearance on

[1] Sharp, *The Discovery of the Pacific Islands*, p. 202.
[2] Duperrey, *Mémoire*, p. 51.

30 May of a three-masted American whaler, the *Boston*, from Nantucket, commanded by Captain Joy. While his men went on with their task of boiling down a recently caught whale, sending a thick nauseating smell of burning fat across the water, the captain

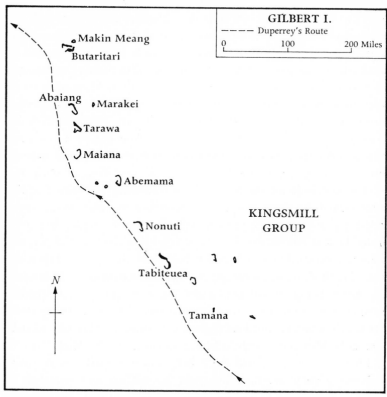

Map 6. Gilbert Islands.

came aboard the French ship. He had seen the *Coquille* some weeks before as he left the Bay of Islands and now was able to pay a courtesy call and also bring some interesting news.

Captain Joy has already collected 600 barrels of oil . . . He had followed the coast of America, obtained most of his catch off the coast of Japan and gone down to New Zealand by way of the Sandwich and Tonga Islands. When he left the Bay of Islands he followed much the same route as we have done, with weak breezes and frequent showers. . . .

He is on his way to Japan where he plans to fish between the twenty-fifth and thirty-fifth degrees. In October he is to go to the Sandwich Islands to refresh his men and if his ship is not full he will complete his load in the region of the Kingsmill group where whales are very plentiful. . . . About four or five days ago, Captain Joy discovered a small group which he called Nantucket Islands. It consists of eight small islands in a horseshoe pattern thirty miles round, with an opening in the NNE. The natives came out in canoes and behaved with him as they did with us. He had ascertained his position the day before and the position he worked out would be 165° 50′ east of Paris and 4° 45′ north.[1]

Joy had discovered Ebon, which answers his description and is the nearest land to the position assigned.[2] Duperrey himself had passed far to the east of it on the same day. The two men amicably parted company, the glare of the *Boston*'s furnace remaining visible for most of the night. The French were now proceeding almost due west towards the Carolines. At 11 a.m. on 3 June, high land was sighted in the far distance; they reached it at 4 p.m., seeing but a few natives assembled on a beach. In the morning they started looking for an opening in the reef; Blosseville and Bérard were sent in turn to investigate. It was not until the 5th that the *Coquille* was able to sail through a pass 'into a perfectly sheltered harbour which we named Coquille Harbour. . . . One can imagine the keenness with which we stepped onto this island where Europeans were landing for the first time. Natural-history excursions began at once. We obtained from the islanders everything that attracted our attention; we went all round the island in the small boat and entered into every harbour to examine every detail'.[3] Bérard and Lottin in fact spent two and a half days on a complete survey of the coastline of Kusaie, as the island was called, although, as d'Urville points out, the native name was Ualan. It had been sighted by the American captain Crozer of the *Nancy* twenty years earlier, but the French were indeed the first Europeans to step ashore, as the enthusiasm and curiosity of the natives clearly showed. 'Our arrival at Lele [the main village]

[1] Blosseville, Journal, 30 May 1824.
[2] Sharp, *The Discovery of the Pacific Islands*, pp. 207–8.
[3] Duperrey, *Mémoire*, p. 54.

caused extreme joy: men, women and children rushed up to us in a body. They were particularly surprised by the colour of our skin which they touched with their hands or faces, uttering at every moment shouts of admiration.'[1]

Lesson, accompanied by the indefatigable Blosseville, travelled overland to a central village where a crowd of over 500 men and women welcomed them. 'We had gained their full confidence, the women no longer hid as we approached . . . They believed at first that our skin and our clothes were similar and, when they drew aside our shirts to see our chests or our sleeves and trouser legs to uncover our arms and legs, they took the greatest precautions to avoid hurting us.'[2] Later, they were received by an elderly chief, too frail to rise from his sickbed but still energetic enough to insist on going through Blosseville's pockets; as these contained geographical instruments, the young Frenchman objected as politely but as firmly as he could; the incident cooled the atmosphere, and Blosseville considered it wiser to decline an invitation to spend the night there. 'Those are the changes which self-interest and unwise gifts had wrought in a short space of time . . . the feeling of wonder had gone; we were now simply men with a skin of a different colour.' As for Lesson, he was to regret the expedition. On the way there they had had to wade for some distance along a meandering river with water up to their waists, and this gave Lesson an attack of rheumatism from which he was to suffer for the rest of the voyage and many years after. Lesson claims that it was this illness which incapacitated him on occasions, leading Dumont d'Urville in his harsh and unsympathetic manner to criticize him in his *Voyage pittoresque*. 'If I had Mr. d'Urville's character', said the doctor, 'I could cruelly revenge myself, but I spurn such methods.'[3]

The French left this pleasant island on 15 June. They now had good supplies of bananas, breadfruit, coconuts, and fish, for which they had given nails, knives, axes, bottles, and two pregnant sows. Their route led them in a north-westerly direction through the main body of the Caroline archipelago. On the 17th they came in

---

[1] Duperrey, *Mémoire*, p. 56.   [2] Blosseville, 'Notes, Île d'Oualan', p. 2.
[3] Lesson, *Voyage*, vol. ii, p. 480.

sight of Pingelap, which they passed at a distance of two miles, sailing slowly in a very light breeze. Natives came up to them in canoes, and threw coconuts on the deck, seemingly expecting nothing in exchange, but when one islander, bolder than his fellows, clambered on board and was presented with fish-hooks and axes he danced his joy and slid down singing to return to his friends. The islands which hove into view the next day did not appear on any chart; three in number they were enclosed by a reef through which no entrance could be found to the deep and placid lagoon inside it. Yet, if geographers had not heard of them, European civilization had passed close by: 'the first proas which came up to us had ten men on board; one of them showed us an iron adze made of a piece of hoop from a cask, which goes to show that they must have had some communication with Europeans or obtained this metal from a neighbouring island'.[1] The islands were named Îles Duperrey, but they have reverted to their native name of Mokil. Nothing else was sighted for several days— until late on the 23rd when in poor visibility a low island was seen to the south-west, which was called Île d'Urville. This was again something of a new discovery, for it is the first firm report of Losap-Nama, which may possibly have been seen by Saavedra in 1528. The next cluster of islands, quite high compared with Losap Atoll, as d'Urville points out,[2] was undeniably Truk. Two of the Englishmen on board the *Coquille* were granted permission to land here: 'the two Englishmen, O'Brien and Scott, one being from Port Jackson, the other from New Zealand, were allowed to remain on these islands. [But] they were given no implements likely to assist them in retaining their European character and enable them to improve the productions of the natives and render them important services'.[3]

The *Coquille* now bore north-west and sighted on 30 June three low and wooded islands, passing less than a mile from the southernmost. Duperrey counted twenty-seven canoes making towards his ship, with large numbers of islanders, some of whom came on board, selling fish, coconuts, and artefacts for knives and

[1] Ibid., vol. ii, p. 527. [2] Journal, 24 June 1824.
[3] Blosseville, Journal, 25 June 1824.

fish-hooks. These islands—Pulap Atoll—had been discovered by Arellano as far back as 1562; the next atoll, Puluwat, sighted later the same day, remained unknown until 1795, when Captain Mortlock, of the *Young William*, reported the presence of a low island to the south-west of Pulap. Rain blotted out the horizon until 3 July, when the French were able to glimpse an island in a position evidently that of Pikelot; two days later they traded under more rain with natives from Satawal Island. Nothing more could be done in these parts; the rain continued, the sea rose, and for nearly a week it was impossible to take the customary noon reading. Duperrey altered course to the south-west. On 15 July, when the weather began to clear, the expedition was once more crossing the Equator and well on its way to New Guinea. The Schouten Islands were just visible on the 21st, when the rain returned. Duperrey sailed westwards for several days more, sighting the New Guinea coast briefly on the 24th and finally dropping anchor two days later in Port Dore, by Manokwari on the north-east coast of New Guinea's westernmost peninsula. The ship was soon surrounded by canoes, and a brisk trade began. The Papuans, displaying both skill and good faith in their dealings, paddled from neighbouring islands to sell birds of paradise, tortoise-shell, pigs, fish, and fruit in exchange for coins and cloth. The scene was peaceful and pleasant in spite of the stifling heat which was reflected and increased by the mirror-like surface of the harbour; but it was an unhealthy spot where dysentery affected nearly the entire crew. The French left the bay on 9 August, followed even as they made for the open sea by a flotilla of small canoes laden with fruit and fish. The *Coquille* was now making for Surabaja by way of the Halmahera Sea, passing like so many milestones the long chain of Indonesian islands: Rawak, Wajag, Gebe, Pisang, and Buru. Surabaya was reached on the 29th, the French being warmly welcomed by the Dutch Resident and paying a courtesy visit to the Sultan of Madura.

All that now lay ahead was the homeward journey. Java was as always an unhealthy spot, and dysentery soon reappeared. Cutting short his stay, Duperrey sailed out on 11 September, leaving behind at their request two more of the English hands.

By the 17th he had passed Sunda Strait. On 3 October he arrived
in Mauritius, which the French still referred to as the Île de
France. There were French merchantmen among the two-score
ships in port, but a visit by a naval vessel was a rare occasion—
almost as soon as the *Coquille* had tied up, the wharf was thronged
by visitors queuing up to be allowed on board. The British, it
was clear, had still not succeeded in severing the islanders' links
with France. Duperrey took the opportunity to replace his stores,
for nearly all the rice he had bought in the Dutch East Indies had
to be jettisoned and half the biscuit was mildewed or worm-
ridden. The corvette herself was repainted so that she might
reach European waters with none of the scars of her long voyage.
Six weeks later, on 16 November, she sailed for nearby Bourbon to the sound of a twenty-one-gun salute. The Governor of
Bourbon was Henri de Freycinet, who was anxious for news of
the voyage; Duperrey stayed a week, sailing on the 23rd with
six extra passengers—convicts who were to be taken to France
to serve their sentence.

Apart from a brief sight of the coast of Africa in mid December,
the next six weeks were uneventful. On 3 January 1825 the
Coquille entered Jamestown Harbour in St. Helena. It was a busy
port, with frequent arrivals and departures, and a place of
refreshment where men could go on shore leave and working
parties obtain water, firewood, and fresh vegetables. It was also
the place where Napoleon had been imprisoned and had recently
died. The French went on a pilgrimage:

When we visited the house, on which a great misfortune has shed
lustre, a shameful state of disorder, worse than utter neglect, had led
to its being used as a bolting mill where they sifted the grain for those
workers of the colony who were restricted to this part of the island.
A manger filled the spot where Napoleon's bed had once been, and
his bedroom had been turned into a stable! No hangings were left, no
wainscoting; nothing in this building showed that it had ever been the
place of refuge of an Emperor sent by Kings into exile. Alone the
barriers which had restricted his walks remained around the house, and
this labyrinth was still an annoyance to visitors . . . Soon, at last, we
were about to enter the valley where Napoleon's ashes were lying

under a few stones . . . 'Your permit, gentlemen!' shouted a soldier
who bore on his cap the word, 'Waterloo' . . . This sentry and his box,
a few tall weeping willows, a flat stone still quite white in the midst of
the green grass, a tomb among the flowers and the ruins of nature, iron
bars around an oblong platform—an incongruous mixture if there ever
was one . . . struck our eyes. It was the tomb of Napoleon Bonaparte.[1]

In this sad and romantic mood, the French sailed for Ascension
Island, stayed ten days, and left on 28 January for Europe. They
entered the Straits of Gibraltar on 9 March and dropped anchor
in Marseilles on the 24th, after a circumnavigation which had
lasted over thirty-one months, including 521 days under sail, and
covered nearly 25,000 leagues. No serious damage had been
incurred, not a single life had been lost.

The aims of the expedition, it will be remembered, had been
largely scientific and Duperrey had well carried out his instructions in this respect. The Académie Royale des Sciences heard on
25 August 1825 a report from Arago, Cuvier, Humboldt, and
Rossel, among others, which praised his achievements.[2] It spoke
of the hydrographic work and of the 'grave errors' which the
fifty-three new maps and charts would rectify, especially in the
Society Islands and the Carolines, both by the elimination of non-
existent reefs, such as the Trépied off the coast of Peru, and the
discovery of new islands. These latter we now know to be fewer
than was at first claimed—a common occurrence in the history of
exploration—but they were nevertheless quite considerable. They
include Reao in the Tuamotus, Marakei in the Gilberts, and
Mokil and Losap-Nama in the Carolines. Meteorologists expressed gratitude for the valuable data which emerged from the
regular series of six daily observations of the temperature of the
atmosphere and the sea and of air pressure, spread over a period of
thirty-one months. Physicists welcomed the appraisement of
earth magnetism, which they hailed as an important contribution
to a still puzzling problem. The geologists thanked Lesson especially for the 300 samples of rock he had brought back. D'Urville

[1] Lesson, *Voyage*, vol. ii, pp. 536–7.
[2] The 'Rapport à l'Académie' was reprinted as an Introduction in Duperrey's
Voyage.

was praised for his botanical work, and the Muséum d'Histoire Naturelle received with gratitude 1,200 insects, 450 of which had not been available before, most of them collected by d'Urville. There were in addition 264 birds and quadrupeds, 63 reptiles, and 288 fishes, more than 80 of them new specimens. As well as this mass of biological samples, there were reports on anthropology, Polynesian vocabularies, and numerous sketches of clothes and weapons.

There were secondary results. Duperrey had not discovered a suitable site in Australia for a convict settlement and it should have been obvious that the British would raise immediate objections if an attempt were to be made to send French convicts to Western Australia; yet Blosseville drew up several plans for such a scheme, the first for the Minister of the Interior in 1825, the second for the Director of Police the following year, a third for the Minister of Marine in 1829. When they became finally convinced that a settlement in Australia would not be possible, the penal reformers—for such they were at the time—looked to New Zealand and the Pacific. For some the aim was to use convicts to open up new territories; to others deportation and isolation were more important, and these included among their number Blosseville, who felt that the fear of cannibals was the beginning of wisdom.[1] Dumont d'Urville was to be charged with investigating the question further, and various alternative locations were proposed. In the end the only real French convict settlement was to be a short-lived one in New Caledonia.

In an indirect way, Duperrey's voyage has been held partly responsible—or has received part of the credit—for the arrival of French Catholic missionaries in the Pacific in the early 1830s. It has been claimed that his letter praising the work of the Protestant missions in Tahiti, printed in the *Moniteur* and in the *Annales maritimes et coloniales*, aroused feeling among religious circles in France and that out of the consequent discussions proposals emerged for remedying the situation.[2] There is little evidence to

[1] Faivre, *Expansion française*, p. 287.
[2] 'It was only towards 1824, following a favourable report from Cap. Duperrey on the results obtained by the British in Tahiti that concern began to be felt in

justify this belief, no correspondence in the daily press, no editorials in Church newspapers, no recognition by Duperrey's contemporaries of his alleged role in this respect. It is enough to say that this letter and his expedition as a whole played their part in drawing French attention again to the Pacific, its problems, and its potential. In a similar way, Duperrey could claim a distant parentage with the ill-fated 'Free Colony of Port-Breton' which a crooked promoter, the Marquis de Rays, set up in 1877. Rays had read the accounts of Carteret, Bougainville, and Duperrey, and quoted—or misquoted—the latter's comments on Port Praslin in New Ireland. The natives had indeed been friendly, the weather had been fine during most of the time the *Coquille* spent there, and the call had undeniably been beneficial to the crew exhausted by weeks of battling through mountainous seas, but this hardly justified the sending of ill-provided and impoverished colonists to a narrow stretch of land overlooked by precipitous jungle-covered slopes. Hundreds of colonists died, the rest being repatriated or making their way to Australia, and thousands of dupes were ruined.

The repercussions of the voyage thus obscured in some ways Duperrey's achievements. If some claimed too much for it, others —d'Urville in particular—unfairly disparaged it. Duperrey emerges as an upright, modest, and truthful man of greater than average ability, possibly lacking in imagination, but precise in the carrying out of his duties. There is in some explorers—d'Urville and Bougainville come to mind—a touch of the flamboyant, a flair for publicity, tactfully exercised but none the less effective. Duperrey lacked this and may suffer by contrast, and it is for us to restore the balance.

What could be asked is whether Duperrey and a number of those who sailed after him could really be called explorers. To many people an explorer is a discoverer, a navigator in search of the unknown, who adds new names, including often his own, to the map of the world. New lands, new tribes, new customs, titillate the popular imagination and supply new topics of

France about the work of the English missions in Oceania' (Russier, *Le Partage de l'Océanie*, p. 125).

conversation in fashionable *salons*. Less dramatic is the slow, determined, and thorough examination of a coastline or of an archipelago which some earlier discoverer once sailed past on a longer voyage; but the exploration of the imperfectly known is as valuable and as necessary as the first sweep across the totally unknown. For the next fifteen years navigators of many nations were to show how much still had to be done before the chapter of Pacific exploration could really be closed, by which time explorers were already moving on to the real southern continent—the Antarctic.

BOUGAINVILLE

As far as the French were concerned, Pacific exploration was to be dominated from this point on by the austere figure of Dumont d'Urville. His personality, as well as his achievements, overshadowed secondary navigators whose quite valuable undertakings have consequently tended to be overlooked. This was the case with Bougainville's son, Hyacinthe, whose expedition of 1824-6 deserves to be rescued, if not from oblivion, at least from relative obscurity.[1] The sons of famous fathers often have to pay a high price for their birth: their achievements can seldom hope to be as notable, and any success which may be theirs runs the danger of being ascribed to the direct or indirect effects of nepotism. Louis de Bougainville's two sons became equally prominent in the spheres they had chosen: Hyacinthe, the elder brother, became an admiral, and Adolphe a general; but both must have found it difficult to still the voices of envy. When Hyacinthe was chosen at the age of 18 to join the Baudin expedition, it had been widely believed that he had been selected because of his father.[2] But he later proved himself in numerous naval engagements during the Napoleonic Wars, in the course of which he rose to lieutenant-commander (in 1808) and commander (in 1811), finally being taken prisoner by the English in 1814. By 1821 he was a post-captain and soon was given the command of the *Thétis*.

This was a frigate built in 1822 and intended for a circumnavigation. 'Our expedition', as Bougainville himself states, 'had been decided upon for a long time.' But first she went on three successive missions to the Mediterranean and the West Indies. Then the major voyage was approved with unexpected suddenness:

I do not know through what mischance, but preparations were made as in great haste. [The voyage] offered a valuable opportunity for

[1] The article under his name in the *Dictionnaire de biographie française* does not even mention his circumnavigation.

[2] Faivre, *L'Expansion française*, p. 117.

scientists and naturalists who could expect all kinds of rich crops, yet none came forward and not even one artist was taken on . . . so that, had it not been for M. de la Touanne, faithful companion of my travels,[1] nothing today would bring back these distant countries to our eyes.[2]

The delay had been due in part to Duperrey's voyage and in part to the political aims of the expedition. By his instructions, Bougainville was required to go to Cochin-China in an attempt to re-establish diplomatic relations and French influence, and to this end was given official letters which made of him in fact a plenipotentiary. It was the latest in a series of moves aimed at gaining a foothold east of British Singapore, less for reasons of prestige than as a commercial base for trade with China and the Philippines. The first Frenchman, a missionary, had landed at Tourane—or Da Nang—in 1615; by mid century there were close on a hundred thousand Christians in the country. The first trading post was opened in Tonkin in 1684, and a French establishment on the island of Pulo Condor, south of Saigon, was suggested two years later. In 1748 Pierre Poivre went to Annam at Dupleix's request, was granted an audience by the King, and signed a trade agreement. The weakness of the French India Company and of Pondicherry, added to the troubles in Europe, nullified French hopes in Indo-China and adjacent Siam until the end of the eighteenth century. But in 1787 Nguyen-Anh, an exiled prince from the former ruling family of Annam, with the active assistance of Pigneau de Behaine, Vicar Apostolic of Cochin-China, Cambodia, and Tonkin, went to France and signed a treaty of mutual assistance. In practical terms, this amounted to the loan of two ships in the charge of a group of French adventurers and volunteers, mostly from Pondicherry, which finally reconquered the country for Nguyen-Anh, who, under the name of Gia-Long, became emperor. Thus were laid the foundations of French Indo-China, for in exchange for their help the French were to be granted sovereignty over Pulo Condor

[1] Edmond de la Touanne, promoted *lieutenant de vaisseau* during the voyage, was a friend and protégé of Bougainville, with whom he had been sailing for four years. See Bougainville, *Journal*, vol. ii, p. 2.
[2] Bougainville, *Journal*, vol. i, p. 23.

and considerable rights over Tourane Bay, including a trading post and facilities for ship repairs. The European wars effectively barred France from the Far East and prevented her from exploiting this advantage. Pigneau himself died in 1799, and by 1815 only two French advisers, Chaigneau and Vannier, remained at Gia-Long's court. Attempts to renew political contacts in 1815 and 1816 ended in failure, but Balguerie and Philippon, both of Bordeaux, sent two ships, the *Paix* and the *Henry*, to seek new trade outlets. At the same time Richelieu, Minister for Foreign Affairs, similarly desirous of encouraging trade, procured a lowering of the tariff applicable to goods imported from Indo-China and dispatched Captain de Kergariou in the *Cybèle* on an official mission to the Far East.

Kergariou's instructions were to collect information of value to French traders, offer protection to French vessels he might meet in eastern waters, obtain an audience with Gia-Long, bring him news of the Restoration, make him certain gifts, and ask him to safeguard the interests of any French citizen who might visit his dominions. He was also to furnish the Government with a report on the state of European settlements in the Far East. Kergariou was an experienced captain who had joined the navy in 1787 and had just returned from Newfoundland. He sailed from Brest on 16 March 1817 direct for Pondicherry, where he arrived on 1 July, reached Malacca in August and Manila at the beginning of September. There he met the captains of three French merchantmen, all from Bordeaux, who were engaged in the sugar trade, refitted, and sailed for Macao on 19 November. After a brief stop off the island of Hainan, he made for Tourane Bay, where he anchored on 30 December. The *Paix* and the *Henry* had been gone only a few days; the mandarin in charge of Tourane was friendly, and it seemed as if the mission was to be a success. But Kergariou was merely to witness the beginning of a long process of prevarication and evasion that was to go on until the French lost patience and started on the military occupation of the country—which was precisely what Gia-Long and his advisers were seeking to avoid. On 1 January he landed and paid a visit to the chief mandarin. Conversation was not made easier by the system of interpretation which required the missionary Brossot to translate from French into Latin, a Christian Chinese to translate this into Chinese, and a local interpreter to render this into the local language. In time other officials arrived from the court at Hué, accompanied by the Frenchman Vannier. The Annamites explained that, as Kergariou had no letter from his King, etiquette could not allow him to meet the Emperor. Kergariou offered to supply extracts from his instructions, witnessed and sealed, as evidence of his mission; these were made and certified and sent on to Hué, but after further delays the council of mandarins made it known that this alternative was unacceptable. Kergariou had failed. He sailed on 22 January, made his way slowly down the coast, and finally left from the Mekong river mouth a fortnight later. He was back in Brest on 19 October 1818. His voyage had not been a total failure: he had shown the flag in the China seas and brought back valuable geographical information on Hainan and the coast of Indo-China.[1] The mandarins had been willing enough to trade and had not withheld supplies. Balguerie indeed sent back two more ships in 1819, in one of which Chaigneau returned to France, whence he was sent back with the title of consul-general at Hué. Trade was therefore possible, but diplomatic relations were much harder to establish.

The French Government made one further effort in 1821 with the dispatch of the *Cléopâtre* to Indo-China under the command of Courson de la Ville-Hélio. By now Gia-Long had died and been succeeded by his xenophobic son, Minh-Mang. La Ville-Hélio sailed from Brest in July 1821, called first at the Île de Bourbon, then, by way of Timor and Amboina, went up to the Philippines and arrived on 28 February at Tourane. In spite of his new official status—indeed, possibly because of it—Chaigneau's influence had waned. He was unable to arrange a meeting between the Emperor and La Ville-Hélio, who sailed for home on 14 March 1822. Soon after this the British, concerned at these obvious attempts to get a foothold in Indo-China, sent John Crawfurd from Singapore to obtain most-favoured-nation conditions from Minh-Mang. This had the effect of increasing the Emperor's

[1] See *La Mission de la* Cybèle *en Extrême-Orient*, Paris, 1914.

anxiety and determining the French to make further efforts to overcome the Annamites' objections. The dispatch of a frigate, accompanied by a corvette, was meant to overawe the mandarins; the appointment of Bougainville as plenipotentiary was planned to override their objections. Bougainville was given a letter signed by Louis XVIII and countersigned by the Vicomte de Chateaubriand, the new Minister for Foreign Affairs. For the rest, his instructions required him to sail to Bourbon and Pondicherry, and call at Manila and Macao before going to Tourane; but, apart from going to Java on the way home, he was given the choice of returning direct or by way of Cape Horn. It was obvious that he would choose the Pacific route in order to see some of the places his father had visited. Hydrography and the natural sciences were not excluded from the aims of the expedition, but clearly the real purpose was to show the flag and make a further and, as it turned out, a final attempt to alter Minh-Mang's attitude. If anything, this was underlined by the appointment of Nourquer du Camper as captain of the *Espérance*, for he had sailed in the *Cybèle* as Kergariou's first officer and thus could claim to be something of an expert.

The *Thétis*, commanded by Bougainville himself, with Captain Longueville as his second, carried 44 guns and had a total complement of 320. The corvette *Espérance* carried 20 guns, with 150 men and 13 officers. Among the lieutenants of the *Thétis*, Jeanneret had already sailed with Freycinet in the *Uranie*, and Joseph du Bouzet, as yet only 19, was to sail with Dumont d'Urville in the *Zélée* in 1837, command the *Allier* in 1841 on her voyage to New Zealand, and subsequently become governor of the French possessions in the Pacific. Bougainville was especially proud of the fact that the *Thétis* was only the second French frigate to engage on a circumnavigation, the other of course being his father's *Boudeuse*. He sent the *Espérance* ahead, fixing a rendezvous at Bourbon, and sailed himself from Brest on 2 March 1824. With him went an unusually large number of passengers, including young missionaries on their way to Siam, Tonkin, and Cochin-China.[1] Their tribulations began almost at once, for the frigate

[1] Bougainville, *Journal*, vol. i, p. 27.

met a storm on the 7th, to which she stood up well, although she was heavily laden with supplies for the French colonies as well as for the voyage, her waterline being ten inches below the surface.

Tenerife was sighted on the 13th. The French anchored for two days at Santa Cruz, and sighted the Cape Verde Islands on the 19th. On the evening of the following day, a sailor fell overboard but was rescued within a quarter of an hour. On 26 April and again on 2 May the same incident occurred. The men were both careless and fit: they were mostly young and raw, for the previous crew of the *Thétis* had suffered severely during an epidemic in the West Indies. But one man did die on 24 April, of pleurisy. Bougainville himself was unwell and it was with a real feeling of relief that he arrived at Bourbon, where the *Espérance* was awaiting him.

The poor state of my health which had been bad since our departure from Brest compelled me to remain ashore for some time. I hoped a rest would be sufficient to restore it, but this did not happen and I was forced to remain in my room for nearly the whole duration of our stay: the bracing air of St. Denis, which is excellent for those whose constitution is strong, does not seem to suit those whose nervous system is affected, as mine was.[1]

The passengers and their luggage, which cluttered up the ship, were taken off 'to the great satisfaction of the officers'. The colony seemed prosperous: sugar production had more than doubled since 1820; there were twenty-five merchantmen at anchor, most of them French. Supplies were not hard to come by, although expensive. Bougainville had not intended to buy very much, as his next port of call was to be Pondicherry, but a large proportion of the tinned food was found to be in a poor condition. He sailed on 9 June, now joined by the *Espérance*, and reached Pondicherry on the 29th. The crossing had been uneventful, except that yet another sailor had fallen overboard, and, like the others, been rescued. The passengers who had been taken on at Bourbon disembarked, and a house was sought ashore for the sick. Most of the latter seemed to be suffering from stomach trouble—two of

[1] Ibid., p. 65.

them died of 'an inflammation of the intestines', which could be taken to mean food poisoning caused by some of the tainted meat which Bougainville had been reluctant to discard. Pondicherry, from which he sailed on 30 July, he found more populated and prosperous than before, but still cramped and overawed by British power. Among the French vessels anchored in the estuary he noted Freycinet's old ship, the *Physicienne*.

Quickly crossing the Gulf of Bengal, the French sighted the Nicobars on 4 August and Pulo Penang a week later. On the 14th a 'frightful storm' assailed them. The cables broke and the two ships collided, the *Espérance*'s bowsprit breaking under the impact. The damage was repaired at sea and in Malacca, where Bougainville spent four days. Two sailors had lost their lives: one as the result of a sunstroke; the other, ominously, of a stomach ailment. In Singapore, where the ships arrived on the 30th, Bougainville met a French trader, a M. Borel, agent for a large Bordeaux firm, who wished to return to Cochin-China. He offered him a passage and used his knowledge of Malaya to draw up a detailed report for the Minister on the trade and administrative problems of Singapore and the neighbouring states, which secret instructions had asked him to prepare.[1] Manila was reached on 17 September after a rapid crossing during which one more man died—as a result of drinking too much coconut wine. Bougainville was a little concerned that recent French intervention in the Spanish revolution might cause him to be unwelcome in the Philippines, but in this he was mistaken. There were ten French trading vessels in port, none of whose captains had any cause for complaint, and, in spite of a strained atmosphere at a reception where Bougainville met a number of supporters of the defeated party, every assistance was offered to him. The *Espérance* still needed repairs, but things were not improved by a typhoon at the end of October which caused further damage, snapping off both her mainmast and her mizzen. Unfortunately 'we were in the hands of the laziest workmen in the world, and in a country where there are nearly

[1] 'I desire you, under some pretext or other, to stop at this port' had said the Minister in a confidential note dated 17 Feb. 1824 and marked 'Most Secret'. See Faivre, *L'Expansion française*, p. 260 n.

as many public holidays as there are saints in the calendar'. Borel
had already left in a brig from Bordeaux, the *Courrier de la Paix*,
and on 12 December Bougainville decided to sail alone for Macao.
It was an unfortunate decision: as she left the coast of Luzon the
Thétis was struck by a new storm which ripped most of her sails
to shreds. She limped into Macao on the 25th and was at once
surrounded by boatloads of Chinese offering fish, oranges, and
small curios, which the young sailors, excited by their first real
glimpse of the East, snapped up so eagerly and at such unreasonable prices that Bougainville had to order the boats away. He
wanted also to avoid desertions, but in spite of all his precautions
he lost two men whom the Portuguese authorities were unable to
recapture.

A boat came up to take off two missionaries who were on their
way to China and Tonkin; another had already been left at
Malacca to start his journey to Siam; a fourth, Régeraud, remained to be disembarked, if possible, in Cochin-China. Bougainville met, a few days later, the famous French missionary, Father
Lamiot, who had been in China since 1791 but was now under
an expulsion order. The elderly priest was living in Macao, still
ministering as best he could to his flock with the complicity of the
Portuguese. The latter did not want to anger the Chinese by
sheltering him, and Father Lamiot's chief purpose was to obtain
Bougainville's written refusal to accept him as a passenger—after
which he returned happily to end his days in Macao. Bougainville's report on the trade potential for France was not very
optimistic. The French did not drink much tea and they had lost
their right to share in the opium trade. Nevertheless he considered
that a French consul should be appointed in Canton to develop
what possibilities China did offer.

When he finally sailed from Macao on 2 January 1825, he
turned for the first time to hydrographical work: Kergariou's
survey of the coast of Hainan needed verification. This he did by
sailing slowly off the coast, and proved to his satisfaction that his
predecessor's work had been reliable. On the 11th he sighted
Annam close by the estuary of the Hué river and the following
day he entered the wide bay of Tourane. The *Espérance*, which

had been given this bay as a place of rendezvous, was not there. This was a disappointment, for advance notice of Bougainville's arrival would have enabled Chaigneau to prepare for his mission; as it was, Bougainville would have to rely on the *Courrier de la Paix* and on Borel to prepare the ground. But, as he soon found out, Borel had not arrived either. Furthermore Chaigneau and Vannier had left Hué for Saigon with their families in the hope of finding a passage to Singapore. The attitude of the new Emperor had made their work impossible and they considered they had no alternative but to leave. No one was available to assist Bougainville. All he could do was to send a letter to the foreigners' mandarin, announcing the arrival of the *Espérance* and his own ship, and asking for permission to proceed to Hué with an official party. While he waited for the reply, the *Courrier de la Paix* and the *Espérance* made their appearance. Borel had been set down at the Hué river mouth. On the 22nd two messengers came to request Louis XVIII's letter to Minh-Mang, but Bougainville, who had been instructed to hand it over in person, refused to part with it. They were followed by Borel, who had disposed of the *Courrier de la Paix*'s cargo without difficulty, and by a guide sent by two French missionaries to lead Régeraud to them; he had to be landed by night as religious persecution was rife. On the 30th two mandarins appeared with an answer from the court. A meeting was held on the poop:

A quarter of an hour went by before they opened their mouths. I remembered the story of the Chinese envoy and the Governor of Java who, trying to outdo each other in diplomatic caution and gravity, remained together for twenty-four hours without saying a word and parted in the same way. As I was in no mood to undergo such a test, I started the conversation by asking the mandarins what news they brought me from the court and what had been decided. After consultation, Pali finally spoke up and told me that the Emperor could receive neither the gifts nor the letter since Messrs. Chaigneau and Vannier had left and no one remained in Hué who could translate it and explain its import; but that His Majesty hoped this refusal, which was beyond his control, would in no way harm the friendly and commercial relations which he strongly wished to see maintained between the two countries.[1]

[1] Bougainville, *Journal*, vol. i, p. 276.

Bougainville pointed out that Borel understood both languages and had been accepted by officials in Hué as a reliable and trustworthy person, and that anyhow the gifts could be sent to the Emperor without the letter. Every time he made this point, the mandarins simply repeated their previous answer, parrot-fashion, 'precisely in the same words, as if the interpreter had learnt it by heart'. After three hours of this, Bougainville was informed that they also had a message for him from the foreigners' mandarin, which they would deliver the next day. Wine and cakes were then provided for all, including the soldiers, whom the weary Frenchmen described as being 'passably dressed like monkeys one sees taken round the streets'. The mandarins themselves, he noted, were none too clean, and vermin could be seen crawling in the folds of their blue silk robes, red trousers, and black hats. When the message from the foreigners' mandarin turned out to be couched in exactly the same terms as the earlier one, Bougainville realized that Minh-Mang had been frightened by Crawfurd's visit and the British attack on Burma. Without Chaigneau, the mission was sure to fail; even had the elderly consul been present the result would probably have been the same. Bougainville's visit anyhow was not a total failure: the flag had been shown, the Emperor had been reminded of France's continued interest and power, Borel had been able to sell his goods without trouble, and other French traders could expect a similar treatment. It was as much as could be hoped for under the circumstances.

When they realized their visitors were not going to insist, the mandarins brought forward cattle and poultry, fruit and vegetables —supplies which had been set aside soon after their arrival—and entertained the French at a banquet. Relations at least were friendly. Bougainville sailed, a little consoled for his failure, on 17 February 1825. He followed the coast southwards for a few days until he met an American three-master from Philadelphia, which he avoided because he wanted no awkward questions from her captain. On 1 March he altered course for the Anambas, a little-known group of islands situated off the main shipping routes between Malaya and Borneo. He had expected a cluster of unattractive rocky islets and was surprised to discover on the 3rd, in 3° 35′ north, a large archipelago of green-clad islands which would offer any ship good shelter during the monsoons. Sending du Camper ahead in the *Thétis*, he found a pass on the eastern side and sailed 'through a passage formed on the one side by the main mass of the land and on the other by a group of three islands which make up the north-eastern part of the Anambas, to the south of which lie two small round islands encircled by white sand and coral reefs . . . these were named the Two Brothers'. The following day, Bougainville and du Camper went to a nearby island to see what it had to offer, but the islanders were too interested in the French: the two officers had to retreat when they found it impossible to keep them away from their yawl and, indeed, most difficult to stop them making off with it altogether. The French had a totally erroneous impression of the Anambas. They had thought that because the islands were off the beaten track the inhabitants would be simple and unaccustomed to European goods and customs, whereas they travelled considerable distances and traded a great deal. Two canoes came up in the afternoon to inspect the ship and no doubt to initiate negotiations, but the large stock of arms on board, placed within immediate reach for fear of trouble, frightened them off; the next day the ships sailed south and were accosted by two more canoes offering fruit in exchange for hatchets and biscuits, but the natives rejected with contemptuous laughter the cheap trade fish-hooks the French were trying to sell. Bougainville anchored close to Doni-jong, a small island in the channel south of the Brothers, where trade was again sluggish. Prices were much higher than he had anticipated; it was not until the 6th that the French were finally tempted by offers of fruit—coconuts, pineapples, and enormous bananas, some of them eighteen inches long—and by a one-man canoe. A day was spent surveying the area: a fine harbour was discovered on the western shore, which they named 'Port de Clermont-Tonnerre', and a nearby island was christened epheme-rally 'Île de Bougainville'. But the currents and numerous dangers ruled out this part of the archipelago as a place of refuge or refreshment. It was anyhow far too close to the Dutch empire, and Bougainville, 'wishing to travel incognito through these islands', had covered up the names of his ships and flew no flags.

His route had taken him down the eastern side of Matak and Siantan, the two main islands of the north-eastern group, and west of Pendjalin and Badjau. Clermont-Tonnerre is a wide and pleasant bay on the east coast of Siantan. The reconnaissance was not a thorough one, but it was a group about which the French in particular knew very little. On the 8th the two ships sailed out of the strait, going south. Sight of the Anambas was lost in the afternoon, although a further cluster of high-peaked islands— Airabo—was seen to the south and south-west in the afternoon. They now made for the Java Sea and the Dutch settlements. Bangka was seen for a time on the 13th, but the weather became cloudy as they entered Gaspar Strait. Bougainville, who had no confidence in the islanders, set up guards at night to warn against a sudden attack. Progress was good, however: he got through the strait in twelve hours, which compared most favourably with the several days some ships had to take. The weather worsened on the 16th and yet another clumsy sailor who fell overboard two days later was lucky to be saved. The ships were now sailing on an easterly course along the north coast of Java. Picking up a pilot from a small village on Pangkah Point, they sailed without difficulty into Surabaya where they anchored at 5.30 p.m. on 20 March 1825.

This was Bougainville's first contact with Europeans since his departure from Macao nearly four months earlier. The first thing he learnt in Java was the news of Louis XVIII's death and the accession of Charles X. Gathering together the officers of both ships, he ordered a period of mourning to cover the entire period of their stay. There was another motive: the need to minimize contact with the shore, for Surabaya's reputation was as bad as ever—worse if anything, since cholera had swept through it in 1822 and killed 3,000 people. The King's death thus provided him with a pretext to enforce some form of quarantine to which his young sailors would find it more difficult to object. While the flags flew at half-mast and guns sounded every quarter of an hour, boatloads of Indonesians selling fruit were driven off, as were—

though with more difficulty—two boats crammed with women. Fortunately a storm broke over the city on the first afternoon, to be followed by a spell of almost continuous bad weather which turned the streets of the city into impassable and evil-smelling stretches of liquid mud. Officials came on board, offering the Governor's services, but for all their goodwill there was little worth while in Surabaya. Anything which came from government stores was subject to a surcharge of 25 per cent; what the Chinese merchants supplied was expensive and poor in quality: their biscuit was simply ship's biscuit which had gone bad and been recooked, the meat was short-shipped, the wine was sour, and the rice so bad that Bougainville refused to have it on board.

The first signs of dysentery made their appearance on 20 April. Preparations were made for an early departure; on the 23rd the two ships sailed into Madura Strait, which it took the French a week to negotiate. It was too late to escape the ravages of the disease—six men died,[1] all of them from the *Thétis*. On 4 May Kangean Island was sighted but the breeze was still weak and changeable, so that only slow progress was made towards Lombok Island and into Alas Strait; a week later, the ship dropped anchor near Pidjoe on the south-east coast of Lombok. The natives came forward and set up a market, revealing themselves honest and friendly, in sharp contrast to the Chinese traders of Surabaya. This was a good opportunity, thought Bougainville, to get his men on shore without the danger of dysentery or other diseases developing.

Our crews went ashore in landing parties to bathe and wash their belongings in soft water: we were careful to warn the officers not to allow the men to go too far into the river, which, so we had been told at Peejow [*sic*], is full of caymans . . . That same day we, Mr. du Camper and I, wanted to go hunting on the banks of the river which meanders through a thick wood and seemed to promise us a pleasant outing: my gigsmen being ashore, they had been replaced by rowers unused to the long pointed oars, so that as we reached the bar the boat broached to because of their clumsiness and we were completely sub-

---

[1] Bougainville, *Journal*, vol. i, p. 398.

merged by the breakers. I was thrown into the sea with one of the men but remained only a minute in the water.[1]

Thus Bougainville experienced at first hand the lack of seamanship of his young sailors and realized why so often they lost their footing and the shout of 'Man overboard' resounded through the ship. However, no harm was done, the other man was picked up by the longboat, and clothes quickly dried out in the hot sun. The local chief and dignitaries brought forward gifts of fruit and artefacts, receiving in exchange a French flag.

The *Thétis* and the *Espérance* sailed on the 18th with a good south-easterly breeze and soon entered the Indian Ocean, speeding under full canvas in a southerly direction. On 5 June Bougainville reached the latitude of Rottnest:

One may presume that the French Government had no knowledge of [the British] intention of settling so soon on this part of the coast and it thought it could establish a colony here without giving umbrage to them; for the instructions from the Dépot des Cartes invited me to complete a survey of the dangers surrounding Rottnest and Buache islands; and I would have gone there soon after turning North-West Cape, if the delays I had encountered earlier had not made this impossible. . . . The enormous swell we feel more than a hundred leagues from this land and in such deep waters was enough to make me realize what it would be like in shallower waters.[2]

But the British had been advised by their ambassador in Paris that the French were thinking of a penal settlement in New Holland; the news of Bougainville's expedition and of the projected departure of Dumont d'Urville's had further shaken British composure.[3] British possession of the whole of Australia had never really been challenged, but it had not been officially recognized either over areas where physical occupation had not yet been possible. As late as 1824, British administrators in New South Wales laid no claim to jurisdiction beyond the Nullarbor Plain; and it was not until 1826 that an attempt was made to establish a settlement in King George Sound, and 1828, again

[1] Ibid., pp. 413–14.   [2] Ibid., pp. 425–6.
[3] Brookes, *International Rivalry in the Pacific Islands*, p. 4.

as a result of reported French plans for this area, that steps were taken to settle the Swan River district. Nevertheless, as Bougainville and the French ministers knew, the likelihood of a French colony being allowed in Western Australia had always been very remote. This was why Bougainville made no attempt to alter course as he reached the latitude of Rottnest, but made promptly for Tasmania, which he sighted on 19 June. The weather was so frightful—it was the winter solstice—that on the third day he gave up all hope of entering d'Entrecasteaux Channel or finding shelter anywhere else, and made for New South Wales. No sooner had he given orders for the necessary manœuvres than a young sailor from St. Malo fell overboard and this time, in spite of all efforts, the man was lost; whereupon the storm abated, although the weather remained cold. This was a blessing: 'The only benefit we received from the cold and the inclement weather to which we had been exposed for so long was the almost complete destruction of a multitude of enormous cockroaches we had acquired in the Indian Ocean—a real Egyptian plague from which it is nearly impossible to protect oneself in hot countries and even more difficult to get rid of.'[1] One may be permitted to doubt that the *Thétis* had taken on these insects in India: she had been infested by cockroaches even in 1823 during the voyage to the West Indies. Subsequent fumigation at Brest, prior to the circumnavigation, had probably not been effective.

The French reached Sydney Heads on the 28th, but the weather was again bad and a fresh gale blew steadily from the land. A pilot came out to them on the 29th and helped them to enter the channel. They finally anchored in Port Jackson on 1 July 1825. Bougainville had been here twenty-three years earlier with Baudin. The city and his own circumstances had changed to a considerable extent:

Outlawed by my chief—but in good company, to be frank—I had left Sydney under threat of a disgrace which might have blocked my advancement at the start of my career; and I now returned at the head of an expedition which, if it could in no way stand comparison with the first one, was nevertheless no less attractive and certainly most

[1] Bougainville, *Journal*, vol. i, p. 438.

honourable for the one to whom the Sovereign had deigned to entrust it. I hope these thoughts may be forgiven me . . . for if the voyage of the *Thétis* and the *Espérance* was for all of us a time of happiness—and that I can state without fear of contradiction from anyone—the fruits it bore have proved more bitter than sweet for the commander who finds himself far indeed from the hopes which his future seemed likely to justify and to which he seemed to have some claim. *Sic voluere fata!*[1]

The stay in Port Jackson, which was to last almost three months, may also have inspired some melancholy thoughts among the young sailors, who might have felt justified in looking forward to Sydney as a place where they could relax from the rigours of the long voyage. But Bougainville was determined to shield them from temptation and at the same time avoid desertions, which he believed to be often caused by 'dangerous contact'. The men were allowed ashore to wash their clothes and exercise, but mainly on the deserted shores of Neutral Harbour, and at nights dancing sessions were organized on deck. It is not hard to imagine their feelings, for hornpipes and the like pale into boring and sterile insignificance when one is within earshot of the grog-shops and dance barns of a main port. But Sydney was, to all intents and purposes, out of bounds. 'None of them set foot in Sydney except for the needs of the service and under the supervision of the *élèves de la marine* who were in command of the fatigue parties and the boats.' He took similar precautions against allowing on board men who might be escaped convicts, and refused to take on discharged convicts even when they were able to produce a certificate. The only time he relented was on an excursion to the Blue Mountains when he met a 25-year-old French convict 'whom an over-impetuous passion for a pretty resident of London had sent to Botany Bay'. He obtained remission of his sentence and subsequently took him back to France. And although he could not altogether avoid desertions—one whose loss he particularly regretted was the *Thétis*'s chief boy, 'a very wide-awake boy who was debauched by the belles of Port Jackson'—the thorough precautions he took to keep off stowaways were completely successful: 'Before we sailed out of the Heads, a careful search was

[1] Ibid., p. 471.

made to ensure that no convict had hidden aboard. This was the twentieth search because I was very anxious that neither of our ships could be accused of having provided an opportunity for the escape of a single man, and this aim I achieved.'[1]

Bougainville's first call had been naturally on the Governor, Sir Thomas Brisbane, with whom he made arrangements for supplies and for repairing the ships. He found him at Paramatta, engaged on scientific experiments in his garden. Sir Thomas went to Sydney only once or twice a week, justifying Dunmore Lang's description of him as 'a man of the best intentions, but disinclined to business', but he had little incentive to work at the time, since, embroiled in a struggle for power between the Exclusives and the Emancipists, he had already been recalled to England and was to leave within a few months. The observatory on which he was working when Bougainville called on him, and which he was having built at his own cost, was to be a more lasting memorial to his years in Australia.

The ships needed refitting, especially the *Espérance*, which had to be beached and was discovered to have suffered an unusual mishap, having been 'struck violently (one cannot say when or where since no shock was noticed by anyone on board) by a sea monster whose natural weapon had broken off against the bows of the ship, after penetrating deeply. The stump, protruding by an inch, four feet below the waterline, had gone completely through the oak planking'.[2] Geoffroy St. Hilaire later identified it as belonging to *Istiophorus gladius*, known also as the Indian or Banana sail-fish, found in Indian and Pacific waters, which can attain a weight of several hundred pounds and a speed of sixty miles an hour.[3]

Supervision of the repairs, arranging for supplies, and duty calls on officials kept Bougainville busy for the first month. But in time he was able to go on a few excursions to the Nepean River and the Blue Mountains; to Windsor, Richmond, Pitt-Town, and the Hawkesbury district, to Liverpool and Kirkham; and to

---

[1] Bougainville, *Journal*, vol. i, p. 539.   [2] Ibid., p. 484.
[3] The other possible genus would be *Tetraptusus* or spear-fish. Damage to ships by these fish was not such a rare occurrence.

Frenchman's Garden, on which occasion he took with him La Touanne, Boissieu, and the hospitable Captain Piper. The copper plate affixed on Governor Phillip's orders to a tree overlooking Father Receveur's grave was still missing, but d'Urville's inscription on the tree itself was still quite legible. Bougainville felt that something more permanent should commemorate the arrival of the first Frenchman, and, at his request, Brisbane granted a concession of land and the services of the colony's architect for a memorial, the first stone of which was laid by Bougainville a few days later.

Bougainville met a number of the interesting personalities which made up the somewhat mixed society of Sydney. They included a lady, Betty Abel, who had met Napoleon; Francis Rossi, a Corsican, brother of Bougainville's first officer in the *Thétis* in 1823 and now superintendent of the local police force; and Samuel Marsden, the chaplain and educator of Maoris, at his seminary in Parramatta, some of whose pupils came with him on board, 'observing everything with a look of keenness and intelligence seldom found among primitive people. They then performed on the quarter-deck a kind of vocal concert with a strange and typical pantomime which greatly amused the crew. . . . After a good lunch . . . I gave them a crystal sweet box, some prisms, and phosphorus tinders'.[1]

The weather had remained fine for most of August, but September was marred by rain and strong winds. Nevertheless it was time to go. The two ships sailed away on the 21st in a strong but favourable gale. A course was set for South America—there never had been any doubt that Bougainville would choose the Cape Horn return route. His only regret was that his instructions did not really leave him free to call at Tahiti on a sentimental pilgrimage. He hoped, however, to stop at Pitcairn and Easter Island, and, indeed, to emulate in some way his illustrious father, for, as he explained, he kept to the thirty-third parallel not just to find a steady westerly wind, but 'to see if I might not succeed in finding along this route some small island or rock of which we might have the honour of being the first discoverers'.[2] This course

[1] Bougainville, *Journal*, vol. i, pp. 524–5.   [2] Ibid. p., 545.

took him approximately 150 miles north of New Zealand—he crossed the longitude of North Cape on 28 September—and thence south of the Kermadec group into the empty seas of the South Pacific. The weather improved slightly until the end of the month when a violent storm snapped off the gaff sling and sent it hurtling down to within inches of where Bougainville was standing. Also damaged were the wooden cages built on the quarter-deck to accommodate the emus, kangaroos, and black swans he was bringing back to Europe, most of which were to die on the way. The storm affected some of the crew, which still included four cases of dysentery: one of these, a corporal, died on 9 October. The storms abated for a while, but returned on the 15th: 'pouring rain, diabolical sea'. Bougainville decided to seek higher latitudes, although this meant forsaking his chance to land at Pitcairn, but he now encountered fog as well as rain. 'Our sailors [are] always in water and under water, soaked by both the sea and the showers.' He was making such slow progress as the ships wallowed in mountainous waves that the proposed call at Easter Island had also to be abandoned.

Friday, 4 November was St. Charles's Day—the King's fête day—and the crew danced on deck in the evening, encouraged by double rations of wine, in spite of the constant rain from which the awning only partly protected them. Two days later, in dense fog, the *Thétis* lost sight of the *Espérance* for the first time since their departure, and this was capped by the discovery that the ship was making water at the rate of six to eight inches an hour. The leak was stopped within twelve hours, and the *Espérance* was sighted anew on the 9th, but the fogs returned a few days later. There was no possibility of seeing Juan Fernandez Islands, which were best avoided under such conditions, and Bougainville made straight for the mainland, which he sighted on 22 November. The two ships dropped anchor in Valparaiso harbour that evening.

Chile was still troubled by wars. On this occasion, General Freire was about to attack the island of Chiloe, still held, if rather half-heartedly, by a Spanish garrison. Trade, however, was recovering slowly, helped to some extent by the presence of French and British naval units. France had a frigate, the *Marie-*

Thérèse, commanded by Admiral Rosamel, a corvette, the *Lybio*, and a schooner, the *Aigrette*; with three more corvettes on the way. Britain had the *Cambridge* and the *Blonde*, Captain Byron, grandson of the circumnavigator. 'By a somewhat strange coincidence the descendants of two of the first navigators to have explored the Pacific met in this very ocean, both in command of frigates, both having just erected memorials to some of their illustrious countrymen who had found their death within its limits'—a reference to Byron's erection of a monument to Cook in Hawaii, and of course to Bougainville's own stone-laying in New South Wales. After the necessary exchange of courtesy visits, Bougainville travelled to Santiago to arrange for the purchase of stores. La Touanne, moved by the spirit of adventure, set off for Rio, where he planned to rejoin the expedition after crossing the Andes and the plains of Argentina on foot and on horseback. Others, moved by a different spirit, deserted: four men from the *Thétis*, two from the *Espérance*. Dutoya, a promising young *élève* from the *Thétis*, recently promoted to *enseigne*, died of an undisclosed illness. There was indeed little in the way of celebration during this somewhat dreary stay. Weariness was setting in and everyone was waiting for the final passage home, but when they sailed, on 8 January 1826, it was realized that no provision had been made, when the ship was outfitted, for a descent into the cold latitudes. 'Preparations for our campaign had been so hurried that they had forgotten to supply us with the high boots and watch-coats normally provided for ships that have to go by way of Cape Horn.' Bougainville hoped to visit the Falkland Islands, where his father had once established a French colony, but here again his hopes were dashed. Fog hung heavily around the islands, obscuring the landmarks and forcing him to 'renounce this call which held interest for no one apart from me . . . I therefore bore away to the north, with a feeling of wonderment towards destiny which was causing me to miss most of the places which I had most set my heart on visiting'.[1] A few days later, as if to punish him for his lack of perseverance, the weather cleared and the sun shone out of a cloudless sky, but even as he rued his luck the

[1] Bougainville, *Journal*, vol. i, p. 583.

clouds returned and two successive storms struck the expedition. By the end of February the two ships had again lost touch and did not meet again until early April—in Rio harbour.

In Rio, which Bougainville describes as 'the saddest and most depressing city in the world', he met quite unexpectedly Sir Thomas Brisbane, who was on his way back to England; but there was little to do there but pay a few courtesy calls, take in stores, and visit the botanical gardens. The return journey, which began on 11 April, was marked only by the loss of a sailor who fell overboard and the constancy of the unfavourable winds; it ended on the morning of 24 June when the ships dropped anchor in the port of Brest: 'When we returned to port, after an absence of twenty-eight months, our troubles, our setbacks, our feelings of impatience, were forgotten—the same thing happened to the voyage.'[1] The touch of despondency in this comment reflects more Bougainville's lack of political success than a real lack of appreciation of what the expedition had achieved. The collection of natural-history specimens was described as 'one of the most precious and important we could hope to receive'. The account of the voyage was ordered to be printed 'par ordre du Roi', and in spite of delays—for it did not finally appear until 1837—it was well produced, with no indications of petty parsimony. Bearing in mind that the prime object of the expedition was not exploration and that the younger Bougainville was not allowed the same freedom of action as his father, the results are by no means inconsiderable:

Although he boasted he had been, with his father, the only officer who had gone round the world in a French frigate, his expedition did not add much to our knowledge of the Pacific Ocean. But the political, strategic and commercial information he brought back are of the highest order and moreover correspond to the main aims of the mission: and Bougainville was the first explorer of the Anambas.[2]

There were two reports. The first, dated 22 August 1826, was written in response to the secret instructions handed to Bougain-

---

[1] Bougainville, *Journal*, vol. i, p. 667.
[2] Faivre, *Expansion française*, p. 268.

ville before his departure; in it he gave a survey of the colonial possessions held by European powers in Asia, the military strength of Manila, Singapore, the Australian colonies, and Spanish America, the relative value of various harbours likely to be of use to French naval units, and the routes followed by vessels trading with India and China. Clearly, the French were bringing up to date their commitments and strategic plans in the East and the Pacific. A few days later, Bougainville was asked for his comments on a report received from T. A. Hervel, nephew of the shipowner Martin Lafitte, who had been trading for ten years in Australia and the Dutch East Indies. Hervel wanted France to appoint consular representatives in Hawaii, California, and Sydney—he was angling for the latter post himself—and urged the establishment of a number of colonial settlements. Bougainville in his reply expressed some reservations, especially in respect of California, about which he knew very little, and Hawaii, which he rightly judged to have fallen too far under Anglo-American influences; in the case of Sydney, Hervel's plan rather boomeranged, for Bougainville agreed so fully that the city needed French representation that he advised against the appointment of an interested trader like Hervel.

It was plain that commercial interests would continue to press for government support in the Pacific, but although sympathetic towards the powerful traders—it was proposed to appoint Hervel at least an honorary vice-consul while taking no further action as far as his report was concerned—Crousol and his successors at the Ministry of Marine wished to direct their main effort to large-scale voyages of exploration. Strategic studies and information of commercial value would take a secondary, even an unavowed, place. And by now Dumont d'Urville was on his way.

DUMONT D'URVILLE

'In accordance with my wishes, I was given the corvette *La Coquille* which was renamed *L'Astrolabe* in memory of Mr. de la Pérouse.'

D'URVILLE had a nice sense of drama. He had triumphed over enemies and dilatory officials; now, less than twelve months after the *Coquille*'s return to France, he had been given permission to take her out again, on a long voyage of exploration of his own planning. The change of name was both a symbol of the break with Duperrey and a challenging proclamation of his success, justified by instructions which requested him to pursue the search for traces of the lost explorer: 'Your voyage will have added interest if you succeed in discovering traces of La Pérouse and his unfortunate companions. An American captain reports seeing a Cross of St. Louis and medals which seemed to him to have originated from the shipwreck . . . in the hands of natives living on an island situated between New Caledonia and the Louisiades.'[1]

D'Urville's first proposals had been placed before the Minister of Marine on 23 May 1825. He had been awarded the Cross of St. Louis only the day before, but there was no sign of his expected promotion to *capitaine de frégate*. 'This [decoration] was far from acceptable and I insisted that I should be given the rank of commander. In spite of the Institute's pressing recommendations, in spite of the support of some distinguished people, I was unsuccessful.'[2]

The trouble was seniority. Duperrey, as leader of the expedition, had been promoted first and elected to the Institute, which, in spite of its support of d'Urville's other hopes, did not invite him to join its ranks now or indeed ever. D'Urville was a proud man with an unshakeable confidence in his own ability—a trait which, however justified, could not fail to irritate many who came in contact with him. Neither was he helped by reports of strained

[1] *Voyage de . . . la corvette* l'Astrolabe, vol. i, p. liii.
[2] Quoted by Vergniol, *Dumont d'Urville*, pp. 80–1.

relations with Duperrey which members of the *Coquille* expedition, excluding her captain, had brought back:

The understanding which prevailed between the two heads of the expedition rapidly began to fade after the first few months of the campaign, to be replaced by feelings the opposite of those which had at first united them towards a common goal. Restless and impressionable, the head of the expedition felt continually embarrassed by the cold, tenacious, and peremptory character of the second-in-command; the result was a series of wranglings and ruffled susceptibilities which added to the usual strains which are the normal outcome of restricting to narrow cabins officers full of energy and ambition but constantly in each other's presence. The antipathy between the leaders gave rise in turn to disagreements between their subordinates who took one side or the other. Mr. d'Urville nevertheless lived at peace embedded with his superior in the military hierarchy . . . He soon ceased working, like the others, on astronomical observations and devoted himself entirely to natural history.[1]

Knowing this, the authorities could scarcely grant d'Urville everything he asked for without appearing to side with him against Duperrey. But as a sailor and a leader he was respected—and he had useful friends and was indefatigable in his lobbying. His plan for an expedition was read with care and endorsed by Rossel, whose role in formulating the eventual instructions was considerable. D'Urville was asking for the *Coquille* for a period of twenty-six to twenty-eight months in order to explore mainly the coasts of New Guinea, New Britain, and the Louisiades. Meanwhile the results of his botanical work had appeared in the *Annales des sciences naturelles*, and his *Flore des Îles malouines*, to be published by the Linnean Society, was already in the press. The summer passed. Rosily of the Dépôt de la Marine was consulted. D'Urville was asked to elaborate his plan, which he did in a memorial dated 3 November entitled 'Campagne d'exploration projetée à la Nouvelle-Guinée, la Nouvelle-Bretagne et la Louisiade'. Provisional approval was given a week later; the next day he was at last promoted *capitaine de frégate*. The voyage was finally approved on Christmas Day. D'Urville was allowed to

[1] Lesson, *Notice historique*, pp. 55–6.

choose officers who had sailed with him in the *Coquille*, Jacquinot as his second-in-command, Lottin as third officer, Adolphe Lesson, younger brother of the surgeon; the ship's name was changed: d'Urville had triumphed.

The instructions, dated 6 April 1826, followed d'Urville's original plan, but Rossel had added New Zealand, Tonga, and the Fiji and Loyalty Islands. The *Coquille-Astrolabe*, slow and heavy but dependable—it puts one in mind of Cook's stolid *Endeavour*—was to sail by the Cape route to Australia, go on to New Zealand, northwards to Tonga and the Fijis, veer west to New Caledonia, the Louisiade archipelago, and New Guinea, where she would spend five or six months exploring the little-known southern coast, refresh her crew in Amboina, return to New Guinea on her way to the western Carolines, and sail home by way of Surabaya and Mauritius. The complement at seventy-nine officers and men was slightly larger than on the previous voyage, the difference being mostly in ordinary seamen; this increase proved a wise move, for eleven were to die, mostly of dysentery, fifteen to be left behind through illness, and three to desert, representing over a third of the total. Their quality, in d'Urville's opinion, was mediocre. 'I found myself compelled to accept men who were in no way suitable for such a campaign.' But they proved better than he had expected, their skill and endurance being put to the test within a few hours of sailing from Toulon—on 25 April 1826—by a wild storm which blew up and contrary winds which forced the ship to spend twenty-seven days fighting her way as far as Gibraltar. After a brief respite, the expedition set off for Algeciras. The westerly winds blew without a break. Eighty ships had now gathered in the Straits, trying to make their way into the Atlantic. They were unsuccessful until 6 June; the *Astrolabe* had thus spent forty-three days on the 700-mile passage from Toulon to the Atlantic.

After a brief stop in Santa Cruz de Tenerife, where d'Urville was able to fulfil a long-standing ambition to climb the Peak, the expedition made for the Cape Verde Islands, reached on 29 June, then for Trinity Islands, briefly sighted on 31 July. The crew seemed even healthier than at Toulon and the weather had been generally good. The fig and olive trees d'Urville was taking to Captain McArthur in Port Jackson were covered in attractive leaves. 'In the middle of the dreary, monotonous Ocean this vegetation pleases the eye . . . If I were in command of a frigate or a ship of the line, I would enjoy decorating my cabin with a few boxes of flowers, irrespective of their cost, just for their green appearance.' But by mid August the weather began to deteriorate and the picture changed. 'The squalls which have been assailing us and the present temperature which maintains itself at 8 or 9° [C.] have struck a fatal blow at my little nursery. The fig trees are dead and the olive trees have suffered considerably.'[1] There was little improvement in September. A man was swept overboard and lost in spite of every effort. On 28 September the sea was 'monstrous, the waves have once more turned into real mountains'. Water poured in everywhere, soaking d'Urville's books, maps, and spare clothes. The coast of Australia was sighted with relief on 5 October—Cape Leeuwin faintly visible in the north-east. Two days later the *Astrolabe* dropped anchor in the shelter of King George Sound.

D'Urville went botanizing along the shore, took on wood and water, and assessed the sound's likely worth as a port. It was still deserted, although an expedition under Major Lockyer was even then preparing a settlement and would arrive a month later. One aborigine appeared, was loaded with gifts and invited on board, then more were seen, equally friendly and similarly welcomed. Gaimard, the chief surgeon, elected to spend the night ashore with the young lieutenant Lottin and the artist Sainson, in the hope of learning more about their customs. They went up to the native camp, where they found about a dozen men and two boys.

When they noticed their compatriot covered with clothing and decked out with necklaces, mirrors and the thousand trinkets we had given him, their gaiety knew no bounds. They all started to yell and sing together. . . . We soon understood that our hosts wished to exchange names with us. This custom which travellers have encoun- tered throughout the archipelagoes of the Pacific surprised us among these wretched people who seem so little endowed intellectually.

---

[1] D'Urville, *Voyage*, vol. i, p. 78.

It reveals a fairly advanced state of society and we could scarcely expect to find it among a nomadic band in this wild country. However the exchange took place to their great satisfaction and several of them sang appropriate songs in which we were able to recognize our names.[1]

In the morning a boat appeared, manned by eight sailors who claimed to have been abandoned along the coast by a sealing vessel. D'Urville offered to take them to Port Jackson, but only three accepted. A few days later two battered whaleboats brought more marooned sailors to the bay. By now d'Urville suspected that most of his visitors were escaped convicts or at the best men of a type he did not want in his ship. Leaving on 25 October, he made for Port Western instead of Port Dalrymple, which his instructions had laid down as a port of call. So far he had strictly adhered to them, but he was already over a month behind schedule and the official visits he would have to make in the Tasmanian settlement would only delay him further. Port Western, however, was uninhabited—except for a few sealers who came up to him offering their services and showing their papers; d'Urville accepted the former and returned the latter, pointing out that he was not on a policing mission. His next call, from 26 to 29 November, was in Jervis Bay, totally deserted except for aborigines, some of whom spoke English. Again they were most friendly and the French equally kind. At this stage, d'Urville records his pride at the 'noble zeal and boundless devotion' of all his officers. The sailors were no less praiseworthy, displaying once more their generosity towards the natives: they shared a successful fishing catch with them, causing such an outburst of shouting that d'Urville on board the corvette thought his men were being attacked.

When he reached Port Jackson on 2 December, he discovered that his desire for quiet uninhabited bays had given rise to suspicion. Governor Darling was polite, but cool; he expressed surprise at the calls d'Urville had made without the assistance of a pilot and pointedly asked whether the French had met the brig which had left for Port Western and King George Sound. A local newspaper had already announced that the *Astrolabe* had raised the

---

[1] Sainson, in d'Urville, *Voyage*, vol. i, pp. 187, 189.

French flag in both these places—which may well have been true
but was certainly not the symbolic gesture the report implied. The
colonial authorities, however, had been disturbed by renewed
French activity in Australian waters, particularly Bougainville's
visit coupled with the news of d'Urville's preparations. They had
acted to forestall French settlements, sending Lockyer in the
Amity—not perhaps the happiest of names in the circumstances—
with a detachment of soldiers from the 39th Regiment and a party
of convicts. If any French were found, these were to be told that
'the whole of New Holland is subject to His Britannic Majesty's
Government'; should Lockyer get there first he was to make it
plain to any French expedition that this was British territory and
'avoid any expression of doubt of the whole of New Holland
being considered within this Government, any division of it,
which may be supposed to exist under the designation of New
South Wales, being merely ideal'.[1] Now it appeared that the two
expeditions had not met and consequently France had not received
the intended warning. As d'Urville went about his business,
paying official calls, buying vegetables, salt, and tobacco, inviting
Samuel Marsden to his table, and talking blithely about an early
departure for New Zealand—yet another area where Britain had
potential claims—Darling watched him with growing apprehen-
sion and perplexity. D'Urville needed two anchor chains; they
were slow in coming. Yet should not Darling allow them to be
supplied to a ship belonging to a friendly power, patently on a
scientific mission, and commanded by an officer whose consuming
hobby was natural history? D'Urville went about in full uniform,
accompanied by officers in similar dress: there was none of that
informality which he assumed on board ship, where he was often
to be seen wearing 'a shapeless straw hat, an old jacket, cloth
trousers and neither cravate nor socks, and looked more like
a market gardener than a naval officer'.[2] Undisturbed by official
coolness he bought a chain cable for £160 from the captain of

[1] *Historical Records of Australia*, Darling to Lockyer, series i, vol. xii, p. 701.
[2] Lesson, *Voyage*, vol. i, pp. 288–9. Cp. O. Wright, *New Zealand 1826–1827*,
p. 19, which gives the traditional picture: 'Always in uniform, judging by the
illustrations . . .'.

the *Regalia*—who also took his letters for France—ordered rum, coffee, sugar, and salt provisions. Darling had second thoughts; nothing seemed to indicate that the French had intended to establish a settlement in Australia, for if they had they would have done so already; and yet d'Urville seemed to be in a great hurry to depart for New Zealand—were there not political aspirations in that quarter?[1] Gradually the Governor relented and d'Urville was able to purchase a light and a heavy chain. Then, on 19 December, after a stay of only seventeen days, leaving Darling's doubts unresolved, the French sailed from Port Jackson. Two sailors had deserted a few days before, both 'fairly undesirable characters' whom d'Urville was not sorry to lose, but local residents, attracted by the routine offer of a reward and presumably not anxious to swell the already large number of undesirables in the colony, promptly sent them back.

The weather remained unfavourable. 'Seventeen days after our departure from Port Jackson, we had scarcely covered 130 leagues in a straight line.'[2] The constancy of the easterlies in a sea where westerlies usually prevail surprised d'Urville, but this was the beginning of summer, when easterlies are not infrequent. He had definite plans for New Zealand, which Cook seemed to have made his own special preserve but which no French navigator had ever explored in detail:

although my instructions required me simply to pass through Cook Strait and survey a few points along the north-east coast of the North Island, being convinced that Cook's work could only have been very incomplete and being anxious to offer an equally interesting contribution to geography, I had planned to approach New Zealand by Chalky Bay, make a short stay there, then follow the entire western coast of Tavai-Pounamou [the South Island], pass through Cook Strait and survey the whole of the east coast of Ika-Na-Mawi [the North Island] as far as North Cape.[3]

This plan was a clear challenge to Cook, which throws light on d'Urville's character: nothing less than a survey of half the entire coastline of New Zealand, the most comprehensive exploration

[1] Darling to Hay, 4 Dec. 1826, *Historical Records of Australia*, series i, vol. xii, p. 730.   [2] D'Urville, *Voyage*, vol. ii, p. 8.   [3] Ibid., pp. 8–9.

of the islands since Cook's death, something which could hardly fail to leave a mark on the geography and possibly the history of New Zealand. Had Darling been fully aware of d'Urville's intentions, his suspicions might have been less easy to allay.

On 8 January the *Astrolabe* was fighting her way along the forty-third parallel, making for the South Island. D'Urville by now had decided to give up the stay in Chalky Bay or Inlet and veered east-north-east to seek a point close to the north-western opening of Cook Strait. Land was sighted two days later, to the south-east, having the appearance of 'a tall island with jagged peaks. As we approached it spread out more and more, but its summit remained jagged like a sharp-toothed saw.'[1] More land appeared to the east-south-east, seeming to be separated from the rest as by some harbour. The most southerly point was in 42° 28', just south of Greymouth. From here Gressien, the young *enseigne*, began a careful charting of the coast, hampered by torrential rain, frequent squalls, and mists. On the 13th he climbed on the cross-trees to get a better view of a large inlet which seemed to offer the possibility of a good anchorage, but the only entrance was through a narrow and almost completely blocked channel. This was Whanganui Inlet, just south of Cape Farewell. The *Astrolabe* turned the cape on the 14th, Guilbert taking over the charting from Gressien as the ship made her way into Cook Strait. Admiralty Bay and Queen Charlotte Sound having been surveyed by Cook, 'I thought that we should render greater service to geography by taking the corvette to anchor in Tasman Bay, which so far had not been made known by any expedition'. Guilbert was sent ashore with Quoy, Gaimard, and Dudemaine. The accompanying sailors, prowling about, discovered some abandoned Maori huts from which they carried away a number of artefacts. D'Urville, now as later, was not to countenance behaviour which was both dishonourable and dangerous. 'I spoke very seriously to them about this and threatened to punish very severely any who in future might dare to take such liberties. One can scarcely doubt that most of the regrettable quarrels which have occurred between the Savages and the Europeans owe their origin to causes of this kind.'[2]

[1] Ibid., p. 11.   [2] O. Wright, transl. in *New Zealand 1826–1827*, p. 73.

The first natives were seen a few days later near another group of huts. The *Astrolabe* was by now sailing slowly along the coast a couple of miles from shore. By the end of the day, d'Urville had made his first contribution to the geography of New Zealand: he had proved to his satisfaction that Tasman Bay was not as 'indicated on Cook's map . . . a slight indentation only a few miles in breadth and depth . . . [but] of enormous extent. This unexpected discovery was a source of the liveliest satisfaction to us all'.[1] On the 16th Maoris came out to the ship in two canoes and were persuaded, after a little initial reluctance, to climb on board; d'Urville conversed with them without too much trouble, using a vocabulary compiled by Marsden's missionaries. The visitors told the French that their canoes would return the next day 'with women, as if that ought to be of special interest to us'; one may presume that not every Frenchman was uninterested, but it was not a promise which held a great deal in store, for when three canoes came out in the morning bringing forty people, including a few women, the latter remained hidden under mats for as long as the canoes were near the ship and once back on land fled precipitately into the undergrowth. D'Urville landed and climbed a high hill from which he could survey the whole bay. Proceeding on his easterly route, he named a small inlet Croisilles Bay after his mother's maiden name. He had already given the name 'Separation Point' to the tongue of land which forms the western arm of Tasman Bay, and was soon to have occasion to add more names to the map of New Zealand. Ahead lay a succession of small islands and a deeply indented coastline with violent tidal currents. It appeared to him that a channel led directly from Tasman Bay into Admiralty Bay; he steered the *Astrolabe* towards it:

We coasted less than two miles from the shore, although the breeze was fitful and threatened at times to leave me at the mercy of the swell. At four-fifty in the afternoon [of 23 January] we had reached a point opposite the entrance to the channel; and I was going in at full sail, when the lookout in the cross-trees sang out that the passage was blocked by reefs not more than two or three cables away from the

[1] Wright, *New Zealand 1826–1827*, p. 74.

ship. Instantly M. Guilbert rushed up to the crow's nest and confirmed the report. There was not a moment to lose; immediately every sail was furled and the leeward anchor was cast at seventeen fathoms, roughly in mid-channel and a mile at the most from each of the two heads.[1]

Lottin and Gressien, sent ahead in two boats, reported that the channel did in fact lead into Admiralty Bay, but that a reef running from the north-west headland reduced the entrance to a narrow passage through which flowed a violent current. The situation was not helped by a gale which blew up in the evening, sending heavy breakers crashing over the forecastle. In the morning it was found that one of the cables was cut. Nevertheless, since the wind had moderated, the *Astrolabe* entered slowly into the narrow channel 'resembling a gorge, between two ranges of high mountains'. The central section of the channel formed a basin which was calm enough at first but into which 'the tidal rip suddenly rose like a seething sheet and the water rushed into the basin forming whirlpools of incredible violence'. The corvette swung round and round, coming to within a few yards of the rocky shore. Only speed and seamanship saved her. But her situation remained precarious in the extreme; with great coolness, d'Urville sent the artists and naturalists ashore, mainly in order to lull the sailors' fears 'by demonstrating that investigations were going on just as they did under the happiest circumstances of our voyage. It is the method I have constantly adopted and I believe it to be indispensable, especially with such cowardly creatures as were the majority of our hands'.[2] He himself investigated the pass, going several times in the whaleboat and once climbing a high bluff to get an overall view. He was fully aware of the risks:

Looking straight down on to the channel from this hill, I was convinced that it could be navigated if great precautions were taken. Yet I did not shut my eyes to the fact that this enterprise might have sinister consequences. As I looked back towards the corvette, I could not help thinking, try as I would, that this very vessel, so well organized, so imposing and intended for a long career, might in a few moments and solely as the result of my wishes, be hurled to destruction on the

[1] Ibid., pp. 87–8.   [2] Ibid., p. 91.

rocks at my feet. Ten officers, a complete crew, the people of that floating city which had become their fatherland, might they not within a few hours be reduced to trying to find their salvation on a bare inhospitable coast; with nothing before them but to drag out a miserable existence, or perhaps to perish there without ever seeing their family or their friends again? Such thoughts weakened my resolution for a moment; but very soon it was steadfast once more and I returned to the ship quite determined to tempt fortune.[1]

He was displaying less rashness than might at first appear. He had spent four days in the pass, exploring it from every angle and planning exactly what he would do and when. At 7 a.m. on the 28th the *Astrolabe* began to move towards the narrow opening. The wind proved fickle and the tidal currents showed little mercy; the ship struck twice, lying for a few seconds on her beam ends, but she lifted off and floated majestically into the calm waters of Admiralty Bay. The episode remains famous and was the subject of a celebrated engraving. D'Urville had proved that the land north-west of Tasman Bay is really an island, which his grateful officers named after him until such time, he adds, 'as the name given to it by its inhabitants be discovered'; it remains D'Urville Island to this day. The channel has similarly retained its name of Passe des Français in the translated form of French Pass.

Now carried by the fast-flowing current, the *Astrolabe* made good speed before a pleasant westerly breeze. Within a few hours she reached the entrance to Queen Charlotte Sound, where Cook had so often refreshed his men. Very slowly, for the wind became erratic, d'Urville approached Cloudy Bay. Night caught up with him and in the morning the current had borne the ship too far to the west. He accordingly made for Cape Palliser, on the North Island, which he found 'a most attractive sight. No rocks, no obvious dangers, clear lofty hills . . .' A canoe came from the shore with six men, all of whom came on board; when it left, d'Urville discovered that two men, a chief and his attendant, had elected to stay behind. It was now impossible to land. The bay was too open and a heavy surf broke all along the coast. In a fit of pique, d'Urville gave 'this miserable basin the name of Useless

---

[1] Wright, *New Zealand 1826–1827*, p. 98.

Bay'. The name has reverted to Palliser Bay, although its usefulness has not increased. As he left the strait, he could not resist
making a passing comment on Cook's pioneering work: 'As at
last I left Cook's Strait behind, I could not refrain from expressing
my surprise at the errors which had crept into this part of the
great man's records. His configurations were extremely inaccurate and the errors in longitude made in the first voyage were as
high as one degree and sometimes more.'[1] But d'Urville, as
Duperrey had discovered, never found it hard to depreciate the
work of others. The two Maoris, who had remained quite cheerful as long as the *Astrolabe* was in the neighbourhood of Palliser
Bay, began to show signs of disquiet, especially as the sea became
rough and they were affected by seasickness; but they could not
be sent off now. D'Urville tried to distract them by asking them
to name the main points they were passing, but this proved of
little help. The chief resorted at first to caresses and supplications,
then flew into a towering rage, then wept. 'It was indeed a
strange sight to see this savage, who on a battlefield would no
doubt have faced death without flinching, so crushed by grief
that he abandoned himself to his sorrow and whined in a plaintive
voice like a sulky child.'[2] In time the two men resigned themselves
to their fate: they were to spend over a week in this ship which
they had obviously thought was going to anchor near their
territory.

Guilbert had completed his charting of the Cook Strait area.
It was Lottin's turn to take over. The *Astrolabe* hauled north along
the east coast to Castlepoint and Cape Turnagain. The wind made
it unwise to anchor in Hawke's Bay, which had seemed to promise
a good anchorage. On 4 February, nearing Tolaga Bay, a European ship was sighted, a small schooner which first skirted the
shore and then suddenly headed out to sea and disappeared,
'a course I could only explain by supposing that for reasons of its
own the ship found our visit unwelcome'. A large number of
Maoris came on board shortly after and were given presents; the
two involuntary passengers who had refused earlier invitations
to land on what d'Urville later realized was enemy territory now

[1] Ibid., p. 106.   [2] Ibid., p. 109.

accepted his suggestion that they leave the *Astrolabe* at this point. Throughout his stay in New Zealand waters, the Frenchman was to be considerate and understanding towards the native inhabitants, trading with them, making them gifts, and questioning them about their country and their tribe, although their numbers were often so great that the din of their shouting and their jostling of the sailors impeded the work and irritated him. His respect for them is reflected by his insistence on using Maori place-names whenever these were known to him. His forbearance on occasions when visitors became too noisy is even more creditable when it is remembered that he was far from well during this period: his extraordinary fondness for highly spiced meals was always more easily indulged once fresh provisions became scarce, and from the end of January he began to complain of pains in his abdomen and chest.

On 6 February, off Tokomaru Bay, he was able to buy a number of pigs brought out by the local chief, Oroua. The surrounding country, with regular lines of small huts forming an amphitheatre, reminded him of Greek villages he had seen during his voyage to the Aegean Sea. This comparison with the cradle of European civilization induced in him a flood of reflections on the future of New Zealand:

If, as everything leads one to think, Australia is destined to become the seat of a great empire, it is inconceivable that New Zealand should not follow her impetus, and her children, civilized and intermingled with the posterity of England, will themselves become a powerful and formidable people. . . . Then these shores, at present without human habitation, except for a few isolated *pas*, will be alive with flourishing cities; these bays of unbroken silence, crossed occasionally by frail canoes, will be highways for ships of every type. And a few centuries hence, were it not that henceforth printing will record by its indestructible means the deeds and discoveries of modern times, future members of the Academy of New Zealand would not fail to question or at least to argue laboriously about the narratives of the earliest explorers, when they found them speaking of the wilderness, the lands, and the savages of their country.[1]

[1] Wright, *New Zealand 1826-1827*, pp. 127–8.

While he was setting down these thoughts, the *Astrolabe* continued on her way 'amid enchanting weather', turning East Cape and following the coast at a distance of ten or twelve miles. He had hopes of hugging the land a little more closely but intermittent calms made this unwise; anyhow, within a day or so, the weather had so changed that 'a frightful sea got up' which battered the corvette and flooded d'Urville's cupboards, causing considerable damage to his books, effects, and maps. Two days later, on 12 February, waves still rose to an enormous height about the ship. Coping with the storm was one thing; keeping on course was another. From East Cape d'Urville should have stood north-west: the storm had driven him north-north-east. 'I realized with sorrow', he wrote, 'that with continually strong contrary winds, counter-currents, and such a rough sea, it would be impossible for us to continue our survey. In spite of the acute regret which I felt, I was greatly tempted to abandon our work on East Cape and to take advantage of the first favourable breath of wind to go to the Bay of Islands.'[1] Tempted he may have been, but determined he remained. The weather cleared, a south-easterly breeze set in, and he was able to return to the coast and start following it to Cape Runaway. It enabled him to compare, not altogether fairly, his own expedition with both Freycinet's and Duperrey's.

Already my companions and I had learnt by painful experience what an enormous difference there is between carrying out easy expeditions like those of the *Uranie* and the *Coquille* across open seas without any detailed investigation, without a single hydrographic observation; and on the other hand, working all the time at a geographical survey of dangerous and often unknown shores, and struggling against hostile elements in an endeavour to fulfil the purpose of one's instructions.[2]

Although no one could challenge d'Urville's daring and persistence, his delight in 'grazing the shore', it would have been preferable had he elected to stand on his own merits and not work off his accumulated grudges against his former friends. His seamanship was soon again to be tested and his skill displayed. From Cape Runaway he sailed on some distance off White Island, which was half-hidden by what he took to be the dense smoke of Maori

[1] Ibid., p. 132.   [2] Ibid., pp. 132–3.

fires but was in reality the result of regular eruptions from this volcanic island. Had he known this at the time, he would have made for it to examine the phenomenon and so have avoided being caught in an exposed position by the storm which was even then blowing up. On the afternoon of 15 February the sky darkened and a light rain began to fall. All landmarks were blotted out; all he knew was that he was in the neighbourhood of Mount Edgecumbe, near which the coast is a capricious sequence of low-lying land and steep cliffs with occasional reefs. Somewhere ahead, as the *Astrolabe* struggled to make for the open sea, lay Mayor Island. In the morning, the storm had risen to a raging tempest; the wind was blowing from the north and north-east, holding the ship against the unseen coast; the jib was slashed to shreds and for a time it looked as if the mast would break. This perilous situation lasted four hours, but when visibility improved it was seen that the ship was making straight for a reef less than a mile away. All possible canvas was unfurled in a matter of seconds and the *Astrolabe* passed within a few yards of the seawardmost spur of reef. Soon after, Mayor Island became visible; in a quietening sea the corvette was able to sail out of the bay.

The route led east of the Alderman group and towards Mercury Bay; d'Urville's original intention had been to anchor in Whiti-anga harbour, but unfavourable winds and the delays he had already encountered decided him to make for the Hauraki Gulf. The sea was now 'as smooth as the surface of a pond' and the islands scattered across the entrance to the gulf looked green and attractive in the late summer sun. 'Here again Cook's work was very inaccurate and a new survey was indispensable', but the wind changed and kept him from entering the harbour; he thought instead of making for Whangarei—this time the wind dropped altogether. D'Urville anchored in a fairly exposed position, but was able to get ashore in the whaleboat and explore on foot a part of the coast. The inter-tribal wars which had been raging among the Maoris had left their mark: 'while prowling about in the neighbourhood, I soon discovered, under the rough growth that covered the soil, the scattered remains of many huts. A village had once stood on this hill and its inhabitants had been wiped out or

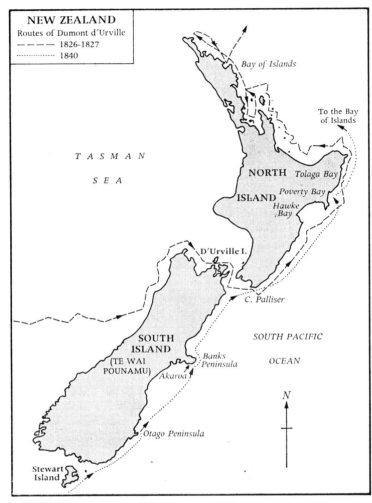

NEW ZEALAND

Routes of Dumont d'Urville

— — — — 1826-1827

· · · · · · · · · · · 1840

Bay of Islands

To the Bay
of Islands

T A S M A N

S E A

NORTH *Tolaga Bay*

ISLAND *Poverty Bay*

Hawke
Bay

D'Urville I.

C. Palliser

SOUTH PACIFIC

**SOUTH
ISLAND
(TE WAI
POUNAMU)**

*Banks
Peninsula*

OCEAN

Akaroa

N

Otago Peninsula

Stewart
Island

Map 7. New Zealand. Route of Dumont d'Urville

had fled into the interior.' On 23 February he was able to take his
corvette into the gulf and begin the survey. He went on botanizing walks, nearly losing himself in the swamps. The excellence of
what was to become Auckland Harbour was clearly apparent as
the *Astrolabe* sailed slowly through the various channels over a
placid sea. Maoris came out in numbers, although it was clear that
the bay was not heavily populated. Nearly a week was spent in

this area; then on 28 February the French continued on their way north to Whangarei and North Cape. On 6 March they were passing the wide opening of Doubtless Bay and could just distinguish the heights of North Cape in the far distance. At four in the afternoon of the 7th they hove to, two miles due north of the cape, and started operations to fix its position with all possible accuracy. The weather was fine and calm, and great numbers of porpoises, gannets, petrels, and kingfishers played near the surface of the water, watched on the periphery by a few large sharks. Then d'Urville slowly made his way back towards the Bay of Islands, where he planned to refresh his crew and lay in a few stores before leaving New Zealand. The breeze was weak and inconstant, so that he did not reach his anchorage until the 12th; he put the delay to good use by buying pigs and potatoes from local Maoris, knowing that he could get them far cheaper in isolated coastal areas than in the bay itself, which had now become a European settlement and a regular port of call for whalers and sealers. The French remained a week in the Bay of Islands, sailing out on 19 March 1827. The time was filled with visits to the English missionaries and excursions around the bay. Their departure was delayed, the feebleness of the breeze keeping them within sight of New Zealand until the 22nd, and five days later they had not progressed more than forty leagues.

These delays gave them the opportunity to take stock. Most of d'Urville's plans for New Zealand had been fulfilled, often against considerable odds; careful charting had been carried out; several new discoveries, such as French Pass and D'Urville Island, could be claimed. Much had been learnt about the local inhabitants and products. Stocks of fresh food and meat had been purchased and the crew refreshed—not fully, since there were three cases of venereal disease and three of stomach ailments, but these were more diseases of affluence than of scarcity. One Maori had joined the crew, whom d'Urville called Kokako,[1]

a slave of the Kororareka tribe from childhood. After seeing his companions offered as sacrifices at the obsequies of the last *rangatiras*, he

[1] D'Urville adds that this is the name of a sea-bird, but the kokako is the native crow, *Calleas*.

was afraid of seeing his turn come and knew that he would be next. . . .
Touched by his persistence and moved by the thought of the fate
which awaited him, I thought that it would be a humane act to take
him with us, as we could always drop him elsewhere, if he wished.
As soon as he received permission to stay with us, the poor fellow let
himself go in demonstrations of the most exuberant joy; then he pulled
himself together, assumed a more confident manner, and announced
in the most resolute tone to the natives, who were waiting for him in
their canoe, that he was now a *Youroupi*, and consequently very *tapu*.[1]

He proved to be a willing and cheerful worker, displaying constant goodwill towards his new masters, often doing his work
'better than several of our men'. D'Urville at this stage was expecting to return to New Zealand in 1828, when he would be able to
land Kokako on some suitable point of the coast.

On 1 April a fresh gale enabled the *Astrolabe* to make progress.
The intention was to make for Esperance Rock and the Kermadec
group. Nothing was seen of the former, but Curtis was sighted at
dawn on the 2nd, then Macauley on the starboard side, some three
miles off. The rest of the day was spent verifying d'Entrecasteaux's
positions for these islands. The next day, the French saw Raoul
Island in the distance as they sailed north-north-east towards
Tonga. The winds became less favourable, the humidity was high
and the heat oppressive. 'Everything seems to be uniting against
me in an effort to keep me away from Tonga Tabou', wrote
d'Urville. He began to consider seriously a change of plan. He
was distressed by the death of two birds he had brought with
him from New Zealand, a tui and a kaka. On 15 April he found
the currents were driving him further off course. 'All this proves
how, in undertakings of this kind, good will is not enough if one
is not helped by good fortune.' At last, at midday on the 16th, he
sighted the low islands of the Nomuka group, but continued to
make very little progress: he was in the unenviable situation of
being practically becalmed in the vicinity of a reef-strewn archipelago. Not until the 20th could the *Astrolabe* enter the channel
between the north-west coast of Tongatapu and its offshore
islands. The weather became overcast and squally, and the sea

[1] O. Wright, transl. in *New Zealand 1826–1827*, pp. 201–2.

discoloured. Lacking a pilot, the French lost the channel and the
ship struck the reef, though not heavily; they anchored somewhat
precariously among the coral. Natives came out to them in canoes,
accompanied by a young Englishman, John Read, a shipwrecked
sailor who had settled in Tonga a few years before. He was
followed soon after by Singleton, another shipwrecked mariner,
who had been in the islands for twenty-three years. Both were
engaged as interpreters, enabling d'Urville to converse with the
local chiefs—Palu, who had known d'Entrecasteaux, and Tahofa.
In the morning the situation was unchanged. The weather, still
menacing, might worsen at any moment: even if a sudden storm
did not arise to snap the cables and drive the corvette on a
nearby reef, the squally gusts which blew up without warning
would make it equally dangerous to raise the anchors and seek
refuge nearer the land. D'Urville decided to land all the men
he could spare to lessen the loss of life should the ship strike
at night. This was announced as a simple precautionary measure,
but plainly most of the crew considered that the final loss of the
Astrolabe was very likely:

In spite of the instructions I had given, it was found when the time
came to place their parcels into the longboat that most of them were
enormous and weighed from forty to fifty pounds; not satisfied with
putting all their belongings in them, several had added filthy rags no one
would have bothered to pick up off the ground; others added piles
of shells and souvenirs. In short there was not enough room in the
longboat to take these enormous sacks as well as the men. The operation
had to be stopped. All the sacks were emptied one after the other in the
presence of the officer.[1]

The watching natives seemed to imply by their attitude that
they shared the sailors' pessimism. When the transfer was resumed in the afternoon, involving forty-two people including
Lottin and Lesson, two Europeans sent on board by the local
missionary, Thomas, exclaimed that d'Urville was sending them
all to their death: there was no doubt in their minds that the
Tongans lined up along the shore would attack and rob them as

[1] D'Urville, *Voyage*, vol. iv, p. 33.

soon as they landed. D'Urville decided to cancel his plan; he contented himself with sending various instruments and documents to the missionaries for safe custody. That night, half the crew, together with Bertrand, Quoy, and Sainson, who could not swim, slept in the ship's boats. The *Astrolabe* was now only ten or twelve feet away from the reef. D'Urville was anxious to discover which of the three main chiefs was the most important and the one whose protection he should seek. Lavaka's influence was more of a religious nature; Fatu, son of Mulikiha'amea, had granted land to the missionaries in 1820 and could be presumed to be kindly disposed towards Europeans; but Tahofa might prove more powerful—indeed, if the man referred to by this name was Taufa'ahau, he was to become King of Tonga as George Tubou I. There was at the time no supreme chief, no Tu'i Tonga, and, even if there had been, his authority would have been nominal. The Reverend Thomas, who had arrived in the island only in 1826, was unable to help, having neither knowledge of the situation nor real authority over the chiefs. D'Urville decided to try to warp his way out with the help of the boats, but the *Astrolabe* moved along for only eight or ten minutes; the depth ahead was only four feet and the corvette was found to be resting on the reef. She was not stuck fast, but completely at the mercy of the weather. With the assistance of Singleton, d'Urville addressed the chiefs together: since he could not find out who was the most influential, he would seek the protection of all three.

In order to add greater solemnity to our conference, I made these men sit in front of the portrait of the King, to whom I referred as the supreme égui [Hou'eiki, or chief] of the French, who was capable of rewarding them handsomely for their generosity towards us, just as he was of extracting a full revenge for any excesses they might allow themselves to commit. Then, through Singleton, using a firm, resolute tone of voice, I admitted that the corvette was in a most critical situation, and that I anticipated her going down during the night; I pointed out that we could no doubt land on their territory with our arms, challenge all their forces, and resist them till victory, but that I preferred to trust in their good faith and place myself and my companions under their protection. All I asked of them was to respect the life of the

Frenchmen who had been entrusted to me and guarantee that we could
retain ownership of the small quantity of goods useful to us in our new
situation. In return I would leave them, without any restrictions, the
arms and numerous valuables, such as iron utensils, glass trinkets, cloth
and mirrors, which were on board. In addition, I asked them to keep
away from the corvette all those natives whom greed was attracting
to all this wealth, and on this point I skillfully made them understand
that their interest coincided with ours, since their share would be
reduced to very little if they allowed all these natives to clamber
unchecked on board when the ship was wrecked. The three chiefs
listened to me most attentively; they received my proposal with much
seriousness and dignity, and solemnly undertook to become my allies,
swearing that they would rather die themselves than allow us to be
sacrificed or even illtreated by the other chiefs of the island.[1]

However, the ship did not sink in the night. It was found
possible in the morning to float her off and return her to the
earlier position. D'Urville, watching the chief's expressions as
this operation was being carried out, was gratified to see them
smile with apparent satisfaction. The next night, half the crew
again slept in the boats, but the weather was improving; on the
23rd one of the anchors lost when some cables had snapped was
retrieved; on the 24th with a light breeze the *Astrolabe* was able to
be moved slowly into a place where she was at least partly protected from the open sea. Finally, on the 26th, a week after his
arrival at Tonga, d'Urville was able to anchor opposite Nukualofa.
The missionaries returned the ship's papers; presents were made
to the chiefs; a brisk trade in pigs, chickens, yams, and fruit was
carried out between ship and shore. Everything seemed to promise
a pleasant and restful stay after the recent dangers. An elderly
chief from Pea called and talked of d'Entrecasteaux and Kermadec,
whom he had met and who were known locally as 'the two
brothers' from their habit of walking arm in arm. D'Urville paid
return calls on the missionaries and the local chief, and expressed
delight at the friendliness which had developed between his men
and the people. 'There has been no quarrel between them and our
sailors. It is true that I allow on board only the principal chiefs

[1] D'Urville, *Voyage*, vol. iv, pp. 49–51.

and their children and a very small number of women. Tahofa faithfully keeps us company, but we do not see his two colleagues any more.'[1] He remembered that his instructions had urged him to obtain any information he could about La Pérouse. The late Tu'i Tonga's granddaughter told him of a tradition that two ships had anchored in Nomuka before d'Entrecasteaux's visit, that they flew a white flag, and that its officers were known as Louadji— which he felt might conceivably be a corruption of Vaujuas. This was insufficient evidence that La Pérouse had returned to the islands after his stay in Botany Bay. The report might even refer to the voyages of Bligh and Edwards of 1789 and 1791, telescoped into one. D'Urville had then no idea that Dillon had already discovered the remains of the lost expedition and was now on his way back to Vanikoro; his theory was still that La Pérouse had sailed to Fiji and been lost on one of the many reef-fringed islands —a belief based on reports that the natives of Lakemba owned a small anchor. However unsubstantial this evidence, he considered it desirable to make for this island and see whether there was any justification for such a rumour.

Speculation of this sort was stopped, however, by a message sent by Thomas warning him that a number of sailors were planning to desert with the connivance of the natives. 'This piece of information led me into sad and serious reflections. As a natural consequence of the extreme indifference of the leading authorities in Toulon towards the equipping of the *Astrolabe*, I had found it impossible to select a satisfactory crew for the corvette. I had been forced, to make up the numbers, to take on men who had been arrested for theft or desertion or who had a bad reputation.'[2] D'Urville set up a guard on deck and decided to leave a day earlier; but the news got abroad, and a group of Tongans captured the yawl and its occupants who had been sent ashore for a last supply of swabbing sand. The longboat was sent in pursuit with twenty-three men and two officers, but only the yawl was found. Seven sailors, together with the *élève* Faraguet, were missing, and one man, Simonet, had deserted from the longboat. A few huts had been set on fire 'to intimidate' the

---

[1] Ibid., vol. iv, pp. 86–7.   [2] Ibid., vol. iv, p. 121.

Tongans. But it was difficult to get the undisciplined sailors to keep together and advance in orderly fashion; conscious of the danger they ran of being attacked singly as they wandered into the bush, d'Urville sent a force of petty officers under Gressien to carry out reprisals and compel the Tongans to give up their prisoners. Two villages were burned down and some canoes destroyed. The incursion was met by fire from the interior, and a corporal who had ignored orders and left his companions to pursue a fleeing native was killed. D'Urville came to the conclusion that only the threat of a bombardment would cause the natives to give up their prisoners. Shortly after, Faraguet arrived with the Englishman Singleton, bringing the information that the raid was Tahofa's work and that the Tongans would release those men who indicated a clear wish to return to the ship. D'Urville replied that, unless all the prisoners were sent back, he would attack the sacred burial ground at Mafanga in the morning. A further message from Thomas asked him to delay any operation as it was hoped that the men would soon be freed. Again d'Urville stressed that they all had to be sent back.

At seven on the morning of 15 May, the *Astrolabe* sailed to Mafanga and anchored a quarter of a mile from the shore. A number of white flags appeared, whereupon d'Urville sent Guilbert to negotiate, but he was fired on. Nothing further was done. On the 16th a meeting of officers was held; it was agreed that only a show of strength would have any effect. The first shot broke the quiet of the bay at 10.30—it snapped off a branch from the large tree under which the ceremonies were normally held. Thirty shots were fired in the morning and twenty-four in the afternoon; but they appeared ineffective—during the night the islanders were heard felling trees to repair the damage done to their defences. At dawn the French were able to discern a double row of ramparts built of tree-trunks and earth. 'My only hope is to exhaust the patience of these islanders and especially see dissensions develop between the chiefs.' He was going to need all the patience he had. Rain started to fall. Seventeen shots were fired at irregular intervals to keep the natives on the alert. The weather worsened; torrential rain almost obliterated the land from view and only one shot could be fired on the 18th and none the following day. The corvette's own position was far from safe, for, if a cable broke, she would almost certainly be unable to avoid drifting on the nearby reefs, whereupon her crew would be at the mercy of the Tongans. Since rumours had it that, with two exceptions, the missing sailors had been planning to desert and had merely been helped by Tahofa, d'Urville's insistence on all his men being returned, in spite of the risks he was running, was largely motivated by a desire to avoid losing face. Ships—as he well knew—were constantly losing deserters in the islands of the Pacific. The Tongans had offered from the start to return some of the men—clearly those unwilling to desert. D'Urville could have accepted the proposal and left the others to their fate. As it was, he was not merely endangering his ship, but also running the risk of losing more would-be deserters. Lottin warned him that whispers of new desertions were spreading through the crew, and the captain agreed that he could stay only one day more and would leave Tonga on the 20th if the wind was favourable. The threat which the weather represented to the safety of all on board could not be met by any new measures. There was no possible hope of pacifying the islanders whose sacred meeting-place had been bombarded. D'Urville instructed the *élève* Dudemaine to blow up the *Astrolabe* if she were to be driven on to the reef: he had no intention of falling alive into his enemies' hands.

Late on the 19th one of the prisoners came on board and a cease-fire was agreed to, although d'Urville, who mistrusted him, refused to let the man speak to any of his crew. 'It was really time for all this to finish, as my position in front of Mafanga was no longer tenable. A talk this morning with Collinet, the boatswain, had convinced me that there were scarcely five or six sailors I could depend on; all the others would joyfully have joined the natives.'[1] Tahofa was claiming—and this seems reasonable— that two of the deserters, unwilling to be sent back, had fled to the interior. He had undoubtedly intended to retain the Frenchmen as advisers and helpers, and for the prestige which Europeans attached to his party would bring at a time when he was

D'Urville, *Voyage*, vol. **iv**, p. 121.

prosecuting a political struggle for supremacy among the chiefs; now he was in danger of losing ground, since the islanders would blame him for having caused trouble with d'Urville. Therefore, as soon as the latter agreed to take his sailors back, less the two deserters, the six men were promptly sent to him. The dispute was at an end. The *Astrolabe* made her way through the northern pass on 21 May 1827, leaving behind the man Reboul, 'a fool [but] a passable sailor and fairly quiet by nature', and Simonet, whom d'Urville considered the ringleader. But Simonet was not destined to disappear without trace, as did so many other ship jumpers and beachcombers. He was to marry a Tongan girl and eventually to found a dynasty of traders, planters, and officials, with branches in various parts of the Pacific.[1] D'Urville himself was to forgive him when he met him on a later voyage.

The *Astrolabe* proceeded north-west by north, towards Hunga Ha'apai and Hunga Tonga. Cook's Turtle Island, Vatoa, was sighted on the 24th, then a succession of small islands belonging to the Eastern Group of Fiji. D'Urville's descriptions are accurate, so that tracing his route presents no difficulty: Ogea Levu and Ogea Driki, two islands encircled by a common reef, appeared to the north-north-west; Fulaga lay a little to the west, covered with dense vegetation and also sheltered by a circular reef; to the north-west the Yagasa cluster spread out its dangerous coral tentacles, among which Wilson had nearly lost his ship in 1797. Gressien worked on the chart as the *Astrolabe* sailed cautiously on a north-easterly route, past Namuka-i-lau, with Marobo, Karaba, and Wagava in the distance, past Komo to Lakemba, where the French anchored on the morning of the 26th, Gressien's work now being hampered by light rain. D'Urville had on board two men who had joined the ship at Ogea Levu: one was a Tongan, Muki, who had settled in the Fijis after an adventurous career which had taken him to Port Jackson, New Zealand, and Tahiti; the other was a Spaniard from Guam, who remembered seeing the *Uranie* there and talking to Quoy and Gaimard, and had been abandoned by—or had deserted—a Spanish sandalwood trader on Vanua

---

[1] A biographical note on Simonet will be found in O'Reilly and Teissier, *Tahitiens*, pp. 426–7, and in *Journal de la Société des océanistes*, vol. xix, p. 17.

Levu. Both were useful as pilots and interpreters in these unsafe waters, and d'Urville had readily agreed to take them at least as far as Lakemba. When he arrived there, the Frenchman was met by three more Spaniards, from the same sandalwood ship, who begged him on their knees to be taken on and were overjoyed when he granted their request. The rumoured anchor turned out to be a relic of a shipwrecked American whaler; d'Urville sent Lottin and Dudemaine, with Muki and the Spaniard as interpreters, and a detachment of ten men in the hope of buying it. To quote Lottin:

The sea, breaking over the outer reefs, rose to a height of eight or ten feet and fell back nearly vertically, so that a rampart was formed behind which the water was as smooth as in a pond: some thirty women were fishing there. Nearly completely naked, black, old, and ugly, they were in the water up to their middle and were dragging fishing nets behind them. They greeted us with a storm of insults, accompanied by various gestures implying contempt, like beating their hands together, throwing water at us and smacking their buttocks. The shore was deserted, the tide was out and a stretch of mud about three cables wide was visible below the forestline, with a few huts and sheds similar to those of Tongatapu. We landed at the spot which seemed the most appropriate. . . . While we were taking these precautions to tie up safely, natives were beginning to arrive little by little and started to talk with the pilot who was standing forward in the boat, unwilling to set foot on land. In vain did I finally get the Spaniard to ask him where the anchor was, whether the natives were prepared to hand it over, what they wanted in exchange . . . I received no clear reply. . . . Meanwhile the natives were growing in number, the new-comers being armed with bows, lances, and clubs, and their heads covered with a piece of white cloth. There were about two hundred of them. I sought in vain among these heads for a Tongan face: the pilot had misled me on this. The natives, now noisier, advancing in the water, were gradually surrounding the canoe, leaning on the wash-strokes and staring inquisitively at the inside of the boat. The depth of the water prevented them from coming aft where I held the grapnel rope ready to haul it in. . . . I repeatedly asked to speak to a chief, for there were no doubt some in the crowd, but no distinguishing mark was apparent. Finally the pilot, turning towards us, warned us that the chiefs wanted four of us to land. They had selected those who stood out, namely Mr. Dudemaine, the boatswain, a helmsman and me. I found this kind of order a little peculiar and asked that a chief should remain in the boat while we were away. After a discussion a man came forward as hostage, whom the pilot declared to be a chief; but at the same moment, the Spaniard, tugging sharply at my coat, told me that it was a commoner. Unsure of what I should do, I was about to leave the boat in charge of Mr. Dudemaine and go to see for myself where the anchor was, when some thirty children in the crowd fled spontaneously, and several climbed trees near the shoreline: at the same time, all the natives came closer, and the pilot hid under the seats of the boat without being able or willing to explain what all this meant. For my part, I naturally concluded that they harboured hostile intentions.[1]

Lottin's conclusion was natural enough, although the Spaniard felt that there was more evidence of a natural curiosity than of any clear hostility. Muki blamed his lack of success on the absence of the Tongan friends he hoped to find there: his nervousness was probably due to taunts shouted at him by the crowd, for Tongans and Fijians were often enemies and the men of Lakemba were the most warlike in the archipelago. They had full confidence in their visitors and, seemingly quite unperturbed by this incident, soon went again on board the *Astrolabe*. Eventually one of them, claiming to be the chief's brother, offered to bring the anchor to the ship, but the weather deteriorated before he was able to redeem his promise. The French sailed on the 28th, going north-north-west towards Nayan and Cicia. The sky was overcast, a strong south-easterly was blowing, and there was a heavy swell, all of which gave rise to anxiety in view of the uncertainty of the currents in the Koro Sea. The next day, when the corvette passed to the west of Vatu Vara and Yacata, the wind had reached gale force. The high peaks of Taveuni could just be discovered to the north, but it was too dangerous to seek a refuge there. Sailing a more westerly course, d'Urville sighted the centrally situated islands of Koro and Nairai; unsure of what lay ahead, he decided to seek Namuka Passage, which would lead him out of the Koro Sea into safer open waters, but it was here in 1797 that Wilson's *Duff* had so narrowly escaped disaster. Visibility was poor and

[1] Account taken from Lottin's Journal, in d'Urville, *Voyage*, vol. iv, pp. 691-5.

the charts were unreliable. D'Urville kept the whole crew on deck overnight in case of need. He identified Naitauba and Vanua Balavu to the west and Qamea and Laucala to the north-east, but conditions did not warrant his hazarding his ship any further. On the 31st the *Astrolabe* turned south, d'Urville noting in his journal: 'In accordance with the wish expressed by Mr. de Rossel in the instructions he drew up for the voyage of the *Astrolabe*, I gave back to these islands the name of Prince William's Islands, which the famous Tasman, their first discoverer, had assigned to them, and I gave the name of that skilful navigator to the canal which separates Qamea from Taveuni.'[1] The name Tasman Strait remains, however, for the true passage between Taveuni and Budd Reef, rather than the reef-sown pass which d'Urville selected.

The French were now making for the Moala group in the southern Koro Sea. D'Urville's desire was to get rid of the Tongan and Fijian passengers to whom he had promised a passage to Taveuni; even so, it took him two days to land them safely on Moala. They parted with mutual relief; and no sooner had this been done than the storm returned—he turned north again, towards Gau, passing to the south of this island and making for the south-east coast of Viti Levu. The weather was improving, which was fortunate because the *Astrolabe* was about to meet another danger. On the evening of 5 June d'Urville altered course in order to survey the Kadavu group, south of Viti Levu:

The *Astrolabe* was sailing quietly at a rate of three knots . . . with an inconstant south-easterly breeze and a fairly heavy swell. As was my custom, I was lying down on one of the hen coops and, tired after the day's work, I had been sleeping for about an hour when, at 10.15, I was suddenly awakened by the terrible shout of 'breakers on the lee!' . . . It is easy to imagine what I felt when I discovered, less than three cable lengths on the lee a long silvery stretch rising and falling at long intervals. Until that moment dark clouds concealing the moon had hidden these breakers from us and it was only when the rays of that planet were able to reflect on the tops of the foaming waves that they could be seen. A few minutes more in darkness and the *Astrolabe*

[1] D'Urville, *Voyage*, vol. iv, p. 422.

would have crashed into these new dangers. . . . At 10.40 we passed
about a cable's length away from the easternmost point of the breaker
and we then saw, with the greatest joy, that it fell away in a different
direction from that of our route. . . . I had no reason to expect such an
encounter. These dangerous breakers were therefore a discovery of the
Astrolabe's; they received the name of our corvette which had nearly
paid so dearly for such an honour.[1]

Astrolabe Reef was indeed a new discovery and its name remains
today in commemoration of that night in June. It consists of two
reefs—North Astrolabe and Great Astrolabe—separated by a
mile-wide stretch of clear water, now known as D'Urville Channel.
Having narrowly avoided it, the French swung out to the south
of Kadavu Island, then north to Vatu Lele, thence to the south-
west coast of Viti Levu. Bligh had already sailed along the
Kadavu coast in the *Providence*, but had not surveyed it in any
detail; Vatu Lele appears to be a new discovery, as d'Urville
himself claimed: 'No traveller had ever mentioned this island',[2]
for Bligh had continued in a south-westerly direction, passing
too far from it to notice it on the horizon. D'Urville had the
advantage of a calm sea and 'superb' weather. When he was but
a few miles off Viti Levu fifteen canoes came out to the corvette
and islanders climbed aboard, selling pigs, coconuts, and fowls
for axes, scissors, and powder. The wind had now almost completely dropped. The *Astrolabe* sailed slowly towards the Malolo
group, a few miles from the west coast of Viti Levu, which was
reached on 10 June. There was a possibility of surveying these
small islands, and the French actually edged for a while along the
Malolo Barrier Reef, but the weakness of the breeze and their
lack of knowledge of the currents led them to abandon this
operation and sail for the Loyalty Islands. The last island they saw
was Viwa, which stands a little to the west of the main Yasawa
group.

Futuna in the New Hebrides appeared on 13 June, and Aney-
tum at dawn on the 14th; Tana remained hidden in fog. D'Urville
fixed the position of the islands as precisely as he could in order

---

[1] D'Urville, *Voyage*, pp. 435–7.   [2] Ibid., vol. iv, p. 443.

to use them as reference points for the Loyalties, whose true position was in question: 'My only thought was now to make for the space occupied on Arrowsmith's English map by the ill-defined Loyalty group. Krusenstern, so thorough about everything that is already known, could give no details on their position or their extent. Mr. de Rossel had even some doubts about their existence. This was therefore a most important point to settle.'[1] Sailing south-west and south-south-west with a fresh easterly, he had no difficulty in finding them. His first landfall, on the 15th, was an island he named Britannia, after Captain Raven's ship, the group having been first reported by him in 1793.[2] This island can be identified as Maré, the easternmost of the group. D'Urville now slowly followed a north-westerly course, discovering or positively reporting for the first time the entire archipelago: Ile Boucher (Tiga); the three small islands Hamelin (Leliogat), Lainé (Uo), and Vauvilliers, the only one to retain a name given by him; the offshore islet of Molard (Ndunduré); a much larger island which 'by common consent' they named Chabrol, after the Minister of Marine, and which is in fact Lifu, the largest of the group;[3] Halgan (Uvea); and Beautemps-Beaupré. Four days were spent on this exploration, in spite of a brief spell of rain. 'We felt a deep satisfaction when we saw that the exploration of the Loyalty Islands was gaining an importance which we had never expected: these islands were henceforth to constitute a fairly remarkable archipelago, instead of the insignificant group we anticipated meeting in these waters.'[4] Halgan seemed clearly to be a new discovery, seen neither by Raven nor by d'Entre-casteaux's expedition; to mark the dangers which the latter had run just before its discovery of Beautemps-Beaupré, d'Urville named the western headland of Uvea 'Cap Rossel'. The other name given in this area, les Pléiades, to a group of islets off the west coast of Uvea, can only apply to the reefs and tiny low atolls on the far side of Uvea Bay.

[1] Ibid., vol. iv, p. 462.
[2] Sharp, *The Discovery of the Pacific Islands*, p. 176.
[3] Names given to various points on the island have remained: Cap des Pins, Baie Chateaubriand, Cap Bernardin, Cap Escarpé.
[4] D'Urville, *Voyage*, vol. iv, p. 469.

There was a possibility that La Pérouse's two ships had struck these unknown dangers. 'Our eyes were anxiously scanning these shores to discover some trace of the stay of the Frenchmen.' The *Astrolabe* herself was sailing towards possible destruction. Having left Beautemps-Beaupré and now believing themselves to be entering the open sea, the French were roused at dawn on the 20th by a shout of 'Reefs on the port side!'; d'Urville ordered a course to be set for it, to the crew's distress. Their nerve was beginning to fail them:

Having only just escaped from the close dangers of New Zealand, Tonga, and the Fiji Islands, these poor people dreamt of nothing but reefs, and it was easy to tell that their morale was seriously affected by the nature of their voyage. Misled by the accounts they had heard of the easy expeditions of the *Uranie* and *Coquille*, which they regarded as mere excursions, they imagined that it would be the same with the *Astrolabe* and they had just been cruelly disabused by an experience which had been repeated several times.[1]

D'Urville seizes this opportunity, as he did others, to draw attention to what he felt was a slighting of his endeavours: 'I do admit today, however, that if I had then foreseen that such hardships and trials were to be received by the Ministry of Marine with so much indifference, I would have taken greater care of my travelling companions' safety.'[2] The immediate situation was met with an astute move—he offered a piastre to the first man who discovered a new islet or a reef, and in this way turned routine duty into eager anticipation. The promise was not an empty one, for the reefs, approximately thirty miles from Beautemps-Beaupré Island, were extensively scattered athwart their route. A new discovery, they were named—and remain—Astrolabe Reefs. From this point on, the *Astrolabe* was in charted waters: d'Entre-casteaux Reefs and Huon Island led her into the open spaces of the Coral Sea which she crossed in six uneventful days, reaching the Louisiades on 29 June 1827.

The first landfall was a low coral strip topped by a few trees, which d'Urville named Île Adèle; this was followed by Cap de la

[1] D'Urville, *Voyage*, vol. iv, p. 475.   [2] Ibid., p. 475.

Délivrance. The instructions required him to enter Torres Strait, but this was plainly unwise after the loss of anchors and cables. The alternative was to sail north to New Ireland for firewood and water, both of which were running low, and thence to New Britain and northern New Guinea. This route would enable the French to verify the position of Laughlan's Islands, discovered by the British vessel *Mary* in August 1812. The Laughlans, or Nadas, lie to the west of the large Woodlark group; the *Astrolabe* sailed past them on 1 July; d'Urville counted nine separate islets, all apparently uninhabited. The sea was running high, and it proved too dangerous to lower a boat, although a supply of coconuts would have been welcome. A small island was discovered nine miles to the west of this group, totally isolated, fairly high and brush-covered, 'which had not been seen by Captain Laughlan. I gave it the name of Cannac, to mark the good services of this young man on the *Astrolabe* expedition'.[1] D'Urville now sailed almost due north for Cape St. George in New Ireland. His health, never very good after he had been at sea for a prolonged period, was causing him anxiety: 'I have experienced today even more than on previous days a general feeling of discomfort and a stiffness in all my limbs, which are certainly due to a need to breathe land air and to take some exercise.' The crew, however, were generally fit, and the water and biscuits were still in good condition, but the men did need a rest. It was with relief therefore that they sighted Cape St. George on 5 July. D'Urville's intention was to anchor in Carteret Harbour in preference to Port Praslin. As if the gods wished to warn him against staying here, a sudden squall blew up and a heavy shower obliterated the whole coast. Lottin was sent ahead to find the pass; a new shower hid the yawl from those still in the ship. Brief respites between the showers were marked by an almost total absence of wind, so that the corvette fell to the mercy of the currents. D'Urville considered abandoning his plan and sailing for New Guinea, but he was unable to recall Lottin and the yawl. The anchor was finally dropped outside the harbour itself. After a night of tropical

[1] Ibid., vol. iv, p. 489. Jean-Victor Cannac was one of the crew. The name remains in use to this day.

downpours, d'Urville went in the whaleboat to seek a safer anchorage; when he returned it was to be told that the anchor cable had snapped: he now had only three anchors left. The corvette had drifted round in the currents and the cables of two of the other anchors were so entangled that both had to be raised together. This operation, especially exhausting to the men, took two and a half hours. When it was completed, d'Urville moved the ship to a safer position. The weather began to improve, but there were more troubles ahead.

A gun had been fired to call whatever natives might be in the vicinity. As the rain abated, a few came out to the ship in canoes to sell fish. D'Urville went ashore, accompanied by a sailor, in the hope of relieving his pain by a change of air. When he returned, he found the deck heaped up with the trunks of cycas trees. He asked what they were for.

Mr. Jacquinot replied that Béringuier, our chief carpenter, and his assistant had cut them down according to my instructions to give them to the crew. I did indeed remember that upon landing I had shown Béringuier some arecas and told him to select the largest and cut them down so that their tops could be used in lieu of palm-cabbages. The poor man had cut down the wrong tree and had attacked the *cycas*, of which he had brought down an enormous number. Not satisfied with this, he and his assistant had eaten some, and I must admit that, in order to do that, one needs a great deal of courage or an incredible appetite for fresh vegetables; for, when I tried to taste one, I found the taste so repellent that I had to throw it down at once. I tried to have it boiled . . . but in vain. Finally, I had it all thrown overboard. . . As for Béringuier and his assistant Chieusse, they were punished by their rashness. This deadly food caused violent stomach pains, especially to the former, which subsided only after repeated treatment by Doctor Gaimard; and even then Béringuier was never completely cured and died three months later. For my part, having scarcely tasted this harmful substance, I felt an immediate nausea, which did not last: however one cannot be sure that it did not play a part in the terrible ills I suffered a few days later, and which have developed so to speak into a chronic condition.[1]

---

[1] D'Urville, *Voyage*, vol. iv, pp. 503–4. *Cycas circinalis* is so poisonous that the water in which the kernels are soaked is fatal to animals. Only after

The natives had little to offer in the way of food—the French sailors' fishing equipment was superior to theirs and fish could be as easily caught as bought—but they did bring to the ship one pig for which they were given an axe. Apart from that, the chain of misfortunes remained unbroken. D'Urville's pet cockatoo, a malicious animal', escaped and flying around the main cabin smashed the only marine barometer his master had succeeded in obtaining from the authorities at Toulon. By the 11th the temperature had risen to 85° in the shade, with scarcely any breeze. D'Urville began to be attacked by severe stomach pains; the next day he once more resorted to his walks on shore and went hunting, but after a short time he was forced to return and take to his bed. Gaimard diagnosed enteritis and prescribed enemas and leeches. The night of the 13th was 'dreadful'. In the morning, d'Urville, thinking that his illness might prove fatal, drew up a schedule of instructions as a guide for Jacquinot. Hot baths gave him some relief from pain, he was able to sleep a little and take some liquid nourishment on the 15th and 16th, but was compelled to postpone the departure of the expedition until the 19th. No sooner had the *Astrolabe* inched her way out of the shelter of the bay than the sky became overcast and it became almost impossible to distinguish the main features of the coast. Soon everything was blotted out by 'incredible showers'. Not surprisingly, d'Urville had caustic comments to make on de Brosses's choice of New Britain as the possible site for a colony:

One must say that a land drowned by such frequent and extraordinary downpours offers man a place of residence which is hardly pleasant or healthy. And accordingly I have changed the favourable opinon I had formed of New Britain from Dampier's account and President Desbrosses's [*sic*] conjectures. If the latter had only shared the hardships of our campaign, he would certainly not have chosen this country as a seat for the colony he wanted to found in this part of the globe. Never have I seen in any country anything like the torrents of rain which poured down on us for twelve whole days.[1] Bougainville and

repeated soaking and frequent changing of the contaminated water can the kernels be ground up into meal and dried for future use.

[2] The annual rainfall along the south and south-east coast reaches 245" and d'Urville was there during the south-east monsoon, which is the wettest season!

d'Entrecasteaux suffered the same fate in their anchorages at Praslin and Carteret. Luckier, it is true, in the *Coquille*, we had had generally fine weather in Port Praslin. But it seems that these cases are rare and one should not count on it.[1]

Fortunately, there were few cases of sickness on board; but poor visibility greatly hampered the survey work, so that the expedition's charts of the archipelago are less reliable and thorough. Nevertheless, the French sailed slowly along the south coast of New Britain, making for New Guinea. As they progressed, the weather started to improve; by early August it was no longer a hindrance to hydrographical work. On the 2nd they entered Dampier Strait, keeping close to the coast of New Britain, a course which again was not free from dangers: 'Suddenly the lookout is heard shouting hoarsely and incoherently, a sign of great fear.' There was a reef ahead, just hidden by unbroken water. The keel scraped twice over it, then the *Astrolabe* was once more in clear water. Rounding the southern cape, the French sailed north towards Sakar, giving the name of Île Tupinier[2] to a small island close to it. Lottin Island, slightly to the west of it, is modern Tolowika, reached by the *Astrolabe* on the evening of 3 August, Île Longue is Long Island still, and Île Couronne Crown Island. This route led the French direct into Astrolabe Bay in New Guinea, from which point they proceeded along the coast towards the Dutch East Indies. D'Urville had always hoped to survey this area which navigators, on their way home or to a place of refreshment after a hard voyage, had a tendency to neglect.

I have never been able to understand, and never shall understand, how Mr. Duperrey could have coasted this part of New Guinea from twelve or fifteen leagues off, under the most favourable circumstances, without wanting to survey it; all the more so since all his officers were burning with a desire to visit this large country. Anyhow, the memory of the bitter regrets I had myself at the time led me to make every possible efforts with the *Astrolabe*.

---

[1] D'Urville, *Voyage*, vol. iv, p. 531.
[2] After Baron Tupinier, *directeur des ports et arsenaux*, an able administrator and author of several books on port administration and shipbuilding.

The shortage of anchors and cables did not help matters: it was dangerous to venture much nearer to the shore than six or seven miles. A few days later, d'Urville seems to have had second thoughts about Duperrey's behaviour; his former colleague was possibly less inefficient than his earlier strictures indicated:

I should point out here that, in spite of the great distance at which Mr. Duperrey passed from the western Schouten Islands, the work done on board the *Coquille* differs very little from the *Astrolabe's*. Nevertheless, on board the former vessel there were never any geographical stations and the compass was ordinarily used only for bearings; whereas in the *Astrolabe* the greatest precautions were taken to ensure the utmost precision in our work. This does show that in many cases the simplest and quickest methods often produce a result which is close enough for the requirements of navigation.[1]

There was only one incident—near Mount Eyries, close to the present settlement of Krukru. The natives, who had hitherto paid no attention to the French ship, approached in some fifteen canoes; after a great deal of shouting and inviting the French to land, one man shot an arrow at the ship, which struck the deck at the feet of a group of officers; d'Urville, who suspected the natives of thinking that the ship was in trouble, had a few shots fired over their heads; they dispersed promptly and the *Astrolabe* went on her way.[2]

At midday on the 12th the expedition entered a wide bay which was given the name—which it has retained—of Humboldt Bay, after 'the only scientist who was actively interested in the voyage of the *Astrolabe*'. D'Urville rightly assessed the value of this bay to future settlers, commenting 'it is a point . . . which will probably assume great importance when New Guinea becomes of interest to commercial operators'—and, indeed, it became the site of the administrative capital of Dutch New Guinea, Hollandia, later known as Sukarnopura. A little later, another opportunity arose of paying a tribute to a friend of the expedition. Naming the next bay Anse Matterer, he said: 'Mr. Matterer . . . far from displaying the ungenerous selfishness of the other captains in

[1] Ibid., vol. iv, p. 554.
[2] Account in 'Extrait du journal de M. Quoy', in ibid., vol. iv, p. 740.

[Toulon], promptly transferred to me two sailors who had volunteered to serve under me. Had I everywhere found the same noble attitude, the crew of the *Astrolabe* would have been quite different and I and the brave officers whose task it was to assist me would have been spared much trouble and anxiety.'[1] Next, d'Urville was able to honour Captain Gauttier, who had surveyed the coasts of the Mediterranean and of the Black Sea in 1816–20, and whose pupils had included Jacquinot, Lottin, and Gressien. Possibly at their suggestion a high range of mountains was named after him—the Gauttier Gebergte, which rise inland up to a height of 6,000 feet. It was then the commander's turn to have his name recorded: the very distinctive Cape d'Urville forms the northernmost point of the main New Guinea land mass. From this cape the coast falls away to the south-west; the *Astrolabe* sailed on towards the Schouten Islands, and through the Straits of Japen to Dore Bay, where the expedition dropped anchor on 25 August. D'Urville had been there three years before in the *Coquille*. The natives came out in droves to the French vessel and treated the visitors 'like old acquaintances'. Unhappily, there was little fresh food available, little to vary the monotonous diet of beans and salt pork, except a few coconuts and some fish. The only supplies the port could provide were fresh water and firewood. 'As the plan of Dore harbour drawn by the *Coquille*'s officers leaves nothing to be desired, we must avoid all hydrographic work.' D'Urville, still far from well, remembering the pleasant stay enjoyed by the men of the *Coquille*, went ashore on a hunting expedition. He found this tiring, but was adhering to his policy of getting away from the sea air whenever he could. The district, however, is enclosed by a range of high mountains inhabited by warlike tribes; one of a party of sailors on a water fatigue was wounded by an arrow fired at them by raiders from the hills, and warnings had to be issued not to venture inland.

Twelve days later, surrounded by a flotilla of small canoes, the *Astrolabe* put to sea. D'Urville planned to pass through Dampier Strait between Waigeo and Batanta, but contrary winds forced him to beat to the north and follow 'the route which so many

[1] D'Urville, *Voyage*, vol. iv, p. 563 n.

navigators have used' by way of Gebe and Pisang to Amboina, where he arrived on the evening of 24 September. For the first time in many months he was received by Europeans. His feelings were mixed. The Dutch authorities were cordial and helpful. Food supplies—expensive though they were—were purchased with little difficulty. Two cases of sickness were transferred to the local hospital. Three of the Spanish sailors taken on in the Fijis were discharged at their request, as they were hopeful of finding a ship bound for Manila, their home. The Maori Kokako, meeting four of his fellows from the British whaler *Castor* bound for the Bay of Islands, succumbed to home-sickness and was allowed to join the whaler's crew. Amboina was therefore a place for re-organization as well as refreshment, but there were drawbacks. D'Urville, still weak from his stomach condition, could not stand the receptions and the heavy dinners his Dutch hosts arranged for him. Tobacco smoke in particular upset him. The Dutch seemed to be perpetually puffing away at heavy pipes filled with dark tobacco from the islands and emitting an acrid smoke which hung over the guests in the hot, calm night. He had no patience with the tales they told him with solemn seriousness, especially on the reproductive powers of pearls fed on rice; he found it difficult to hide his scorn when they showed him 'breeding pearls' nestling in tiny bowls of rice. To avoid social occasions and to rest, he remained on board whenever he could and sent his officers on errands. On 10 October he sailed. Five of the men were sick, including Béringuier, the edacious carpenter who died at the end of November. One of the most experienced men on board, he had sailed under Freycinet in the *Uranie*, under Duperrey in the *Coquille*, and finally under d'Urville in the *Astrolabe*. He had survived storms and a shipwreck, had avoided dysentery in the East Indies, and had lived for months running into years on ship's biscuit, dried pork, and near-stagnant water, only to fall a victim to a simple misunderstanding; 'much mourned', especially by d'Urville, for his personality, his 'blameless conduct . . . limitless zeal and devotion', he was consigned to the sea—not, as he might have hoped in view of his career, to the Pacific, but to the Indian Ocean, for the *Astrolabe* had been held back by contrary winds and

calms, and had barely covered 180 leagues in six weeks. The plan
had been to sail to Tasmania along the western coast of Australia,
a plan the winds had soon thwarted. It had just been possible to
reach the Rowley Shoals, approximately 150 miles west of
Dampier Land, but from there the French had to sail west-south-
west in search of a favourable wind, then south and south-east
a great distance from the Australian continent until the latitude
of southern Tasmania was crossed, and thence east. It was again
a route many others had followed before and for the same reasons.
The westerlies sped the corvette towards Hobart, but were accompanied by rain and high seas, so that it was with some relief that
they finally sighted the Mewstone on 16 December 1827. They
sailed into D'Entrecasteaux Channel and as they approached
Hobart a pilot came to their assistance; he was soon replaced by
the harbourmaster himself, for this was the first visit to Hobart of
a French warship since its foundation and the citizens wished to
pay it every respect. With his help, the *Astrolabe* anchored on the
20th half a mile south of the town.

Even before then, d'Urville had learnt about Dillon's discoveries at Tikopia.[1] The first version was given him by the pilot
and perhaps not surprisingly was garbled: the Prussian Burkhardt
was referred to as a member of La Pérouse's crew. The harbourmaster was able to clear up this misunderstanding; he expressed
full confidence in Dillon, but the French soon realized that the
settlers were divided on the Irishman's claims. Told that Dillon
'was mad, was an adventurer, that his so-called discovery was a
fable', d'Urville felt his enthusiasm cooling: it seemed scarcely
warranted to alter his present plan—a further exploration of the
New Zealand coast—in order to go off on what might prove a
foolish wild-goose chase. The Governor's secretary, Burnett, and
the Chief Justice, John Pedder, added their adverse comments on
Dillon; and indeed the absurd imbroglio with Dr. Tytler was
hardly likely to strengthen one's faith in the man. Yet, when he
read the newspaper reports on the affair, d'Urville began to feel
that his duty lay more in the neighbourhood of Vanikoro than in
New Zealand. His instructions were so precise that they did not

---

[1] See *supra*, vol. i, pp. 333–5.

allow him to ignore an opportunity of finding traces of La Pérouse unless he was quite certain that the reports were false. The *Coquille*, after all, had been renamed partly to underline this fact. What would be said of him if he had simply sailed to New Zealand while Dillon went to Vanikoro and there found some survivors? It was not a risk he could take—unless Dillon himself had second thoughts and abandoned his scheme. This, Dillon's opponents realized, was crucial, and they showed d'Urville a letter purporting to be signed by Dillon, in which he stated that, having reached the Bay of Islands, he would not now go on to Vanikoro; but d'Urville believed this to be a forgery and that, even if it were not, it was still his duty to go there. Pedder, with whom he dined soon after this episode, saw 'with sorrow that I am persisting in abandoning my brilliant explorations in order to visit Vanikoro'. But Pedder was to be further discomfited on 1 January when two ships arrived from the Australian continent, bringing a copy of the New South Wales *Advertiser* in which it was reported that Dillon had been to Vanikoro and had returned with relics of the French expedition. There could be no more indecision: on 6 January 1828 the *Astrolabe* sailed from Hobart. The departure was not untimely, for the crew had been involved in a resounding brawl ashore on Christmas Eve and a new outbreak of trouble with the local colonists could occur at any time.

D'Urville set a north-easterly course which would take the corvette to the neighbourhood of Norfolk Island, but a steady northerly breeze delayed her. It took over ten days to reach the latitude of Sydney. Norfolk was sighted on the 20th, tiny Matthew Island, east of New Caledonia, on the 26th, and two days later the peak of Futuna appeared to the west-north-west. The heat had become oppressive as the *Astrolabe* entered the belt of equatorial calms. The expedition steered east to avoid the reef-strewn New Hebrides, then west and north to Tikopia, and was in view of the island on 9 February, but 'the breeze was so weak we were approaching Tikopia with disheartening slowness'. During the afternoon of the next day, three canoes came out, in one of which was Burkhardt himself, who confirmed everything Dillon had said as well as the report of his recent return visit. The Prussian agreed to accompany d'Urville to Vanikoro on condition that he was allowed to bring his wife and their luggage, since he now wished to leave the islands. 'I was particularly reluctant to receive on the corvette a young woman whose presence could give rise to disorderly conduct among the crew. However, so that I would not be deprived of the assistance of such a useful guide, I promised to take his wife with him and see that she was respected on board the *Astrolabe*.'[1] However, at the last minute, Burkhardt changed his mind, to the great joy of his wife, who had no wish to leave Tikopia. The *Astrolabe* sailed without him, having on board instead two deserters from the whaler *Harriet*, who had been in the island for nearly a year, and a Tikopian to act as guide and interpreter. Arriving off Vanikoro on 14 February, d'Urville was at first unable to find an anchorage or a pass through the reef. Lottin, sent with one of the deserters and the Tikopian to establish contact with the islanders, reported unfavourably on both people and island. Meanwhile the winds were gradually driving the corvette towards the reef. D'Urville, assured that Taumako was only a day or so's sailing away and would provide a safe anchorage, agreed to leave; he returned within a few days—not having found Taumako—and dropped anchor in Tevia Bay late on the 21st.

It took the French several days before the islanders even agreed that there had been a wreck or that Dillon had recently visited them. Responses varied from silence and frowns to a few inconclusive answers. At Peou all the natives fled when they approached, except an elderly couple too frightened to speak. At Nama and Vanu a few items were bought, but no information could be obtained. Gressien, who had been sent to make a complete circuit of the island, was no more successful than d'Urville. Part of the reason seemed to be Dillon's recent visit, for, having received a generous grant from the East India Company, he had distributed large quantities of European goods and iron; consequently the natives disdained much of what the late-comers had to offer; and if they had been given to understand by the interpreter that these were of the same nation as La Pérouse the fear of vengeance must have increased their reluctance to trade. It was

[1] D'Urville, *Voyage*, vol. v, p. 111.

not until Jacquinot went in the longboat to Nama in the hope of locating the wreck that any progress was made: in exchange for red cloth the natives agreed to take him to the exact spot. An anchor, a few guns, some lead and porcelain were raised from the sea floor. D'Urville erected a cenotaph on the northern reef, for which kauri timber obtained in Kororareka the previous year was used. So as to avoid the islanders' destructive cupidity, the memorial was put together without nails, but the commemorative plaque had to be of lead; it read simply: 'To the memory of Lapérouse and his companions. *Astrolabe*. 14 March 1828.' D'Urville himself being laid low by a fever, Jacquinot went down to the reef with part of the crew and carried out a solemn unveiling. 'Three men went past three times in respectful and solemn silence and three times fired their rifles, while from the ship a salvo of twenty-one guns echoed over the hills of Vanikoro.'[1] But the weather was deteriorating and an increasing number of men, including the ship's surgeon Gaimard, were affected by the fevers for which the island was feared. The natives were showing obvious signs of interest if not downright satisfaction at this, and d'Urville, suspecting that they were contemplating an attack on the corvette and her weakened crew, abandoned his search for further relics and put to sea on 17 March. There were now forty cases of sickness.

At first a course was set for Taumako, but the *Astrolabe* was pitching and rolling so heavily through the mountainous seas and so many men were unwell that d'Urville decided to go to Port Jackson for rest and refreshments. Changing course to east-south-east on 20 March, he sailed past Tikopia on the 22nd and continued southwards, retracing the route he had followed a month earlier. 'Navigation painful beyond anything that can be imagined.' Only Gressien and Guilbert were unaffected: twenty-five men were totally unfit for service and half the remainder were intermittently affected. After a few days d'Urville realized that the route to Port Jackson was impossible and that the only alternative was to take advantage of the prevailing winds and make for Guam. There was no hope of any hydrographic work

[1] Ibid., vol. v, p. 200.

on the way there. By 28 March the number of serious cases had risen to thirty-five; they had been joined by Gressien, only Guilbert being fit enough for service. One of the watches was being taken by the boatswain Collinet. Two days later an order to haul in the mainsail in the face of a threatening squall could not be carried out; it was thus necessary to reduce canvas to a minimum, although this meant slowing down the ship when the winds moderated; they gradually fell away to nothing, leaving the *Astrolabe* almost completely becalmed, 'a floating hospital ship'. On 17 April d'Urville wrote in his diary 'already a month has passed since our departure from Vanikoro and we have not covered more than four hundred leagues in a straight line'.[1] Ten days later he sailed through the Carolines, east of the Truk group, and on 2 May anchored at last at Guam.

The Governor was still that same Medinilla who had treated Freycinet so well and been rewarded by the Legion of Honour. Hospitable as ever, he placed his home at the disposal of the officers and turned the old convent into a hospital to which forty men—all fever-stricken—there were no cases of scurvy—were promptly transferred. The first to die was one of the *Harriet*'s deserters, Hamilton, so recently taken on board, and immune, one might have expected, from the sickness which the French had brought with them from the Santa Cruz group. More fortunate, the last of the Spanish sailors from the Fijis landed safely in his native Guam. The respite and the refreshments—in spite of a shortage of supplies caused by a prolonged drought—were beneficial: when the *Astrolabe* sailed on 30 May, only seventeen men were still incapacitated. The thought that they now were going home must have raised their morale, but d'Urville could see opportunities for more geographical work.

My plan was now to make for Amboina by way of the Moluccas; but I wanted my crossing of the western Carolines to be of value to navigation. Consequently I proposed to explore the large Egoi group, shown tentatively on Mr. Freycinet's little sketch map of the Carolines, the great island of Yap, the Matelotas group, and the Pelew archipelago.

---

[1] D'Urville, *Voyage*, vol. v, p. 241.

With a crew as weakened as the *Astrolabe*'s it was impossible to think of stopping in any of these islands, but at least we could determine new positions based on Umata, and these results did not lack interest.[1]

The French therefore sailed in a south-westerly direction, reaching Fais on 1 June, and Ulithi the next day. They passed between these two islands, but natives who came out to the ship from the latter were nonplussed by the word Egoi. When Yap was reached late the next day, canoes came out in spite of heavy rains; these islanders spoke some Spanish but denied any knowledge of an island called Ulithi—although they did claim that 'Hogoi' could be found to the east-south-east. The French, not surprisingly, were puzzled. The explanation was that Ulithi had been discovered by Bernard de Egui in 1712, a fact of which the Spanish-speaking Yap islanders were aware. As for the wrong direction in which some were pointing, it can be blamed on a long-standing confusion of Farauler, to the south-east of Ulithi, with Falalap, one of the islets which make up Ulithi Atoll; with the natives speaking a mixture of Spanish and their own dialect, crowding around the French and pointing to different points of the horizon, confusion was to be expected—the Egoi group itself did not really exist.[2]

When he returned to France, d'Urville was faced with another puzzle. In Duperrey's chart of the Carolines, which appeared while the *Astrolabe* was in the Pacific, there was shown a small island named D'Urville, approximately forty miles east of Truk.

The two officers from the *Astrolabe* who had been with me in the *Coquille* had no more knowledge than I did of the discovery of this island. However, when I read my private journal I saw that on 23 June 1824, at sunset, the lookout had indeed reported a low island on the horizon. Had I known of this during the voyage of the *Astrolabe*, I would have altered my course so as to pass near there and find out whether D'Urville Island really exists. It would have been easy to do, since on the 25th [April 1828] we cannot have been more than six leagues north-east of it.[3]

[1] Ibid., p. 386.
[2] On Faraulep-Falalap see Shirp, *The Discovery of the Pacific Islands*, pp. 90–1.
[3] D'Urville, *Voyage*, vol. v, p. 243.

On 5 June a number of low-lying islands were sighted to the north-west, the Ngulu archipelago; then, two days after that, the first of the Palaus. There was time for some hydrographical work, but the *Astrolabe* had now entered the doldrums and the currents were driving her towards the north-east. The number of sick had been falling gradually, but soon after crossing the line, on the 19th, a case of dysentery was diagnosed. On the 20th Waigeo was sighted, low on the horizon. The heat was great and the breezes inconstant and weak. On the 24th the first case of dysentery died; the disease was now spreading through the crew; a *novice* died a few days later. But on the 30th the expedition anchored in Buru.

The Dutch were again hospitable and supplies of all kinds—eggs, poultry, fish—were bought at most reasonable prices. Once these stores had been taken in, the *Astrolabe* sailed for Amboina, where she arrived on 10 July for an eight-day stay. Governor Merkus invited d'Urville to accompany him to Celebes, 'an island about which Europeans know little', on his way to Batavia. When d'Urville agreed, this piece of news was not received by the naturalists and officers 'with the enthusiasm it would not have failed to arouse just six months earlier'. The gloomy atmosphere was certainly not relieved by the absence of news from Paris and especially of promotions. The two ships—the *Astrolabe* was now accompanied by the Dutch vessel *Bantjar* with Merkus on board—were piloted by a Frenchman, Barbier, who had served in the French Navy, including a term in the *Sémillante* on her Indian campaign, but had been dismissed in 1815 for his Bonapartist leanings and was now captain of a trading schooner in the Moluccas. The expedition reached Manada, the northernmost port of Celebes, on 27 July, just as one of the dysentery cases died. Another man was to die a few days later.

Merkus organized several excursions for his guests and went to considerable pains to help the naturalists. Guides were provided for the botanists, while the local poeple were instructed to bring him any interesting sample of local fauna. The latter included two live babirusas, the rare wild pig of Celebes, for which a special cage was built, 'one of the most precious acquisitions the Museum of Natural History could receive'. On 5 August the *Astrolabe*

sailed from Celebes, making for Batavia, where she arrived on
the 29th. The city was, fortunately for the men, a far healthier
place than it had been in the eighteenth century, and dysentery
did not cause the ravages one might have feared. But there was
still no news from Paris, no promotions or rewards for any
member of the expedition. From this point, complaints of neglect
by the authorities became more frequent: d'Urville had followed
fairly closely the instructions he had received, the main variations
being his decision not to risk his ship in Torres Strait and the
voyage to Vanikoro, both forced on him by circumstances beyond
his control; but the route he had most recently followed—the
Carolines and back to the Dutch East Indies—conformed to what
had been laid down. He felt therefore that there should have been
no problem with the dispatch of mail to his various ports of call.
The final stages of the return journey began on 2 September 1828
when the expedition sailed from Batavia, making for Sunda
Strait and Mauritius. When the French arrived at the latter place
on the 29th, there was once again no news from the Minister of
Marine. Several weeks went by before anything was received.
When news finally came, Pâris and Faraguet were both promoted
from *élèves* to *enseignes de vaisseau*, while Quoy and Lottin were
raised to a higher grade in the medical service; there was nothing
more spectacular, nothing as yet for the commander.

Nearly everyone was now suffering from weariness and exhaustion. Twelve cases of dysentery had been sent to the hospital
at Port-Louis; but a seven-week stay did little to improve either
physical or mental states: 'Our crew is reduced to an extreme state
of weakness and discouragement; far from reviving at the thought
of a prompt return home, the morale of these men appears to be
falling more and more. It might be said that their minds, filled
with all the dangers they have encountered, are obsessed by the
thought that the *Astrolabe* is fated not to see France again.'[1] When
d'Urville went on to Bourbon, where he stayed from 19 to 24
November, fourteen men had to be left behind at the hospital,
including Gaimard and Faraguet. 'If I were to stay ten days in
Bourbon,' said d'Urville, 'they would all finish in the hospital.'

[1] D'Urville, *Voyage*, vol. v, p. 537.

Things did not improve until the *Astrolabe* entered Atlantic waters after a brief stay at Cape Town. The year 1828 had been a hard one: when 1829 dawned, hope revived. The stops at St. Helena, Ascension, and Gibraltar were but brief episodes of no significance or interest in the voyage home; all the sailors cared about was Marseilles and Toulon. The former was reached on 25 March 1829. The large collections of natural-history specimens were unloaded and sent on to Paris. When this was done, the *Astrolabe* sailed for Toulon, where the men were paid off.

Thus ended the most important French expedition since that of La Pérouse. The results from the point of view of geography and science were very considerable. The islands of Totoya and Makutu in the Fiji group, as well as the great Astrolabe Reef off Vatu Lele, and Cannac Island near the Laughlans, were new discoveries; the Loyalty group had been explored with great thoroughness; the New Zealand coast, especially the southern part of Cook Strait, had been surveyed with similar care; everywhere the *Astrolabe* had sailed, elaborate charts had been prepared often in the face of great dangers. Peter Dillon's claims were fully confirmed and the mystery of La Pérouse's disappearance had been solved. So much material had been collected that the Museum found itself embarrassed by this unexpected wealth.[1] There were nearly 500 species of insects, mostly collected by d'Urville and Lottin; 525 sheets containing 3,350 drawings of a total of 1,263 animals; 900 samples of rock; nearly 1,600 botanical specimens, including many totally new ones collected in New Zealand. The Institute in its various sectional reports showered praise on the benefactors. Public opinion endorsed their views, in spite of a fairly heavy cost in men, which reflected the strain of a hard voyage: only fifty out of the original complement of seventy-nine had completed the voyage. But officialdom was slow in recognizing the merit of those who had taken part. D'Urville's main complaints had been with the delays that had occurred in granting the promotions he had asked for. La Pérouse, d'Entrecasteaux, and Baudin had had all their recommendations automatically ac-

[1] See Cuvier's report to the Académie des Sciences, 26 Oct. 1829, in d'Urville, *Voyage*, vol. i, p. xcix.

cepted, so that in fact it could be said that they had made their own promotions; but, although on arrival he had asked for advancement or honours for Jacquinot, Lottin, Guilbert, Bertrand, Sainson, and three of the men, nothing had been done; there was nothing for him either. Downright and outspoken to the point of rudeness, he was particularly indignant when he considered himself slighted.

People at the Ministry of Marine were almost indifferent about the achievements of the *Astrolabe*. They were not even sufficiently inquisitive to ask me about the accidents and manœuvres of our hard voyage and satisfy themselves that the claims I was making on behalf of my companions were well founded. The Ministry and the Institute, who saw in me neither a favourite nor indeed a creature, showed themselves very cold and casual. Only Mr. de Rossel, moved by a sense of justice that was natural to him and out of concern for the progress of navigation, and Mr. Tupinier, whose enlightened mind could better appreciate the importance of our work, took any active step on behalf of the *Astrolabe*.[1]

D'Urville's proud manner did not help his case. He had written to the Minister of Marine soon after his return: 'It is now up to Your Excellency to show to the learned men of Europe the value you are willing to place on such a work.'[2] But the Minister was no longer that Chabrol de Crousol under whose aegis Duperrey, Bougainville, and d'Urville had sailed, but Neuville de Hyde, who was perhaps more concerned with the current political instability than distant voyages; he took no action until just before he left office, on 8 August 1829, when he promoted d'Urville to the rank of *capitaine de vaisseau*—post captain—and finally approved the official publication of an account of the expedition 'on the most splendid scale'. Possibly there had been more prevarication than sinister plottings by jealous rivals, but d'Urville could not be persuaded that this was so. He undeniably had a gift for making enemies; Duperrey's friends blamed him in particular for having disparaged the earlier expedition: 'Mr. d'Urville was

[1] 'Conclusions et réflexions sur les voyages de découvertes', printed as an appendix to vol. v of d'Urville's *Voyage*, p. 589.
[2] Vergniol, *Dumont d'Urville*, pp. 105-6.

quite wrong to try to discredit the voyage of the *Coquille*', wrote Lesson.[1] 'No educated person will believe that the skies retained their splendour and their calm for the *Coquille* alone for a period of three years.' When Neuville's successor, the Baron d'Haussez, granted the remainder of d'Urville's recommendations, with the exception of Jacquinot's promotion (he received a medal instead) and the decorations requested for the crew, d'Urville continued to press for the balance to the point of importunity, whereupon the Minister's manner 'cooled markedly'. Even his own promotion was marred for him by the fact that Legoarant de Tromelin had also been promoted. 'So the Minister of Marine was placing the voyage of the *Bayonnaise* on the same footing as the *Astrolabe*'s; certain people even gave a clear preference to the former.'[2] The comment is unfair, for Tromelin was d'Urville's senior by seven years.

But by now d'Urville had other things on his mind. Rossel died in December 1829 after a long and distinguished career. This left a vacancy at the Institute, for which d'Urville allowed his name to be put forward. He was defeated by Baron Roussin, who had been an admiral since 1822 and was to be French ambassador in Constantinople and eventually Minister of Marine. D'Urville was bitterly disappointed: 'It was at first believed that I was sure of a large majority. But a powerful clique suddenly brought out an unexpected rival, and worked so well that he was elected by an immense majority.'[3] Among his enemies, d'Urville soon numbered François Arago, whom he accused of having disparaged his work on sea temperatures. There was little else for him to do now but devote himself to the task of writing the account of his voyage. 'I felt I was condemned to absolute obscurity and must think of nothing but my work of publication.' It was a monumental publication, which took him over five years; related accounts and especially his *Voyage pittoresque autour du monde* ensured him a wider public; even members of the Académie des Sciences realized as the volumes of the *Voyage* began to appear

[1] *Notice historique sur Dumont d'Urville*, pp. 94–5.
[2] D'Urville, *Voyage*, vol. v, p. 590 n.
[3] Ibid., vol. v, p. 592.

that they had underestimated his achievements. But the real reward for all his endeavours and undeniable talents was to be a second expedition to the Pacific, which established his reputation beyond anything his enemies—or he himself—could do to undermine it.

LAPLACE

AFTER d'Urville's first expedition, subtle changes which had been developing below the surface began to crystallize.

Exploration for its own sake, for science, for the advancement of geographical knowledge and of navigation, played a continually decreasing role. Scientific expeditions—indeed, expeditions of any type—became less frequent: there is a four-year gap between the return of Laplace in 1832 and Vaillant's departure in 1836, and of the subsequent expeditions d'Urville's of 1837–40 stands out as a lone voyage of exploration amidst a series of politically motivated undertakings. The rise of the propertied middle class, which had already made its power felt under Charles X, was completed under Louis-Philippe. Commercial activity in the Pacific after 1826[1] reflected the energy and determination of the mercantile class. Fourteen vessels from Bordeaux were sent to the South Seas in 1826 alone; forty-three sailed during the next three years; and, of course, others were dispatched from other ports. Among them were numbered the *Comète*, which went to Valparaiso, Callao, and Honolulu in 1827, the *Héros*, which completed a circumnavigation from 1826 to 1829 under Captain Duhaut-Cilly, as did the *Algérie* from Marseilles under Darlue, the *Péruvien* from Nantes, the *Romilly* under Beaufort, the *Duchesse de Berry* under Mioté. Roquefeuil's second-in-command, Salis, returned to the Pacific as captain of the *Péruvien* and later of the *Adhémar*. Mauruc in the *Courrier de Bordeaux* spent several years in the Pacific, going in particular to Tahiti—where he helped Moerenhout, later French consul in that island—and keeping a valuable record, now lost, of his navigation in the Tuamotus. The former Spanish colonies provided the basic market for these merchants, buying wines, clothes,

---

[1] Kotzebue mentions the presence of a Bordeaux trader at Honolulu in 1824, but does not name her. See *A New Voyage round the World*, vol. ii, p. 159. It is the only reference to French commercial activities there before 1826.

French perfumes, millinery, and even sugar from the French West Indies, in exchange mainly for precious minerals, but also for such local products as chinchilla, cinchona, and indigo. The islands of the Pacific provided an additional source of revenue, and, for those who could satisfactorily undertake the voyage, the Chinese market was often a valuable outlet.

Traders in distant, often strife-torn, lands needed protection. The promulgation in 1825 of a law 'for the safety of navigation and trade', largely drawn up by Portal, was symptomatic of growing concern for the interests of France's sea-borne trade. Admiral Rosamel had sailed for Chile and Peru the year before and by a judicious mixture of force and tact had assisted French traders who had fallen victim to piracy, a corrupt administration, and the aftermath of civil disorders. But diplomacy was the only satisfactory method to adopt in countries which had so recently shaken off colonial rule and would soon come to resent a show of force by foreign powers; consular representatives alone could serve the more permanent interests of France. The difficulty was that the appointment of consuls would entail *de facto* recognition of the new states—and this meant affronting Spain, with whom Charles X, a devout and ultra-conservative king, wished to maintain close relations. A compromise was found in the selection of agents-general and inspectors-general who were 'introduced' by commanders of naval units, instead of being officially appointed by the French Government. This fooled neither the Spanish, who protested violently, nor the local authorities, who often refused to recognize the representatives of a government unwilling to grant them an official commission. But it was an interim measure. In October 1827 Chaumette, then 'Inspector-General of French Trade', was appointed consul-general of France in Peru, and in the same year de la Forest was named consul-general in Chile.

The appointment of consuls-general in Peru and Chile certainly benefited our prestige and the defence of our commercial interests. In 1828 the captain of the *Moselle* declared: 'our consul seems more highly esteemed [by the Peruvian Government] than those of other nations'. When, in 1829, Danycan, commanding the *Durance*, arrived in Guayaquil where Bolivar was then living, the latter, having laid aside all his suspicions, welcomed him in a most flattering manner.[1]

Thus trade led to what was euphemistically called naval protection and to the establishment of naval stations, eventually replaced by permanent diplomatic representation; and, inevitably, it gave rise to thoughts of imperial expansion. In this France was not alone. By 1830 the British had completed the occupation of the Australian continent, establishing, sometimes painfully and impermanently, settlements on Melville Island, at Western Port, at King George Sound, and at the mouth of the Swan River. Meanwhile whalers, sealers, and sandalwood traders were setting up seasonal bases along the Australian and New Zealand coasts, spreading to Fiji, Tahiti, and Hawaii, crossing the path of American vessels, many of them from New England, sailing in search of the bounties which the Pacific trade seemed to offer. English missionaries were turning Tahiti into a focal point for protestant and British endeavours, becoming increasingly linked with Port Jackson, and helping to foster the emergence of Australia as a Pacific power. The Dutch were spreading eastwards to New Guinea and consolidating their hold on Sumatra, gaining the British ports on the west coast of that rich island in exchange for recognition of British preponderance in the Straits, where Singapore was rapidly becoming the key port in east-Asian trade. Further north, the Russians were attempting to perserve for themselves the entire Northern Pacific from the coast of northern Japan to the shores of southern Alaska. The struggle between the major powers still remained well below the surface, hidden by apparent preoccupations about the safety of navigation and the interests of geographical research; but complaints about the rights and proper treatment of nationals were becoming increasingly loud and pointed, whether from traders or from missionaries.

National interests were served in part by scientific and near-scientific expeditions, but it is interesting to note that between 1815 and 1830 France had led her rivals by sending out seven expeditions[2] to Russia's six, Britain's and America's three, and

[1] Faivre, *Expansion française*, p. 329.
[2] If one includes *Le Bordelais*, the other six being those of Freycinet, Duperrey,

Prussia's one, the latter distantly foreshadowing German penetration into the Pacific. Lord Byron had sailed to Hawaii in the *Blonde* in 1825, bearing the bodies of King Liholiho and his queen, who had died on their ill-fated visit to England; Captain Beechey in the *Blossom* had made a number of discoveries in the Tuamotus in 1826 before going on to Honolulu and the Bering Sea; but the major British expedition of the period was to be the voyage of the *Adventure* and the *Beagle* under Robert FitzRoy, which had the distinction of including Charles Darwin among its members.[1] Rather more commercial and expansionist were the voyages of the American brigs *Seraph* and *Annawan*, and of the *Vincennes*, in 1829–30. With John Downes's circumnavigation of 1831–4 in the *Potomac* and Charles Wilkes's voyage of exploration in the *Vincennes* in 1838–42, the United States displayed a greater awareness of the possibilities of scientific expeditions.[2] The Russians had to their credit—in addition to Kruzenstern's expedition of 1803–6—the great voyages of the *Rurik* and the *Nadesha* under Otto von Kotzebue in 1815–18 and of the *Predpriatie* in 1823–6, of the *Kamchatka* under Vasily Golovnin in 1817–18, of the *Vostok* and *Mirnyi* under Thaddeus Bellingshausen in 1819–21, and of the *Senyavin* and the *Möller* under Fedor Lütke in 1826–9—none of them the result of pure altruism since imperialist considerations were not absent, but each one without doubt a notable contribution to science and exploration.

Thus, in the first quarter of the nineteenth century, exploration was becoming gradually tinged with expansionist policies. Greater knowledge of the Pacific, coupled with considerable advances in navigation, shipbuilding, and marine hygiene, had opened the way for occupation and colonization. In Paris, permanent civil servants such as Fileau St-Hilaire, *directeur des colonies* at the Ministry of Marine from 1826 to 1842, and Catineau-Laroche, head of the trade section at the Ministry of the Interior

---

Bougainville, d'Urville, Tromelin, and Laplace. There were in addition purely commercial expeditions.

[1] The Pacific section of the voyage belongs to the 1831–6 period.

[2] While not losing sight of expansionist opportunities, as Jore vehemently argued in *Océan Pacifique*, vol. i, pp. 361–2.

from 1826 to 1828, actively promoted a policy which for reasons of diplomacy the Government could not openly espouse. Commercial interests, government officials, and politicians all proceeded with caution. There was little hope of gaining a foothold in South America, and the opportunities further north were only slightly greater, for France would then clash with American and British interests; but there seemed to be some possibility in the Hawaiian Islands. There the impetus was given less by traders than by missionaries—for the religious fervour of Charles X, coupled with a genuine revival which spread through much of Europe in the 1820s and the missionary zeal of Pope Gregory XVI, proved as effective in distant fields as it was to be disastrous at home. The King's clericalism may have cost him his throne, but neither his successor, Louis-Philippe, nor, indeed, later governments with decided anti-clerical views were to withdraw their support from French missionaries overseas. Expansion and colonialism were to be based on the twin pillars of commerce and religion. In each case the immediate consideration was assistance to French nationals faced with the opposition and arbitrary actions of native populations or of other Europeans (either trade rivals or missionaries belonging to non-Catholic groups); but the ultimate consequence, which was annexation or attempted annexation, expressed the views on colonial expansion which France held under Charles X, who initiated the conquest of Algeria, and Louis-Philippe, who completed it. Traditional spheres of influence were retained and, if possible, strengthened: this was the case, in time, with Indo-China. But new opportunities were not neglected. The departure of Legoarant de Tromelin for Hawaii in 1828 proves this. Tromelin—who was to return to the Pacific as admiral commanding the French naval station—was then in Callao with his corvette *La Bayonnaise* which formed part of the French naval unit stationed in South America. He was instructed to return to France by way of the Sandwich Islands and Vanikoro. He was to examine the political situation in the islands and report on the position of French residents who had recently settled there; an attempted agricultural and trading settlement having failed, these now consisted of a group of missionaries who had landed a bare eight months before *La Bayonnaise*'s arrival in Honolulu on 21 March 1828.

I paid a visit to the small group of French Catholic missionaries who came to this island a few months ago in the ship *La Comète*. It consists of three priests and three workmen [lay brothers] one of whom devotes his time to agriculture. The Director tells me that at first he laboured under great difficulties; that at the instigation of a missionary belonging to another religion, an attempt was made to refuse them permission to stay in the island and that it would not have been granted without the generous intervention of the British and American consuls, but that now their situation was improving day by day, and they are satisfied of their undertaking and are hopeful of achieving some success.[1]

Tromelin wrote a number of other reports during his month's stay, expressing confidence in the future of the mission, if not in the Sandwich Islands as a place for a possible settlement. He paid a number of official calls: on Queen Kaahumanu Kamehameha's widow; on Boki, the Governor of Oahu; and, of course, on the British and American consuls. It was enough at this point to survey the position and show the flag, for the *Bayonnaise* was only the second French naval vessel to visit the islands—after Freycinet's *Uranie*— and only the fifth French ship. 'I think that I am entitled to tell Your Excellency', he wrote to the Minister on 15 April, 'that the visit of the *Bayonnaise* to Honolulu has shown with honour the King's flag and helped in no small way to create a good opinion of our Nation and of the respect due to the flag of the Sovereign by whom she has the good fortune of being governed.'[2] Yet the impression he made was much slighter than he imagined. Almost no trace remained of Freycinet's visit—Kalanimoku, whom Quélen had baptized, was now dead, and his brother Boki, although still a friend of France, had become a protestant. As the French missionaries began to gather converts around them, their American colleagues put pressure on the queen regent to forbid her people from attending any Catholic ceremony: the

[1] Tromelin to Minister of Marine, quoted in Jore, *Océan Pacifique*, vol. ii, p. 19.
[2] Ibid., vol. ii, p. 20.

law was promulgated by Boki himself on 4 August 1829—less than sixteen months after Tromelin's departure. Thus began a long struggle for religious freedom and for the recognition of the rights of French residents, tinged with hopes of eventual annexation, in which Laplace, Vaillant, and Tromelin himself, among others, were to be involved.[1]

Tromelin sailed, feeling satisfied and confident, on 17 April 1828; he went south to Fanning Island, which he surveyed from 28 April to 2 May, then on to Rotuma, where he stayed for three days—from 26 to 29 May—and to Tikopia, reaching Vanikoro on 17 June. Both Dillon and d'Urville had long since departed and little remained to be done. He questioned a few natives, visited the place where the wreck had occurred, and added a plaque to d'Urville's monument. He returned home by way of Guam, Buru, Timor, and Bourbon, where he took on Gaimard, the *Astrolabe*'s surgeon who had been left behind on account of ill health. He was back in Toulon on 19 March 1829.

The voyage of the *Bayonnaise* had been motivated partly by the situation in the Sandwich Islands, and partly by Dillon's discoveries at Vanikoro. The Laplace expedition, on the other hand, was related to Hyacinthe de Bougainville's, which it resembled and was to complement. The spur was the desire to re-establish French influence over Indo-China: the Pacific was to assume importance only if Laplace, like Bougainville, elected to return home by way of Cape Horn. The route laid down in a letter from the Minister of Marine, Baron d'Haussez, dated 15 December 1829, was to take Laplace to Tenerife, Bourbon, and Pondicherry, thence through the Straits of Malacca to the Anambas, which Bougainville had brought to the notice of the authorities and which in spite of appearances warranted further exploration; from the near-by Natunas the expedition was to sail to Cochin-China, Hainan, and Macao, to Manila for a refitting, back to the Natunas, to Samarang or Surabaya, and to Timor, where the captain would decide his own return itinerary. The draft instructions based on this outline added dates: Laplace was to reach

[1] See *infra*, chapters on Laplace and Vaillant.

Pondicherry by 1 April 1830; if he selected the Pacific route, he
was to make for Hobart and Port Jackson, tarrying there no later
than June 1831, and sail either north or south of New Zealand,
or through Cook Strait, to Valparaiso. The 'Mémoire portant
instructions pour la campagne'[1] was the work of Daussy, the
Navy's chief hydrographer, and was checked by Beautemps-
Beaupré; but hydrographic work was only incidental. The
verification of a number of longitudes was prescribed almost as
a matter of course—the same duties would have been expected
from any naval vessel on an official mission. What was more
important was to show the flag in eastern and other waters, and
to protect French traders whenever any of them were in need of
assistance. The hold was no longer filled with trinkets to amuse
natives and buy supplies from them, but with 'luxury weapons,
clocks and jewellery, porcelain, crystal ware and other products
of French manufacture, which it was desirable to make known
in far-away countries'. At every port of call, Laplace was to
obtain information of value to merchants, such as customs and
harbour regulations, conditions of entry for French and European goods, types of products most likely to find a market, local
goods one could obtain by barter, and the time of the year most
suitable for trading operations. In Cochin-China he was to give
support to Eugène Chaigneau, who, after his voyage to Vanikoro
with Dillon, had returned to France, but was now about to sail
in the *S. Michel* with the title of royal vice-consul. If he found that
Chaigneau had been accepted by the authorities, he was to show
him every mark of respect so as to strengthen his position; if not,
he was to find out the reason. Finally, almost as an afterthought,
the officers were encouraged to carry out work of interest to
natural history. Laplace may also have been given secret instructions—they are crossed out in the original, but whether this was
because they were cancelled or simply to prevent their inclusion
in the official account is not clear: 'It would be most useful to
know, in the many archipelagoes one finds in the middle of these
seas, about points which are not yet under occupation, and where
naval vessels could gather . . . in order to sail together on an

[1] In Laplace, *Voyage*, vol. i, pp. xvii–xxv.

expedition . . . to neighbouring areas. That is the particular value of an exact description of the anchorages and ports of the Anambas and Natunas.'[1]

Cyrille-Pierre-Théodore Laplace had already behind him a long career which justified the confidence the Minister placed in him. He had the unusual distinction of having been born at sea, on 7 November 1793; he had joined the Navy as *aspirant* during the Empire and had fought in the Indian and Atlantic Oceans and in the West Indies. He had been promoted to *lieutenant de vaisseau* in 1823 and to *capitaine de frégate* in 1828; cited as 'full of zeal and highly resourceful', he had been given the Cross of St. Louis in 1825. He had in addition the good fortune of being the brother-in-law of the *directeur des ports et arsenaux*, of that very Baron Tupinier whom d'Urville had praised for his sympathetic attitude towards the *Astrolabe* expedition. Through him and through other colleagues, Laplace was able to obtain adequate supplies—six months' ammunition, spares of all kinds for one year, food for seven months, wine for seven, and water for four. He had been given a free hand in the selection of his officers: Verdier, his second-in-command; Frederic Sholten, a Danish officer; Edmond de Boissieu, who had sailed with Bougainville in the *Thétis*; Edmond-François Pâris, who had also sailed with Bougainville and was to return to the Pacific in the *Artémise* and reach the rank of rear-admiral. Adolphe Thiers, one day to be elected President of the Third Republic, applied to join the expedition as official historian, but a sudden worsening in the political situation changed his mind for him—the distant South Seas were no place for a promising young politician when there was a crisis at home. The total complement, including surgeons, the artist Barthélémy Lauvergne, petty officers, sailors, cooks, and servants, was 177. Nine others would be taken on in Chile and Cochin-China. Twenty-one were to die or be left behind on account of illness. The corvette allocated for the expedition was *La Favorite*, of 680 tons, carrying 24 guns; she was quite new, having been launched in Toulon on 11 June 1829. After a trial cruise to Sardinia and Italy in August, and some delay caused by the troubles in Greece, which gave rise

---

[1] Quoted in Faivre, *Expansion française*, p. 262.

to the possibility of direct French intervention, she sailed from Toulon on 30 December 1829.

Laplace met none of d'Urville's initial setbacks, for he took only a week to reach Gibraltar and sail through the Straits into the Atlantic. The Peak of Tenerife was sighted a few days later, but the wind was weak and inconstant, so he decided to make instead for the French settlement at Gorée in Senegal, a region he knew well, having spent a number of years there in command of a schooner. After a week there, he continued on his way south, crossing the Equator on 4 February and sighting the Cape of Good Hope on 6 March. The weather was menacing, with strong north-westerly winds, a cloud-laden sky, and high seas, and he found it wiser to omit the scheduled stop in Cape Town and proceed without delay to Île Bourbon. The *Favorite* was then forced south by the winds almost to the fortieth degree of latitude (15 March) and slowly made her way back to the low thirties, where, on the 28th, she was struck by a hurricane. Reaching Bourbon on 1 April, the French realized that they had been on the edge of the storm, which, striking the island with all its fury, had destroyed plantations and homes. Two days later the approach of another hurricane sent the *Favorite* out to sea in great haste, abandoning an anchor and a chain cable. Laplace went to Mauritius for a few days, Port-Louis being a much safer haven for shipping. He found considerable dissatisfaction among the people, for not only was British rule resented, but there were serious economic problems due, in the main, to over-production of sugar coinciding with a sudden collapse of the world market price. The position in Bourbon was little better, but good prices for coffee provided some compensation; Bourbon anyhow had never been as prosperous as her sister isle, so that the fall in living standards was less drastic, and there was naturally no serious political problem, no occupation by a former enemy power. There was the irritant of a trade ban between the two islands, but the residents of Bourbon could make up for this by trading with near-by Madagascar, where French influence was continuing to make itself felt. Indeed, the people he visited on his return talked above all of a recent attempt by the French to establish a base on

Madagascar. A frigate from the Brazilian station, the *Terpsichore*, under Captain Goubeyre, had sailed from Bourbon in August with the transport *Madagascar*, the sloop *Colibri*, the storeships *Infatigable* and *Chevrette*, and the *Zélée* of later Pacific fame. The division had succeeded in occupying the port of Tintingue, but Queen Ranavalona had refused to grant any concessions, and in time the French, decimated by sickness, had withdrawn.

All this Laplace set down in the reports he prepared at Bourbon almost daily as his officers supervised the loading of supplies— no easy task in St. Denis, where the port facilities had always been inadequate. The difficulty of communicating with the shore led to tragedy: two sailors attempted to desert by swimming ashore—sharks killed one; the other was injured when the surf threw him against the rocks. And Laplace was unable to recover the anchor he had lost. On 1 May 1830 he sailed for India.

His first hydrological task, as set down in his instructions, was to check the position of the Île de Sable, a sandbank in latitude 150° 53′ which had first achieved notoriety in 1767 when the *Utile* had been wrecked on it. This done, he went on to Mahé in the Seychelles, another former French possession. A pleasant six days were spent in this quiet place which provided a plentiful supply of fruit and helped the growing number of sick to recover; but another anchor was lost, caught and broken in the coral. There was worse trouble ahead. The *Favorite* sailed through the Maldives and along the east coast of Ceylon, reaching Pondicherry on 9 June for a stay of ten days. Here as elsewhere Laplace observed, asked questions, and filled his notebooks with information on the trade and customs of the city. A few days later he was doing the same in Madras, where he was also able to buy two anchors and a cable to make up for his recent losses. He left on 28 June; on the night of the 29th the *Favorite*, running too close to the land, grounded on a mudbank.

This first moment was terrible. The night was dark, the breeze, which was very fresh, increased the strength of the waves which broke on the bar around us, making a frightening noise. The rudder, torn from its braces, made us fear for our poop over which the sea was crashing furiously. I felt, in these critical circumstances, how an organized body of men helps to enforce discipline and always retains a valuable unity: there was not the slightest disorder or the least uncertainty among the crew; my orders were carried out in silence and with remarkable speed; the sails were furled in a flash and everything was put in order . . . the corvette's gentle motion, followed by her stillness, had told me from the start that she was grounded in mud: I then felt hopeful of getting her out of this unfortunate predicament. Dawn, so ardently awaited, finally broke: before us, two miles to the north, lay a very low sandy coastline, almost drowned by the waters of a river whose mouth, not far distant, I could clearly see on our right.[1]

Getting the ship off was not easy. In the late afternoon an attempt was made with two anchors and the help of the high tide, but although she moved she did not come off. The night presented dangers, lessened by the anchors which prevented her from settling further into the bank. In the morning Indian fishermen arrived in a catamaran and Boissieu was sent ashore with them to seek help. Meanwhile a second unsuccessful attempt was made to refloat the corvette, held fast by a quantity of mud which every breaker increased. The next day Boissieu was seen approaching with two fishing-boats, but the Indians were not prepared to risk crossing the bar in such heavy seas and they all went back. It was not until 6 July that enough help arrived to make another—and successful—attempt to free the ship. Three days later, the slight damage she had sustained was made good, although a large anchor had been lost in the mud.

Laplace called briefly at Mazulipatam to thank the British authorities, who, having learnt, rather late, of his mishaps, had sent an offer of assistance. He went on to the French port of Yanaon, but decided not to visit Calcutta as he had now wasted more time than he could afford and was anxious to reach the China Sea before the onset of the typhoon season. He sailed from India on 2 August, rapidly crossed to the Straits of Malacca, thanks to the south-west monsoon, called briefly at Malacca, and obtained a pilot for the rest of the journey to Singapore, where he arrived on 17 August. Once more he made notes on the town, its trade and administration, and its masters, whom he found to be,

---

[1] Laplace, *Voyage*, vol. i, p. 257.

as in India, a solemn and dull crowd. Meeting the best people
at an official reception was usually more soporific than relaxing:
'Interminable sonatas on the piano and arias from English grand
opera amused me but slightly and did not in the least cause the
cold and unprepossessing countenances around me to unbend.'[1]
He left on the 25th and, leaving the exploration of the Anambas
until later, crossed the South China Sea in cloudy and stormy
weather; it did not improve during most of his stay in Manila,
which lasted from 8 September to 1 November. A number of
officers and men developed colds and fevers, some becoming
dangerously ill. Even the chief surgeon Eydoux was affected, but
he continued his work with the assistance of Laplace himself.
When things improved on board, they worsened on land: cholera
was diagnosed, spreading from the slums to the better residential
quarters. 'Every hour the convent bells told us of a new death or
of another funeral; our own misfortunes forced us to see to our
own safety: on 28 September a young and vigorous sailor, whose
health had so far been excellent, died within three hours of an
attack of cholera.' He was the only victim from the *Favorite*; the
epidemic abated just as Laplace was about to sail to a healthier
place. Within a matter of days the city passed from a mood of
sorrow and panic to one of wild celebration: a new archbishop
was being consecrated. It was an occasion for rejoicing, possibly
too for thanksgiving on the part of those who had survived.
There were fireworks displays, illuminations, parties of all
kinds. The Spaniards of Manila were far less sombre than the
British in Singapore—the contrast was almost too great for
Laplace, who was shocked by the worldly behaviour of the
monks, especially the Augustinians—although these had a special
reason for celebrating, since the new archbishop belonged to their
order. 'The regimental band was playing alternately waltzes and
quadrilles. I noticed, in a large side room, the officers and the
élèves of the *Favorite* teaching the steps and figures to some young
Augustinian brothers . . . I returned, but alone, to my carriage,
thinking very seriously about people's strange customs and deciding for the hundredth time that one should be surprised at nothing

[1] Laplace, *Voyage*, vol. i, pp. 342–3.

in this world.' He had been courteously received by the Governor and by the Governor-elect, General Henrile, and he felt confident of the success of his mission as far as helping French traders was concerned:

[The goodwill of the Governor] proved auspicious for the affairs of several French merchants, including a shipowner from Bourbon for whom I obtained a special favour which altered completely the outcome of his voyage. The services I was able to render to our commerce seem to show how soundly based are the continual claims of our merchants for the protection of warships in these distant countries, where arbitrary decisions and temporary gains often cause customs and duties to be changed several times a year. This lack of stability, which could be made to operate in favour of our trade, works nearly always to its disadvantage if it is allowed to go on unchecked.[1]

The visit to Canton, next on his programme, was to be equally successful. The *Favorite* sailed from Manila on 1 November 1830 and anchored in Macao on the 21st after a notably rough crossing. Laplace went to Canton with Sholten and Boissieu to discuss with the authorities the difficulties which some French traders were struggling against, especially in the face of British near-monopolies. He had lunch on board the *Castle Huntly*, which was then loading for the United Kingdom, spent the night at the French consul's house, and the next day attended a ceremonial Chinese multi-course dinner, coping valiantly with ivory chopsticks and innumerable toasts. As usual he took copious notes on everything he saw—the food, the clothes, the customs, even the music. After a few days he sent back his two officers and was then joined by Eydoux, Pâris, and another lieutenant, Gustave Serval. He had written to the local viceroy to thank him for having punished a band of pirates who had attacked the crew of the French vessel *Le Navigateur*, and at the same time to ask for most-favoured-nation terms on behalf of French merchants. A couple of weeks elapsed before the reply arrived, but when it came it was couched in unusually courteous language, the Chinese granting without any difficulty the conditions the French traders were

---

[1] Ibid., vol. i, p. 452.

seeking. Thus Laplace had every reason to be satisfied with his
stay in Canton, which had lasted twenty-two days; the Chinese
obviously were pleased by the possibility of using the French as
a counter to growing British power in the East.

On 18 December the *Favorite* sailed for Indo-China almost due
south, then south-west past the coast of Hainan and on across to
Tourane, where she arrived on the 21st. Now Laplace was to
meet the first of a series of setbacks. In the first place, instead of
finding the *S. Michel* at anchor, he found only her crew, 'short of
everything, affected by sickness and all kinds of privations, a
victim of the insolence of the local authorities'. The *S.Michel* had
been wrecked on arrival, and Laplace was compelled to cram all
the survivors as best he could into the already cramped quarters
of the *Favorite*. 'It is sad to have to add that, in spite of all the
cares lavished on them, several died as a result of the hardships
they had suffered earlier or of illnesses caught in an unhealthy
country; the others vied in zeal and devotion with their comrades
from the *Favorite* and I have always reckoned them among my
best sailors.'[1] Unfortunately, shipwrecked and landing in a foreign
country without supplies and gifts, compelled even to buy
clothes from local merchants, Chaigneau had lost face as soon as
he struggled ashore. The mandarin in charge of foreign relations
had contemptuously rejected his credentials and made it plain
that he tolerated his presence at Tourane purely as an act of kindness and only until an opportunity arose of his being taken off
by a foreign ship.

Almost from the start, the presence of the *Favorite* worried the
authorities. They were already suspicious of foreign powers and
were endeavouring to seal their country against outside visitors.
The *Favorite* was an imposing warship, with a large crew
strengthened by the men from the *S. Michel*. The situation was
complicated by the large-scale buying of supplies, not just for
the daily needs of the two hundred Frenchmen, but as a reserve
for the long voyage ahead. The mandarins, amazed at the quantities of stores being taken in, suspected that a large army was
concealed in the hold. In consequence, soldiers were brought to

[1] Laplace, *Voyage*, vol. ii, p. 267.

Tourane to watch every move the visitors made and contain them along a part of the shore and outside the city. And in time, news came from Hué in reply to Laplace and Chaigneau's messages:

I received official notice that a leading mandarin, who was the King's favourite, had arrived at Tourane to discuss with me the reasons for my stay in Cochin-China. A large wooden hangar hung with mats, a kind of common house which occupies the centre of nearly every Cochin-Chinese village, was selected as the meeting place and surrounded by troops brought from several parts of the province to act as a guard of honour for the sovereign's envoy. . . . I had to struggle against a host of obstacles: I countered guile and duplicity with frankness and firmness; but as the King of Cochin-China's policy towards the English . . . was an unsurmountable obstacle to the success of my negotiations, every argument I could put forward simply caused additional worry to the court at Hué about this present danger, and prevented it from deciding in favour of a nation of whose power it was unaware, and which being in fact still too weak in these distant seas could only send belated and inadequate assistance. The meeting perforce concluded fairly coolly, since neither side was satisfied; however, to remove any likelihood of my appearing dissatisfied, I accepted the bullocks, pigs, and poultry, as well as the jars of local wine, which were offered me on behalf of the King.[1]

Laplace's protestations of friendship and his request for a reconsideration of Chaigneau's rejection as French consul were sent to Hué. Meanwhile there was nothing for it but to wait, watched and followed at every turn by the local soldiery. Almost the only event to break the monotony was the departure for Singapore of the captain and officers of the S. *Michel* in a corvette belonging to the Emperor,

who must have felt most satisfied at having her in such good hands since several of his ships, no doubt unable to find their way in the straits, were failing to return. This vessel was due to exchange her cargo of sugar in Batavia for diamonds and pearls, and if possible a steam ship—the latest whim of the Emperor who, according to his travelling mandarins, had thought of this method for transporting more rapidly from Hué to Tourane and to other parts of his kingdom his floating

[1] Ibid., vol. ii, pp. 337, 341-2.

harem, a sort of Noah's ark in which he places his women when they
follow him on his maritime excursions.[1]

The preparations for this voyage and the ceremonial surrounding
the departure provided entertainment for a whole day. A trip
ashore, organized in great secrecy to foil the watching guards,
supplied a little more relief a few days later, but nearly ended in
tragedy. Two boatloads of officers and men left early in the
morning with Chaigneau as interpreter in case of need. The
weather was fine in spite of a fresh breeze, and the plan was to
row up a small river a little distance off and picnic by the Marble
Mountains, five high rocks jutting out above a peninsula. When
Laplace's boat reached the river mouth it was swamped by high
waves breaking over low sandbanks; the sailors just managed to
get it ashore, but the incident had alerted the neighbourhood and
all hope of privacy had to be abandoned.

   Minh-Mang's attitude showed no sign of relaxation; his
xenophobic policy, justified by the desire to defend Cochin-China
from the kind of fate threatening Burma and China, could not be
relaxed even in favour of France, in whom his father had found
an ally in times of trouble. No doubt the Emperor remembered
that Gia-Long, while urging him to be friendly with the French,
had also warned him to grant no extra-territorial rights and no
trading privileges to any European nation. Unfortunately for the
country, his persecution of Christians, soon to be intensified, was
eventually to produce the very result he was striving to avoid.
Laplace decided to leave, his diplomatic mission a total failure;
but the stay itself had not been a complete waste of time. The
crew had been refreshed, less perhaps by relaxation ashore than
by the boredom which inaction engendered, making them now
eager to sail forth into lesser-known seas; firewood and water
supplies had been replenished; and Pâris had completed a detailed
plan of Tourane Bay 'as handsome a piece of work as it was
useful'. Furthermore, by sailing north into the Gulf of Tonkin,
on 24 January, Laplace hoped to gather more geographical
knowledge, as these waters were by no means well known to

[1] Laplace, *Voyage*, vol. ii, p. 350.

Europeans. It was his intention 'to devote the month of February, the only time my mission allowed me to spend on this kind of work, to drawing up a map [of the gulf], but unhappily insurmountable obstacles prevented us from undertaking this task, which might have been of such value to navigation, and I abandoned it only when squalls, which were greatly imperilling the corvette on those wild shores, had made me lose every hope of success'.[1]

The *Favorite* therefore turned back to Tourane Bay, where she put in for wood and water, greatly alarming the Cochin-Chinese authorities, who thought they had got rid of the French for good. Attempts to buy food in Tourane market were hampered by continual harassment by the local mandarins, who forbade merchants to sell them either pigs or bullocks. Laplace's patience was at an end and the need for diplomacy was gone: he threatened to send an immediate message to the Emperor complaining of discourtesy and provocations. Almost magically, oxen, pigs, and ducks filled the market place, and rice spilled in abundance at the feet of the officers.

On 5 March the expedition sailed for the south without any pangs of regret. A week later, the Natunas came into sight, a long and narrow stretch of land to the south-west. Close to, they looked unattractive: a barren coast surrounded by reefs over which the sea broke angrily, rising to low wooded hills shrouded in misty rain. It was Shrove Tuesday and the crew, leaving Pâris to chart the area as best he could, celebrated the traditional carnival with games, a special dinner, and extra rations of wine. The weather cleared on the Wednesday, enabling Pâris to complete his survey of the northern group, but the fog returned as the *Favorite* approached Great Natuna. At one stage the channel ahead seemed to be closed off by reefs. Boissieu climbed aloft to direct operations. He found a clear but narrow passage between the main reefs which line the coast of the various islands as far as the eye could see. Only the calls of the men who were sounding and the crash of the waves over the reefs broke the deep silence which fell over the ship at this moment. The depth decreased

[1] Ibid., vol. ii, p. 364.

gradually to thirty feet, then began to increase: they were through. The *Favorite* entered a maze of small islands, which had the effect of reducing the swell. Laplace was able to anchor in safety, as the setting sun transformed the appearance of the barren islands about him, creating 'a scene of enchantment'. Naming the channel 'Canal de la Favorite', the French proceeded with their hydrographical work. Boatloads of islanders now began to circle the ship, coming in the main from one of the smaller islands. Laplace landed with Chaigneau and called on the local headman, whom they found surrounded by 'a large number of individuals whose appearance inspired in my companion and me some anxious thoughts', but the reception was friendly and marked by gifts of coconuts and by local songs, and the village, set in greenery, was most attractive. The French returned to their ship with the chief, only to find the *Favorite* crowded with natives who proved difficult to dislodge, as they all claimed to belong to the chief's bodyguard. Laplace was rather concerned, owing to the Malays' reputation for piracy, but gifts of swords and bead necklaces established the friendliest relations and the visitors departed without difficulty. Trading carried out in his absence had resulted in useful purchases of fowls, ducks, and goats. Pleased with both the islanders' welcome and the pleasant appearance of the island, the French named it Île Belle.[1] They sailed at dawn on the 18th, entering 'the two-mile-wide channel separating the south-west point of Great Natuna from a group of islands to which I gave the name of Îles Duperré in the honour of the admiral who had just shed new lustre on the name of the French Navy at the siege of Algiers'.[2] The channel itself was named after Laplace. The *Favorite* sailed slowly through it to enable the officers to complete their charts, then proceeded eastwards along the south coast of Great Natuna. The survey was completed by the evening of 22 March, when Laplace steered west-north-west to seek the Anambas.

These came into view the next morning. The plan was to

[1] It is situated at the mouth of the wide Binjai river in Great Natuna.
[2] *Voyage*, vol. ii, p. 399. The name has remained. Duperré (1775–1846) had already had a glorious career under Napoleon.

enlarge on Bougainville's work, following 'his fine example', and paying particular attention to the central and western islands which the earlier expedition had been unable to survey. The first day was devoted to the determination of the positions of the northernmost points, thus tying Bougainville's work with the

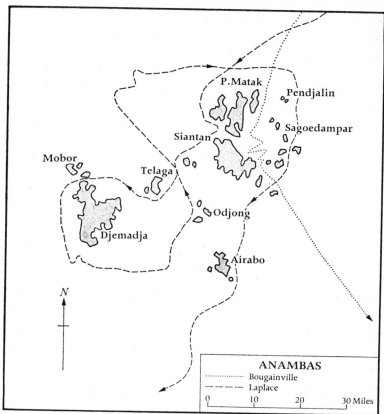

Map 8. Anambas. Tracks of Bougainville and Laplace

new; then the *Favorite*, struggling against a south-westerly current, made for western Siantan. The islanders, it was noted, drove harder bargains in their dealings with the visitors, a consequence of easier and more frequent intercourse with traders in Singapore. Laplace, again accompanied by Chaigneau, made an official call on a local village chief who claimed to be the nephew of the Sultan of Rhio, titular lord of the Anambas and Natunas. Laplace presented him with a pair of pistols in a case, although the chief coveted a watch which, however, the Frenchman could not spare. From Siantan, he sailed south of Pulo Telaga, the central group of islets, and towards Djemadja, where he anchored for the night. The weather had so far been magnificent, but on the 28th the wind rose and the sky filled with clouds. There was time, nevertheless, to complete the survey of the central group, which he named Îles de Rigny 'in honour of the admiral under whose orders the French naval forces had fought at Navarino'.[1] On 4 April, his work finished and his supplies dwindling—there was only enough food for twelve days—he sailed south-east for Karimata Strait and Surabaya. As the *Favorite* neared the Equator the breezes weakened and the heat was magnified by the sea, which, now mirror-like, reflected the sun. Laplace took advantage of the corvette's slow progress to have the exterior repainted 'so as to maintain with honour the reputation of our Navy in Surabaya roadstead'. Pulo Karimata was sighted on the 6th and three days later the expedition entered the Java Sea. Almost another week went by before they reached Surabaya.

Laplace was disappointed to find that once more—as in Manila —there were no dispatches for him from Paris. But there was news from France, startling news indeed: Charles X had been overthrown by the July Revolution which had brought Louis-Philippe to the throne, an upheaval by no means kindly regarded by other European Governments. Laplace found himself faced with the difficulty of discovering from the limited information available to a foreign visitor in the Dutch East Indies whether it was safe for him to declare his support for the July monarchy, or whether a counter-revolution was likely to bring the legitimate Bourbons back to the throne before the *Favorite* reached France. There was no possibility of equivocating, for the Revolution had also overthrown the Bourbon flag.

Our situation had nothing reassuring about it: the conflicting reports I kept receiving on such extraordinry events, the rumours which illwill

---

[1] Henri-Daniel de Rigny (1782–1835). The name did not remain.

and fear magnified, at first caused me considerable worry: the *Favorite* with just a few days' supplies on board was in the midst of territories which belonged to a nation that was displeased, which believed itself to be on the verge of declaring war on France, and displayed both jealousy and coolness towards us. However, I had to preserve the corvette for France, which may change her institutions and her sovereign, but must always remain her children's true fatherland. I waited for news from Batavia, the chief administrative centre of the colony; and when I became convinced that the French Government, by sending no instructions or orders of any sort, had fully entrusted me with the fate of the *Favorite*, I ordered the tricolour to be flown from all masts: it was raised to the sound of gunfire and of cheers from the crew who, from that moment on, were charged with defending it against every enemy . . .[1]

Politically this was a sound decision, but it did not gain Laplace the sympathy of the Dutch merchants, who believed that a European war involving the new French Government was inevitable. It was only when French traders came forward to accept his bills of exchange that he was able to obtain the food and refreshments he needed so badly. As might be expected, life in Surabaya had nothing to offer to the officers, who found themselves virtually ostracized. The only social event of the stay was a visit to the Sultan of Bangkalan in early May. Laplace stayed three days as the Sultan's guest with Pâris, Eydoux, Sholten, and two *élèves*. When the rounds of banquets and dancing displays were completed, the Sultan and his suite came on board the corvette. But Surabaya was still an unhealthy place. Dysentery had made its appearance, and the number of sick was growing rapidly. The *Favorite* sailed on 10 May, struggling through Madura Strait in the face of easterlies which forced the men to remain on duty too long for their health. A five-day halt was made at Besuki on the north-east coast of Java, where Laplace was able to obtain water, bullocks, sheep, and fruit, but waited in vain for a shipment of wine he had ordered from Samarang. The epidemic was worsening—a young sailor 'whom a gentle nature and good behaviour had endeared to his superiors as well as to his comrades' died soon after their

[1] *Voyage*, vol. iii, pp. 2–3.

departure from Besuki. Entering Bali Strait at the end of the month, Laplace anchored in Banjuwangy.

The day before our departure, the chief caulker, a good and strongly-built man, died within a few moments of cholera. Others suffered from dizziness, with violent headaches and nausea. The number of dysentery cases kept on increasing, several officers were sick, I myself had to fight against upsets of varying seriousness, and yet we had to undertake a long and difficult crossing of the southern ocean during the winter of these stormy regions. It was under sad auspices that the *Favorite* sailed on the morning of 1 June to complete the journey through the strait. Contrary winds and calms forced her to go back and forth from the sandy and deserted shores of this part of Java to the dark mountainous coast of Bali.[1]

Finally, on the evening of 2 June, the *Favorite* was out of sight of land. Laplace aimed to make for Hobart as quickly as he could, but easterly winds and heavy seas delayed him and forced him off course. As the expedition approached the higher latitudes, cold and rain made conditions increasingly unpleasant. Morale began to break:

Most [of the men] young and with no experience of their trade were depressed by the slightest indisposition and at once gave up hope of ever seeing their homeland again. The death of one sailor often brought about the death of his friend, the latter falling into a deep melancholy and a real stupor. In vain did I use every means of consolation and encouragement: the unhappy youth soon reached the last stages of homesickness, without appearing to be suffering from any other illness, and then died in a matter of hours from an attack of dysentery. Each day was marked by another loss; and as the large number of sick did not allow us to take the precautions customary on board a warship in such circumstances, the unfortunate victim died almost under the eyes of his companions who were affected by the same illness; and the few men who were still in a fit state to be on watch at night were present, in spite of all we did to prevent them, when the last respects were paid to the dead.[2]

Sixty men were unfit for any duty, many others were in a weakened condition, supplies were running out—all the fresh food obtained in Java had been exhausted—medical supplies were

---

[1] *Voyage*, vol. iii, p. 132.   [2] Ibid., vol. iii, pp. 135-6.

dwindling. Laplace could not understand why things were so bad. There were daily inspections to ensure cleanliness; braziers were kept burning between decks to reduce the humidity; Eydoux, the surgeon, although affected as well, devotedly tended the sick. The drinking-water, kept in iron casks, had a slight flavour of iron oxide, but the men drank it mixed only with lemon juice or brandy. The only reasons he could find for their low powers of resistance were weariness and the fact that the wine ration had had to be cut by two-thirds. At the beginning of July, however, beyond the fortieth parallel, the winds at last turned westerly and the corvette began to speed towards Hobart. The Mewstone was sighted on the 6th, but the winds moderated and veered northerly just as the expedition was preparing to enter d'Entrecasteaux Channel. Two men died as the ship lay at anchor outside Storm Bay; they were buried on Bruny Island. Then on 11 July the *Favorite* was at last able to enter the channel and reach Hobart. The next day all the sick were taken to hospital. Those who were fit were able to relax and enjoy the hospitality of the local citizens, whom they found courteous but somewhat solemn and dull. But dysentery continued its ravages; three deaths occurred in the hospital, and Laplace decided to seek the warmer climate of New South Wales. Misfortune struck again when he was preparing to leave: two men were lost as they tied up a boat in which Laplace had just returned. The bodies were not found, so that the French believed them to have been attacked by sharks, although this seems unlikely in such cool waters in midwinter.

The expedition sailed from Hobart on 7 August and arrived in Sydney, after once more battling against heavy seas, on the 17th. The weather was warmer, the number of dysentery cases began to decrease rapidly, and spirits rose again. Visits were made to country homes: to Sir John Jamison's estate by the banks of the Nepean river and to Blaxland. Back in the town, 'banquets and balls took up our time', including a reception on board the *Comet*, a British corvette which had been in Madras at the same time as the *Favorite*, fourteen months before, and was once again riding at anchor beside her. The French themselves gave a ball on the eve of their departure, followed by supper and a fireworks display. But behind this social life, which Laplace interpreted as marking the final stage in the development of Sydney, they guessed the presence of all the petty jealousies and manœuvres of a colonial and provincial administrative centre, fanned while they were there by the forthcoming arrival of a new governor. When Laplace sailed from Sydney, to a salute from twenty-one guns, on the morning of 21 September 1831, he did not realize that he was himself to be the next subject of gossip and rumour in the society which had so welcomed him. His immediate thoughts were concerned with the crossing of the south Pacific, which in view of the condition of his crew, now mostly free from dysentery though still weak from its after-effects, he proposed to break with a short stay in New Zealand. He reached Three Kings and North Cape on the 30th, was held up for a while by inconstant breezes, and finally anchored in the Bay of Islands on 2 October. A large crowd had gathered on the shore to watch the new arrivals, but 'no doubt intimidated by the corvette's guns and numerous crew, or worried, as I later learnt, by false rumours', few approached. Those who did all claimed to be important chiefs and insisted on liberal gifts. Some, on the other hand, made no claims but could not be kept away:

The sentries whose task was to warn the officer on watch of approaching boats had been on duty for two hours, and only the distant calls of the Sirens disturbed the deep silence which had fallen over the *Favorite*, when several canoes, too small to cause any anxiety, and which the clear and noisy voices of their many passengers showed to be friendly, simultaneously approached the corvette from all sides. This surprise assault was all the more difficult to avoid in that the enemy, displaying an agility which easily defeated the questionable surveillance of the sailors on watch, climbed up the chain-wales and, led by accomplices, rapidly invaded the lower parts of the ship. In such a critical situation, M. Verdier displayed a zeal and a strictness of principles which deserved better success; but treason had corrupted every heart. My own authority was invoked but I went back to sleep to avoid seeing such a spectacle; and the next morning when I wanted, perhaps a little belatedly, to defend the virtue of my crew, the female cohort had disappeared.[1]

[1] *Voyage*, vol. iv, p. 49.

Laplace had soon less reason to feel indulgent. The very next day a victorious war party returned from a raid on a southern tribe, bringing back a number of bodies, which at once provided a cannibal feast. The French sailors, seeing their fair visitors of the previous night taking part in the festivities, developed feelings of aversion for them which facilitated the watch officers' work in the future. A 'haka' with which the warriors entertained the French did nothing to erase the horror and repugnance created by the earlier scenes:

No words could describe the frightful appearance of these abominable scoundrels. Their bodies, completely naked and painted red, white and black, their tangled hair dusted with yellow ochre, their extravagant attitudes and frightening grimaces gave them an appearance of demons. Some, standing in the bow of their canoes, held out before us on bloodstained poles the heads of the enemy chiefs killed in the battle; others, brandishing their weapons, executed dances which aged crones, squatting in the bottom of the canoes, accompanied by beating their hands. All of them were yelling war chants and tried to outdo each other with extravagant contortions. I should like to know what one of these philosophers who consider man in his wild state to be a model of innocence and goodness would have said if he had been present at this spectacle. For our part, having been able for nearly two years, living sometimes among wild tribes and sometimes among civilized nations, to look at the question from every angle, we found that such a scene helped considerably to sicken us of this savage country and to make us desire to leave it as soon as possible.[1]

A visit by Pomare and Rewi did nothing to alter these views. The former's reputation among Europeans was unsavoury and Rewi's appearance did not inspire confidence. Laplace reacted by making a few niggardly presents, thus ensuring that they would not return. The Ngapuhi chief, Rewa, on the other hand, he had already met in Hobart and liked; he gave him muskets and powder 'as he was preparing a formidable expedition against tribes in the Thames-river district, who had not been satisfied with eating, a few months earlier, a hundred or so raiders from the

---

[1] Ibid., pp. 51–2.

Bay of Islands, but had promised to do the same to the friends and relatives of the victims'.[1] But before they sailed, on 11 October, the French had carried out a number of observations, Pâris in particular making a detailed plan of the Kawakawa river and carefully charting the shoal that lies between Manawaora Point and Waihihi at the mouth of the river, which he named 'Banc de la Favorite'. These activities, innocuous though they were, involving nothing more than the erection of a temporary observatory on Kairoro Island, had repercussions of which Laplace, sailing for South America, remained quite unaware. A fortnight after his departure from the Bay, the English cutter *Fairy* arrived in Port Jackson with news that the French had taken possession of New Zealand. The rumour, and the excitement this caused in Sydney, were symptomatic of Australian nervousness about the future of New Zealand. The New South Wales Executive Council felt that the rumour was unfounded, but the possibility of Laplace's having deceived everyone in the colony about the true purpose of his voyage to New Zealand could not altogether be discounted. A report was sent to London, and meanwhile Saumarez was ordered to proceed to New Zealand in the sloop *Zebra* to investigate the situation and inform Laplace—if he were still there—'that the British government had taken the islands of New Zealand under its protection at the request of the Maoris and would not tolerate the intrusion of any other nation'.[2] It was discovered that Laplace had indeed landed guns (the muskets he had given to Rewa) and set up some flags (in order to carry out his survey); but there was nothing whatever to support the view that he had ever intended to take possession.[3] The British Government had nevertheless been sufficiently alarmed to ask its ambassador to Paris to report 'after confidential inquiry' and was reassured to hear that Laplace had no orders authorizing him to take possession or form an establishment of any kind in New Zealand. But before the storm died down a dozen chiefs had been moved to sign a letter addressed to King William IV, asking for his protec-

[1] *Voyage*, vol. iv, p. 13.
[2] Brookes, *International Rivalry in the Pacific*, pp. 54–5.
[3] Bourke to Goderich, 23 Dec. 1831, *Hist. Records of Australia*, I, xvi, p. 483.

ion, as they were in great fear of 'the tribe of Marion'.[1] Thus, the
eventual colonization of New Zealand had taken one more definite, if scarcely perceptible, step forward.

Unaware of all this, Laplace was sailing on a westward
course between the thirty-third and fortieth parallel. A fresh
north-easterly at first ensured rapid progress, then easterlies and
storms held the expedition back. Laplace had toyed with the
thought of calling at Easter Island, but dysentery reappeared and
he considered it far wiser to make for Valparaiso with all possible
speed. On 13 November he sighted Mas Afuera, the weather
having cleared and the wind moderated. South America was
naturally of considerable importance to French trade. Chile was
barely recovering from the after-effects of the 1829 revolution
which had overthrown Freire, and trade was still languishing, but
whalers were now joining ordinary merchantmen, driven into
the Pacific by the exhaustion of the South Atlantic hunting-
grounds, and encouraged by a system of bonus grants begun in
1829. French influence was also making itself felt in the cultural
sphere, through the establishment of the French-run schools that
have remained a feature of Chilean higher education. Thus, when
Laplace arrived in Valparaiso on 14 November, he found a
number of his compatriots:

the corvette . . . anchored by two French naval brigs whose captains
and staffs welcomed us with the kindness and eagerness we expected
from fellow countrymen and friends. Our voyage of exploration was
ending in Valparaiso: we were here in a country which its trade and
its revolutions had made widely known to the old world, and we saw,
with a joy which it would be difficult to describe, our national emblem
flying on warships and merchantmen; the kind of virtual isolation in
which we had been living since our departure from Bourbon had at
last ended. Our homeland was still very far away, but we were speaking
about it with fellow citizens and friends. How pleasant to the ear of an
exile is his mother tongue! It has harmony, an expressiveness of feelings
which no other idiom can offer him . . . each day I renewed the pleasure
of the company of Post-Captain de Villeneuve, officer commanding
our station, and of my old comrade-in-arms, Commander du Petit-

[1] Brookes, op. cit., p. 55.

Thouars, commanding the brig *Griffon* whose guns a year later protected efficiently and brilliantly the interests of our shipowners against
the rapacity of the Peruvian authorities.[1]

News of the break between Belgium and Holland and the
possibility that this might develop into a major conflict led the
captain of a Bordeaux three-master, the *Ernestine*, to request
Laplace's protection as far as Rio. Thus on 10 December 1831 the
Favorite sailed from Valparaiso escorting the merchant ship. All
the damage caused by storms in recent months had been repaired,
there was on board a four months' supply of food, including fruit
and green vegetables for the sick, whose 'numbers were unhappily
all too great'. There were also two passengers on board: one a
young man from Hobart who had taken passage for Europe, the
other the head of an English firm established in China. The
latitude of Cape Horn was reached at the beginning of January
in a wild north-westerly storm; the cape itself was passed on the
6th at a safe distance, out of sight behind a rolling bank of fog
and a flurry of snowflakes—although it was midsummer. The
Favorite then steered north to the east of the Falkland Islands and
reached Rio on the 23rd. A number of ships there were flying the
tricolour, including *l'Herminie*, a frigate of sixty guns, commanded
by Villeneuve de Bargemont,[2] head of the French naval station.
When Laplace left, on 9 February, the band of H.M.S. *Warspite*,
flagship of the British station, honoured him by playing a series
of French airs: he felt as if he had already returned to Europe.
The remainder of the voyage, apart from delays caused by the
lack of winds along the Equator, was uneventful. The Straits of
Gibraltar were reached on 11 April, the snow-covered peaks of
the Pyrenees became visible a few days later, and the *Favorite*
anchored in Toulon harbour on the evening of the 21st after an
absence of twenty-eight months. She had spent 482 days at sea
and travelled 56,000 miles.

Politically, the expedition had not been unsuccessful. It had

---

[1] *Voyage*, vol. iv, pp. 65–6.

[2] Not the Villeneuve whom Laplace had met in Valparaiso commanding the
brig *Nisus*; the *Herminie*, however, had been recently in the Pacific as the naval
station there was a subdivision of the main French naval station in Brazil.

failed in Cochin-China, but elsewhere it had shown the flag,
strengthened French influence, given protection and encouragement to French traders, and obtained valuable information on

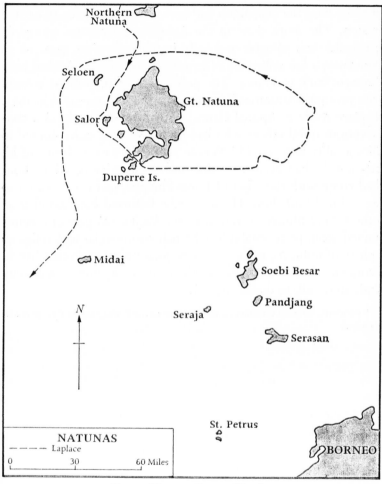

Map 9. Natunas. Route of Laplace

the commercial potential and the military strength of all the
places visited. In Canton especially, the value of the *Favorite*'s
visit was immediately felt, and nearly everywhere her presence
had proved effective. The cost had been fairly heavy: twenty-one

men had died, mostly as a result of sickness; but there were no
deserters, an indication that Laplace had shown himself a firm and
not unpopular captain. The hydrographic work was thorough
and reliable, although not spectacular—but no one had expected
it to be since the expedition had been required to keep to known
waters. The work done in the Anamba and Natuna groups in
particular was valuable and fully justified the time spent on it.
Similarly, a fair collection of natural-history specimens had been
brought back to France. The publication of the official account
was promptly authorized and the first volume appeared in 1833.
Laplace made no special claims; he had acted merely as a conscientious naval officer who had carried out the tasks allotted to
him as ably as he could.[1] Within the fairly narrow limits of his
mission, he had been successful, and the merchants, whose hour
had come with the reign of Louis-Philippe, had every reason to
be satisfied with him. He was to be followed by a number of
others—and himself to return to the Pacific—as part of a determined attempt to establish a French commercial and religious
sphere of influence in the southern ocean; but first France had to
reorganize herself after the overthrow of the legitimist monarchy
and, above all, to digest Algeria.

[1] Modesty, or even humility, is the keynote of the Preface to his *Voyage autour
du monde*.

VAILLANT

THE new Orleanist monarchy did not turn its attention to the Pacific until 1835. Algeria had loomed far more in the minds of the French Government after 1830, when Charles X had first sent troops across the Mediterranean, and the Navy had been occupied ever since in ferrying more troops and protecting the army's supply lines. When the Government began to turn to more distant fields the first few expeditions were mainly of a political nature; without the influence of Admirals Duperré and Ducampe de Rosamel, who held the position of Minister of Marine, the first from November 1834 to September 1836, the second from then until March 1839, the geographical and scientific components of the expeditions which did leave for the Pacific might have been even less significant. In 1835, when Duperré was sending Vaillant to the Pacific, the main aim was clearly a political—one cannot yet say an expansionist—one:

> The purpose of the expedition is to settle various diplomatic and consular representatives in the different posts of South America, in Chile and Peru; then, in the interests of trade, to make an appearance in the Gulf of California in Western Mexico, in the port of San Blas and even in Mazatlán; if this does not delay too much your crossing of the Pacific, to stay for a short time in the Sandwich Islands; and thence to sail for Manila to land the two consular agents appointed to that post.[1]

The appointment of consular agents in South America was, as we have already seen, the outcome of a policy which had been slowly maturing over the years, involving final recognition of the independent states of South America and the consolidation of French commercial influence. The stay in Hawaii—the term used is 'station'—reflected the serious situation in the archipelago as it affected French missionary endeavours and French nationals.

[1] Archives de la Marine, BB4 1007, 'Notes sommaires sur les instructions . . .'.

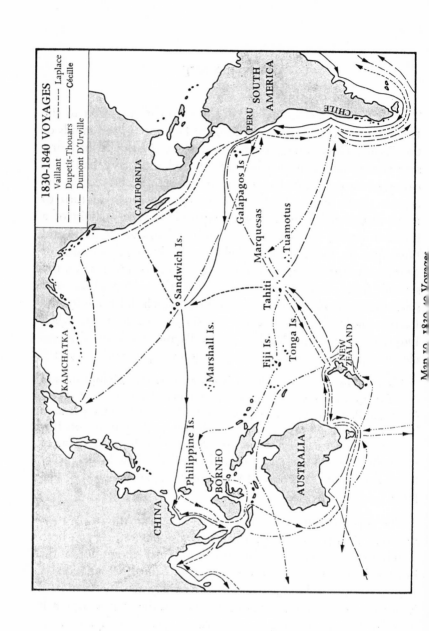

Map 10. 1830-40 Voyages

1830-1840 VOYAGES

Vaillant ——— Laplace
Dupetit-Thouars —·—·— Cécille
Dumont D'Urville ·······

Much had happened there since Tromelin had called in 1828 and his fairly complacent report had long been out of date.

French interest in the Sandwich Islands went back to Jean-Baptiste Rives, the strange unkempt figure whom Arago had derided. Rives had accompanied Liholiho to England and, following the latter's death, had gone on to France, where he had canvassed for support from traders and missionaries. A 'Mémoire sur les Îles Sandwich, la Californie et la Côte Nord-Ouest de l'Amérique' drawn up in November 1824 had received no official support, but he had succeeded in interesting a firm of Paris bankers, Javal Frères, who approached the French Government for the loan of a corvette. The Minister of Marine, Chabrol de Crousol, declined, stating, reasonably enough, that 'the Royal Navy can intervene in commercial undertakings only when it has to extend over them all equally the protection of its guns'.[1] This did not deter the Javals, who bought a ship of 370 tons, the *Héros*, which they fitted out, and which sailed from Le Havre on 10 April 1826 under the command of Auguste Bernard Duhaut-Cilly. The expedition was a purely commercial one: French missionaries responding to Rives's call were compelled to seek another ship. But, even so, the backers—who had been joined by the bankers and shipowners Martin and Jacques Laffitte —realized that the profits might well be small or non-existent:

A treaty under which Mr. R . . ., acting in the name of the government of the Sandwich Islands, granted enormous benefits to the parties concerned was signed in Paris towards the end of 1825. It promised, among other things, a high return on any goods which might be sent, the development of vast areas of land which he claimed to own in these islands, a monopoly of the sandalwood trade which is their main source of wealth, and many other dazzling advantages. Without having complete faith in these brilliant results, we believed, however, that it might be possible to establish with that archipelago a connexion which could assume considerable importance for our trade in general; but this scheme had hardly been set in motion when a greater knowledge of Mr. R . . .'s character led us to fear that we had become involved without sufficient consideration with a man whose

[1] Quoted in Jore, *Océan Pacifique*, vol. i, p. 132.

speech revealed with increasing clarity a lack of caution and of means which later became quite evident. Nevertheless, unwilling to break commitments into which they had already entered, the heads of the expedition proceeded with their plans; but they decided to remove him entirely from the management of the undertaking, and it was then that they offered it to me in addition to the command of the ship.[1]

Duhaut-Cilly, who was then 36 years of age, had had a brilliant and lively career during the Napoleonic Wars, sailing for a time in the Indian Ocean with the famous privateer Robert Surcouf. He had long since joined the merchant navy, but, strangely enough, was compelled to address his assembled crew just before departure and deny rumours which had become current in Le Havre that the *Héros* was about to engage in piracy. Her complement of thirty-two presumably reassured, she sailed, reached Rio on 25 May, turned Cape Horn on 14 July, and dropped anchor in Valparaiso on 3 August. After a brief respite, the *Héros* continued on her way up the coast in order to dispose of as much as possible of the cargo she had brought from Europe. At San José del Cabo, at the southern tip of Lower California, in late October, Duhaut-Cilly was authorized to trade, but found the rate of duty so high that little was achieved. Rives for his part went to Real San Antonio with one of the officers, Le Netrel, then on to Mazatlán, where things improved a little. In San Lucas, Duhaut-Cilly met the captain of the brig *Waverley*, a vessel engaged in the Sandwich Islands trade, who confirmed his worst fears about Rives. 'From that moment, I resolved inwardly to seize every opportunity of disposing of the cargo.'[2] In fairness to Rives, it must be said that he was doing his best to find suitable markets for Javals's merchandise, spending most of January to April 1827 visiting mission stations and outposts along the coast of California, with Duhaut-Cilly following him in the *Héros* and sending him goods for sale in the ship's boats. They had left San Lucas on 29 December, had gone to San Francisco on 26 January,

[1] Duhaut-Cilly, *Voyage autour du monde*, vol. i, pp. 4–6. Duhaut-Cilly in his account reveals a literary gift for description which is fairly rare among heads of commercial expeditions.
[2] Ibid., vol. i, p. 280.

then to Santa Cruz, Monterey, Santa Barbara, and San Pedro, reaching San Diego on 18 April. Duhaut-Cilly made a second attempt to sell goods in Mazatlán; this time he was unable to land anything and returned to San Diego. Rives then went on to Santa Barbara and the Santa Clara mission. These various comings and goings make it clear that the French were as keen to dispose of their cargo as the authorities were unwilling to allow it to land; there was, moreover, a great deal of competition—but worse was to come. On 20 August Duhaut-Cilly sailed for Monterey, where he arrived on the 26th—and there he found another French ship, the *Comète*, which like the *Héros* had sailed from France bound for the Sandwich Islands. But there was a difference: the *Comète* was already on her way back from Hawaii!

The presence of a competitor was made worse by the fact that his arrival was due to Rives, one of whose aims, it will be remembered, was the introduction of French missionaries in the islands. Javal Frères had restricted themselves, wisely, to the promotion of trade. However, Rives's proposal had not been lost: the Superior General in charge of foreign missions had forwarded it to the Vatican; there, as in France, the climate of opinion was favourable towards an expansion of missionary endeavour or, in the case of the Pacific, a resumption of Catholic efforts in an area where such activities had lain dormant for half a century. Father Coudrin, founder of the Congregation of the Sacred Hearts of Jesus and Mary, had offered the services of his priests, known as the Picpus Fathers, for any new field being opened up for missionary activity. An apostolic prefecture was created, centred on Hawaii, and placed in the care of the Picpus Fathers; but the problem of transport remained unsolved. Javals refused to provide a passage for missionaries, and even the intervention of the Minister of Marine had no effect: the presence of Catholic priests on board the *Héros*, they felt, could only antagonize the powerful American mission in Hawaii and jeopardize the success of the venture. In May 1826, after the *Héros* had sailed from Le Havre, Father Coudrin was approached by Catineau-Laroche, the head of the trade section of the Ministry of the Interior, with an unusual proposition. Catineau-Laroche, acting on behalf of Rives, offered to provide transport for the missionaries and even build them a house and a church, as long as six lay workers could accompany them to form the nucleus of a French settlement. Father Coudrin succeeded in keeping separate his own spiritual undertaking and Catineau-Laroche's commercial and imperialist aims. A three-masted vessel of 600 tons, the *Comète*, was chartered with the backing of the shipowning firm of Changeur, and placed under the command of Captain Plassiard. Nominally in charge was Catineau-Laroche's nephew, Philippe-Auguste de Morineau, aged 23, watched jealously by the newly created Apostolic Prefect, Father Alexis Bachelot, his two assistants, Fathers Armand and Short, and three lay brothers. The expedition sailed on 26 November 1826 and reached Valparaiso on 8 February 1827.

News of the undertaking had long since reached London and was even now on its way to Hawaii and Australia; and, as it travelled from one official to the next, so it grew in importance. In November 1826 W. Alers Hankey, the London treasurer of the London Missionary Society, wrote to the Foreign Secretary, drawing his attention to the departure of 'two large merchant ships, bearing six priests and a precut church', and sailing under the protection of the King, the royal family, and the Archbishop of Paris, the aim being not merely to supplant 'Protestantism by Popery' but to lay the foundations of a settlement. Canning took no notice, whereupon the London Missionary Society wrote to Samuel Marsden in Sydney, who asked Governor Darling to intervene. On 30 July 1827 Darling reported this to R. W. Hay, Under-Secretary of State for the Colonies, but added he was not sure what might be done to prevent this invasion—for by now rumours had magnified the expedition to four ships with from fourteen to eighteen priests. Other details were equally exaggerated:

Besides the passengers already mentioned, there were Engineer Officers with Artillery and ammunition, Artizans of every description, agricultural implements, etc., in short everything necessary for forming a Colony, and which it is understood is to be formed at Tahiti. There were also on board two sugar refiners for Oahu with the requisite utensils. There was also a Cotton Press for the same place. We are informed that the Vessel is, in the first instance, bound to Lima, and will afterwards touch at Sansanato and the coast of California, then to proceed to the Sandwich and lastly to the Society Islands. On board the above-mentioned Vessels have been shipped what may be called the paraphernalia of Popery, consisting of splendid vestments, crucifixes, etc. There is also an elegant temple or Church in frame and a great variety of philosophical apparatus, including galvanic instruments, etc. The Priests, who are of different Orders, we understand, were selected for their imposing personal appearance and captivating address. They are accompanied by numerous attendants. Another vessel connected with the Expedition is expected to sail for the Pacific in May next.[1]

Meanwhile, the *Comète* had sailed to Quilca and then to Callao, where news of the priests' arrival caused a different kind of concern among the authorities—they feared a 'Jesuit-led' uprising. After spending four weeks in Peru, Plassiard went on to Mezatlán, arriving on 27 May, and then to Honolulu, where he anchored on 7 July 1827. The success of the expedition hinged on what Rives could do for it, but Rives had not arrived and his influence seemed to be nil. The Queen Regent, Kaahumanu, was not prepared to allow the French even to land, but they did so. She then pressed Plassiard to take them back. He refused, being interested only in disposing of the cargo. Father Coudrin's caution in keeping the temporal and the spiritual apart was now justified: Bachelot was able to reject all responsibility for the likely failure of the commercial side of the voyage. Morineau, who was to stay behind in the islands until the end of the year, realized that the undertaking had failed. On 24 July he wrote to his uncle: 'Rives planned this operation for no other reason than to swindle you out of a few thousand francs. . . . Now, here we are abandoned without resources in the Antipodes [*sic*] of our homeland. It is at the same time most unfortunate for Messrs. Changeur and Plassiard, and such roguery destroys the confidence of our traders.'[2] Rives may not have been the rogue every one now thought him to be, for he does seem to have owned property[3] and no doubt, when Kamehameha was alive, he had had some influence. He may have

[1] *Historical Records of Australia*, I, vol. xiii, pp. 475–6.
[2] Quoted in Jore, *Océan Pacifique*, vol. i, p. 151.
[3] See Yzendoorn, *History of the Catholic Mission in Hawaii*, p. 29.

been attempting to recover it with the help of the French; but his gamble certainly never came off. Morineau himself clearly believed that trade with the Sandwich Islands was possible and likely to prove profitable, for when he returned to France he requested official support and an appointment as French consul, which would have strengthened his hand in difficult negotiations with the local chiefs. There was a plan for him to sail back in the corvette *Dordogne* due to take a group of French missionaries to the Pacific in June 1830, but the Algerian campaign and the overthrow of Charles X caused it to be abandoned.[1]

The handful of artisans whom Morineau had brought with him soon dispersed. Two sailed in a Mexican ship at the end of October, the others disappeared over the next three years. Morineau himself left at the end of 1827. He had secured, so he claimed, a piece of land for the French missionaries who remained on the island with the three brothers. Even this property was to be the subject for a lengthy dispute, settled only in 1842 when a court of inquiry presided over by Captain Mallet of the corvette *Embuscade* rejected Morineau's claim of ownership. The priests were left to settle down in Honolulu, the object of suspicion but undisturbed as long as they restricted their ministrations to the small group of foreign-born Roman Catholics living in the district. This is how Tromelin found them when he called in the *Bayonnaise* in March and April 1828. As for Captain Plassiard, he had left Honolulu almost as soon as he realized that Rives was not to be found and that there was no hope of selling any of the cargo, and consequently none of buying sandalwood with the proceeds and sailing to Canton as had been the original proposal. Plassiard anchored in Monterey harbour, and there on 26 August 1827 he met the *Héros*. Duhaut-Cilly was completely unsympathetic towards his commercial rivals:

I will not enter into any details of this strange expedition; I shall only say that Mr. R . . . had been its instigator, and that it had been organized by the head of a department at the Ministry of the Interior, who had been a party to all our secrets and had taken advantage of them in this

[1] See G. W. Blue, 'The Project for a French Settlement . . .', *Pacific Historical Review*, vol. ii, pp. 94–5.

way. This undertaking made plain Mr. R . . .'s irresponsibility and bad faith and, had his intentions been realized, the *Héros*'s voyage would have been totally disrupted . . . We left [the *Comète*] after a few days in port in the greatest embarrassment, her captain having absolutely no idea what to do with the remainder of the cargo.[1]

Plassiard did in fact what Duhaut-Cilly had been doing: he sailed down the American coast, selling what he could where he could; having reached Valparaiso he sold the *Comète*, which had become unseaworthy, chartered another ship, and returned to France to report to his principals. Duhaut-Cilly had not yet despaired of covering his own losses, but at this moment Rives considered it prudent to disappear: entrusted with a stock of goods which he was to dispose of in California and in the Russian settlements along the North-West Coast with the assistance of Sumner, the captain of the *Waverley*, he chose to go to Mexico. When Duhaut-Cilly, who had gone down to Peru in October, returned to Monterey in May 1828, there was no sign of Rives.[2] The *Héros* continued to sail between the various settlements: Bodega, the Russian settlement near San Francisco, Santa Barbara, and San Diego in July. Most of the goods had now been sold, although this had taken so long that it was now a question not of making a profit but of cutting losses. The only purpose in going to Hawaii, where Duhaut-Cilly arrived on 17 September, was to obtain evidence which would exonerate him from any responsibility for the losses by placing the blame squarely on Rives's shoulders. The arrival of a third French ship within a period of a little over twelve months may have caused the Hawaiian rulers to use caution in their relations with the French priests, which, under pressure from the protestant missionaries, were becoming increasingly strained. But Father Bachelot and his colleagues, whom Duhaut-Cilly visited soon after his arrival, were unaware that their activities were the subject of an official

---

[1] Duhaut-Cilly, *Voyage*, vol. ii, pp. 118–19.

[2] In fairness to him, it must be said that the bulk of the goods had been confiscated by the Mexicans, who in 1838 agreed to pay an indemnity of 90,000 frs. to the heirs of Rives, who had died five years earlier. No one seems to have worried about the fact that the goods in dispute had not belonged to Rives in the first place.

investigation, and he reports that he found them happy although lacking comfort, careful to avoid attracting attention, and engaged in learning the language. His other calls bore fruit: 'I received written proof of [Rives's] bad faith, signed by the Regent, the consuls of Britain and America, and the Interpreter.'[1] This done, he sailed on 15 November 1828 for Canton, which he reached on 26 December. He left after a stay of three months, passed through Sunda Strait, called at Bourbon and St. Helena, and was back in Le Havre on 19 July 1829.

By then Father Bachelot's position had seriously worsened. Queen Kaahumanu had prevailed on Boki, Governor of Oahu, to issue a proclamation forbidding the islanders to attend Catholic services. This was done in April 1829, but Boki, having been once a Catholic, however nominally, remained in sympathy with his former co-religionists, and the law was not enforced until the end of the year, when he left Hawaii. The protestant missionaries, knowing that persecution merely encourages proselytizing, urged the Regent to expel the French; accordingly, in April 1831, they were ordered to leave. Father Bachelot refused and, thanks to the scarcity of ships and the unwillingness of passing captains to become involved, was able to hold on until the end of the year, when he and Father Short were placed on board the *Waverley* and taken to California. But by this action a new situation had been created: French nationals had been expelled from a native kingdom, not for any misdemeanour, but for preaching the tenets of the established religion of their country. The major powers began to react and the first steps were taken which would lead, in time, to intervention and annexation. The American Government was anxious to preserve the right of peaceful foreigners to settle in the islands—when Commodore Downes visited Honolulu in the *Potomac* he expressed his disapproval of the policy then being followed and obtained some lessening of the anti-Catholic persecution. At this stage, however, the French Government had no real wish to become involved, realizing after the failure of Javal and Changeur's attempts, that the Sandwich Islands were poor prospects for French traders, and having no immediate plans for the

[1] Duhaut-Cilly, *Voyage*, vol. ii, p. 325.

Pacific in any case. The missionary authorities, aware of this, were adopting a cautious policy: since one of the brothers, Melchior Bondu, had been allowed to remain in Hawaii, they sent first, in 1834, another brother to join him, then in August 1835 an Irish brother, Columba Murphy, to report on the likely success of a new attempt to establish a mission. As soon as his true identity and purpose were discovered, Murphy was expelled; but another Irishman, Arsenius Walsh, landed in Honolulu a year later—he was the first ordained priest to set foot in the islands for five years. It was hoped that a British subject might have a better chance of success than a French one, but Walsh was promptly ordered to leave. This time, however, the British consul intervened, claiming that the expulsion order violated an agreement made in 1794 between Vancouver and Kamehameha I.

This then formed the background to Vaillant's visit to the Sandwich Islands, although his instructions were couched in general terms because the French Government had no knowledge of more recent events. Broadly, he was to obtain, wherever he went, up-to-date news and information of value to French traders and to the Minister for Foreign Affairs; and if there were occasions when science and hydrography could be served he was not to neglect them:

The voyage you are going to undertake does not have a scientific purpose; the limited amount of time you will be spending in each of the places to be visited would not allow you to carry out any important hydrographic work. . . . You will, however, find frequent occasions to render useful services to the various branches of science . . . Your voyage will not be unfruitful if the observations carried out on it enable you to correct the position of some little known points, to give additional details on some localities which have been imperfectly described, to make better known the dangers one can encounter in parts which have been seldom frequented, to make a series of observation on meteorology, physics, electricity, and magnetism, and to add a few new specimens to the collections of the Museum of Natural History—in a word to bring back information of value on all these fields of study.[1]

[1] Vaillant, *Voyage autour du Monde*, vol. i, pp. xiv–xv. (Although written by La Salle, this work will be referred to as 'Vaillant'.)

Beautemps-Beaupré drew up the detailed recommendations on hydrographic work.[1] Baron Hamelin added a note on compass variations, Arago outlined tasks to be done in the physical sciences, Mirbel saw to botany, Cordier to geology, and Blainville to zoology: the Académie des Sciences responded as on previous occasions to the Ministry's call for advice. Equally precise were some of the political questions Vaillant had to answer. Could a consular agent be appointed in Guaymas in Mexico and in the Sandwich Islands? What advantages could be gained out of the current disputes between the British and the Chinese? What hope was there of a resumption of trade with Cochin-China? Vaillant was also to give assistance to any French trader or captain who asked for it, to act as consular agent and press for a reparation of any harm which seemed to him to have been done to French interests, 'in brief to act in such a way as to give a correct impression of the power of France and of the vigilant solicitude of her government'.

The man chosen to carry out these tasks, Auguste-Nicolas Vaillant, was in his forty-third year. Like his contemporaries he had served in the Napoleonic Wars; he had risen to the rank of post-captain, and was to become rear-admiral in 1849 and Minister of Marine two years later. The *Bonite*, allocated to the expedition, was not a war vessel, but a heavily built corvette of 800 tons, intended for the transport of troops and supplies. She was neither as elegant as an ordinary corvette, nor as fast as a frigate; but she was solid and spacious: one is reminded again of Cook's stolid bark. Preparations took over three months—from October 1835 to the end of January 1836. The officers began to gather in Toulon. The first officer, Louis-Augustin Pironneau, had already served under Vaillant, in the *Actéon*, and was appointed at Vaillant's request. The second officer was Prosper de Brégéas. There were several specialists: Yves Chevalier was a geologist and hydrographer who had done valuable work in the Plate estuary; Joseph Eydoux, the surgeon, had already sailed with Laplace—as had Barthélémy Lauvergne, the artist—and

[1] 'Note sur les opérations hydrographiques à exécuter dans le voyage de *la Bonite*' (Nov. 1835), Marine BB4 G1007.

been praised for his contributions to zoology; Charles Gaudichaud, the botanist and now a *professeur-pharmacien*, had sailed as
a young man with Freycinet; Benoît-Darondeau was appointed
as a supernumerary *ingénieur-hydrographe* and was fully to justify his
appointment. One notes the presence, among the young *élèves*,
of a future admiral and Minister of Marine, Louis Pothuau.
The passengers numbered sixteen—nine consular officials and
seven servants—and their luggage, described as 'fabulous' in
size and amount, caused dismay when it arrived and was piled
up in an untidy heap on the deck. Vaillant, like so many others
before him, complained of the quality of the crew: 'It scarcely
included any men suitable for the duties of able seamen; most
of them knew neither the name nor the purpose of the various
manœuvres.'[1]

Soon after the departure of the *Bonite*, at 8.30 on the morning
of 6 February 1836, the crew and passengers were put to the test
by rough weather which kept the latter below decks for several
days; but, driven by a strong gale the ship made good progress,
reaching Gibraltar in a week and Cadiz two days later. The
Canary Islands were sighted briefly on the 21st, the Line was
crossed on 7 March; the ship anchored in Rio de Janeiro on the
24th. While she was being repaired and cleaned, an observatory
was set up ashore and considerable scientific work was carried
out; Vaillant drew up his first report—on the commerce and
administration of the Rio district. Leaving on 4 April, the expedition was assailed by two *pampero* storms, but the slight damage
sustained was soon put right in Montevideo. Sailing south again
on 28 April (and leaving behind his first deserter) Vaillant speedily
reached the latitude of the Falklands, had a brief glimpse of
Staten Land, and turned Cape Horn on 16 May. The weather was
stormy and cold, ice and snow covered the deck and rigging.
Icebergs appeared, which remained in the neighbourhood of the
corvette for a week, at times dangerously enshrouded by fog.
Soon, however, helped by a strong breeze, the *Bonite* was able to
reach a milder latitude and clothes and supplies were dried out.
The crew was in better shape: 'whenever we looked at these

[1] Vaillant, *Voyage*, vol. i, p. 53.

sailors, now tested by several months of often arduous navigation, accustomed to a rigorous discipline, and grown familiar as a result of frequent exercises with every aspect of the work one has to do on board a ship, we found it difficult to recognize the men, so raw and clumsy, we had known in Toulon.'[1] But the winds fell away as the weather became warmer, so that the expedition did not reach Valparaiso until 10 June.

The first two consular officers, Cazotte and Blanchard, were landed here: the appointment of French representatives seemed justified by the presence of four French merchant ships in the harbour—three from Bordeaux and another from Marseilles—one of which, the whaler *Geneviève*, certainly needed assistance, for its entire crew had deserted! Vaillant gave her three men he had taken on at Rio for the *Flore*, a unit of the South Seas naval sub-station, and helped the captain to complete his complement with locally recruited British sailors. However, the *Bonite* herself was affected by desertions: one sailor disappeared on 14 June and seven went missing two days later, taking one of the ship's boats with them. Three were soon recaptured and another three were set upon and robbed by bandits who left them at the mercy of a search party sent out by the governor. The two ringleaders were keel-hauled, the rest received twelve lashes each. Before the sentences were carried out, the *Narval* from Dieppe arrived in port, similarly affected by insubordination—her leading trouble-makers were taken to the *Bonite* to witness the punishment of the earlier offenders 'pour encourager les autres'. While all this was going on, supplies were being purchased, and the usual round of official visits and receptions took up the rest of the time. Vaillant dined with Captain Beechey, who had returned to the Pacific with the *Sulphur* and the *Stirling* for a survey of the coasts of Chile, Peru, and California. He then left on the 24th for Cobija at the request of Cazotte, who wished to take to the French representative in Bolivia the ratification of a commercial treaty recently signed with France. 'Nothing was sadder or more miserable in appearance than this town'—civil war had ravaged the district. As the port was seldom visited by foreign ships, the

[1] Vaillant, *Voyage*, vol. i, p. 283.

French had no plan of the bay, and Darondeau drew one up, while Gaudichaud went exploring ashore and captured a rodent of an unknown species. After two days the French went on to Callao, where they arrived on 11 July and found the *Flore* under the command of Captain Daguenet. An observatory was set up, water was taken on, the officers rode to Lima. The *Bonite* sailed for Payta on the 21st, anchored beside two French ships, *l'Aigrette* and *le Sylphe*, and then went on to Guayaguil. De Mendeville, the new French consul, was taken off with two secretaries and a servant. There were the customary dinners and balls, and Darondeau once again went surveying.

Vaillant wanted to visit the Galapagos Islands, where a colony named Floriade had been founded by one Willimi, a native of Louisiana who had risen to the rank of colonel in the Ecuadorian army; the semi-independent status of the colony was unclear, and Vaillant felt that the political and diplomatic implications warranted an investigation and special report. To reach the colony he sailed west from Guayaquil River, aiming to sail south of the group, but the sky was overcast so that no reading could be taken for four days; it was then discovered that the ship was a full degree further north and thirty-three minutes further west than her estimated position. This meant that she was already east-north-east of the Galapagos—the French had overestimated the strength of the north-west current. Bearing in mind that his instructions did not require him to call there anyhow, Vaillant decided against turning south and west and probably wasting a couple of days on the effort. As the expedition neared the Equator and found itself slowed down by intermittent calms, the health of the crew deteriorated: 'the hospital was filled with patients whose number grew day by day, in spite of the precautionary measures which the captain insisted on. Everyone was more or less affected by the humid heat in which we were compelled to live . . . Everything in the ship was mildewed; the food was rotting; even metal fixtures, unless they were thickly covered with grease to shield them from the air, rusted in a matter of hours.'[1] The calms, however, enabled the scientists to carry out a number of experiments,

[1] Ibid., vol. ii, p. 161.

in particular recordings of the temperature of the sea at various depths. During the first fortnight of September, progress remained slow until, reaching the seventeenth degree of latitude, the *Bonite* found the trade winds and sped northwards.

The high peaks of Hawaii were sighted on 29 September 1836; two days later the French reached Kealakekua Bay. A large number of canoes encircled the new arrivals and several natives came on board. They were joined soon after by an English pilot bearing a document signed by Kuakini, known as John Adams, the Governor of Hawaii; with his help, the *Bonite* entered the bay and anchor was dropped at 3 p.m. on 1 October. Kapiolani, an influential chieftainess, promply sent supplies—pigs, cabbages, and sweet potatoes, all much appreciated by the sick—and Vaillant went to see her the same afternoon to express his thanks 'with the respectful politeness of the French knight'. What Vaillant did not know when he arrived was that his visit had been interpreted in the light of the recent expulsion order affecting Father Walsh; Vaillant had no knowledge of this until Walsh himself told him, although he did know that French missionaries had found it impossible to remain in the islands. His expedition certainly benefited materially from the Hawaiian concern at his arrival; Kuakini arrived on board on Monday, 3 October with a large following and quantities of food; the next day Kapiolani paid a visit accompanied by the missionary Forbes and his wife; on the Wednesday Kuakini returned, gave Vaillant a ceremonial feather cloak, and they all went in a group to visit the Cook memorial erected by Byron of the *Blonde* in 1825; they dined at the Forbes's in the evening. Vaillant for his part had been careful to observe the rules of etiquette: he had paid an early call on the American missionary and even accompanied him to church with Kapiolani. He realized furthermore that final decisions were not made in Hawaii but in Oahu. He accordingly sailed on the 6th, going first to Kailua, a short distance along the coast, so that Eydoux could attend to Kuakini's wife. Eydoux, however, considered she was not so much ill as 'succumbing under the weight of her own obesity'. The only remedy was dieting, which he felt was impossible in view of Hawaiian traditions. Kuakini himself

was so fat he walked only with difficulty while his wife reminded
the French of a stranded sea lion.

When the *Bonite* arrived in Honolulu, on the 8th, she found a
United States corvette, the *Peacock*, two Hawaiian ships, and
several whalers. Her arrival was marked by a twenty-one-gun
salute. Father Walsh came to see Vaillant within a matter of
hours; and, soon after, Melchior Bondu, the lay brother who had
been virtually in charge of the tiny mission since Father Bachelot's
departure, came to offer his services and his house as a site for the
observatory. The *Peacock* sailed on the 9th, leaving Vaillant to
defend the interests of the French, just as her own captain had
been putting pressure on the King on behalf of American residents.
Vaillant did not begin by broaching the question, but decided to
wait for a suitable opening. 'Mr. Vaillant proposed to give the
Sandwich Government a better idea of the greatness of our
country and to take advantage of the prolonged relations he
would have with Kamehameha III to inspire in that prince a
salutary fear of the power of France, while at the same time his
attitude towards him would give rise to feelings of friendship
towards French people.'[1] The first step was an official visit, with
everyone in full dress uniform. Vaillant began by a series of
compliments, culminating in an expressed desire to take back
with him portraits of the King and the princesses. The audience
was therefore suspended while Lauvergne, Touchard, and Fisquet
busily sketched the royal family; when it was resumed, Vaillant
formally invited the King to visit the *Bonite*. Kamehameha came
two days later and was entertained by a series of military exercises
including—pointedly—manoeuvres around the guns. At dinner,
still feeling uneasy about the French priests, he asked Vaillant to
provide him with a certificate to the effect that the *Bonite* and her
complement had been well treated. This supplied Vaillant with
the opening he needed: he pointed out that a well-armed warship
received every courtesy from the Hawaiians, but that harmless
and unarmed French individuals such as the missionaries did not.
Kamehameha 'readily agreed to leave the two lay brothers in
peaceful possession of their property and to afford them suitable

[1] Vaillant, *Voyage,* vol. ii, p. 237.

protection; and furthermore to receive with particular good will all French subjects who might come to his dominions. As to Father Walsh, the King withdrew the order of expulsion against him and agreed to his remaining in Honolulu, but only on condition that he should not give religious instruction to any native Hawaiians.'[1] At the same time, he asked the French for advice on the administration and the economic development of his kingdom.[2] The agreement was sealed by a feast, a *luau*, whereupon Vaillant prepared to leave. As he did, on 24 October, H.M.S. *Acteon*, commanded by Lord Edward Russell, arrived. Vaillant did not delay his departure—he merely sent a message of apology, hopeful that the British would take Walsh's side with a firmness which as a Frenchman he would not himself display.[3]

All this had delayed him. As he had no other plan than to sail with all possible speed to the Philippines, he sought the eighteenth parallel to reach a belt of north-easterlies free from islands and reefs. All went well until the end of the month, when the expedition encountered heavy south and south-westerly storms which slowed progress. Vaillant wanted to check the position of Asunción and Agrihan in the northern Marianas, which he finally reached on 17 November; various readings and observations were made; he then continued on his way towards the Babuyans, sighted the group on the 27th, and entered the South China Sea by way of the Balintang Channel. Turning Cape Bojeador the next day he sailed down the west coast of Luzon, encountering a fierce storm which tore the main topsail to shreds and snapped off a number of yard ends; he struggled to enter Manila Bay, where he finally succeeded in dropping anchor on 7 December. It was here that Vaillant disembarked his last passengers. These were Adolphe Barrot, the newly appointed consul in Manila; Chaigneau, his first secretary, who had failed to reopen relations with Cochin-China; their two servants; and Hébert, a representative of the Ministry of Commerce, whose mission it was to

[1] Kuykendall, *The Hawaiian Kingdom*, p. 147.
[2] As, apparently, did the council of chiefs. Vaillant, *Voyage*, vol. ii, pp. 273–4.
[3] In fact, the French believed, wrongly, that Kamehameha broke his word and that Walsh was forced to sail in the *Acteon*.

obtain for France silkworms and mulberry plants from the Philippines. Barrot's position was in fact much more important: he was to become 'Consul général de l'Indochine'—a term embracing most of South-East Asia—while Chaigneau opened a consular post in Singapore.[1] French trade with the Philippines was booming, and the opening-up of European trade in Malayan territories offered additional possibilities. Barrot's appointment was an attempt to capitalize on this, but he did not find it easy to maintain his position in the face of Spanish suspicions. Vaillant helped him to establish himself—or rather to re-establish himself, since he had already been stationed in Manila—by paying a number of calls and displaying all the might and pomp he could, not forgetting to visit the Archbishop, who was almost as powerful as the Governor. The latter authorized Gaudichaud and Eydoux to travel inland, where foreigners were seldom allowed to go because of the unsettled state of the country; the two men called on a French planter, M. de la Gironnière, in the Laguna district. Vaillant's own mission in Manila was soon completed—far more accurate and detailed reports than he could prepare would soon be dispatched by Barrot—and when he had repaired the damage to the corvette he sailed on 21 December, for Macao.

His purpose in the Portuguese colony—where he arrived on the 31st and was greeted by a twenty-one-gun salute—was to examine the consequences of the recent war between Britain and China, review the position of a number of French missionaries now in Macao, and obtain from the Chinese payment of an outstanding indemnity owed to the dependants of sailors from the *Navigateur*. As in Hawaii, his interest in the missionaries could only be justified by their French nationality: the matter of religion and of religious disputes was strictly none of his concern. He had to tread warily because there were two distinct groups of French missionaries: the Lazarists, and those who belonged to the Missions étrangères. Both complained of harassment by the Portuguese authorities, possibly because of jealousy on the part of rival Portuguese orders. Their position was made less secure by the fact that they held their residence permit from the Governor

[1] Faivre, *Expansion française*, pp. 373–4.

of Goa. Vaillant called on the Governor of Macao, who agreed to help, but as he was due to return to Europe the improvement could only be temporary. Vaillant then turned his attention to French trade with China, which was at a low ebb: there was only one French vessel in Macao harbour and that one had merely put in for urgent repairs; total exports through Canton amounted to a mere fifteenth of what Britain was sending and imports were half that figure.[1] Barrot was to take steps to improve matters, but several years elapsed before there was any appreciable change. All Vaillant could do was to travel to Canton with the French consul Gernaert and several of his officers: Gaudichaud, Eydoux, Lauvergne, and Fisquet. The report he drew up as a result of this visit and his interviews with Chinese and European traders was one of the most thorough France had received in many a year, but the conclusion was still that Britain held too many trump cards and that French captains and French merchants lacked experience. There might be some opportunities in the rising tension between China and Britain, but it was just as likely that the French would be regarded as equally obnoxious foreigners. The feeling was likely to be mutual—when Vaillant returned to Macao he found that one of the *élèves* had gone for a walk in the country with a missionary and had been attacked and robbed; he obtained compensation, while scolding the imprudent youth; but the French were becoming irritated by the attitude of both the Portuguese and the Chinese. 'I do not know what would have happened if the expedition had had to remain any longer in Macao', wrote Vaillant as the *Bonite* sailed on 21 January 1837. But since they were sailing towards xenophobic Cochin-China their patience was to be tried even further.

Hainan was sighted the next day—Tonkin Point, the eastern headland, just rising out of the mist—the *Bonite* continuing on her way down the coast and across to Tourane, where she dropped anchor on the 25th. Three officials came on board, accompanied by Vannier's son, now an ill-paid interpreter at court; they requested details of the ship and reasons for the visit, and wanted to know why the French were flying a tricolour—an indication

[1] Faivre, *Expansion française*, p. 382.

of how far out of touch they were. Vaillant told them of the
Revolution of 1830 and showed them a portrait of Louis-Philippe:

a fine full-length portrait of the King, which adorned the corvette's
main gallery and before which the mandarins bowed respectfully. One
ought to point out that this portrait had always a great effect on the
foreigners who visited the *Bonite*; whence Mr. Vaillant concluded that
it would be advisable to place on every occasion in ships sent on
missions similar to his a richly framed picture representing the French
sovereign in ceremonial dress and with all the symbols of his power;
for indeed nothing impresses more nations who are still at a low level
of civilization.[1]

The mandarins pointed out that foreigners were not allowed to
land; this was to cause trouble both for the sailors, who found
themselves surrounded by soldiers whenever they were sent to
get fresh water, and for the naturalists, who were even less able
to persuade the guards of the importance of their work: the
solution was to take no notice of the Vietnamese and to go ahead
and set up the necessary observatory. Vaillant himself was invited
to a reception in Tourane on the 27th; both banks of the river
were lined with soldiers, so that it looked more like a defensive
operation than a social engagement. New mandarins appeared
almost daily, obviously sent from Hué to report on French
activities. The courtesies and constant formalities concealed a very
real anxiety. When Vannier sailed for Singapore with two of the
emperor's ships, the visitors were left without an interpreter, a
situation which suited Vaillant, who was now able to smile and
pretend not to understand their questions, while observing and
noting everything he saw. But nothing justified his remaining
much longer. There was no likelihood of his being allowed to
proceed to Hué, and, even if he had, he would have come face to
face with an emperor who had no intention of easing restrictions
on foreigners and who had been systematically massacring those
of his subjects who had embraced Christianity. Cochin-China
was now completely sealed off from the outside world—'no
European may enter, on pain of death'—with Tourane as the
only point of contact; and there was no reason for trading vessels

[1] Vaillant, *Voyage*, vol. iii, p. 261.

to call, as the emperor had set up a trade monopoly and sent his vessels to trade in Singapore. There was nothing for it but to sail. The *Bonite* left on 4 February but was held in the bay by variable weak breezes until the 6th; she reached Singapore on the 17th, stayed five days, and went on to Malacca and Penang.

Vaillant's instructions had made no mention of Singapore, but it would have been impossible for him to ignore this rapidly developing commercial centre, the key to Far Eastern trade. 'Without any fear of being accused of exaggeration, one can say that it is marked out for a most brilliant commercial future', he wrote in his report.[1] Penang, on the other hand, with its chief town Georgetown, was of far less importance, except to French missionaries, for this was their main staging-post for Siam. Vaillant met there Mgr. Bouchot, the Catholic Bishop of Siam, who showed him the mission-run boys' school, girls' orphanage, old people's home, and seminary attended at the time by fifteen Chinese or Indo-Chinese students and one Thai. From here Vaillant sailed direct to Bengal, anchoring in the Hoogly river on 5 April. Through the good offices of Bédier, the Chief Resident at the French river port of Chandernagore, he obtained mulberry plants and silkworms. Having agreed to take supplies of rice to Pondicherry, then in the grip of a severe famine, he sailed on 4 May, and was first held in the river by contrary winds, then struck almost immediately by a violent storm, the worst, he considered, he had encountered in his career. One of the boats was carried away and a number of spars were snapped. After a lull of a few days, the storm revived—'monstrous seas' battered the corvette, the tiller broke as did three makeshift substitutes, and another boat was lost. The *Bonite* limped into Pondicherry on the 28th and had to stay a fortnight for repairs. She then sailed for Bourbon, where she arrived on 11 July. Anchored in the road was the corvette *L'Aube* and several French merchantmen; the expedition had now almost come to an end—all that lay before it was routine. Vaillant drew up his final reports and took on supplies for the final part of the voyage. Brégéas, suffering from acute dysentery, had to be left behind with three other cases of sickness,

[1] Quoted in Faivre, *Expansion française*, p. 371 n.

but eleven passengers had to be accommodated. The only one of note was Saboureau, a navy pharmacist; the remainder consisted of six indigents being repatriated and four convicts going home to serve their sentences in state prisons. An even less fortunate passenger was a panther, a gift from the Iman of Muscat to the Governor of Bourbon, which was to be taken to France: after sailing, Vaillant realized that there was no fresh meat on board and the poor animal had to be killed and stuffed. It would probably have met this fate anyhow, since a storm struck the *Bonite* near the Cape and caused the death of all the poultry. Vaillant was thus compelled to seek supplies in St. Helena, where he arrived on 5 September.

The French made the traditional pilgrimage to the tomb of Napoleon I at Longwood; in 'this now sacred place . . . they bowed their heads before the revered tomb'.[1] They sailed the next day. A few weeks later they were delayed by calms, and scurvy began to develop rapidly. The number of sick grew so fast that the ship's hospital could not accommodate them all— a rare occurrence by that time, when civilization had multiplied her outposts and science was providing better remedies—but when the *Bonite* reached Brest, on 6 November 1837, there was no loss of life to report.

It had been basically a successful voyage. Hydrography had benefited from Darondeau's brilliant work; the investigations on terrestrial magnetism were among the most thorough made by any expedition so far; and, although the principal aims of the voyage had forced scientific work into the background, the scientists had collected 3,500 natural-history specimens, including 600 which were so rare that the Museum had none in its collections or only damaged specimens; there were in addition 1,300 samples of rock. As Blainville, who had rather mildly drawn up the instructions to the naturalists, reported to the Académie des Sciences, what had been done by far exceeded expectations: 'When we drew up at fairly great length the main *desiderata* of science and of our collections, we were far from thinking that, in

[1] Vaillant, *Voyage*, vol. iii, p. 494. Volume iii was published in 1852—under Napoleon III—by which time the Emperor's ashes had been returned to France.

a voyage which was to be carried out so rapidly and the main aim of which was not scientific research, our hopes and needs would be fully met . . . [but] we hasten to declare that the *Bonite* expedition has, in zoology, considerably exceeded our expectations.'[1]

The expedition had been fully successful in the political and diplomatic field, except, predictably, in Cochin-China. Vaillant had shown the flag, extended protection to a number of French subjects, helped to restore discipline on board merchantmen and whalers, and drawn up comprehensive reports on the countries he had visited. In the case of the Hawaiian Islands these, added to Barrot's equally authoritative statements, helped to influence and shape French policy.[2] The expedition was considered important enough to justify the official publication of the scientific results— entrusted to Gaudichaud and Eydoux—and of a more general narrative—which Vaillant could not spare time to undertake himself and which was left to La Salle, a head clerk in the Ministry of Marine, whose style was, in keeping with his occupation, somewhat pedestrian. Vaillant, before returning to his duties, summed up his achievements in a lengthy final report, concluding:

I shall always claim the honour of having led the first expedition around the world undertaken, and most happily completed, under the reign of H.M. Louis-Philippe I, and of having been the first captain of our Royal Navy since 1830 to have been entrusted with the task of making the King's flag and the noble colours of France known in distant countries where they were totally unknown and in several others where they appear only at very long intervals.[3]

Speedy, short, and efficient, with neither loss of life nor serious setbacks, nor marked by any great achievements, save in the work of a few determined individuals, Vaillant's voyage was essentially a pioneering incursion, the first survey by a new government which, slowly but with gathering determination, was turning its eyes in the direction of the Pacific, where as in Africa and in the East the foundations of a new empire might be laid.

[1] Quoted in Vaillant, *Voyage*, vol. i, pp. 432–3.
[2] Blue, 'The Policy of France toward the Hawaiian Islands', *Pacific Historical Review*, Mar. 1933, pp. 61–3.
[3] Brest, 20 Nov. 1837, quoted in Faivre, *Expansion française*, p. 413.

DUPETIT-THOUARS

A SECOND expedition left France for the Pacific in the year 1836. It was to be a far more leisurely voyage than Vaillant's, and to be more eventful and fraught with greater political implications. The personality of its leader helped to shape, no doubt as much as circumstances, the near-interventionist character of the voyage, for Abel Aubert Dupetit-Thouars, the nephew of that Aristide who had so gallantly tried and failed to sail in search of La Pérouse, was an authoritative man who, without being overbearing, had never been afraid to act firmly when the interests of France required it. Born in 1793, he had joined the Navy at the age of eleven, been appointed *aspirant* in 1808 and *enseigne* in 1814. The Restoration, far from delaying his career, had enabled him, as a member of a patrician family with a tradition of service to the old Royal Navy, to rise to *lieutenant de vaisseau* in 1819 and to *capitaine de frégate* in 1826. The fall of Charles X in no way affected his future, for he was by then engaged in the expedition against Algiers, in which he added to his reputation. The July monarchy sent him to serve with the French naval station in the Pacific, whose chief described him as 'suitable to fulfil any kind of mission'. The Pacific seaboard of South America seemed about to erupt in a series of wars; he tried to mediate whenever he could, and used tact and firmness when the interests of French commerce and French citizens were in danger. The French Government had been trying, without marked success, to foster a whaling industry. Dupetit-Thouars, on his way home after four years in Pacific waters, was asked for advice. He replied that it was essential to assist the captains of whalers to maintain discipline—the work was hard, the voyages usually dreary, the rewards uncertain. It was also necessary to protect the whalers and their crews from the vexations inflicted on them by minor officials in foreign ports. To achieve this it was necessary to send, at regular intervals, naval units to visit the various fishing-grounds. The information obtained by these vessels, he added, would be of value to French commerce and diplomacy.

It was a sensible and practical recommendation. The Government acted with remarkable speed: the report was received in October 1836 and its major points were embodied in the instructions issued to him on 21 December—for the Minister had decided that Dupetit-Thouars was eminently fitted to lead the kind of expedition he had suggested. At the same time, Laplace—also a veteran of the Pacific—was ordered to effect a circumnavigation, but from the west, and 'seek the areas where French whaling ships are concentrated'. A third expedition, Cécille's, was to sail in July. The French were now serious about the whaling industry and about the Pacific. Dupetit-Thouars was to sail to the various areas frequented by whalers, afford them assistance and support when required, and make to the Government such further recommendations as might prove beneficial to the industry, 'which has been almost at a standstill'. This, it was stressed, was the primary purpose of the expedition.

Dupetit-Thouars, however, in the frigate *Vénus*—size becomes important at this stage of Pacific history, since national prestige was at stake—was also required to assist French traders in South America and in Mexico, where commercial interests had been clamouring for support for some time. The volume of trade remained comparatively small—what else could it be in the midst of so much political turbulence!—but it was hoped that firmness or even the mere appearance of a frigate with her large complement might help it to develop. 'So great is the Government's concern for commerce, that, with no further thought for economies which might prove disastrous . . . it has decided not to abandon finally to their own resources captains and supercargoes who are exposed to all types of vexations and exactions on those distant shores.'[1] He was accordingly to sail in the first instance to

---

[1] The instructions are reprinted in Dupetit-Thouars, *Voyage autour du monde*, vol. i, pp. xi–xxii. They are signed by the Minister of Marine, Ducampe de Rosamel, himself a former commander of the Pacific naval station, whose role in redirecting French attention to the Southern Ocean may have been more considerable than is often realized.

Rio, Valparaiso, and Callao, go from Payta to the Galapagos whaling-grounds, then proceed to the Mexican coast and north-ward to California and beyond, to the Russian settlements along the North-West Coast, and across by the Aleutians to Kamchatka; he would return by way of Hawaii to Chile, then along the southern fringe of the Dangerous Archipelago to Port Jackson, and to France by the western route. He was allowed to depart from these instructions if he considered it necessary but, as we shall see, further orders were issued to him in Valparaiso.

The *Vénus* was thus to be the first French vessel to visit Kam-chatka since La Pérouse's expedition exactly half a century before. She would pass through stretches of ocean seldom visited by naval units, and it could be expected that much scientific know-ledge would be gained in consequence: there were to be, for instance. hourly readings of the temperature of the air and the sea throughout the voyage; hydrography would gain from the pre-paration of accurate charts; the usual reports on local conditions, native peoples, and openings for French traders were called for. Research in the field of natural history was entrusted to the chief surgeon, Adolphe Néboux, and to Émile Fillieux, the supply officer; and two of the eleven *élèves*, Masselot and Mesnard, were to act as draughtsmen. Dupetit-Thouars was finally requested to look for suvivors from the merchantman *La Nouvelle-Amérique*, which had sailed from Bordeaux in November 1835 and was presumed lost in the neighbourhood of Cape Horn.

The men, for once, seem to have pleased their captain. Although young and lacking experience, they appeared promisingly zealous. Including cooks and tradesmen, there were 445 of them, making with the officers an imposing complement of 468. The first officer was Chiron du Brossay; the senior *lieutenant de vaisseau* was Léon Dalmas de la Pérouse, the explorer's nephew, and the *ingénieur-hydrographe* was a skilled and hardworking specialist named Dortet de Tessan.

The *Vénus* sailed from Brest on 29 December 1836. A brief storm was encountered without impeding her progress, for on 9 January she was already in sight of the Canaries. As thirty-seven men were suffering from colds and fevers, Dupetit-Thouars decided to call at Tenerife and obtain refreshments. Oranges and bananas were bought at reasonable prices, and in addition the presence of another French vessel reduced the loneliness and homesickness of the younger sailors. This was the *Delphine*, a merchantman from Bordeaux, which had suffered in the same storm as the *Vénus*; her ultimate destination was Chile and Peru, where she was taking silk from Lyon as well as several missionaries from Paris—including the future bishop Pompallier—bound for Polynesia.[1] The French parted from them the next day, continuing their route for the Cape Verde Islands and Brazil. In the small hours of 16 January the master carpenter fell overboard; three boats were at once lowered but they saw no sign of him; the *Vénus* remained in the neighbourhood until 1 p.m., then went on her way. Although this episode cast a cloud over the early part of the voyage, this was to be the only life lost in this way: a sailor who fell overboard a few days later was rescued.

Cape Frio was sighted on 3 February. The French anchored in Rio harbour the next day for a twelve-day stay, then went down to the Plate estuary, and sailed on the 24th for Cape Horn. A fortnight later they were becalmed west of the Falkland Islands and spent their time taking the temperature of the sea at various depths and dragging the bottom, bringing up nothing more exciting than grey sand with a little mud and a few shells. Soon after this, they saw in the distance what seemed to be a reef on which the sea was violently breaking: they sailed slowly towards it and saw a large school of whales estimated at over two hundred. On 11 March, in worsening weather, they sailed slowly along the east coast of Staten Land, hoping for signs of wreckage or of survivors from the *Nouvelle-Amérique*, and firing a gun at regular intervals. There was no response—the coast was as bare and as inhospitable as ever. Dupetit-Thouars, who knew the *Nouvelle-Amérique*'s captain, Chabrié, continued the search for some time and went down as far as the sixtieth parallel. There was nothing to be seen but the angry waves lashing at the base of an occasional ice-floe. An island was reported to lie in 58° 22′ south and 82° 40′

---

[1] It was the *Delphine* which, two years earlier, had taken Mgr. Rouchouze, Vicar Apostolic of Oceania, to Valparaiso with five other missionaries.

west of Paris, but the French found no trace of that either. Finally, on 1 April, they gave up and veered north, beating up against unfavourable winds.

They reached Valparaiso on the 26th, and found there the French frigate *Flore*, Captain Lemarrant, the corvette *Ariane*, commanded by Duhaut-Cilly, and the brig *Dassas*, Captain Daguenet, as well as the United States corvette *Peacock*, commanded by Commodore Kennedy, which had sailed from Honolulu on the very day of the *Bonite*'s arrival. The harbour was a scene of great activity, for fifteen armed merchantmen lay at anchor there, equipped to take part in the war which had just broken out between Chile and Peru. Dupetit-Thouars had no wish to become involved in this struggle; he had considerable experience with South American politics and was determined to preserve complete neutrality. He set up an observatory on land, including an apparatus for measuring the tides, took on supplies, and repaired the frigate. Even so, he had to stay longer in Valparaiso than intended, for the city was struck by two violent storms in quick succession. Finally, on 13 May, he sailed for Callao, leaving until later his planned survey of San Ambrosio and San Felix. He sent Tessan and one of the lieutenants, Lefebre, to chart the shoal Hormigas off the north point of San Lorenzo Island, while he went on to Lima to call on Santa Cruz, the 'Protector', and on Garcia del Rio, the Minister of Finance, whom he had met in Guayaquil in 1833. He then returned to Callao to prepare to receive Santa Cruz on board the *Vénus*. But it was getting too late to go to Mexico:

After 1 May it is too late to go north by the Gulf of Panama. Had I sailed there, I would have found myself on the whole coast of Mexico in the dead season, at the time of the year when the coast is empty of its inhabitants. Worse still, owing to the time it would have taken me to sail in this direction against the prevailing winds, I would have scarcely reached Monterey when I would have been forced to retrace my steps or sail to the Sandwich Islands. Taking advantage therefore of the discretion left me by my instructions, I thought it was better at this time of the year first to visit the Sandwich Islands and Kamchatka where, with luck, I could arrive towards the 15th August. If I got there by that date I could spend September going to one of the Aleutians and to Sitka, before proceeding to California.[1]

Leaving Callao on 14 June, he sailed due west to check whether the island of St. Paul, found on some old charts, did in fact exist. His method was to sail by dead reckoning, which the old navigators had used. In this way, he would be able to compensate for the effect of the currents. But when he had by these means reached the position assigned to St. Paul, there was no sign of land and he changed to a northerly course. On 7 July he saw Hawaii to the south-west. By the following day he was at anchor off Honolulu and already involved in the bitter struggle between the French missionaries and the Hawaiian authorities. The situation was now far more complicated. Fathers Bachelot and Short had returned to the islands on 17 April 1837 in the *Clementine*, a brig owned by Jules Dudoit, a French national born in Mauritius in 1803, who had settled in the Sandwich Islands in 1835. Kekuanaoa, the governor, ordered them to leave at once; Kamehameha confirmed the banishment order, but the priests were not willing to comply and Dudoit assisted them by refusing to allow them back on board his ship. Interpreting this—correctly—as a conspiracy to defeat the expulsion order, the Hawaiians forced a showdown and escorted Bachelot and Short to the *Clementine* and compelled them to go on board. It was a high-handed action, but the islanders' right to decide who might and who might not reside in their country seemed unchallengeable. The point at issue was that the *Clementine* was a British-registered ship, and as such protected by the agreement signed between the Hawaiians and Britain. Declaring that the use of force was an attack on British property, Dudoit—who seems to have enjoyed a convenient dual nationality—appealed to the British consul, who supported him. Protests were made on all sides, with the advantage slightly on Dudoit's side since he was supported by the islands' weekly news-sheet, the *Sandwich Island Gazette*, which was violently opposed to the American missionaries.[2] On 6 July 1837 the *Sulphur*, Captain Belcher, and the *Sterling* arrived from Chili. Belcher came out

---

[1] Dupetit-Thouars, *Voyage*, vol. i, p. 315.
[2] Yzendoorn, *History of the Catholic Mission in Hawaii*, pp. 104–6.

in support of Dudoit and made arrangements to take over the *Clementine* and escort Father Short—who was a British subject—ashore. It was at this point that Dupetit-Thouars arrived. He was at once approached by Dudoit, now stressing his French birth, who offered him his home for the duration of his stay and told him in a few words of the French missionaries' plight.

When I landed, I almost immediately met Mr. Charlton, the British Consul, who was on his way to see me, and I learnt from Captain Belcher, commanding the corvette *Sulphur*, who came to join us, that within one hour he would recapture the *Clementine* . . . He also told me that he intended to land Mr. Short whom in accordance with the treaty recently signed between the Government of the Sandwich Islands and Captain Lord Russell, of the British corvette *Acteon*, he was entitled to bring back to land; and that had the *Vénus* not appeared he would have extended the same protection to Mr. Bachelot.[1]

Dupetit-Thouars and Belcher agreed on joint action. Their main concern was for the protection of their nationals and of the rights of traders: neither the Frenchman, who was aware of the implications of supporting a purely missionary undertaking, nor the Englishman, who can have had little sympathy for Roman Catholics, was anxious to be drawn into a sectarian struggle; but there was also the possibility of reducing or breaking the influence of the American missionaries, led by Hiram Bingham, and of delaying or preventing the ultimate annexation of the islands by the United States. It was a struggle in which every move counted. Belcher and Dupetit-Thouars went to see the Queen—for Kamehameha was away—but supported by Bingham, who acted as interpreter, she refused to allow Short to remain and Bachelot even to land until he could find a passage for Valparaiso. Accordingly, on the 11th, French and British sailors escorted the two men ashore, Bachelot going to Dudoit's home. Belcher then sent the *Clementine* to fetch the King and, on the 20th, a meeting was held.

When we presented ourselves at the court gate which leads to a small straw-coloured house where we were to be received, we found the

---

[1] Dupetit-Thouars, *Voyage*, vol. i, pp. 327–8.

ceremonial increased for the occasion; the Governor of Oahu in full dress uniform came to meet us and carried out the duties of the protocol official who introduces ambassadors . . . We were led into a large room, hung with maps, which took up nearly the whole house . . . As soon as we came in, the King advanced towards us and begged us to be seated. He was surrounded by his sister, Queen Kinau; his wife, Princess Kalama; Kaukini, Governor of Hawaii; Opili, Governor of Mawée; the Governors of Morotoi, of Oahou[1] and many other chiefs, male and female. All the ladies were lying down on their stomachs or on their side on a bed of mats which also served as a seat for Queen Kinau, Princess Boki, and the other Governors I have named. The King was seated in an armchair in front of the Queen who dictated to him what he had to say; for her part she received her instructions from the leader of the missionaries, Mr. Bingham, who was present and stood behind her.[2]

The two captains could scarcely object to Bingham's presence, much as they disliked his influence, for the King was entitled to select his own advisers—but Dupetit-Thouars attempted to use Father Bachelot as interpreter instead of the American. Kamehameha, utterly unco-operative, defeated this move. He firmly made his point that the Protestant missionaries had been the first to land in the islands, that he was satisfied with them and wanted no others in his dominions. Dupetit-Thouars refused to be led into a discussion on the merits of the two religions—a few weeks earlier, to avoid involving the French Government in the religious dispute, he had refused Father Maigret a passage from Valparaiso to Honolulu. He urged the King to regard Bachelot simply as a French citizen. This paralleled Belcher's plea that Father Short, as a British subject, could not be banned from the island. But Kamehameha insisted on calling them both Frenchmen on the grounds, he admitted, that he regarded all Catholics as Frenchmen. Dupetit-Thouars pointed out that the French Government might object to his calling Frenchmen people he obviously wished to treat as enemies, but the King simply repeated that he wanted the two priests out of his territories and that since one was French

---

[1] The correct names are Hoapili, of Maui, and Molokai, of Oahu.
[2] Dupetit-Thouars, *Voyage*, vol. i, pp. 335–6.

and the other British the two ships could take away one each. The meeting dragged on into a deadlock and ended with a somewhat ridiculous scene:

I handed the King a written note containing the same demands as I had just formulated. At first the King took it, but some of the chiefs and missionaries blamed him for accepting it; the British consul, who happened to be near him at this moment, took it out of his hands—for what reason I do not know. But the King appeared very frightened and was unwilling to touch it again; the British consul placed this note on the King's knees, but it slipped down; an officer picked it up and gave it back to me, whereupon I handed it once more to the King, but he took it on this second occasion only with a feeling of fear which nothing could justify.[1]

The King certainly had some justification for his anxiety, but, when the meeting was resumed the next morning, his determination remained. He sensed that neither the French nor the English were prepared to use force to impose on him the presence of two missionaries. Bingham's advice may have been that their respective governments would not support such an action and that the end of the virtual imprisonment of the two priests on board the *Clementine* was all the two nations would really require. Kamehameha therefore agreed that the priests might remain, but only until some opportunity arose of their leaving the islands for good. Belcher and Dupetit-Thouars each signed an undertaking on behalf of their nationals, the former adding, 'I guarantee in addition that he [Short] will not countervene the laws of the country', while Dupetit-Thouars was even more specific: 'Meanwhile, Mr. Bachelot will not preach.' As far as the English were concerned, the incident was closed; but Dupetit-Thouars was anxious to obtain the same conditions for French nationals as Captain Lord Edward Russell had obtained for the British in November 1836. Kamehameha raised no objections and a convention was signed on 24 July, the important clause of which was that 'the French may go and come freely in all the states which compose the Government of the Sandwich Islands; they will be

[1] Ibid., vol. i, pp. 339–40.

there received and protected, and they will enjoy the same advantages as the subjects of the most favoured nation'.[1] This was a significant gain for French commercial interests, if not—as yet—for the missionaries. Dupetit-Thouars was later blamed for not having firmly enough defended the latter and for agreeing to Bachelot and Short's expulsion, thus appearing to side with Kamehameha,[2] but he realized that only the use of force could have gained him every point and—even if the Hawaiians did not undo his work after his departure—he had no authority to impose conditions. As it is, even his appointment of Dudoit as French consul, intended partly to protect him from possible reprisals, was not something he was empowered to do; as it turned out, his action was promptly confirmed by the French Government.

The Catholics kept their word. Short sailed for Valparaiso in the brig *Peru* at the end of October, and Bachelot in the mission schooner *Notre-Dame de la Paix* (formerly Dudoit's *Honolulu*) in November, dying at sea a fortnight later; but by then more missionaries had arrived and the religious dispute was to continue for some time. However, all that Dupetit-Thouars felt he could do had been done. He had hoped that Kamehameha might visit his ship—indeed, the King had expressed a wish to do so and had been at once invited—but no doubt Kinau or Bingham pointed out to him that this might be politically unwise, for he never came. The *Sulphur* sailed on the 24th, followed a few hours later by the *Vénus*.

Dupetit-Thouars's next port of call was to be Petropavlovsk, and he set a north-westerly course which would take him through seas rarely visited by French ships. He had a number of hydrographical points to check, one being a reef reported by Kruzenstern and named after him. Making very careful checks of his position, using all five chronometers on board, he reached its neighbourhood on 31 July, the weather being fine, as it was to be, except for occasional patches of fog, for most of the crossing; but the sea remained empty. He continued sailing along the same parallel for another day, then concluded that the reef did not exist.

---

[1] Kuykendall, *Hawaiian Kingdom*, p. 150.
[2] Dumont d'Urville, *Voyage au Pôle Sud*, vol. iii, p. 191.

Similarly, on 8 August, he sailed over the reported position of Patrocinio Island, supposedly discovered by Manuel Zipiani of the *Nuestra Señora del Pilar* in 1799, but again there was no sign of land. The following day, a whaler was sighted, the *Hesper* from Newhaven, the two ships passing at some distance without attempting to communicate. On the 25th land appeared 'in the shape of a cloud', and at sunset the French recognized Cape Porotnoï. However, they could not enter harbour for another five days as fog came down almost immediately and hid the coast from view. Finally, on 31 August, it cleared sufficiently for them to approach the Heads and, with the assistance of the deputy Governor who came out to them in a boat with greetings from Governor Shakov, to make their cautious way to a safe anchorage.

The Russians gave the French 'the most gracious welcome one could expect'. A twenty-one-gun salute was exchanged in the morning, then Dupetit-Thouars went with all his officers to call on the Governor. Shakov, being a naval man, was most interested in the expedition and in the frigate, which he visited at the earliest opportunity. It was, as he pointed out, the largest naval vessel ever to call at Avatscha. He placed a house at Dupetit-Thouars's disposal to be used as an observatory, and organized hunting excursions for the officers. On one of these the French caught a bear who soon became tame, 'good company and a source of amusement for the entire crew'. On a visit to the town district, they were introduced to an elderly Russian who had known La Pérouse; Dupetit-Thouars invited him to the *Vénus* to meet the navigator's nephew. The stay came to an end on 16 September, when the expedition set sail for the Aleutian Islands. The first task was to investigate the existence of Nuniwak, an island which appeared on a number of recent British charts, but on the 21st the frigate sailed across its assigned position which it had checked 'by astronomical calculations of the greatest accuracy'. Soundings taken four days later revealed a depth of 2,200 fathoms, although this was probably excessive since the frigate was making good progress and the line could scarcely have been vertical at the time. Travelling well to the south of the Andreanov group, the French next looked for Saavaty Island, said to have been discovered by some Japanese sailors, but there was nothing to be seen and the vagueness of the report precluded a more thorough search. The *Vénus* now steered for California, assisted by steady south-easterly and south-westerly winds. There were few incidents on the way, apart from one sailor falling overboard, but in spite of heavy seas he was quickly hauled back.

The coast of California was sighted at dawn on 18 October 1837; in the same afternoon the frigate dropped anchor in Monterey Bay near two American whalers and the *Kamamalu*, a trading vessel from the Sandwich Islands. Dupetit-Thouars's first care was for his sick; most of them had suffered gashes or minor injuries which had refused to heal. They were accommodated in a large empty house which he turned into a hospital. They began to improve rapidly, except for one who had contracted tuberculosis and died a few days later, being buried in the grounds of San Carlos mission. It was here that La Pérouse had been so well received half a century earlier, but Dupetit-Thouars found it in ruins, with only a handful of monks and a few Indian families left. The entire district was poverty-stricken.

Before our departure from the Sandwich Islands, I had sent notice to the effect that we would be calling at this time; I was therefore expecting to find, when I arrived in this port, food supplies collected for the frigate. Although I did not count too much on the efficiency of the people who had undertaken to provide these supplies, I was disappointed to find nothing or practically nothing for us; I had expected more from them. Orders had indeed been sent forward, but the usual laziness of these inhabitants had triumphed over their interests and had not yet allowed them to carry out the plan they had of having biscuits and salt provisions prepared for us. Only a few kilos of biscuit had been made.[1]

Dupetit-Thouars was thus compelled to waste time organizing his own supplies. He scoured the countryside for wheat and set day and night shifts of bakers to making biscuits. He regretted not having gone to San Francisco, because the summer at Monterey had been particularly dry, and refilling the water casks was both arduous and slow. The *Kamamalu* being about to sail for

[1] Dupetit-Thouars, *Voyage*, vol. ii, pp. 79–80.

San Francisco, he asked her captain to bring him back some water
and also to take with him a hydrographic party which could work
in San Francisco while he remained in Monterey. The *Kamamalu*
left on 20 October and returned on 2 November, saving Dupetit-
Thouars a great deal of time and energy. He was concerned to
compile detailed and accurate reports on the Californian coast, on
every bay which might become 'a useful place of call for our
whaling ships'. He was therefore anxious to refit his ship and
refresh his men as quickly and as completely as possible. Finally,
on 14 November, he was able to begin this work. 'The *Vénus*
was thus going back to sea being, when she left Monterey, fresh
and graceful, proud of her now experienced crew, shining with
youth, and eager to meet new adventures.'[1]

The expedition first sailed south to Guadalupe Island. Dupetit-
Thouars sighted it on 17 November, but calms held him until
the 19th, when he was able to circumnavigate it from the north
and east, determining its position precisely. In the evening, this
task being completed, he continued in a southerly direction to
seek the Alijos.

This reef, discovered in 1791, had not been seen again and its very
existence had become so open to doubt that some geographers were
quite determined to suppress it completely from the new charts. On
22 November, at a quarter past twelve, [we were] sailing under full
canvas in fine weather, [when] the look-outs told us of the presence of
two ships ahead of us: these were the Alijos which their appearance had
caused to be thus announced. We had at the time a fresh north to
N.N.E. gale and in a short time we could see the reef from the deck.
It is composed of four main rocks which appeared one after the other
as we approached. The first two, much higher than the others, were the
first to appear; they looked so much like ships under sail that this error,
easy to make at night, would expose a vessel to the greatest peril.[2]

Later the same day, having completed this survey, the French
turned east to seek an unnamed island, reported by an American
'worthy of trust, but no sailor'; there was no sign of it: the island
was probably a distant sighting of Cape San Lazaro. As Dupetit-
Thouars later discovered, Captain Belcher, in the *Sulphur*, had

[1] Ibid., vol. ii, p. 142.   [2] Ibid., vol. ii, pp. 148-9.

also sought in vain for the island, having received a similar report from the same source. The *Vénus* was now to the south-west of Cape San Lazaro, by which she met three whalers, including the *Young Eagle*, of Nantucket, on her way back from Honolulu, whose captain reassured Dupetit-Thouars that Kamehameha was keeping his word as far as Father Bachelot was concerned.

On 25 November the French anchored in Magdalena Bay, still on the west coast of Lower California, which they charted for ten days, then sailed out to seek 'an island called Shelvock. Our trouble was once more in vain; we visited without result the two positions assigned to this island on two different French maps; the results of our search were merely *undiscoveries*, if I may express myself thus—that is to say that there was nothing in the locations indicated'.[1] This was only to be expected: much of the Pacific was now so well known, so 'white with canvas' as was said, that new discoveries were unlikely; on the other hand, rumours, garbled reports, schools of fish even, could still be transformed into sightings of islands or reefs, and needed verification if the charts were to be reliable. Dupetit-Thouars's contribution to this type of work, especially along the Mexican coast, is considerable. It continued the next day, as the *Vénus* sailed south for Cape San Lucas, then along to Cortes Gulf—the Vermilion Sea, which, appropriately, they found to be coloured crimson in large patches by colonies of small red animals—and to Cape Porfia in 22° 57′, before veering north and anchoring in Mazatlán harbour on 12 December. The local people were greatly impressed by the frigate, the first they had seen, and they lined the shore in great numbers; but Dupetit-Thouars had fallen ill and could attend none of the numerous receptions given in his honour. With fresh supplies, and having certainly shown the flag to advantage, he sailed on the 18th for Tres Marias, anchoring off the small island of Isabelle, where Tessan landed to climb the peak and check the detailed features of his chart. Returning to the mainland, they made for San Blas, where they once again met the *Sulphur*; the town was deserted, most of the inhabitants being in Tepic, a few miles away and on higher ground: 'the streets, where weeds were

[1] Dupetit-Thouars, *Voyage*, vol. ii, p. 156.

growing, were deserted. This great solitude gave the streets the appearance of a Turkish town during an outbreak of plague, and gave rise to a feeling of sadness which was hard to overcome.' It was in fact a dying town, its port gradually silting up, its population steadily falling; there was not even enough gunpowder for the customary salute. But it was possible to obtain water, a little flour, and a few bullocks.

The last stage of this survey of the coast ended at Acapulco. The *Vénus*, slowed by contrary winds, took twelve days, from 27 December to 8 January, to cover the three hundred miles from San Blas. Acapulco, where the Manila galleon had once brought wealth and excitement, was now just another stricken city. The population, which in days gone by had steadily remained at 6,000, except when people from outlying districts coming to town to meet the galleon and join in the festivities caused it to swell to 8,000 or 9,000, was now less than 2,000. A desultory trade continued, but affected by the atmosphere of indifference and apathy which pervaded the city. It was, however, a place where the growing number of sick, some affected by scurvy, could be cured; the enforced inaction, the sun, and the warm sea were welcome to the young sailors after their lengthy voyage and the constant manœuvring along the Mexican coast. They were joined ashore by the men of the *Sulphur*—old acquaintances by now—and by those of the small *Clementine*, on her way from Honolulu to Panama, bringing news of Fathers Bachelot and Short's departure from the Sandwich Islands.

After slightly more than a fortnight, Dupetit-Thouars sailed for Easter Island. The crossing was straightforward as far as 3° north, then came the inevitable equatorial calms; once the *Vénus* had struggled down to 4° south—which took her two weeks—she sped easily to Easter Island, sighting land at midday on 25 February. She hauled along the east coast to the northern cape and then down the west coast, at a distance of two miles or less. Large numbers of islanders could be seen on the cliffs, waving and urging the French to anchor; behind them stood the large mysterious statues for which the island was so famous, and one could also make out at infrequent intervals a *ahu*, or temple platform, with its three or four red-topped statues. Soon islanders came out in canoes and climbed aboard, showing themselves to be as friendly—and as thievish—as La Pérouse had found them:

> The men made signs indicating they wished to be shaved, which was done. One of them who then received the gift of a cap and a collar at once put them on and strutted proudly along the deck, admiring himself as if he had been richly dressed. All the natives repeated often and excitedly the word *miru* and became impatient because they saw we did not understand it: this word is the name of the timber used by Polynesians to make their canoes.[1] This was what they wanted most, and they used every means to make us understand this; they refused food and drink; they appeared to be but slightly interested in knives and scissors; fish hooks pleased them greatly, as did mirrors and coloured handkerchiefs. While the crew were busy picking up their linen which had been washed, one of these natives showed himself to be a very clever thief: he sat down, as if he did not know it, on a red cravat which he hid very skilfully in a little wicker bag he was carrying and when he was forced to give it back he showed no displeasure, nor any surprise at being discovered, and at once began the same little game, hoping this time to be more successful.[2]

More surprising was the sight of two islanders swimming apparently astride a piece of broken canoe. Dupetit-Thouars was afraid that they might sink and was about to send a boat to their rescue when he discovered to his astonishment that they were seated in *poras*, or reed boats,[3] and that they were bringing him bananas, sweet potatoes, and yams. Having completed his survey of the northern and western side of the island, he sailed south from Cabo Sur to return to Valparaiso by way of Juan Fernandez, which French newspapers reported as having been extensively damaged—and even destroyed—by an earthquake. When the *Vénus* reached 28° south, a favourable wind rose up which took her speedily to the still extant island group—Mas Afuera on 12 March, Mas a Tierra two days later. Arriving in Valparaiso

[1] *Miru*, found on Pitcairn and Henderson, is used for wood carvings. By the time Dupetit-Thouars arrived this timber was in very short supply.

[2] Dupetit-Thouars, *Voyage*, vol. ii, pp. 227–8.

[3] The presence of these reed boats is considered by some to be evidence of connections between Polynesia and South America, where these are also found.

on the 18th, the French found there the United States ship *North Carolina*, with H.M.S. *Stag*, H.M.S. *Imogen*, and the French frigate *Andromède*, commanded by Henry de Villeneuve, head of the French Pacific naval station, which had now been separated from the Brazil station.

The French spent the following month repairing the ship and buying supplies, their own stocks being now nearly exhausted. The *Imogen*, Captain Bruce, had gone to the Sandwich Islands at the end of September and had been requested by Kamehameha to provide a passage for Father Short; the latter, however, had already made his own arrangements with the owners of the *Peru*. But the *Imogen* had also gone on to Tahiti, where Bruce had appointed the missionary George Pritchard as British consul— and it was to Tahiti that Dupetit-Thouars was now instructed to proceed by new orders sent to him at Valparaiso. The situation he was required to deal with was broadly the same as the one which had developed in the Sandwich Islands. Protestant missionaries had been the first to arrive; they had, after some initial difficulties, established themselves in a position of great influence, and had become the virtual rulers of the islands; faced with the arrival of Roman Catholic missionaries they had strengthened— if not inspired—the Queen's determination to refuse them permission to settle and proselytize; since the priests concerned were French, the question was now one which could affect the rights of all French nationals. Tahiti's equivalent of Hiram Bingham was Pritchard, who had been sent to the Pacific by the London Missionary Society in 1824 and had gradually gained an ascendancy over the young Queen Pomare IV. In 1835, when Father Murphy arrived on a reconnaissance mission similar to the one he was to carry out in the Sandwich Islands, Pritchard and the Queen wrote urging the British authorities to prevent the intrusion of Catholic missionaries in the Society Islands. Three years earlier she had written to London asking that Pritchard be appointed British consul. No notice had been taken of her request so she wrote again urgently pressing for his nomination. It is likely that these requests, premature in the case of the consulship (and patently inspired by Pritchard, since on the first of these occasions the Queen was only 19) and clearly sectarian as far as the Catholic missionaries were concerned, weakened Pomare's and Pritchard's later appeals for support and intervention. In addition to this, Dupetit-Thouars had received unequivocal orders: in Hawaii he had been held back by some indecision and a lack of instructions, but the letter from Rosamel now required him to 'require from the Queen of that island full reparations for the insult France has sustained in the person of three of our compatriots . . . You will understand, Monsieur, how important it is in such circumstances to impress upon the Queen and the inhabitants of Tahiti that France is a great and powerful nation which has the means and the will to ensure that its citizens everywhere are respected.'[1] Having already allowed Pritchard to overstate the case on her behalf, she was now to be left alone to bear the consequences.

The immediate problem—the 'insult'—was an expulsion order issued against Fathers Caret and Laval, of the Picpus Society, who had arrived on 20 November 1836. They were helped by Jacques Moerenhout, a trader of Belgian extraction, who plays in this story a role very similar to Dudoit's in Hawaii. The missionaries had been preceded by their reputation, for they came from the Gambier Islands, where they had been highly successful. The ruler of the archipelago, Maputeoa, had been baptized with 160 of his people on 21 January 1836 and had taken the name of Gregario in honour of Pope Gregory XVI. Obviously, this was not the sort of challenge which the London Missionary Society missionaries, after nearly forty years in the Society Islands, would relish. At first Pomare seemed willing enough to let them stay: she received them in audience without comment. The expulsion order came a few days later, followed by their arrest. As in the case of Bachelot and Short, they were placed on board a small ship, but this time the captain complied and sailed with them to Mangareva. Father Caret returned with Father Maigret a few weeks later, but they were not allowed to land, and Father Caret went on to Valparaiso and Europe, where he was given an enthusiastic reception. In the margin of what could be once again considered a sectarian struggle, a French carpenter named Vincent

[1] Dupetit-Thouars, *Voyage*, vol. iv, p. 48.

who had accompanied Caret and Laval was also expelled, but he does not appear to have belonged to the mission,[1] so that this expulsion could be regarded as affecting simply a French national. It will be remembered that the lay brothers who had accompanied Father Bachelot to the Sandwich Islands had been allowed to remain, and that the Hawaiian ruler's objections were—in spite of some semantic difficulties—directed at the missionaries' function rather than their nationality.

Dupetit-Thouars did not leave at once for Tahiti, nor go to the Society Islands by the most direct route. The matter was not so urgent that he was required to drop everything to go there; he could not know either that this was to be but the first stage of his difficulties with Pritchard, nor that the 'affaire Pritchard' was one day to develop into an international incident. He prepared to sail from Valparaiso on 28 April, agreeing to take with him, at the urging of the French consul, two Picpus fathers, Desvault and Borgella, bound for the Gambiers. On 1 May the *Vénus* was sailing close to San Ambrosio and San Felix, on her way to Peru. She was also moving into a war zone: Chile was blockading the port of Callao. But the European nations did not recognize the validity of this blockade: the *Imogen*, the *Andromède*, the *North Carolina*, and the *Lexington* were cruising round the five Chilean blockading vessels to protect the interests of their respective nationals. The *Vénus* anchored in the port on 10 May in the midst of this unaccustomed activity. External trade was still possible, but local trade was almost at a standstill, and Callao and therefore Lima were at the mercy of a Chilean landing. The *Vénus* hardly helped to calm fears and allay rumours, for Dupetit-Thouars ordered the gunners to start gunnery and target practice! On 3 June the French sailed for Payta, where they remained eleven days, and then made for the Galapagos Islands. Hood was sighted on the morning of 21 June. The expedition sailed on to Charles Island, where they found the whaler *Augusta* anchored close to a small Ecuadorian vessel. Dupetit-Thouars went with the latter's

[1] Jore, *Océan Pacifique*, vol. ii, p. 212. Dupetit-Thouars reports that, in addition, a French sailor engaged in pearl-fishing had been refused passage to Tahiti 'for fear of reprisals' (*Voyage*, vol. ii, pp. 382–3).

captain to visit the settlement of Floriana, which he found to consist mainly of political deportees and criminals. Nearly three weeks were spent on a survey of the island group, which had interested France for some time but had not been carefully charted by a French expedition. Dupetit-Thouars, here as elsewhere, remembered that the main body of his instructions concerned the whaling industry and openings for French trade.

When this work was completed, the *Vénus* left, on 15 July, for the Marquesas. Reaching Fatu Hiva on the first day of August, Dupetit-Thouars corrected its recorded position—finding it to be 11′ 30″ too far north and 8′ 30″ too far east.

Passing very close to the SSW point, formed by a remarkable tall mountain which falls very steeply, we discovered immediately to the west of it a delightful valley at the back of an attractive small bay in front of which is an anchorage: the interior of this valley and the shores of the bay are covered with the most brilliant vegetation and filled with a multitude of Indian huts which add life to this pleasant spectacle. Stopped in front of this bay, we were surrounded by outrigger canoes of various sizes, a few of which were elegant-looking; in them were natives who were not slow in climbing aboard. Generally speaking these Indians were ugly and covered with repulsive-looking scrofulous tumors and ulcers. They seemed used to visiting ships; several knew a few words of English; some showed us certificates from captains who had employed them as sailors in British or American whalers. These natives urged us to go into the anchorage, where we would find abundant water, fruit, and very attractive women. The visit of these islanders, who had brought nothing to barter, was not of interest to us. They are already no longer savages; they have lost all the originality of their primitive character, and as yet all they have acquired from civilization is its vices. Their nakedness, being almost dressed up, is horrible to see; the few clothes they wear are in shreds, cover them inadequately and, being continually worn in the high temperatures one finds in these islands, are so dirty that one is anxious to keep away from them; they offend the sight as much as the sense of smell. We promptly forsook, without any regrets, this degraded society lacking any national colour; we hauled along the coast on a northerly course.[1]

---

[1] Dupetit-Thouars, *Voyage*, vol. ii, pp. 331–2.

On 2 August, having sailed close to the western shore of Fatu Hiva, the *Vénus* proceeded north to Hiva Oa and Fatu Haku. Three canoes came out, again filled with islanders urging the French to land. The two missionaries were tempted to stay there, but Dupetit-Thouars was distrustful and would not let them land. 'Who knows if they might not have been delighted to find such an easy and favourable occasion to rob them and possibly roast them, for they have not yet given up their cannibalistic meals.'[1] But these suspicions were allayed during the next few days. Two British sailors, Robinson and Collins, residents of Tahuata, offered their help, and led the *Vénus* to the anchorage of Amanoa—a poor one which after an uneasy night the French abandoned in favour of the safer one of Madre de Dios. The local chief visited the vessel and soon became exceedingly friendly—Iotete was in fact to sign without difficulty, in 1842, the document establishing French sovereignty over the islands, an attitude which was the combined result of missionary influence, of an uneasy conscience about an American whaler which his people had looted, and of his friendship with Dupetit-Thouars:

Following one of the oldest customs of Polynesia, I exchanged names with the King; he became Dupetit-Thouars, I became Youtati; from that moment there was nothing he could refuse me, I was the master of the island and especially of his valley and of Madame Youtati who came the very next day with the King to remind me that I was Youtati. I received her very courteously, but did not abuse the magnanimity of such a good prince.[2]

These friendly relations were cemented by gifts on both sides— the Marquesan chief, large and heavily built, with a florid profile which reminded the French of the late Louis XVIII, selected a blue and red flag from the *Vénus*'s stock of signals to use as his personal emblem. He also agreed to receive the two missionaries, offering them half his 'palace'—a hut approximately sixty feet long and fifteen wide built close to the shore—until they should

---

[1] Ibid., vol. ii, p. 335.
[2] Ibid., vol. ii, p. 341. The restraint of Dupetit-Thouars towards the new 'Péti-Tua's lady' is vouched for by his companions. See article on Iotete in O'Reilly and Teissier, *Tahitiens*, pp. 222–4.

have built their own residence. A couple of days later, however, he gave them a piece of land 'in the middle of which stood a house, fair enough and in quite good condition: only the roof needed repairs. The ground was partly covered with coconut trees, with a few breadfruit trees, and was big enough for a garden. The King himself traced the boundaries of this property; they were at once confirmed by a more formal demarcation, and the first step was the erection of the boundary walls, which, according to tradition, are made of dry stones.'[1] Iotete was to display a little more indifference later. He had no objection to the priests' condemnation of the old taboos and customs, and their indirect support helped him to keep control over other chiefs; but he was less anxious to adopt new sets of rules himself. However, when the French sailed, on 9 August, he wept copiously—more like a child who is easily upset and who quickly forgets, thought Deputit-Thouars, than on account of any real sorrow; but, as he was to find out in 1842, the regard the Marquesan chief felt for the Frenchman was real; one can only regret that French officials did not display a comparable understanding in their later dealings with him.

The expedition sailed south and west to continue along the coast of Tahuata, then passed through the channel between the island and Hiva Oa, which was named Canal du Bordelais in honour of Roquefeuil. They went on to Ua Huka, Eiao, and Hatutu. Sighting Motu Iti, they continued to Ua Pu and Nuku-hiva. The whole archipelago had thus been completely surveyed and most of the main islands circumnavigated. The next stage was less successful. It was a search for Magellan's Tiburones Island in 10° 40' south, but, having sailed along this latitude for most of 22 August, Dupetit-Thouars found no sign of land and at nightfall made for the Tuamotus. On the 26th, at 10 a.m., he suddenly saw ahead the atoll of Tikahau, one of the westernmost of the group. He sailed west and south to avoid it, reaching Tahiti on the 28th. The firing of a gun brought out a pilot who took the *Vénus* to Papeete. Dupetit-Thouars wasted no time on pre-liminaries: he at once went to see Moerenhout, outlined the

[1] Dupetit-Thouars, *Voyage*, vol. ii, p. 353.

instructions he had received and the steps he proposed to take. The next day, he wrote to Pritchard, as British consul, and to Moerenhout, as United States consul, warning them of the possibilities of hostilities and offering them asylum for themselves and their families on board the *Vénus*. At the same time, he sent a three-point ultimatum to Queen Pomare. This stated that a letter of apology must be addressed by her to Louis-Philippe, the sum of 2,000 dollars paid forthwith as compensation for the treatment suffered by Fathers Caret and Laval, and the French flag raised on Motu Uta, the small island opposite Papeete, and given a twenty-one-gun salute. Failing acceptance of these terms within twenty-four hours, hostilities would begin.

Pritchard came aboard the same afternoon, offering a bill drawn by the Queen in payment of the indemnity; Dupetit-Thouars declined, insisting on dollars or gold. Pomare had in fact blamed Pritchard for having caused all the trouble through his enmity for the Catholics. She had some justification for this view, but even if she had accepted responsibility she would have found it difficult to raise the money so promptly. Pritchard was thus compelled to advance 500 dollars out of his own pocket and borrow the rest from other Protestant missionaries.[1] Having done this, he returned to the *Vénus* with 125 ounces of gold and a written apology. As the Tahitians had no gunpowder for the salute, Dupetit-Thouars agreed to provide it, together with a French flag which a chief came to borrow, and the ceremony was duly carried out. Thus, within three days of his arrival, his mission was fulfilled. 'Harmonious relations having been re-established and all the trouble smoothed over', he went to visit the Queen. She seemed bored by the proceedings. Dupetit-Thouars interpreted this as evidence that she was apolitical and simply Pritchard's puppet, but—however true this may be—he can hardly have expected her to display much animation in the presence of a man who had just threatened to declare war on her.

As he had done with Dudoit in the Sandwich Islands, Dupetit-Thouars appointed Moerenhout as French consul, as much to

---

[1] According to Orsmond, the Tahitians never paid any money to anyone in respect of this indemnity.

protect him from possible reprisals as to have a French representative in Tahiti. Moerenhout had learnt unofficially, a few days earlier, that, following a complaint addressed by Pritchard to Washington, he had lost his appointment as American consul; Dupetit-Thouars's action thus restored his standing in the island. Not surprisingly, Pomare, advised by Pritchard, was reluctant to accept this new nomination: she asked that someone else be appointed, but Dupetit-Thouars insisted. This done, he also obtained from her a most-favoured-nation agreement, similar to the one signed by Kamehameha III, under which French nationals were guaranteed rights of residence in Tahiti.[1]

Political troubles did not impede trade: fresh supplies of beef, oranges, and guavas were bought daily at reasonable prices. Nor was shore leave stopped: forty to fifty men went ashore each day and there were no incidents. Dupetit-Thouars met an old friend of France, now in disgrace, General Freire, the ex-President of Chile, who was living in exile in Papeete; he had originally been sent to Port Jackson, but had found New South Wales inhospitable and too expensive for him. Then, on 9 September, Dupetit-Thouars learnt that two French warships had arrived in Matavai Bay. These were the *Astrolabe* and the *Zélée*, commanded by Dumont d'Urville and Jacquinot. He started off for Matavai the next morning, but met them half-way, coming to see him. He returned with them to the *Vénus*. D'Urville saw no reason why he should not add his own weight to what Dupetit-Thouars had been trying to achieve. They accordingly both went to pay an official visit to the Queen and Pritchard. D'Urville, even more of an authoritarian than Dupetit-Thouars, spoke firmly to them both: 'Tears were beginning to appear in her eyes which she fixed on me with a fairly evident feeling of anger',[2]—but Dupetit-Thouars's attempts to counteract this dismay and anger provide an interesting sidelight on the visitors' attitude towards Pomare and, indeed, on court life in Papeete: 'at the same time I noticed

---

[1] Although freedom of religion was not included. Within a few months a law was enacted, prohibiting Catholic missionaries from preaching. See under Laplace and the *Artemise*, *infra*.

[2] D'Urville, *Voyage au Pôle Sud*, vol. iv, p. 70.

that Captain Dupetit-Thouars seemed to be trying to tone down its effect, by teasing Pomare in a friendly manner, such as tugging gently at her hair or lightly tapping her cheek; he even added in an affectionate tone that she was wrong to be upset in this way, etc.'[1] She declined to visit the *Astrolabe*, just as she had refused to go on board the *Vénus*, on the grounds that she had to breast-feed her child; accordingly both captains refused her gifts of pigs, hens, and fruit.

This strangely informal scene could not be repeated with Pritchard. D'Urville stressed that he was not paying a call on a missionary, but on the British consul. Pritchard, faced with two equally stern visitors, was at first cold and formal.

Mr. Pritchard is a man some forty-five years of age, thin, dry and bilious-looking. His person displays that pride and that cold dignity and reserve which are so natural to Englishmen when Fortune raises them from the lowest classes to a certain level in life . . . [I said to him:] I should like at least to think that from now on, as a British subject, you will have a better understanding of your duties and that you will protect, even at the risk of your own life, all French citizens should they still chance at a subsequent date to be exposed to such affronts.[2]

Pritchard was at first taken aback by this unexpected confrontation, but he undertook to defend the rights of citizens of all nations, whereupon d'Urville agreed to enter his house, and they later parted 'very satisfied with each other, at least in appearance'.

The day ended with dinner in the *Vénus*, the beginning of a series of exchange visits. The officers of d'Urville's expedition were glad of an opportunity to show the results of their work in the Antarctic, although Dupetit-Thouars, to d'Urville's dismay, was more interested in the art work of Goupil and Lebreton than in charts and reports. They went in a group to visit the former chapel near Matavai and later to Pomare II's tomb, where they parted. De Flotte, a young *aspirant* from the *Vénus*, sought and was granted a transfer to the *Zélée*. D'Urville sailed on 16 September; Dupetit-Thouars, after entertaining Pritchard

[1] Ibid., vol. iv, p. 70. D'Urville had been given a stool, but Dupetit-Thouars and Jacquinot were stretched out on a mat near Pomare.
[2] Ibid., vol. iv, p. 71.

and Moerenhout to dinner, one day later. His mission had been successfully and promptly carried out, but its effects were not permanent. When he returned to the Society Islands in the *Reine-Blanche* in 1842, it was to proclaim a French protectorate over

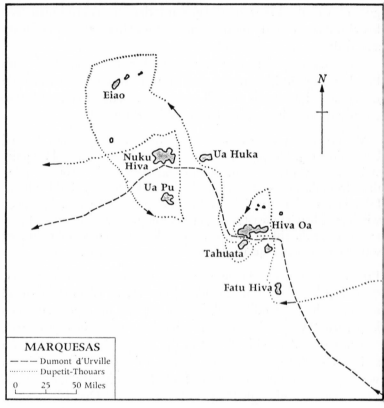

Map 11. Marquesas archipelago

the Queen's possessions, and on his next visit it was for a straightforward annexation: only thus could French missionaries (and French interests) be finally protected.

The next fortnight was devoted to hydrographic work. The expedition sailed west towards Tubuai Manu, then south-west to the Cook group, reaching Mangaia late on 21 September. They sought in vain an island named Roxburgh found on some of their

charts, went on to Rarotonga, and searched fruitlessly for Arm-
strong Island. These were doomed to be 'undiscoveries', which
Dupetit-Thouars set down as faulty sightings of Rarotonga. The
route next led across empty seas to the northern Kermadecs, off
which the *Vénus* remained becalmed in stifling heat for two days.
It was now early October. There was no further work to be done
in these waters. Slowly the *Vénus* sailed south, anchoring in the
Bay of Islands in front of Kororareka on 13 October.

No pilot came to assist the ship to find an anchorage. This
Dupetit-Thouars ascribed to fear of the French, following the
murder of 'Captain Marion du Klémeur' [*sic*].[1] Eventually one
did come who 'could not have timed it better to be useless'; however, John Robertson, as he was called, had been genuinely unable
to come earlier and proved a generous and helpful friend, whose
first gesture was to lend his house for use as an observatory. He
was followed shortly by a local trader, Gilbert Mair, who brought
news of the *Héroine*'s recent departure for the Chatham Islands in
connection with an attack by Maoris on the whaler *Jean Bart*.[2]
Dupetit-Thouars was satisfied that Cécille could deal adequately
with the situation, and devoted his attention instead to the French
whaler *La Manche* which had suffered heavy damage in a storm
and was in danger of being paralyzed by desertions and indiscipline. Expensive repairs were needed, so that the French had to
stay longer than anticipated. The officers occupied their time by
preparing a chart of the bay and 'visiting all the rivers which come
down into it'. There were also visits from local settlers. James
Busby, the British Resident, called twice; he was 'a young man,
pleasant and well brought up, with good manners, and what the
English call a *gentleman*'. Mgr. Pompallier, representing the
Catholic Church, arrived at Dupetit-Thouars's invitation and
dined on board, a man of charm and noble bearing. The elderly
Maori chief Rewa came to lament his poverty: 'in earlier days,
the absolute master of a great part of the land around us, he would
have given proofs of his munificence; he found his poverty
humiliating and it had kept him away from us'. He was consoled
by gifts of axes, shovels, picks, tobacco, flour, and fat. Pomare was

[1] D'Urville, *Voyage au Pôle Sud*, vol. iii, p. 1.   [2] See *infra*, p. 338.

similarly treated, although his complaints scarcely rang true:
'Pomare, like Rewa, complained that the whites had ruined him,
[and that they] did not even allow him to trade in potatoes, pigs,
and women, and gave him nothing in exchange.'[1]

There were various excursions, in particular visits to Maori
points of interest—the account of the stay in New Zealand fills
over 150 pages. Maori tombs, topped by two halves of a canoe,
abounded. On the right bank of the Kawakawa river, Dupetit-
Thouars found one such monument, said to have been erected
over the grave of one of Pomare's ancestors who would have
known Marion du Fresne: 'I bought this mausoleum hoping that
I might bring it back in good enough condition to erect it in the
Paris Jardin des Plantes where I thought it would look striking.
But as it was too large to stow inside the frigate, it was placed in
the mizzen chainwales where, in spite of all our precautions, it was
destroyed when we shipped heavy seas.'[2] Less attractive souvenirs
were also available:

> While the *Vénus* was at Kororareka we saw a small schooner coming
> in to anchor on its way back from the port of Tauranga situated in the
> western part of the Bay of Plenty; this ship was sailing under the New
> Zealand flag[3] and was commanded and partly manned by Englishmen.
> The captain came to offer me a sack full of smoked heads, assuring me,
> in order to decide me, that he would let me have them cheap because,
> he added with regret, several of them had been damaged by rats during
> the crossing. When we were in Rio de Janeiro in 1825 we saw the sum
> of six thousand francs being paid for two similar New Zealand heads
> which were remarkably fine ones on account of the evenness of their
> tattooings and their perfect state of preservation.[4]

Going to the observatory on the 9th with Pompallier, they
discussed the question of land ownership. A local chief reported
that the missionaries were buying up all the spare land they could
because, he claimed, they were anxious to keep the Catholics out

[1] Dupetit-Thouars, *Voyage*, vol. iii, p. 112.
[2] Ibid., vol. iii, p. 109.
[3] This would be the flag adopted by Maori chiefs at the meeting at Waitangi
in 1834, following Busby's attempt to establish a federation of tribes.
[4] Ibid., vol. iii, p. 40.

of the Bay of Islands. Pompallier, who had only recently arrived from Hokianga, on the west coast, where he had established his first mission, was naturally concerned. Robertson, who was also present, offered to give him an entire hillock where he could build a chapel and a presbytery. 'We were very touched by Mr. Robertson's generosity; we thanked him warmly, then begged him to sell us this land, which he agreed to most graciously; he set the price himself at one shilling the acre, which again was a delicate way of giving it to us.'[1] Some land, situated at Waihihi, had been bought by Robertson in association with other European settlers and is recorded as having been sold to Bishop Pompallier for £30 on the very next day—10 November 1838.[2]

By 11 November the work on *La Manche* had been completed and all the charts and surveys finished. The *Vénus* sailed from the bay, making for North Cape, then steered west for Australia. On the 13th the expedition passed between Cape Maria van Diemen and Manawatawi Island and entered the Tasman Sea, which, as it frequently is, was wild and angry. Nevertheless, because of the absence of the predominant south-westerlies, the French reached Sydney in just over ten days. If they had looked forward to a pleasant respite in New South Wales, they were at first sorely disappointed. Dupetit-Thouars paid the customary calls, but with the exception of the harbourmaster and the Catholic bishop, no one was at home.

I had no difficulty in explaining this singular behaviour; it was becoming evident that the letters we had brought from Tahiti, especially those of Mr. Pritchard, must have depicted us as having committed some grievous actions to the detriment of British preponderance in that archipelago . . . The Sydney newspapers soon proved to us that we had guessed the reasons for the attitude of the authorities; I took very little notice of the controversy in these papers, which deserved nothing but contempt, and we turned our attention to the replacement of our food supplies, and the erection of our observatory on Pinchgut Island.[3]

[1] Ibid., vol. iii, pp. 112–13.
[2] L. Keys, *Life and Times of Bishop Pompallier*, pp. 109–10. For Dupetit-Thouars's full dealings with Pompallier, see pp. 106–10.
[3] Dupetit-Thouars, *Voyage*, vol. iii, p. 171.

Nevertheless, the colonial authorities could not ignore the presence of a large French vessel. A deputation of officers from the Fiftieth Regiment came to invite all the ship's officers to dine at their mess. The Australian Club invited them to a function on the 30th at which the Governor, Sir George Gipps, was to be present. The two men met earlier the same day for the first time. Gipps was certainly cool: 'having been informed of the violent hatred he bears towards Catholics, I soon noticed that he had taken Mr. Pritchard's calumnies on trust and shared his feelings towards us'. Gipps may well have felt little sympathy for Roman Catholic interlopers, being himself a parson's son, but his real objection centred on a report that the French had actually taken possession of Tahiti. He began to question Dupetit-Thouars on the steps he had taken at Papeete, but the Frenchman replied that he was not prepared to discuss matters which were no concern of the Governor of New South Wales. They parted, and the evening function was not surprisingly marked by coolness on both sides. On 3 December Gipps wrote to Dupetit-Thouars, through his Colonial Secretary, drawing his attention to the raising and saluting of the French flag at Papeete and to reports made by Pritchard of harsh demands made on Queen Pomare. Plainly, Gipps was concerned about the ceremony on Motu Uta: could this be interpreted as establishing some claim to Tahiti? Dupetit-Thouars had already indicated to the Governor that his primary concern had been to obtain redress for the ill-treatment of Frenchmen; since Gipps now officially referred to Pritchard's letter, he replied mainly with comments on the latter's role in Tahiti, devoting one paragraph each to his various functions—as minister, trader, agent, 'or rather factotum', of Queen Pomare, and interpreter. This was as far as Dupetit-Thouars would go—he not only refused to admit that he was accountable to Gipps for his action, but was careful not to be drawn into a discussion on the possible future of Tahiti. The Governor dropped the subject and relations between them slowly improved. Dupetit-Thouars visited him at his Parramatta estate and found him less formal, but at no stage were the French made to feel truly welcome in official circles.

In December, Dupetit-Thouars went to the La Pérouse

memorial, accompanied by a party led by the Attorney-General, John Plunkett, the Colonial Secretary, Edward Thomson, and their wives. 'We landed near Father Receveur's tomb and paid a visit to La Pérouse's monument . . . Our lunch was a very gay one; confidence had become established as a result of an acquaintance which was now a fortnight old.' But there was no point in prolonging his stay. At dawn on the 9th, the *Vénus* sailed through the Heads and began to make her way south, battling against contrary winds and a wild sea. On 3 January 1839, being then south of Tasmania, she was struck by a violent storm which continued for several days. In almost constant bad weather she suffered considerable damage, the entire foremast structure being endangered by the heavy battering which most of the forepart of the ship was receiving. It was necessary to heave to for repairs, in spite of a heavy swell which caused the bow—and the sailors working on it—to be submerged at regular intervals. By the end of the month the ship was making water at the rate of a foot every twelve hours: the long voyage and the storms were beginning to exact their toll.

Things began to improve on 1 February, after the French turned Cape Leeuwin. Mauritius was sighted on 4 March; they maintained their course for Bourbon, where they arrived on the morrow. No time was wasted: the *Vénus* took in water and fresh food, and went on her way. The repairs appeared to be holding well, but three weeks later when they reached the South African coast they were forced to put into Simon's Bay for further repairs. Dupetit-Thouars rode to Cape Town to obtain supplies of biscuit and whatever else the colony could provide. Deliveries were slow, so that he could not sail until 21 April. By 8 May he was in St. Helena, leaving two days later in company with the *Gange*, a merchant vessel homebound from India. There were rumours of tension between France and Mexico, and latest reports indicated that war had actually broken out and that Mexican corsairs were cruising in the Central Atlantic. Therefore, although this seemed likely to slow him down, Dupetit-Thouars agreed to escort the *Gange* as far as the coast of France. They made their way together to Ascension Island, arriving on 15 May. The *Vénus* was about to fire the customary salute when the Governor sent an urgent message asking the French to omit it: 'It was then the end of the season when the turtles lay their eggs, and it is customary at this time of the year not to fire the gun for fear of frightening the turtles which frequent the bay where they come to lay each night.'[1] The stop was only a brief one, the French sailing the next afternoon. The rest of the voyage was quite uneventful. On 23 June, at the entrance to the Bay of Biscay, they obtained news of the Mexican situation; there was no war and therefore no danger from raiders. The two ships separated, the *Gange* making for Bordeaux, the *Vénus* for Brest. The merchantman had turned out to be a fine sailer which often, with a light breeze, was faster than the frigate. 'We arrived [at Brest] the next day, 24 June 1839, at 6 p.m., after a voyage lasting nearly thirty months, during which we were fortunate enough to lose only one man as the result of an accident and six through illness or desertion.'[2]

The importance of the voyage was recognized at once. Within six weeks the Government authorized the publication of an official account, the first volume of which appeared the following year. Dupetit-Thouars himself was not promoted to the rank of rear-admiral until 1841, but Chiron du Brossay was made an officer of the Legion of Honour, while Néboux, the surgeon, and three of the officers were appointed chevaliers of that order. Only Dortet de Tessan, the hard-working *ingénieur-hydrographe*, was given less than Dupetit-Thouars felt was his due: he received merely an official letter of thanks and commendation. The influence the expedition was to have in the expansionist field was not apparent at first, in spite of all Gipps's suspicions. First impressions were that a fairly firm line had been taken in the Sandwich Islands and a firmer one in Tahiti, and that French missionaries had been well received in one of the Marquesas. But on 22 August 1839 Dupetit-Thouars submitted a report on the Marquesas to the Government in which he commented on their suitability as a penal colony and as a French base. What he proposed was not strictly the first attempt at colonizing the archipelago, for there had been one peculiar plan by an adventurer of French descent,

[1] Dupetit-Thouars, *Voyage*, vol. iii, p. 318.   [2] Ibid., p. 320.

the Baron de Thierry, to take possession of the islands for himself in 1835, but the episode of Charles I, King of Nukuhiva, belongs more to the realm of psychology than to that of colonial history. Dupetit-Thouars, like Laplace before him, considered that a settlement in the Marquesas would not clash with any prior claim of Britain or the United States, as a scheme to settle Hawaii or Tahiti would.[1] The Marquesas, he felt, could become a place of refreshment for merchantmen and whalers second in importance only to the Sandwich Islands, could produce cotton, coffee, and sandalwood for the China trade, and would offer great possibilities for an escape-proof penal settlement.[2] In the same report, he drew attention to the potential of New Zealand, which by now was becoming the focal point of colonial endeavours; but it was too late, and, when the future of New Zealand as a British possession was no longer in doubt, France turned back to the Marquesas and sent him to take them over. But few of the great possibilities he had foreseen for them ever eventuated.

It will be remembered that an important factor in the dispatch of the *Vénus* expedition had been the protection of French whalers. Dupetit-Thouars's 'Rapport sur la pêche de la baleine'[3] was a detailed document covering problems of discipline, the most suitable types of ships to be used, the supplies needed on a voyage, the most fruitful fishing-grounds, and the best places of refreshment. It was a useful and practical document. Although the reference to scientific work in the instructions had been primarily a courteous gesture to the learned societies, the expedition also brought back 'a wealth of precious information' on sea currents, magnetism, barometric pressure, and tides. Some useful work had been done on longitudes, and de Tessan brought back twenty-one valuable charts on Kamchatka, California, the Galapagos, and the South-East Pacific. Although none of the officers had travelled any distance inland, the natural-history specimens obtained were far from negligible. There was a live bear and a

[1] Although he admitted the existence of a possible claim by the U.S. as a consequence of Commodore David Porter's temporary occupation of Nukuhiva in 1813–14.

[2] Faivre, *Expansion Française*, pp. 464–5.

[3] Reprinted in the third volume of his *Voyage*, pp. 345–96.

'magnificent' skeleton of another, obtained by Néboux in the forests of California; there was, above all, a fine collection of 430 birds—'we have seen few ornithological collections in which, in proportion to the total, the number of objects of interest is as high as it is in Mr. Néboux's collection'.[1] There were 1,500 shells, 230 plants from Australia, and 40 from Tahiti donated by Jacques Moerenhout. In addition, there were samples from the sea bottom off Petropavlovsk, rocks from Monterey and Payta, and 140 samples of Peruvian copper- and silver-bearing rock. Dupetit-Thouars and his officers fully deserved the thanks and praise which the Académie des Sciences bestowed on them. But the voyage had shown once again how little there was left to discover. To add new features and new names to the map, explorers would have to seek more distant shores, so often defended by ice, or concentrate with infinite patience on the minutiae of coastal surveys. Never again would they see new islands rise up over the horizon and naked savages assemble in wonderment along the surf-beaten shore. The politicians, the administrators, the 'black-birders', were even now sailing towards the Pacific to weave their patterns of European rivalries across its enormous expanse. D'Urville himself, now engaged on his great final voyage, was to do his best work along the far edge of the Pacific; elsewhere he was, like his colleagues, a mere representative of French political interests; and, when he sailed away, the curtain fell for the last time on the age of exploration.

[1] 'Rapport sur les résultats concernant l'histoire naturelle', in *Voyage*, vol. iii, p. 469.

LAPLACE AND THE *ARTÉMISE*

BEFORE one can deal with the second voyage of Dumont d'Urville, it is necessary to mention the two other expeditions which the French sent to the Pacific in 1837 before his departure in September. The more important of these was undeniably Laplace's, but the aims in each case were non-scientific. His instructions were quite explicit: 'The mission you are going to carry out has as its basic purpose to render to French trade every service in your power, either by obtaining, in the foreign settlements which you will visit, information of value to the commercial operations of the shipowners and traders of our ports, or by offering to their ships the protection which naval units are everywhere called upon to give them . . .'[1]

Once again special attention was to be paid to the needs of whaling undertakings, and as before scientific interests, although secondary, were not to be neglected. In many ways the Laplace expedition was to follow so closely the pattern laid down for Dupetit-Thouars as to become fully complementary to it. There were differences in the itinerary—Laplace was to enter the Pacific from the west, having spent a considerable part of 1838 in the Arabian Gulf, India, and South-East Asia, and omit Kamchatka—[2] but these were planned to cover as large an area of Asian and Pacific waters as possible. The July monarchy was at last turning its full attention to long-distance commerce; having almost digested its earlier conquests in Africa, the throne itself now being secure, it felt confident and eager for further expansion. One could claim that this change of attitude was underlined in the case of Laplace's second voyage by the appointment of the Prince d'Eckmühl as what may be called an auxiliary political observer.

---

[1] Laplace, *Campagne de circumnavigation de la frégate* l'Artémise, vol. i, p. xii. This account, in six volumes, is well written, but precise details and navigational data are relatively scarce.

[2] Although he hoped at one time to be able to go there, see *infra*, p. 334.

The true motive for this is by no means clear—it may be, quite simply, that his mother, the widow of Marshall Davoût and the sister-in-law of Pauline Bonaparte, wished to remove him for a while from the attractions of Paris society, for the young nobleman was leading a fairly rakish existence. He was seconded to the expedition by the Ministry of War and received his instructions from the Ministry for Foreign Affairs; these were to report on the need for French representatives in the Sandwich Islands, in Australia, and in Chiloe, and to draw up a general report on the value of the latter island as a place of refreshment for whaling crews. In Sydney he was to contact Patrick Dillon, whom the French Government were thinking of appointing as consul.[1] As it turned out, Eckmühl did not go beyond Madras.

Laplace's first officer was Esprit-Martin Long, who was promoted lieutenant-commander a few months after the expedition's departure. Among the other officers, one finds François Pâris, who had already sailed in the *Favorite*; Léon Fourichon, who was to become an admiral and a minister of marine under the Third Republic; Edouard de Carpegna, who was to return to Tahiti with Dupetit-Thouars and become harbourmaster of Papeete; Max de Nansouty, who was also to return to Papeete, but to be killed in a riot in 1844; and one name which also belongs to the Pacific, Charles de Surville. The complement, 465 officers and men, included a large number of raw sailors who 'from the point of view of health and physique left much to be desired'. The *Artémise*, a frigate of fifty-two guns, had recently returned from a cruise to the West Indies, the United States, and Canada, although unfortunately for Laplace a high proportion of her men had finished their time and were paid off. But there was nothing unusual in a captain complaining of the presence of new recruits, and in time they proved themselves fully adequate for their work. Laplace seems to have taken particular care of his crew's morale: while at Gorée, in West Africa, he organized a school where they could learn to read and write—but he noted with regret that not all of them availed themselves of these facilities and of those who did not many persevered. He sought to reduce the harshness of

[1] Jore, *Océan Pacifique*, vol. i, p. 187.

traditional punishments and to avoid having to order them by discovering in advance possible causes of dissatisfaction and disaffection. His estimate of their poor physique, however, would seem accurate, for he noticed when fevers, dysentery, and scurvy made their appearance soon after the *Artémise* crossed the Line that the new recruits were almost exclusively the ones affected; the death rate was certainly far higher than it had been during the voyage of the *Favorite*.

Everything was ready by mid January 1837. The *Artémise* sailed from Toulon on the 20th, promptly found a favourable wind, sailed into the Atlantic within a fortnight, and made for the Canaries. At Tenerife on 13 February, Laplace met Mgr. Pompallier, who had left France before him in the *Delphine* on his way to Polynesia, but was now held up through sickness and the need to repair the ship. The expedition next went to Gorée for supplies, then sailed south-west across the Atlantic to within sight of Trinidad and Martin Vas. Storms began to batter and delay the frigate, and sickness spread rapidly. Laplace tried to improve morale by promoting a state 'of mirth as well as contentment among the crew', but it was evident that only the sight of land would reduce the wretchedness of his men. When they reached Cape Town on 1 April, 'abundant refreshments and frequent walks ashore promptly restored the health of the men who were sick when we arrived, and restored everyone to a state of fitness in order to face, without fear of illness, the trials we would have to meet on our way to Bourbon'.[1] Trials began almost as soon as they sailed, on 22 April: gales lasting until 4 May were succeeded by showers and uncertain breezes. 'I was almost consoled by the pleasure I felt in seeing, during the squalls, how our young men had progressed since our departure from Toulon', but sickness returned and one man, Fumelot, 'a gentle man, a wise and able sailor', succumbed to a fever. The weather improved on 24 May and two days later the *Artémise* anchored in Bourbon. Laplace believed that the abolition of slavery, the burning issue of the day, would turn out to be disastrous for the colonies—he had already commented on this at Gorée. The trade itself had been

---

[1] Laplace, *Campagne,* vol. i, pp. 326–7.

outlawed by France in 1818, but the institution remained, to be
finally abolished in all French colonies in 1848. 'It is clear', wrote
Laplace, 'that the settlers cannot avoid utter ruin if the government adopts these fatal measures.'[1] The prosperity of Bourbon,
he considered, compared favourably with the economic situation
in France, where 'our cities and our countryside are full of poor
wretches a thousand times less fortunate than the negroes'—but
the price of wine and flour was so high that he refused to buy any.
Bourbon, anyhow, struck him as dull and provincial; he sailed as
soon as he could for 'the brilliant and gracious Île de France'. He
took with him fifteen coloured youths whom he felt it would be
to the colony's advantage to train in the skills of the sea. This
enabled him to leave behind 'puny and sickly men who, taken on
at Toulon in spite of my protests to make up the numbers, had
quickly fallen victim to the diseases of hot climates'.[2] His losses
at this stage included one death, two desertions at Cape Town,
and two seamen left in the Bourbon hospital; two more were to
desert in Mauritius.

In Port-Louis he gave vent again to anti-abolitionist feelings.
Slave-owners had received an indemnity which had caused inflation, honest farmers found it impossible to employ labour, former
slaves roamed the island, there were not enough magistrates to
deal with the crime wave, and the prisons were overcrowded.
The true picture was visible only to a convinced anti-abolitionist;
more casual observers might fail to notice the evil which was
rampant just below the surface:

this evil was hidden under a varnish of wealth and splendour that was
so seductive, Port-Louis was so brilliant, so animated that without the
deep knowledge I had of the country I could have been misled and
believed that the Île de France was happier and wealthier than ever
before. The capital was the abode of noisy pleasures; there was a daily
round of banquets and balls. A new theatre, built of stone, rather
attractively designed, could scarcely hold all the spectators drawn
thither several times a week by a company of actors from Paris.
Excessive gambling, heavy bets laid at the horse races which had just

[1] Laplace, *Campagne*, vol. ii, p. 39.
[2] Ibid., vol. ii, pp. 59-60.

become fashionable in the colony ... and many other equally expensive forms of entertainment offered to the townspeople opportunities for displaying their prodigality.[1]

Laplace's conservatism was fortunately tempered by his paternalistic concern for his men. But it is clear that he was disappointed by Mauritius. He could not give a reception on board because he could not accommodate all those he was expected to invite, and decided not to risk offending anyone. The situation was complicated by the strained relationship which was all too apparent between island society and the British administration. And in addition the high price of sugar, coming on top of the slave indemnity, had sent up the price of every commodity. Once again, he refused to buy more than the absolute minimum and sailed without delay, on 19 June. His yearning for bygone days was to be satisfied by his next stop, the tiny coral island of Agalega, to which its owner, M. de Saint-Aulaire, had invited him. It was pleasant, peaceful, covered with coconut trees, bathed by the lazy lapping water of a small lagoon, and totally free from economic and political troubles. The Seychelles, where the *Artémise* arrived on the 26th, were less prosperous than he had found them on his first voyage, and this he naturally blamed on the abolition of slavery. His call at Mahé was forced on him by damage to the rigging, which he repaired as quickly as he could because the heat was causing some of his men to fall ill again. Then, after some delay near the Equator, he picked up the southwest monsoon, which brought him rapidly to Trincomalee. There, with the assistance of Admiral Keppel, he could at last buy material at a reasonable price: 'Admiral Keppel did not restrict his courtesies towards me to a kindly and affable welcome. He insisted on the Trincomalee arsenal providing me with the supplies needed for the frigate, and I was thus able to replace an anchor lost among rocks in the Seychelles, and broken or lost spars, as well as a number of items which were becoming short, for all of which I would have had to pay far more everywhere else in India.'[2]

---

[1] Ibid., vol. ii, p. 84.   [2] Ibid., vol. ii, pp. 456–7.

He gave a reception on board the *Artémise* to express his thanks, and made his way to the Coromandel coast, reaching Pondicherry on 4 August. He was writing at the same time a detailed report on trade and social problems in India. Food was inexpensive, as he had hoped, and supplies of good Bordeaux wine had recently been landed. Shore leave and plentiful food restored everyone's health, so that nothing could indicate 'when we sailed, in the evening of 16 August, the cruel losses which, a few days later, were to plunge our ship into mourning'. Cholera broke out two days after a call at Madras. The seriousness of the disease was increased by the effect it had on morale: most of the young crew came from Provence, where, a few years earlier, an outbreak of cholera had resulted in heavy loss of life. This was still fresh in their minds, many had lost close relatives, and this their first voyage already held for them all the terrors of the unknown and the unfamiliar. Fortunately, the first outbreak was mild—only one man died—but when they reached the mouth of the Hoogly, they were held up for ten days waiting for a favourable combination of winds and tide. Laplace was not willing to risk his frigate between the sandbanks without a pilot; as he waited for one of the steamboats to come from Calcutta, cholera reappeared:

Several men [died] and in a short time the hospital was so overcrowded with the sick that I was forced to reserve for them a large area of the battery deck, in spite of all the regrettable physical and mental consequences of this health measure. At the same time weather and atmospheric conditions made our position even worse: the rain falling in torrents almost continually and the roll of the ship, which was both violent and unending, caused by waves stirred up by a very strong wind, forced us to keep constantly closed all the openings through which the outside air could have driven out the poisonous air which infected the inside of the frigate. The epidemic had made frightening progress: fifty sailors were laid low, and several officers were affected by the scourge under whose influence everyone on board was suffering to some degree. The stocks of fresh food were exhausted, even medicine was in short supply, when finally on the morning of the 12th, a favorable breeze having sprung up as the tide was rising, we were able to drop anchor that evening at Sagor, under the lee of the banks.[1]

[1] Laplace, *Campagne*, vol. ii, p. 273.

The epidemic receded and Laplace was able to take the steam packet from Kedgeree to Calcutta. The losses were not too severe: five men had died, but two *élèves* and two youths had already been left behind in the Pondicherry and Chandernagore hospitals. Laplace recruited three men in Calcutta, one of whom deserted six months later. His conservatism returned in Bengal, where he blamed languishing trade on attempts by the British to break down the caste system, or at least their refusal to pay adequate attention to it in their relations with their Indian subjects. What he called 'the baneful effects' of this policy seemed to have been again a shortage of cheap labour on large country estates.

The next few months were spent at various points along the Indian coast. He first sailed towards Sumatra, sighting the northern highlands on 28 October and going down the west coast to Pulau Raya; he then turned back across the Indian Ocean to Ceylon, then on to Calicut and to the French India settlement at Mahé, making calls at a number of points on the way.

The presence of the *Artémise* in every naval sector of Hindustan accessible to our shipowners was having a most beneficial effect on their activities; at the same time the sight of a frigate of such fine dimensions and so carefully fitted out in every respect gave the native a high opinion of this French navy which our rivals were trying to make people believe was now worthless. I was all the more eager to alter this opinion among the Malabar people because France, which has perhaps fallen to a greater extent from its ancient glory along these shores than in Coromandel, has now no possessions left there.[1]

By the end of December Laplace had made his way to Goa, the Portuguese settlement; the political unrest there caused him to be regarded with such suspicion that he was unable to obtain any of the information about trade and local conditions which he sought at every stop. He then went on to Bombay, where he took in stores for his exploration of the Arabian coast.[2]

---

[1] Ibid., vol. iii, p. 201.
[2] It is typical of the carelessness which mars this otherwise readable account that he states that he left Mahé on 25 December, reached Goa on the 30th, but Bombay on the 12th.

The *Artémise* sailed from Bombay on 4 February 1838, going first to Diu, then to Muscat, where she dropped anchor on 2 March. Here one of the men jumped ship—a deserter from the *Néréide* whom Laplace had taken on in Calcutta. It was the first desertion for many months. The expedition reached Socotra Island on 16 March and turned back after reaching Mokha at the end of the month. The British were to capture Aden a few months later, an incident which inspired in him comments which reflect the general attitude of the pro-expansionists of the time:

The painful feeling which this latest invasion by Great Britain has caused was without doubt a natural reaction, for it is hard to see passing daily in this way under the yoke of a rival nation cities, provinces, and entire countries, which with a little foresight we could have placed under our laws. . . . Would it not be better to follow her example, that is to say to play our part in this kind of sharing out of the globe among the great European powers?[1]

Laplace was back in Muscat on 23 April. He stayed there five days, then made for Bander-Abbas at the entrance to the Persian Gulf. Like the rest of the ports he visited it was 'a spectacle of desolation'—barren, parched, and poverty-stricken, burning under a 'truly frightful heat'. After a final visit to Muscat, he set course for Ceylon, sailed through Nine Degree Channel between the Maldives and the Laccadives, sighted Ceylon on 27 May, and anchored in Trincomalee two days later. The Pacific stage of the voyage was now about to begin. It opened with a near-tragedy: arriving at Pondicherry on 4 June, the French went as a party to visit a foundry at Porto Novo; there Pâris caught his sleeve in some machinery and his mangled left arm had to be amputated. In Madras, ten days later, an outbreak of dysentery forced them to leave as quickly as they could, but after a temporary improvement the epidemic worsened as they passed the Nicobar Islands. Held back by contrary winds, the *Artémise* did not reach Pulau Penang until 1 July. The number of sick continued to rise. Hoping Malacca might prove healthier, Laplace continued on his way after a few days, but still struggling against a steady opposing

[1] Laplace, *Campagne*, vol. iii, pp. 488–9.

breeze he did not reach the port until the 15th. Forty sick, the worst cases, were taken to a large house which was converted into a hospital for their use. Fifteen men died between the expedition's departure from Pondicherry and 28 July, when it sailed for Singapore; another four were to die soon after.

The *Artémise* sailed into Tourane Bay on 12 August 1838. The area was deserted, in accordance with the Emperor's policy of forbidding all communication and contact between his people and the outside world. A ship came out of the river mouth, filled with soldiers, which anchored close to the frigate; from that moment no one could land without being accompanied by a detachment of soldiers who were far more efficient than they had been on previous occasions in interposing themselves whenever the French approached the inhabitants. This prevented Laplace from receiving news from the few remaining French missionaries. Reporting on their ill treatment at the hands of the authorities was the main purpose of his visit—'and to put an end, so far as this would be in my power, to a state of affairs which was so opposed to the propagation of the Catholic religion and therefore to our political influence in those parts'. A visit from a mandarin sent by the Emperor brought greetings and good wishes, and facilitated the purchase of supplies from the Tourane markets; but at no stage could he discuss the rumoured persecution of missionaries and converts or receive any firm news. He sailed on 21 August, having achieved nothing of any diplomatic value. Although it is difficult to see what he could have done in view of his ignorance of conditions inside the country and of his inability to obtain any information, his failure was severely criticized: Bishop de Courvoisier, who was in charge of South-East Asian missions, meeting Dumont d'Urville in Singapore in July 1839, 'complained bitterly about Captain Laplace, of the frigate *Artémise*, in connection with his behaviour in Cochin-China, where he could, he added, have saved the life of a missionary under sentence of death, had he wanted to make some kind of demonstration on his behalf'.[1]

The crossing to Manila was uneventful, and most of the sick finally recovered. Laplace remained in the Philippines from

[1] Dumont d'Urville, *Voyage au Pôle Sud*, vol. vii, p. 90.

30 August to 16 October, repairing his ship and laying in enough stores for six months. He then sailed to Macao, going up to visit his former acquaintances at Canton, and went south to the Anambas, through the Straits of Banka, and on to Batavia, where he arrived on 2 December, taking good care, however, to anchor well away from the city and the river mouth so as to minimize contact with the inhabitants and avoid sickness among his men. He left again on the 13th, passed through Sunda Strait and out into the Indian Ocean.[1]

Favourable winds sped the *Artémise* towards Tasmania. At dawn on 25 January 1839, she was in sight of Bruni Island, and the next day she anchored in Hobart. The attractive appearance of the city and its growth were impressive; but the back streets were less savoury. A group of French sailors on shore leave were involved in a brawl. They seem to have come out victorious from this incident, although most of them had to be sent to hospital—'in spite of this, the warlike accounts so inflamed the adventurous spirits of their colleagues that I found myself compelled to confine the entire crew to the ship for several days, otherwise the places of ill repute in the capital of Van Diemen would quickly have been sacked'.[2] Laplace was interested in the Australian prisons, since he had been instructed to report on suitable sites for penal settlements. He also needed supplies of flour and, as these were not immediately available, he was able to visit both Hobart prison and the camp for incorrigibles at Port Arthur. Both places favourably impressed him, especially the former, which was well kept and clean. Many women in Europe, he reflected, even those who were free, did not live in such good surroundings. 'I agreed fully with the head of the establishment who, in reply to several comments by the Governor [of Tasmania, Sir John Franklin], did not

---

[1] This marks the end of the fourth volume of his *Campagne*. The next one did not appear until 1853: 'the blame [for this] can be laid on the revolutions which have disturbed our country.' But seven years elapsed between the publication of the first volume in 1841 and the overthrow of Louis-Philippe in 1848, so that Laplace's tendency to fill his account with personal observations scarcely related to his voyage (e.g. a discussion of penal systems and prisons in the United States, France, and Britain) must bear a share of the blame. As an account of a circumnavigation, *Campagne* could have stood some pruning.

[2] Laplace, *Campagne*, vol. v, p. 46.

hesitate to declare that, in his view, the fate of these ugly creatures was far too happy.'[1] Nevertheless he conceded that the atmosphere of restriction, threats, and punishment counteracted the attractions of a pleasant climate, adequate space, and clean quarters; and he realized that no attempt at reform was ever made, that inmates never heard 'a consoling voice which might awaken in a soul some glimmer of virtue' and that they lacked equally the opportunity to discuss their 'struggles against the spirit of evil' with a religious adviser.

When it was time to leave, the Hobartians presented Laplace with the same kind of problem as he had encountered in Mauritius. According to reports, the citizens of Hobart were divided into warring factions: 'How could I bring together in the same drawing room, side by side so to speak, and especially entertain, families who, having become deadly enemies for more or less serious reasons, refused to meet, but towards whom I had, nevertheless, equal obligations?' However, he felt that he could not sail without formally expressing his thanks to all those who had shown him hospitality and kindness; nor could he hope to thread his way with any hope of success through the involved feuds of a small colonial society. He decided to invite everyone, and requested his officers to display equally to all the guests the utmost charm they could muster. The evening was a great success.

When he left, he took with him one sailor who had transferred from the French whaler *Réunion*, but he had lost five deserters, including one Malcolm Macpherson whose presence in a French frigate seems nowadays somewhat incongruous. When the French arrived in Port Jackson on 2 March, they met a handful of young French settlers who, 'attracted by the brilliant promises made by immigration agents who had come to Paris to recruit colonists for the Southern Lands, had sought fortune on these distant shores'. Most had succeeded in establishing trading houses through which they imported French goods—brandy, liquors, foodstuffs, dresses, perfume, and furniture. One of these was probably Jules Joubert, whose brother was sailing to meet him in the *Héroïne*. Dupetit-Thouars had considered him a suitable

[1] Ibid., vol. v, p. 13.

person to appoint as French consul, but this was not acted upon. Joubert later became the first mayor of Hunter's Hill in Sydney.[1] Laplace also called on friends he had met on his first voyage, but most of the officials were cool:

apart from a very small number of my good friends of the *Favorite* days, among whom I am happy to include Sir John Jamison and Mr. Jones, a member of the Legislative Council,[2] who displayed the same cordiality as in the past, I did not have cause in general to be satisfied with the reception of the remainder of Sydney's high society, including most government officials. The enthusiasm for our July Revolution, which I had found so strong in 1831, had completely vanished, to be replaced by feelings of jealousy and ill-will whose effects I encountered at every step. Heroic France could find admirers among them, but a France which had become great, rich, and powerful, which was trying to compete with Great Britain in commerce and political influence in distant countries, was merely a target for jealousy; we received from those same people whose acclaim had greeted the *Favorite*'s tricolour only a cool and embarrassed reception. Several recent events, admittedly, had further aroused this feeling of national rivalry: never had so many of our warships appeared at the same time on Australia's shores. Firstly the *Vénus*, commanded by Captain Dupetit-Thouars who had made the Queen of Taïti pay dearly for the ill treatment to which, at the instigation of Methodist or Wesleyan ministers, our Catholic missionaries had found themselves exposed in her realm; then the *Astrolabe* and the *Zélée*, both under the command of Captain d'Urville; then the handsome corvette, *Héroïne*, Captain Cécille; and finally the *Artémise* whose captain, although he had arrived after the distinguished officers I have just named, seemed to give no less umbrage to the politicians and saints of New South Wales.[3]

Laplace was partly correct in his interpretation of France's unpopularity in Australia. A powerful reason which he only touches on is the cumulative effect of reports on attempted religious penetration by Catholic missionaries in Hawaii, the Marquesas,

[1] Jore, *Océan Pacifique*, vol. ii, p. 79.
[2] Richard Jones, landowner and banker, appointed to the Legislative Council in 1829.
[3] Laplace, *Campagne*, vol. v, p. 255. The saints referred to are Low Church groups.

and Tahiti, and the general suspicion that the French Government's intervention on their behalf concealed expansionist plans. Laplace himself, having received new instructions from France, was to impose a clause on religious freedom in Tahiti, which aroused considerable indignation in New South Wales. Had he visited Sydney after his stop in the Society Islands, the 'saints' would have taken even greater umbrage.[1] Nevertheless, Laplace was able to give a dinner and ball, and was invited to a number of receptions: if the officials had no wish to appear cordial, they could not show actual discourtesy towards their visitors. He was also able to visit the jail, but this time he was put off by the appearance of the jailers: 'It would be impossible to see coarser, more repulsive, or more sinister faces than those of the keepers of every rank. How they treated the convicts!'[2]

As the *Artémise* prepared to sail, a French whaler arrived in port, forced to put in by a mutinous crew. 'It would be difficult to picture the astonishment of these trouble-makers when they found, at the very place where they expected to carry out their evil schemes, a warship belonging to their own nation; it can be compared to what robbers, about to commit some evil deed, would feel upon meeting policemen.' Laplace sent some of his men over to carry out a few repairs, and officers to admonish the crew. The whaler was able to sail from Sydney within three days, and the *Artémise* followed almost at once. Laplace had begun to feel that the French Government's efforts to assist the whaling industry were not really worth the cost. The undisciplined whaler crews needed constant surveillance, while their ill treatment of natives in the South Seas gave Europeans a bad name, impeded trade, and at times led to reprisals against innocent parties. Desertions were inevitable in trading vessels and, indeed, in his own; this 'plague' cost him five men in Sydney. 'Desertion . . . was decimating our crew, without the police being able to offer me any assistance.' Each day brought forward its ration of troubles

---

[1] Witness this comment in a letter from Captain J. C. Wickham to Stuart Donaldson: 'What do you think of La Place? But I am not astonished at anything done by the Pope through such agents as Frenchmen. Poor helpless Tahitians!' (Mitchell Library Papers on Education 1804–68, p. 216).

[2] Laplace, *Campagne*, vol. v, p. 234.

and weariness: 'I felt as if I were isolated and the object of a kind of continual supervision.' He sailed with a feeling of relief on 18 March 1839.

The route now lay across the Tasman Sea, almost due east to the northern point of New Zealand, briefly glimpsed after a painful battle against contrary winds and a heavy swell. 'Thus it was that, before we had sight of the northern part of New Zealand . . . a sailor, working on the bowsprit, fell overboard when the ship pitched violently and sank so quickly that, in spite of a search by several boats we at once sent to his rescue, he could not be found.'[1] Even after a month, the sky remained grey, and the inside of the ship, soaked by constant rain and heavy seas, could not be dried. Things improved a little when the *Artémise* reached the tropics, sighting Tubuai Manu on 21 April and Tahiti the next day; but the island peaks were still hidden by low clouds when the *Artémise*, having remained hove-to during the night, sailed closer in-shore to continue her route to Point Venus:

> There was no danger shown on the chart; however some *élèves* sent as lookouts to the top of the masts were watching the route ahead of us, while several officers and I standing on the poop were exploring, so to speak, the surroundings. All these precautions were useless; my gloomy foreboding was realized: the mizzen-mast lookout had just called out that there patches on the surface of the water. I had borne off towards the open sea, when the *Artémise*, violently striking a coral reef, had her rudder torn off, and stopped suddenly. There was a fresh breeze coming almost straight towards our stern; heavy rollers lifted the ship, making it roll painfully across the sickbed to which she seemed to be tied.[2]

Laplace had a choice between trying to get over the reef and warping the frigate back. The latter operation would have taken time, have involved struggling against the wind, and have brought the ship into deeper water. Since it could be presumed that she had suffered damage below the waterline and was making water, only the first solution was feasible. He set all his sails, and towed by his boats, and with the help of the breeze and the swell, he

---

[1] Laplace, *Campagne*, vol. v, p. 354.   [2] Ibid., vol. v, p. 357.

managed to struggle over the reef. 'But in what a state, great Heavens! no rudder, part of the keel torn off, and so much water pouring in that a hundred men working at the pumps could scarcely keep the ship afloat.' A spare rudder was hastily fitted, the weather remaining overcast and threatening all the while. In the evening an American whaler appeared, whose captain agreed to accompany the *Artémise* to Papeete and take off her crew should she founder. It was an anxious night—'water below the decks and rain above'. The men worked at the pumps almost continually. At dawn the land was shrouded in fog. It cleared at about ten o'clock, and in the afternoon the *Artémise* was able to approach Papeete and anchor off Taunoa. Two days later she was towed to a more suitable part of the bay where she could be careened. Repairs began at once, with 120 natives employed daily to work at the pumps or do other menial tasks which would free the more skilled sailors for more important duties.

The situation soon looked much brighter. The Tahitians were cheerful workers: 'their dances, their almost continual singing, amused our sailors who, for their part, were living in the most perfect harmony with them and with both sexes of the population of Papeïti and district. The native chiefs accustomed to seeing fights, disorderly behaviour, and scenes of debauchery in their town when a few ships lay at anchor, were astonished when they saw the greatest peace and quiet reigning around them.'[1] There was no shortage of food, since every day the islanders and their wives came up with baskets of fruit and vegetables. There was not even the presence of Pritchard to spoil this idyllic scene, for he was temporarily out of Tahiti. Nevertheless Queen Pomare had left Papeete, and a number of influential chiefs seemed anxious to follow her example. Laplace put this down to rumours spread by the English missionaries that 'as soon as the frigate was repaired violence and spoliation of property' would replace the current pleasant relations. It is more likely that Pomare, remembering the recent visits of Dupetit-Thouars and d'Urville, wanted to avoid yet another unpleasant confrontation. However, there were minor incidents. Some of the local workers, mostly

[1] Ibid., vol. v, p. 364.

Marquesans, went on strike for a short time, while some Tahitians, emboldened by the presence of the French, taunted the occasional missionary who came down to watch the work.

The repairs took nearly two months—the careening had revealed extensive damage along forty feet of keel. When everything was completed and the *Artémise* was once more seaworthy, Laplace took steps to carry out his instructions 'to ask ... reparation for the bad treatment accorded to our compatriots in the Society Islands, under the pretext that they were Catholics; and ask as far as I could for limits to be set to the temporal power which the [British] missionaries had arrogated to themselves in the Society archipelago; so that such happenings should not recur'.[1] On 19 June he requested the Queen to call the chiefs together to hear an important communication. She replied that her health was not good enough for her to travel to Papeete. Laplace then asked her to appoint someone to preside over the meeting in her absence; she selected an elderly relative of hers, 'the governor of the main town and a supporter of my opponents'. On the 20th a large crowd gathered in the Wesleyan chapel. Laplace read a new clause which he wished inserted in the treaty signed by Dupetit-Thouars and Pomare; it provided for the free exercise of the Catholic religion. He left the meeting, with Moerenhout defending his interests. He had other allies: Tati, 'my friend', spoke in support of the clause. A decision was put off until the morrow. Pomare, 'possibly also giving way to feminine curiosity', came to Papeete that afternoon. She met Laplace, who invited her to visit his ship. Charm worked better than bullying; there was furthermore no Pritchard to make up her mind for her; she agreed to the clause on the morning of the 21st, came to see the *Artémise*, and stayed to lunch. The ratification of the treaty was completed that very evening in an atmosphere more friendly than he had ever hoped. 'Victory was decisively ours.' The law prohibiting the teaching of non-Protestant doctrines—what Lord Palmerston had called 'an intolerant and indefensible Edict'[2]—had been repealed. Laplace had every reason to be satisfied with his work

[1] Laplace, *Campagne*, vol. v, p. 395.
[2] Haldane, *Tempest over Tahiti*, p. 101.

in Tahiti. But there was more to be done: he sailed at dawn on the 22nd for Hawaii, where 'I was to find myself faced by opponents who were far more active, far more intolerant, and far more enamoured with temporal power than those against whom I had recently fought'.[1]

The unreliable *Campagne* gives 19 July as the date of arrival at Honolulu, but it is clear that this is an error for the 9th.[2] The King was in one of the other islands, so Laplace presented his conditions to the Governor of Oahu, and at the same time surveyed the fort and planned the landings and strategy he would undertake if his requests were refused. The lightly veiled ultimatum worked once again. Catholics who had been imprisoned for their beliefs were liberated, and the Council, in the King's absence, agreed to grant freedom of religion throughout the archipelago and to a deposit of 20,000 piastres as a guarantee of good faith.[3] The European settlers appeared glad that the power of the Protestant missionaries had at last been broken (no doubt some disliked the restrictions on the sale of liquor, which these had tried to impose). The British Consul came to congratulate Laplace; and a subsequent unofficial inquiry by the American Commodore Read does not appear to have come out in support of the missionaries. On the 13th, a Sunday, the freeing of religious practices was marked by a solemn High Mass celebrated ashore by Father Walsh and attended by Laplace, his officers, a detachment of soldiers, and most of the crew, led by a band. The King himself, who had arrived incognito during the morning, did not seem at all put out by recent events and sent a message to Laplace offering to meet him. The Frenchman agreed at once. Kamehameha appeared, wearing the uniform of an English colonel and accompanied by his two sisters, whose presence kept on distracting Laplace 'or to put it more correctly took up my whole attention . . . two women, still young, at least five foot six high, appropriately proportioned, and blessed with attractions of which the most unbridled imagination could not conjure up the gigantic development'. But he kept enough

[1] *Campagne*, vol. v, p. 428.
[2] See Yzendoorn, *History of the Catholic Mission*, p. 134.
[3] The money was returned in 1846.

presence of mind to obtain from the King a commercial treaty
providing for most-favoured-nation terms and removing the ban
on the importation of certain French goods. This the King ratified
on 17 July 1839. Laplace had again succeeded in ending a long-
standing dispute and in defeating the aims of intolerant missionaries; but two of the clauses in the new treaty seemed to go beyond
establishing equality for French interests. Under Article IV
Frenchmen were removed from the jurisdiction of the King or
his officers: 'No Frenchman accused of any crime whatever shall
be judged otherwise than by a jury consisting of foreign residents,
proposed by the French consul and accepted by the Government
of the Sandwich Islands'; while Article VI prevented the King
from prohibiting the importation of French wines and brandies
and from taxing them at a higher rate than 5 per cent. 'This convention was the beginning of a system of unequal treaties which
fettered the domestic policy and plagued the foreign relations of
the country for many years.'[1] As for the liquor clause, it did little
good because direct French trade with the islands remained
negligible, so that American and British traders reaped the
benefits of the reduced duties in accordance with their own
countries' most-favoured-nation treaties. In addition, 'to impose
by force the admission of the Catholic missionaries and the introduction of brandies was to create a shocking confusion of ideas
in the mind of the people and place a redoubtable weapon in the
hands of the Protestant missionaries'.[2]

Nevertheless Laplace could feel satisfied with his work in the
Pacific. He sailed on 20 July, no longer able, as he had hoped, to go
to Kamchatka, for the accident at Tahiti had so far delayed him
that the season was too far advanced even to think of it, but still
with time enough to sail to the Russian settlement of Bodega on
the Californian coast. He arrived in mid August, and succeeded,
through talks with the Governor, Rotschev, in filling some gaps
in his knowledge of Kamchatka. But Bodega was a melancholy
and deserted spot—the French even sighted wolves along the
coast. On the 20th, his crew healthy after a week of excursions

[1] Kuykendall, *The Hawaiian Kingdom*, p. 166.
[2] Jore, *Océan Pacifique*, vol. ii, p. 46.

and hunts ashore, he sailed for San Francisco. The local authorities were both unprepossessing and disgruntled:

> Neither their dress, which was far too untidy, even for the authorities of a wretched Californian settlement; nor their faces which were rather too tanned and adorned with enormous side whiskers and long mustachios; nor indeed their manners which lacked both distinction and frankness, aroused any hopes in me of pleasant intercourse. However I received them courteously and offered them refreshments, which seemed to please them greatly; particularly as at that time, a war was in progress between Mexico and France who, at that very moment, was shelling San Juan d'Ulloa.[1]

But there was nothing attractive even about the scenery, and Laplace sailed away after buying a few supplies, wondering whether this 'dreary lonely spot' would ever see a busy settlement growing on its shores. He went down to the Santa Cruz mission near Monterey, intending to buy fresh vegetables before making for Peru. The mission looked pleasant enough with its white buildings roofed with red tiles and a little church tower rising above the greenery, but, when he landed, 'a spectacle of poverty and desolation spread before my eyes'. Everything was in ruins. Where La Pérouse had once been so warmly received, a few wretched Indian families now sheltered with one cynical-looking and down-at-heels Mexican padre to attend to their spiritual needs; and there were no supplies to be had. Laplace sailed on to Monterey itself, where the Governor proved a pleasant and helpful man, and fresh food, now Laplace's main concern, could be bought in adequate quantities.

He had encountered fog all along the Californian coast. It persisted in patches until he reached Guayaquil in early September. After spending two days in that region 'worn out by revolutions', he went on to Payta, bought good supplies of fresh meat and fruit, and then 'to the great satisfaction of everyone' weighed anchor for Callao and Valparaiso. He sailed from the latter port for Concepción on 15 December, stopping to see if any French vessel were in port in need of assistance. There was none and, staying only long enough to lay in further supplies for the hard

[1] Laplace, *Campagne*, vol. vi, p. 236.

Horn passage, he sailed south, taking with him the seeds of an epidemic of smallpox which laid low many of his men. Rounding the Horn on 12 January 1840, he decided not to call at the Falkland Islands, where there was now a British settlement to which he had no desire to pass on smallpox. He therefore continued on his way, east of the Falklands, surrounded at times by icebergs 'longer and higher than the Tuileries'. He arrived in Rio on 4 February, stayed a fortnight to restore the health of his crew, and finally anchored in Lorient harbour on 14 April.

It had been without doubt a hard voyage. Thirty-six men had died, eleven had been left behind at various hospitals or transferred to homebound ships, twenty had deserted. The *Artémise* herself, too old to be repaired, was put out of commission and her hulk used as a naval store. Inevitably the officers brought back natural-history specimens for which the Museum was grateful, and the hydrographical and scientific data collected were of considerable value; but it was the political aspects of the voyage which attracted attention. Laplace's reports were voluminous and informative. They ranged from surveys of trade along the coasts of Arabia and Persia, in the Far East, and in South America, to detailed comments on penal settlements and an analysis of the problems facing the whaling industry. They may have been tinged with pessimism, but they were none the less valuable. And no French official could overlook the fact that Laplace had dealt firmly and promptly with the missionary-backed rulers of Tahiti and Hawaii. With the reports of Dupetit-Thouars and Laplace, to which must be added those of Cécille, the French Government now knew a great deal about the Pacific and was able to act speedily and surely in the months ahead. The importance of the expeditions of the *Vénus*, the *Artémise*, and the *Héroïne* in laying the foundations for the subsequent sharing-out of Oceania should never be overlooked.

The voyage of the *Héroïne* marks primarily a stage in the development of fisheries protection. The selection of Cécille as head of the expedition underlines this, for he had been sent on a similar mission in the South Atlantic in 1836. J.-B. Thomas Médée Cécille was 50 years of age, and had been in the Navy since 1810. His experience was wide: in recent years he had sailed to North Africa, Brazil, and the Pacific; and an official report described him as endowed with 'every quality one could wish for in a naval officer'. His original instructions were to sail to the eastern seaboard of South America and to Africa, returning to the area he had successfully patrolled a few years earlier; but these were added to, at the request of the whaling industry, to enable him to enter the India Ocean along the thirty-seventh parallel, making for Hobart and Port Jackson, thence to New Zealand, back to Port Jackson, across to Tahiti 'in order to remind the Queen and the population that France is a great and powerful nation which, all over the globe, watches over the interests of her citizens', returning to France by way of Valparaiso, the Horn, and Rio. The *Héroïne* accordingly sailed from Brest on 1 July 1837, spent a short time in Rio, and sailed by way of the Cape of Good Hope to King George Sound, Hobart, and Port Jackson, but passing through sufficiently high latitudes to sight the Prince Edward and Crozet groups discovered by Marion du Fresne.[1] There was no reason for him to deviate from the route traced by his instructions, and what he found was what he had expected to find: whalers in need of protection, and the ever-growing commercial power of Britain.

One incident earned him considerable publicity. He reached the Bay of Islands on 20 May 1838, sailed down to Akaroa on the east coast of New Zealand's South Island, and returned to the Bay of Islands in August. This complied with his instructions to remain in New Zealand waters until the end of the whaling season and reflected French concern for the future of the islands. There had been a considerable increase in French commercial activities in the region—upward of twenty French ships put into the Bay of Islands during 1838—and growing friction between their crews and local settlers:

Captain Grandsaigne of the whaler *Gange* complains much of the insults and vexations to which the French who put into port in New

---

[1] There is no published account of the voyage, but voluminous reports are held in French naval archives under A.M. BB.4.

Zealand are exposed, and he asks himself to whom that island belongs where the British flag is hoisted everywhere. . . . Some of the new colonists go so far as to try to set the natives against us by telling them that we come to avenge the death of the unfortunate Marion. It is therefore only with mistrust that the New Zealanders agree to treat with us.[1]

Cécille's stay in New Zealand was thus fully justified and resulted in his advocacy of a French establishment there, which later led him to be consulted by the promoters of an ill-fated French colonial company.[2] But his presence also enabled him to intervene in the affair of the *Jean Bart*. While the *Héroïne* lay at anchor in the Bay of Islands, the American ship *Rebecca Sims* brought news of the massacre of the crew of this whaler. Cécille went down to the Chathams with the *Rebecca Sims* and the French whaler *Adèle*. They arrived in mid October and succeeded in enticing a few Maoris on board before the alarm was raised. A detachment of a hundred men was landed under fire from the shore, but the natives promptly sought refuge in the bush, and all the French could do was to burn down a village. One of the captives, E Taka, is reported to have been taken to France, taught to read and write, and converted to the Catholic religion. He was retained by the French Government as an interpreter in the event of a French settlement and, luckier than Ranginui, actually returned to his homeland, where he died in February 1842, his personal effects being then sold and the proceeds handed over to the French state, 'which had paid the cost of his maintenance'.[3]

On 27 November the *Héroïne* reached Tahiti. The French consul, Moerenhout, at once came to see Cécille to complain that he was being harassed by Queen Pomare and that laws were being passed prohibiting the free exercise of the Catholic religion in contravention of the agreement signed with Dupetit-Thouars. Cécille intervened successfully on behalf of Moerenhout, but refused to take any action in respect of the religious struggle, on the grounds that he had no instructions on this from his govern-

---

[1] *Journal des Débats*, 26 Apr. 1838.

[2] Buick, *The French at Akaroa*, pp. 26–7.

[3] According to a report from Captain Lavaud, of the *Allier*, to the Minister of Marine, dated 14 Mar. 1842. Typescript in Turnbull Library.

ment and that his supplies were running short: 'I had hardly
enough food left for two months and I did not know how long
it would take me to reach Valparaiso; this consideration led me to
hasten my departure and I sailed on 4 December.'[1]

The *Héroïne* was back in Brest on 17 July 1839 after a circumnavigation lasting just under twenty-five months. Cécille had
carried out his instructions to the letter and with a thoroughness
which fully justified the confidence placed in him.

Assistance of every kind usefully given to twenty whaling vessels met
at sea and in bays, a constant protection over all their movements . . .
discipline maintained among their crews; twenty-three of their
deserters recaptured; the Chatham tribes punished for their barbaric
behaviour; a powerful moral effect produced on the people of Tahiti
and neighbouring islands through seeing the Chatham chief held a
prisoner; the opinion of the New Zealanders changed in our favour;
some services rendered to religion; twenty-five shipwrecked American
sailors rescued . . . a survey of Prince Edward, Crozet, St. Paul, Chatham
and Bass islands, and charts of the bays of Kororareka, Akaroa, Toko-
labo and Kokorarata drawn up with the utmost precision . . . a new
rock discovered in the Bay of Islands; two collections of thirty-three
species of the most remarkable of New Zealand timbers, the acquisition
of three hundred Chilean araucarias . . . the experience obtained by the
Héroïne's officers . . . and the training of the sailors . . . such is the
balance sheet of a mission which showed that, if the whale hunt was
one school for sailors, the supervision of whaling ships was another.
It was certainly one of the most successful expeditions of the period.
The corvette's visit to the Bay of Islands, the homage which Cécille
spontaneously paid to Mgr. Pompallier, and the presents and courtesies
offered to the Maori chiefs, had played an important part in strengthening the position of the Catholic mission, which until then had been
fairly precarious.[2]

This showed that even a straightforward expedition, with no
geographical aims, could still at this late stage make a contribution

---

[1] Quoted in Jore, *Océan Pacifique*, vol. i, p. 244.

[2] Faivre, *Expansion française*, pp. 417–18. Cécille was made a Count of the
Roman Empire in appreciation of his services to missionaries in New Zealand
and later in China. This second expedition, that of the *Érigone* in 1841, was to
take him once more to the Pacific by way of New Zealand, Tahiti, and the
Marquesas, but these plans were cancelled when he was appointed commander
of the China naval station.

to the knowledge of the Pacific. It had certainly fitted into the expansionist pattern which, by 1840, was so clearly and so finally emerging and which, after the return of Dumont d'Urville, was to dominate French thought in the Pacific.

DUMONT D'URVILLE'S LAST VOYAGE

WHEN Dumont d'Urville at the end of 1836 judged the time opportune for a second circumnavigation, he put forward a relatively modest proposal. No Frenchman since Bougainville had led an expedition through the Straits of Magellan; the Solomons could still provide a rich field of exploration; and survivors from the *Boussole* and the *Astrolabe* might yet be found on Vanikoro—such were the three points on which his plan was based. Louis-Philippe considered it insufficiently ambitious and pointed to the greater opportunities for new discoveries offered by the vast Antarctic.

Whether this thought had occurred to the King without the prompting of his Navy Minister, Rosamel, or whether Casy, the Minister's aide and a friend of d'Urville's, had made this suggestion in the hope of increasing the plan's chances of being accepted, is not clear. Louis-Philippe, in the absence of other evidence, may retain the credit for it. It was certainly a sound idea and showed a realistic awareness of recent developments in the Pacific. D'Urville 'identified [himself] without hesitation with the King's thinking', adding, more romantically: 'haunted by Cook's example, I often thought about that famous navigator's three voyages and nearly every night I was tormented by dreams in which I saw myself on my third voyage around the world. A strange feature of these dreams is that they always tended to bring me towards the Pole. . . . A fact which is no less peculiar is that these troublesome dreams stopped almost as soon as the expedition to the South Pole was agreed upon and never returned.'[1] It was indeed a strange premonition, but what is odder still is his omission of the South Pole from his plan of exploration, in view both of these dreams and, more realistically, of British and American activities in the Antarctic. Weddell had recently discovered the enormous bight which bears his name; the United

[1] *Voyage au Pôle Sud*, vol. i, p. lxiv.

States were preparing to dispatch the Wilkes expedition; and the British Government, urged on by the Royal Society, was about to organize the voyage of the *Terror* and the *Erebus* to be placed under the command of James Ross. And even before Wilkes was able to reach the southern continent Captain Balleny had discovered Sabrina Land. Thus the ancient rivalries of the exploring nations were being transferred to new areas, and Louis-Philippe's suggestion was eminently logical.

Instructions were issued to d'Urville in August 1837, foreshadowing an extensive exploration of Pacific and southern waters involving two ships, instead of the single one he had requested. Although the interests of French traders were not overlooked, the aims of the expedition could correctly be claimed to be 'purely scientific' and hydrographic. D'Urville was to sail in the first place down to the South Shetlands and go south 'as far as the ice permits you', to better if possible British achievements in the Weddell Sea. He was then to sail through the Straits of Magellan to Valparaiso and across to the lonely islands of Ducie, Pitcairn, and Rapa, on to Raratonga and the Fijis, to the New Hebrides, the Banks group, 'of which the only thing known is their name', to Vanikoro, Santa Cruz, and the Solomons. Sailing to Amboina either through Torres Strait or along the northern coast of New Guinea, he was to send the second ship home before going on to Western Australia, Tasmania, and New Zealand, seeking, especially around Cook Strait, suitable localities for French whalers; from there he was to go to the Chatham Islands and northwards to the Gilberts, the Marshalls, and the Carolines, returning to France by way of the Philippines, the Dutch East Indies, and the Cape of Good Hope. D'Urville adhered fairly closely to these instructions, except that the possibility of new discoveries and the news that Ross and Wilkes were on their way led him to make a second and highly successful attempt to reach the Antarctic continent.

Of the two corvettes, one was to be the faithful *Astrolabe*, the other the *Zélée*, of 300 tons, built twenty-five years before as a storeship and only called a corvette as an act of courtesy. Charles Jacquinot was selected to command the second ship, 'no other officer in the entire Navy [having] my confidence to the same extent'. But Lottin, Gressien, and Guilbert all refused to sail a second time with d'Urville. However, among the *Astrolabe*'s eighty-four officers and men were included the noted hydrographer Clément Vincendon Dumoulin, and Pierre Dumoutier, a phrenologist whose inclusion reflected d'Urville's growing fascination with this new field of study. The *Zélée* had a complement of eighty-one, including Joseph du Bouzet, who had sailed with Bougainville in the *Thétis*, Tardy de Montravel, who was later to found Noumea in New Caledonia, and a young *commis* bearing the illustrious name of Louis Huon de Kermadec.

D'Urville spent ten days in London collecting charts and reference works, and endeavouring to obtain information on Weddell's voyage and on British intentions in the far south. When he returned and went to visit his ships in Toulon he found that very little progress had been made in equipping them for their long voyage. It was already early June and he had to reach the Antarctic before the southern summer became too advanced, which meant within six months. Slightly cheered by letters of good wishes from Humboldt and Kruzenstern and by the support of Admiral Jurien, who was now *préfet maritime*, he endeavoured to reorganize the working parties, but even so the ships were not ready until the beginning of September. The final details took a few days more: receipt of special instructions from the Dépôt des Cartes et Plans, arrangements whereby the officers and men were to be paid an extra hundred francs on reaching the seventy-fifth parallel and a further twenty francs for each additional degree, the loading of meat tinned 'according to the new Noel and Taboureau process'.[1] Finally, on 7 September 1837, the two ships sailed for Gibraltar.

The *Zélée*, d'Urville was glad to see, sailed as well as the *Astrolabe* and, indeed, was frequently speedier. Variable winds held back both vessels, which reached Gibraltar on the 20th; fortunately the passing of the Straits was easy, so that he did not have to take

---

[1] Taboureau was a chemist at Rochefort. The meat was salted and sealed with carbon dioxide. It needed prolonged soaking before use, but was deemed superior in taste to ordinary salt meat. Unfortunately the tins were not airtight.

note of that clause in his instructions which urged him to get himself towed through rather than be held back for days as he had been in 1826. But another ten days went by before the ship could anchor in Tenerife. The usual trips and purchases were made and shore leave was granted to a quarter of the crew at a time. 'Most of them drank so heavily that they lost the feeble dose of reason they had been endowed with. Once in this condition they went, in accordance with the worthy traditions of Frenchmen, to quarrel with the townspeople.'[1] The result was jail for some, the cancellation of leave for the rest, and a departure free from regrets on 7 October. According to his instructions, d'Urville should now have proceeded to Cape Verde and Baya de la Praya, but the ship surgeon told him that the young *élève* Le Maistre Duparc was seriously ill with tuberculosis. The captain altered course for Rio de Janeiro, where he handed the young man over to the French consul. 'By turning aside a little from his route', wrote Jean Gourdin, an *enseigne* who was to die on board a couple of years later, 'our commander can save a young officer from imminent death, and if one day the ice of the Pole closes over us there will be one victim fewer.'[2] The stop in Brazil lasted only one day, for it was already November. Contrary winds and fogs had delayed the ships and continued to do so. 'I am increasingly conscious of the fact that I left Toulon too late', commented d'Urville on 28 November when it was discovered that currents had borne them forty-four miles to the north of their estimated position. On 10 December they were still only at the fifty-second parallel. D'Urville returned to his original idea of entering the Straits of Magellan and decided to substitute a halt at Port Famine for one at Staten Land. He entered the Straits on 12 December in rain and strong wind, having recourse to a series of bold manœuvres which he felt were more necessary for reasons of prestige than for anything else:

It proved to everyone that when the occasion arose I would not be found lacking in daring nor in presence of mind, and this was what I wanted the two crews to understand. When the expedition was being

[1] *Voyage au Pôle Sud*, vol. i, p. 18.
[2] Quoted in ibid., vol. i, p. 211.

fitted out and they saw me walking slowly and heavily, because of an attack of gout, they had seemed quite surprised that I was their commander and some had even exclaimed naively: 'Oh, that fellow won't lead us very far' . . . When we left the Straits, the sailors of both ships, talking of our operations in that channel, liked to repeat: '. . . he made us hug the rocks and reefs and the land as if he had never sailed anywhere else in his life.'[1]

The French spent thirteen days in Port Famine, botanizing, gathering firewood, hunting wild geese, and fishing. 'How often have I yearned for the plenty of Port Famine!' the commander said later. They made use of 'Cunningham's letter-box', a small barrel suspended to a tree in which westbound crews could deposit letters to be taken home by passing eastbound vessels—an idea originated by the American captain of that name in 1833. But no trace could be found of the early ill-fated Spanish settlement. On the 28th they went on to Fortescue Bay, where d'Urville was compelled to abandon a botanizing excursion by the most intense cold he had ever experienced. In Peckett Haven at the beginning of January he rescued two European sealers, an Englishman and a Swiss, who had been left behind by their ship. And on the 8th he sailed out of the Straits the way he had come, helped by a fresh west-north-westerly breeze. He had lost a certain amount of time, for Staten Land would have been reached more quickly; but this he had probably made up by the relative shelter of Port Famine which enabled the crew to carry out important repairs far quicker than on an exposed coast. In addition he had accomplished his intention of going into the Straits and had at the same time displayed his coolness and seamanship to his crew and officers. It was therefore with some feeling of satisfaction that he sailed south along the Tierra del Fuego coast. The great adventure was beginning. Le Maire Strait was sighted on the 10th, its waters calm and peaceful; the next day the ships sailed past Cape St. John, the easternmost point of Staten Land; and on the 12th they lost sight of land altogether, and bore east-south-east into fog, rain, and increasing cold. Ice appeared three days later, irregularly shaped floes over which the sea broke as on coral reefs. The latitude was 59° 20' south.

[1] Ibid., vol. i, pp. 88–90.

This ice, the first our eyes had met, was gazed upon with great curiosity by everyone and was the object of numerous comments. This unusual spectacle seemed to move our sailors. It was indeed the advance guard of the formidable enemy they were going to fight; and nothing as yet could guarantee that they would come out victorious from the fierce attacks they would have to mount against it. Twenty minutes later, everyone's attention turned suddenly from these insignificant fragments to a mass a hundred times larger some three miles to windward. It was an immense block [which] seemed to be forty metres high and sixty long; but to our inexperienced eyes it appeared far more monstrous.[1]

The struggle began at once. Hope and despondency seesawed as fog and ice receded and returned. There were two main targets, one to reach as high a latitude as possible, the other to chart the edge of the icefield. He sailed east and east-south-east from the neighbourhood of Clarence Island on the 16th until ice barred his route and forced him to veer north on the 20th. So far he had been able to see very little in the succession of fogs and sleet showers, and he had still only reached the sixty-second parallel. 'I was rapidly nearing the route followed by Weddell.' On the 21st the sky cleared so that he could see icebergs fifteen or sixteen miles away and, without taking great risks, advance at a good pace towards the south-east. 'We have already reached Weddell's track . . . and until this moment no serious obstacle seems to be impeding our plans. Accordingly everyone on board is entertaining great hopes and the least sanguine refuse to restrict their expectations below 80° south. Even I, sharing in the general euphoria, having spent nearly eighteen hours on the bridge, go to bed at 10 p.m. and promptly fall asleep.'[2] But hopes were soon dashed. Woken up by shouts in the middle of the night, d'Urville rushed up on deck to find the icefield stretching across the horizon from the south-west to east-north-east. There was nothing for it but to turn north. Vincendon Dumoulin began to chart the field, although they all knew that the winds and the changing seasons would alter its outline. It would at least give a precise picture of the coastline at a given date. 'Let others follow suit and we may

---

[1] *Voyage au Pôle Sud*, vol. ii, pp. 37–8.   [2] Ibid., vol. ii, p. 47.

possibly obtain in time more satisfactory documents on the movements and evolution of the southern ice.'

By 22 January they had found the northernmost head of the icefield and had succeeded in remaining below the sixty-third degree; but soon they had to creep north again—'a sad omen'. There were large ice-floes on all sides, cracking and crashing with frightening roars in the eerie silence; a smooth line of ice clung to every inch of the rigging; snow had to be swept off the deck at regular intervals, although much of it melted along the companionways and seeped into the cold dampness below. Inexorably the expedition was forced back: 63° 39' on the 22nd, 63° 23' on the 24th, 62° 42' on the 25th. This marked the end of the first stage of exploration. D'Urville altered course for the west and sailed north for the South Orkneys, the tall snowbound peaks of which became visible the next day. Vincendon Dumoulin was at last able to prepare accurate detailed charts of a firm coastline. But the land was even less attractive than the ice. As d'Urville, on the 28th, entered Lewthwaite Strait in the hope of finding an anchorage in Spence Harbour and resting for a few days, he wrote: 'Nothing anywhere in the world could be more gloomy and more repulsive than the aspect of these desolate regions.' The barren and blackened rock stretched out in grim contrast to the ice; for now the sailors, having become accustomed to manœuvring between the gigantic icebergs, had begun to appreciate their austere beauty. But there was no hope of seeking a harbour among the islands: the wind rose, reaching gale force by the 30th. D'Urville, suffering from nausea and migraines, found the unending cold and damp truly intolerable. He could waste no more time: it was imperative to make a second attempt to go south before the end of the short summer. When the winds abated on 2 February, being then in 55° 34' south and approximately 41° west of Greenwich (the unknown effects of the currents and frequent fogs prevented him from being quite sure of his longitude), d'Urville turned south-south-east. Within two days he found himself again face to face with the icefields. Hauling slowly along the barrier, he came across a narrow channel, rashly entered it, and anchored in a kind of interior basin. He was now still only a little beyond the sixty-second parallel. The wind changed during the night and in the morning he found that the ice-floes had closed up the channel:

The *Astrolabe* moved forward a distance of two or three times its own length and stopped. We then had to use every means at our disposal. Men climbed down onto the ice to tie ropes to the large floes and those who remained on board hauled on them to move painfully forward, while others on the ice tried to push aside with picks, pincers and pickaxes the blocks which would form too hard an obstacle for the stem of our corvette. It was a laborious and exhausting procedure. . . . Seeing our two ships working in this way one thought of two crayfish stranded by the tide on a beach full of stones and struggling to move them aside in order to regain the open sea.[1]

But there was no hope. Further attempts to find a way out had to be postponed until the next day as snow started to fall, reducing visibility to a bare two or three hundred yards. Having arranged with Jacquinot to meet in the Falkland Islands should they become separated, d'Urville sailed slowly along the northern edge of the basin until he found a more promising channel. A change of wind suddenly cleared a way for the corvette, but it still took ten hours to advance one mile. The ships finally reached the open sea on the afternoon of 9 February: they had been imprisoned for a whole five days. Long stalactites of ice hung down from every yardarm, the ropes were so frozen that they had to be clipped before they could be used, and there was a growing number of sick in each ship, including the three surgeons. On the 12th snow fell so heavily that the ships remained hove-to most of the day as the men shovelled it overboard. 'This continuous bad weather, the intense cold, the lengthening nights, the almost unending snow and fog, warned me that it was time to give up this kind of navigation.' When the weather cleared for a while on the 13th he was able to fix their position fairly reliably as 62° 21′ south and 33° 40′ west. There was clearly no possibility of going further south. The second chapter of d'Urville's Antarctic exploration was ending in the same manner as the first. He told Jacquinot that

[1] *Voyage au Pôle Sud*, vol. ii, pp. 91–2.

he would either follow the iceshelf as far as the South Sandwich Islands or make for the South Orkneys. The winds made up his mind for him: blowing steadily from the north-east from 15 February, they drove him west towards the South Orkneys. Sighting them on 20 February, d'Urville sailed along the northern coast, as he feared that the south would by now be icebound. When he reached Saddle Island, the weather seemed to be sufficiently fine to send a party ashore. Vincendon Dumoulin went with the *enseignes* Marescot and Gourdin and the surgeon Le Breton. They were joined by du Bouzet and the *Zélée's* surgeon Le Guillou. But the sea proved to be too rough, lashing dangerously at the foot of the steep coast, so they landed instead on Weddell Island and brought back a good collection of geological specimens and some penguins, whose flesh the men claimed was as tasty as chicken. The weather remained fair long enough to enable Vincendon Dumoulin to complete his chart of the group, which the expedition left finally on the 22nd; but the identification of the series of snow-covered islands they passed during the following week, often glimpsed dimly through fog and flurries of snow, is uncertain: Clarence, Elephant, Narrow, Biggs, O'Brien, Aspland, Bridgeman. The South Shetlands appeared on the 27th bearing north-west, then more land bearing east to west-south-west. D'Urville could recognize very little of what he saw around him. Existing charts were too sketchy and inaccurate and, even if the land which now became visible to the south-west was not entirely unknown, he felt that his own survey was sufficiently accurate for him to bestow French names on what lay before him:

The sky having cleared between six and eight in the evening, we were able to see fairly distinctly the full extent of the land we had just discovered. I am using this term because, in spite of all our guesses, we could recognize nothing of what was drawn on Laurie's shapeless sketch-map. . . . To the great high land which stretched out towards the south-west I gave the name of Louis-Philippe to commemorate the name of the King who first thought of explorations towards the southern pole; the low coastline which extended eastward was called Joinville Land. Next the high island which seemed to fill the middle of the channel between these two stretches of land was named Rosamel after the minister who had endorsed my plans and under whose auspices our voyage had been undertaken. The islets scattered along the coast received the names of various members of the expedition. Finally I called Zélée Rocks those which had been the first to appear and Daussy Island the one we had left to starboard.[1]

A combination of impenetrable fog and calms on 1 March gave the French an opportunity to carry out a number of scientific tests. They took soundings, and checked the temperature of the sea at the surface and near the bottom, 180 fathoms down. The fog was filled with the deafening sound of whales blowing around the ships; when it thinned they saw dozens of them disporting themselves nearby. An observation made the next day gave the ship's position as 63° 10′ south and 63° 6′ west—they had managed to remain in reasonably high latitudes. The fogs were caused by a rising temperature which enabled the French to creep down to 63° 17′ the next day and to 63° 27′ on the 5th; but this could not last. 'The doctor advised me that the condition of Lepreux [a sailor from the Zélée] was unchanged and that a dozen sailors were also showing signs of scurvy. . . . To avoid alarming the men it was agreed that the doctor would not use the word scurvy and would put down their indisposition to something quite different.'[2] D'Urville had made up his mind to return to the Antarctic at the beginning of the next season, but he kept this to himself because 'such an announcement would certainly have caused the complete demoralization of the crew'. The ships sailed, all too slowly because of weak and variable breezes, far to the south of Cape Horn and began to bear west-north-west towards Chile. By 20 March there were seven cases of scurvy in the Astrolabe and twenty in the Zélée, whose between-deck, noted du Bouzet, was like a floating hospital. A week later, the Astrolabe had twenty cases of scurvy, while on board the Zélée the situation had so worsened that the officers themselves had to climb aloft and help work the ship. Lepreux was the first to die,

---

[1] Voyage au Pôle Sud, vol. ii, pp. 147–8.
[2] Jacquinot, Journal, quoted in ibid., vol. ii, p. 336.

on 1 April. Meanwhile d'Urville was taking stock of the past three months:

I will admit that this first attempt was a complete failure so far as the chief and almost special aim which had been assigned to it was concerned. It was, as we have often said, to make for Weddell's tracks and try to go beyond them so as to get as close as possible to the South Pole. Far from being able to reach the furthest point of the Englishman's travels, we were repeatedly held up by a solid and impenetrable ice field as soon as we approached the 63rd and 64th parallels of southern latitude. We tried in vain on three occasions to find a way through it; twice we were able to escape without too much difficulty, but the third time we were blocked in and were able to leave our icy prison only through a set of circumstances it would not be prudent to bank on. Finally we passed all the points by which Weddell was able to advance towards the South, and nowhere did the barrier fail to remain impenetrable.[1]

As against this, he could lay claim to the discovery, or charting, of Louis-Philippe Land and Joinville Land—which are, in fact, the northern tip of Graham Land and Joinville Island—as well as to scientific work on magnetism, natural history, and above all meteorology. The achievements were not spectacular, but they were solid. Explorers had still to learn that the Antarctic regions were far more inhospitable than those of the Arctic and that ice defended almost every approach to the land mass. The myth of Gonneville Land had almost vanished, but complete exorcism still required a slow and patient navigation in the highest latitudes. D'Urville's first advance towards the south had served to remind him, and others with him, of what difficulties still lay ahead. But to the casual observer—to the shivering sailors on board—it looked like a failure and, as d'Urville was soon to learn, it would be regarded as such for months to come.

Land was sighted on 6 April. The corvettes made their way, 'fumbling', into Talcahuano harbour the same night. There were by then thirty-eight cases of scurvy in the Zélée and twenty in the Astrolabe. They included Vincendon Dumoulin and Demas, the

<hr>

[1] Ibid., vol. ii, p. 169.

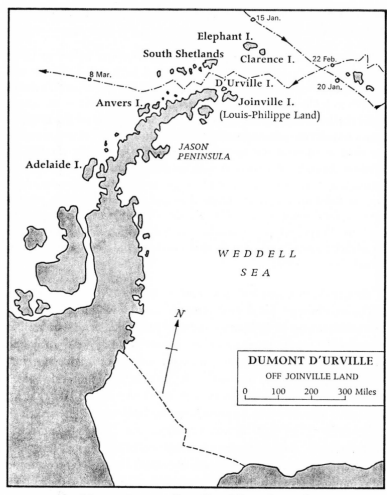

Map 12. Dumont d'Urville off 'Joinville Land'

Astrolabe's second officer, who had to be carried ashore. Arrangements were at once made to obtain fresh food, and a building was
taken over for use as hospital. When his men were being put into
the boats to be taken to it, Jacquinot found them so altered by
their illness that he had to ask them their names.

The French were naturally eager for news. A number of French
whalers were in port, some concerned about indiscipline—those

who so far had not had a successful voyage. The American consul told d'Urville that French missionaries had landed in the Gambiers. 'I promised myself that I would visit them to offer them any assistance I could and, in addition, compare their approach with those of the Methodists.' The British consul informed him that his Government had decided 'to take formal possession of the great island Ika-na-Mawi [North Island] in New Zealand, which in no way surprised me, I had on the contrary been most surprised that they had not done it earlier'. Captain Scott and Rear-Admiral Ross, of H.M.S. *President*, were courteous and praised the French for their endeavours, while being secretly pleased, thought d'Urville, that they had not bettered Weddell's achievements. There were brief botanizing expeditions and, especially, some repairs to the copper sheathing which the ice had damaged. The men recovered, except one who died as a result of eating immoderately too soon after recovering from scurvy. Desertions, on the other hand, began to mount—nine men in all. 'It is really deplorable that for such an important voyage the port of Toulon could not provide us with better people.' The two men rescued from Magellan Strait were landed here, and three sick were left behind. To make up the numbers, d'Urville took on five replacements, all the port could offer. The expedition then sailed to Valparaiso, where he hoped to find more recruits. When he arrived there on 25 May and met Duhaut-Cilly, then in command of the *Ariane*, he asked him whether he could find a few volunteers for him, but Duhaut-Cilly refused. Yet d'Urville was compelled to land and leave behind another five men who had insufficiently recovered, so that he was now, with deaths and desertions, fifteen men short of his initial complement. Duhaut-Cilly's lack of sympathy, indeed his evasiveness, were therefore surprising. It was Jacquinot who discovered the reason:

Mr. Jacquinot told me of the very peculiar and unexpected rumours circulating in the town and mainly in the French ships about our expedition. It was considered a complete failure, I do not know for what reason; people were even going so far as to say that we had not dared to enter the Straits of Magellan and that our corvettes had fled as soon as they had seen the first sign of ice. Thus, to hide my shame,

I had taken refuge in Concepción and did not even dare show my face in Valparaiso. It even appeared that one of the officers from the *Vénus*, where these rumours were most current, had written to one of the *Astrolabe*'s that the only course the commander of the expedition had left to him was to blow his brains out. These allegations were so stupid and so absurd that the only impression they made on me was one of pity and contempt. All I saw in them was evidence of the lowly feelings of jealousy and of a lack of patriotism, which are so common among officers of our nation. In similar circumstances and supposing such facts had been well founded, Englishmen would have endeavoured to conceal them, instead of publicizing them.[1]

It was ironical that the French, who sixty years before had received Kerguelen's claims with such credulity, should be now responding in this way to d'Urville's efforts in the high latitudes; but undeniably his achievements were not spectacular and could not be described in a few boastful sentences. He wisely decided to show the French residents all his charts and read them the report he was preparing for Rosamel. The painstaking work of the last three months thus became evident and moved them from contemptuous silence to admiration. His audience consisted of Duhaut-Cilly, of Cazotte, the acting consul-general, and of several businessmen. One of the latter was Lamotte Duportail, son of a Duportail who had sailed with d'Entrecasteaux; he still had with him an unpublished journal of his father's which he later showed d'Urville. All were now anxious to help. Duhaut-Cilly in particular was embarrassed to admit that he had believed the earlier gossip. Jacquinot acted as an intermediary and saved every-body's face by asking Duhaut-Cilly for volunteers for the *Zélée*. Six men were found without difficulty and they were shared, as if this had been agreed all along, between the two ships. Others made amends in different ways and the next few days were spent attending dinners and receptions. But it was time to leave for the Pacific—to begin that part of the voyage which d'Urville had planned himself. 'At last I had come to the moment for which I had been waiting for so long, when I would see our two cor-vettes definitely making for the islands of Oceania. At that

[1] *Voyage au Pôle Sud*, vol. iii, p. 92.

moment would begin the campaign I had conceived and suggested; for our work in the icefield, however dangerous it had
been and however important its results, had no other aim than
to meet the King's wishes.'[1] The *Ariane*'s longboat towed the
ships one by one towards the open sea, and at 4 p.m. on 29 May
they sailed with a light south-westerly breeze. They reached Juan
Fernandez on 3 June, where they spent a couple of days becalmed.
The winds were unfavourable for Mas Afuera, so d'Urville set
a course for San Ambrosio, but the weak breeze, when it blew at
all, remained westerly and ten days went by before he sighted it
and hauled along its northern coast. 'It was my third circumnavigation and I could not remember a passage as dull, as boring
and as monotonous as this one', wrote Jacquinot, but they had to
wait another month—until 14 July—before they found any
easterlies. Finally, on 3 August, the two ships anchored off
Mangareva.

Christianity had made great progress since Mgr. Rochouze's
arrival in the Gambiers in 1835. Five missionaries and several lay
helpers were now stationed there in addition to the Bishop. The
natives seemed happy and contented, although those were days
when the mass could not be celebrated in the vernacular:

The religious pomp of the new rite appeals to them; they are not
used to it yet, and in their naïve ignorance they are probably more
fervent and more strictly religious than any of the civilized nations of
Europe. They chant and recite at every moment the Latin prayers
which the missionaries have been barbarous enough to make them
learn by heart. Thus I heard a native singing at the top of his voice the
Pater Noster, admittedly disfigured, while he was folding dry pandanus
leaves around a stick to repair or strengthen the walls of his home.
We sometimes sang with them, in which case they ran up from every
side to form a circle and join in. What a strange picture that made!
A crowd of half-naked, wild-looking men, singing, among the trees
of a world which until recently was unknown, prayers of the religion
of civilized peoples, in the language of a nation which had disappeared
from the globe so long ago.[2]

[1] Ibid., vol. iii, p. 109.
[2] Desgraz, quoted in ibid., vol. iii, p. 381.

Admittedly, Desgraz, who was d'Urville's secretary, was something of an anti-clerical. The rivalry between Catholic and Protestant missionaries, which had flared into open war in Tahiti and Hawaii, he considered 'improper' at a time when so many 'idolatrous natives' needed to be converted to any form of Christianity. But d'Urville, more devout, was determined to do all he could to assist the Bishop, whose behaviour was 'exactly that of a father towards his children'; and there was no doubt that the islands were peaceful and prosperous. He had promptly sent Marescot Duthilleul, one of the young *enseignes*, with a message for the Bishop, had visited him on the 5th, and had received him ceremonially on board two days later. Rochouze was accompanied by Father Laval, the missionary who had been expelled from Tahiti two years earlier. The Bishop wore all his episcopal robes, including his mitre, and spent an hour on board each ship, receiving on each occasion a nine-gun salute. 'It was the first time I had seen a bishop in this ceremonial dress outside a church', commented d'Urville's first officer Rocquemaurel, but Desgraz, as usual, showed little sympathy: 'Short and plain, Mr. de Nilopolis[1] is not impressive. His bishop's costume, soiled and faded . . . arouses a feeling of compassion.' But d'Urville knew the difficulties which beset early missionaries in the Pacific. He gave Rochouze a supply of tools and agricultural implements and attended a solemn mass in full uniform accompanied by most of the officers and a large detachment of sailors. Father Laval's reports on Tahiti strengthened his resolve to be firm with Queen Pomare, but firstly he would go to the Marquesas, where 'the people were still in their primitive condition', and give what help he could to French missionaries there.

Another friend of France in the Gambiers was Maputeoa, from whom he received a gift of poultry, bananas, and breadfruit. The chief's messenger had been slow to identify the commander of the expedition: 'He no doubt found it difficult to recognize the powerful chief he was looking for under the informal clothes I was wearing, because he repeated his request three times.' D'Urville's usual shipboard dress, it will be remembered, was

---

[1] Quoted in *Voyage au Pôle Sud*, vol. iii, p. 384. Rochouze was Bishop of Nilopolis.

scarcely distinguishable from the ordinary sailor's working-clothes and included a shapeless straw hat. After an abortive attempt to visit the chief on the 5th—the boat capsized in the surf and the officers were all soaked to the skin—he paid him an official call, accompanied by Jacquinot and the surgeon Le Breton. Maputeoa was waiting on the beach with two missionaries and led him to the royal hut. D'Urville, seated in a ceremonial arm-chair, made a speech on behalf of Louis-Philippe, announced that French ships would call at intervals at Mangareva, and offered presents—a suit,[1] scissors, knives, mirrors, bead necklaces, but especially a shotgun which caused a great sensation. The King gave the French a hundred head of poultry and 'a great heap' of coconuts and bananas. When the expedition left on 15 August, no one had doubts that Mangareva was firmly in the French sphere of influence.

The *Astrolabe* and the *Zélée* sailed north-north-west, passing south of Hood Island in the night, and reaching 20° south on the 18th, when the breeze fell and 'the heat became very troublesome'. They then steered north-east to pass within sight of Minerva and Serles, and continued north and north-west for Nukuhiva. Land was seen in the morning of 24 August—Tahuata. They hauled along its east coast and continued north, although natives came out in canoes, enticing them to land. On the afternoon of the 26th, the two corvettes dropped anchor in Anna Maria Bay. D'Urville had expected to find news of the *Vénus* and to meet French missionaries, but all he found was an American whaler and several European settlers, two of whom, an Englishman and an American, he agreed to take with him. He succeeded in buying coconuts and a few hens, but no pigs. Tardy de Montravel, who had gone to survey nearby Taihoa Bay, did bring back eight of them, but the problem was always the same—the Marquesans insisted on guns or powder. Even firewood was not easy to obtain, the natives bartering it against axes. Water was plentiful, but the most suitable supply was from a pool which, it was discovered, was the islanders' favourite bathing-place. The contrast with idyllic

---

[1] When P. A. Lesson called at Mangareva in April 1840, Maputeoa was still wearing the jacket. See his *Voyage au Îles Mangareva*.

Mangareva was most marked and missionary influence clearly lacking, for, if the men seemed timid and often churlish, the women were troublesome and invaded the ships as soon as the anchors touched bottom:

> Less reserved than the men, the women came up to the corvettes and grasped anything which enabled them to climb aboard. They reached the rail in a flash, but there they found the nets firmly stretched out forming an obstacle which they dared not cross. They would however, without any doubt, have tried to surmount it if we had not told them by signs to remain quiet. As a consolation for these poor creatures I said that I would allow them on board at night; and from that moment they remained quietly standing, talking among themselves and forming around the corvettes a living belt which made a peculiar and unusual effect. . . . I do not find among them those remarkable beauties and those delightful nymphs which several navigators and especially Porter and Paulding described in such pompous terms. It will be said, it is true, that I could be nothing but a stern judge, with my dour outlook and my indifferent health; it was a different matter for these young officers and ardent sailors for whom the stay at Mangareva had merely added to the privations of two months at sea. . . . However, I must say to their credit that they were patient and reasonable. Work proceeded without trouble and the appointed hour was awaited, if not with patience, at least without complaint or breach of discipline.[1]

Jacquinot was less strict. When morning came he sent the women back in the ship's boats, whereas d'Urville told them to swim to the shore. The result was that none came back to the *Astrolabe* for a couple of days and even then only those who were too plain to find favour with the men of the *Zélée*. D'Urville strengthened his reputation as an unchivalrous commander when he saw the *Zélée*'s longboat going ashore to fetch the evening's guests and ordered Jacquinot to stop providing transport for them. Reasonably enough, he had no wish to be accused, when he returned to France, of having ferried native girls for his men. He was, moreover, anxious to leave. By the afternoon of 3 September the green shores of Nukuhiva had disappeared below the horizon. The men

[1] *Voyage au Pôle Sud*, vol. iv, pp. 6–7.

were fit, except for two or three cases of 'routine indisposition', and there was no shortage of fresh food. The main trouble was the heat, especially below decks, and d'Urville took steps to simplify manœuvres to avoid having to wake men in the middle of the night and expose them suddenly to the cool night air. He sighted the edge of the Tuamotus on 5 September, but his main concern was to make for Tahiti as quickly as he could. With the help of a sturdy south-easterly he reached it on the 9th. The morning fog was already clearing and the young sailors could admire 'the fine beaches and pleasant hillsides of this delightful island'. He wanted to reach a point whose position was well determined, and although Papeete, not far away, was a more important centre he made for Point Venus, 'considered with reason among hydrographers as the point whose longitude is the best determined in Oceania'.

His instructions did not require him to intervene in the religious dispute; they merely required him in a general way to provide such assistance as captains of whalers and other French citizens he met might request. He soon discovered anyhow that the matter was being settled by others. A Tahitian who came up to the *Astrolabe* offering goods for sale—at exhorbitant prices—told him that a ship similar to his own was anchored in Papeete harbour. Soon after, the missionary Rodgerson came on board and replied to d'Urville's comments about the ill-treatment of the French missionaries that the objections were no longer valid, since Dupetit-Thouars, whose *Vénus* was the other ship in question, had come to an agreement with Queen Pomare.

A deep feeling of satisfaction came over me when I learnt of this; the French flag was flying honourably on Tahiti; I was freed from the need to take up a hostile attitude which I had no desire to adopt. . . . From that moment I behaved in a quite different way towards the English missionary. I expressed again all the satisfaction I felt that everything had been settled; I was at once prepared to reassume the goodwill and sympathy I had had formerly towards the English missions and which I have expressed publicly in my writings; and I invited Mr. Rodgerson . . . to step into my cabin to partake of refreshments. . . . I shall add that, during my entire stay at Tahiti, Mr. Rodgerson was invariably courteous and extremely obliging towards me. It would be very fortunate for the English missions if they had only people like him.[1]

The stay at Tahiti was thus quite straightforward. Although d'Urville was senior to Dupetit-Thouars, the latter had done everything that could be done to put an end to the struggle between the rival factions. D'Urville seconded him, as we have seen,[2] with his customary sternness, but apart from that the week he spent in the island was marked mainly by social activities. There were exchanges of visits between the ships, d'Urville being flattered by comments on his *Voyage pittoresque autour du monde*, the popular work which had helped to make his name widely known in the years when lack of favour and French inaction in the Pacific had condemned him to what he called 'the obscure duties of a captain in port'. He called on Moerenhout, who was recovering from a recent attack on his life, and on General Freire, the former Chilean dictator, who 'remembered perfectly having already met me in the *Coquille* in 1823, when he was leaving Talcahuano for Valparaiso where he was to take up the reins of government'. Although he met some of the Protestant missionaries, he had only a glimpse of Pritchard. 'We were arriving in front of Papawa when a whaleboat passed fifteen paces away on our right, bearing in the stern a man who turned his head away when he came up to us. . . . Mr. Dupetit-Thouars confirmed it was Mr. Pritchard . . . he was no doubt going to see me in order to lay a complaint against the captain of the *Vénus*.'[3] But, with Dupetit-Thouars in port, there was very little for d'Urville to do. He disliked the Tahitians, whom he considered greedy and immoral, and was not anxious to play second fiddle to Dupetit-Thouars. 'Bathing [in Matavai Creek] is probably the only pleasant souvenir I will have of my brief stay in Tahiti.' He sailed early on the 16th to the north of Moorea, glimpsing the fog-

[1] *Voyage au Pôle Sud*, vol. iv, pp. 60–1.
[2] See *supra*, pp. 305–6.
[3] *Voyage au Pôle Sud*, vol. iv, pp. 64–5. The French held the view that the missionaries hoped that d'Urville, as the senior officer, might be induced to restrain Dupetit-Thouars. They obviously did not know their man.

shrouded shape of Tubuai Manu in the evening, and going on north-west to Raiatea, Borabora, and Maupiti.

He then altered course for Samoa, sighting Rose Island on the 23rd, then Opua and Manua, sailing fairly close to the southern coast. On the 25th he met a whaler, the *Lady Rowena*, which came towards him to offer him the services of a certain Frazer who had been living in Samoa for six years. No sooner had the whaler left than another British pilot came out in a canoe; d'Urville sent him on to the *Zélée*. With the help of these two men, the French were able to hug the shore with confidence, admiring 'the enchanting spectacle offered by this beautiful land', and anchor without difficulty off Apia. He decided to stay six days —he always endeavoured to decide this in advance and told his officers so that they could plan their excursions accordingly. He called on the missionary Mills and his wife, finding clear evidence of their influence in the district: the local women, far from rushing the ships as they had done at Nukuhiva, 'rejected the sailors' serious proposals', but they did point out, for the sake of peace, that a nearby village had not been Christianized and 'from that moment this path was daily trodden by the inhabitants of the corvettes'. There were a few incidents to mar the peaceful days they mostly spent on walks ashore, hunting, bathing, or trading with the islanders: some men from the *Zélée* were involved in a fight with men from Fate-ata; the *élève* Lafond was robbed of all his belongings by a guide who led him into a lonely swamp. Of greater interest was a persistent rumour that three of de Langle's companions had escaped the massacre of 1788 and had been sheltered by friendly Samoans; one of them was said to have married and one of his children was supposedly still alive. But in spite of all their inquiries the French could find no one who had actually met him, and d'Urville decided he was not justified in sending an expedition on the basis of such second-hand reports.

When the six days were up, on 2 October, the corvettes sailed westwards along the coast to Manono, passing between Savaii and Upolu. The French lost sight of the south-east coast of Savaii at dusk and went on to Vavau. They were now nearing the Tonga group, where d'Urville had shelled Mafanga ten years before. He was to find that this episode had not been forgotten, although no one bore any grudge. Soon after he arrived, on the 5th, a young Tongan came on board, claiming to be a son of the chief of Mafanga and asking to sail with d'Urville; his name is given as Mafi-Kelepi on the rolls and the date of his joining the expedition as the 9th. Then, through a Scottish sailor named Mackenzie who was living in the islands, d'Urville learnt of Simonet's presence on Vavau, and the deserter did in fact appear and talk to some of the sailors, but d'Urville, while stating that, after such a lapse of time, he was not prepared to be vindictive, would not allow him near his ships—he still considered him to have been the chief troublemaker at Tongatabu and was afraid he might again encourage desertions. But he was not allowed to leave it at that: the two local missionaries, Thomas and Brooks, coming to pay their respects, complained that Simonet was a bad influence. The commander repeated that he would not send a party ashore to arrest the man, but that if the Tongans brought him to the *Astrolabe* he would naturally be compelled to put him under arrest. Thomas, who, of the two, seemed the more anxious to be rid of Simonet, mentioned this to King Tubou, who, with Queen Salote, was the next visitor to the ship.[1] The Tongans appeared reluctant to make any move, and presents were exchanged without further comment; but d'Urville subsequently learnt two things—that Simonet had been arrested (he was brought on board the next day and put in irons) and that the young Mafi-Kelepi was an enemy of the King, who had sent him in exile to Vavau. Tongan politics were decidedly too involved for the French to fathom. Glad not to be involved to any greater degree, d'Urville sailed on 9 October, taking with him the two missionaries and their families, who had asked for a passage to Fiji. The expedition passed south of Tofua and soon sighted the first of the innumerable islands which make up the Fiji group. D'Urville stopped briefly at Lakemba to deliver a letter to the resident missionary Cargill and took on two natives as guides and pilots—it is interesting to note that Simonet was brought out

---

[1] If Tubou, who was now paramount chief, was that same Tahofa against whom the French had fought, d'Urville seemed unaware of it.

of irons on this occasion to act as interpreter—but the pilots seemed to have little idea of the draught of the two corvettes and d'Urville trembled on more than one occasion as they led them through shallow channels.

His first duty was to avenge the death of Captain Bureau of the *Aimable Joséphine*. Bureau had apparently been trading in the islands and had allowed himself to take sides in one of the inter-tribal wars until one of the chiefs he had served, Takalasale, had massacred him and his crew and captured the ship. When he arrived at the small island of Piva, near Viti Levu, d'Urville was not in a bloodthirsty mood. 'I hope', he wrote, 'that the entire tribe will have taken good care to run away before my men land, so that they will only find huts to burn and there will be no bloodshed.'[1] When the French—a detachment of eighty men under the order of du Bouzet—landed in the morning, they found the village indeed deserted and all they had to do was to burn it down. When this was done, d'Urville landed nearby, at Pao, and addressed an estimated two thousand Fijians, explaining why he had destroyed the village, adding, somewhat strangely, 'I have learnt with joy that Tanoa has condemned Nakalasse's crime, and has already killed and eaten [*sic*] the chief Mala and others who have had a hand in the killing of Captain Bureau.'

On 20 October the expedition arrived in Levuka in the island of Ovalau. D'Urville planned to stay a week, to take in water and give his men a further chance to rest.

Reassured by the peaceful intentions of the natives of Levuka and especially by the frequent contacts they have with Europeans I sent a part of my crew on shore leave. I congratulate myself for being able to give my sailors this pleasure which can only be beneficial for their health; for at least at Levuka they will find none of these numerous taverns which seem to follow civilization everywhere and where sailors, who are always so anxious for new sensations, never fail to leave their reason with the money they have often earned at the cost of fatigue and danger.[2]

The sailors may not have appreciated his solicitude, but his concern for their welfare was evident at every step. This gruff and

---

[1] *Voyage au Pôle Sud*, vol. iv, p. 193.   [2] Ibid., vol. iv, p. 231.

austere, often humourless, man was undeniably fond of the men under his command. On the 27th the French called briefly at Vanua Levu, which d'Urville called 'possibly one of the finest places in the world to found . . . colonies . . . to gather and maintain in a state of plenty the surplus populations of Europe'. The next day they sailed finally from the Fijis. The last two months had not yielded any startling discoveries—the time for this was past—but the expedition had collected numerous botanical and geological samples, while the detailed charts of Vincendon Dumoulin, Duroch, Coupvent, and others had filled the cupboards of the *grande cabine*. The small reefs and tiny islets which appeared for the first time on their charts were not spectacular contributions to knowledge, but such precise and painstaking work was needed before the map of the Pacific could be complete. They made for the New Hebrides and entered the belt of equatorial calms. Aurora was sighted on 4 November—showing that the expedition was making more rapid progress than d'Urville's complaints about weak breezes would justify—then Etoile Peak. The corvettes sailed on north-north-west towards the Banks group, whose peaks were beginning to pierce through the mist, and on the way d'Urville sighted two islets which he identified as Bligh's North Rocks. But the mist returned, the wind was fresh and the sea rough. Unable to survey the group as he had wanted and not knowing how long he might have to wait before the weather settled down, he decided to make for Vanikoro. As it turned out, it was a wise decision, for in the night the wind reached gale force and rain fell in torrents, the instruments on board recording a fall of just under two inches in two hours. When he reached Vanikoro, on 6 November, the sky was still overcast but the sea had moderated. The corvettes hove to in front of Peou Pass and he went in one of the boats to survey the lagoon. The wind was still rippling the surface of the water too much for him to discover any sign of the wreck. He landed on the beach and found an area clear of trees where the French had presumably established their camp, but it was so overgrown with convolvulus that he felt it was impossible to dig for remains. Nearby, however, a large coconut tree had been cut around its trunk and further investigations revealed axe cuts on a number of other trees. 'I had no doubt that it was here that the companions of the unfortunate Lapérouse settled after seeing their ships disappear among the reefs.' All attempts to make contact with the natives failed. There was one hut on the beach, but its inhabitants had fled.

I went, alone and unarmed, along a path which leads to the interior of the island; Simonet, with whom the reader is already acquainted, followed a few steps behind, armed only with a sword. After walking for a short while, I told Simonet to call out in the native style; his shout was at first echoed only by the mountain, but after waiting a few minutes I had the satisfaction of hearing a real native reply, and soon we came across an inhabitant of Vanikoro, of some twenty-five to thirty years of age, who appeared before us dressed in his national costume. . . . Going up to him, I hastened to tell him that I was the *aligui* (chief) of the vessels, that I had already visited Vanikoro and had stayed there for some considerable time. I named almost at once Paiou, Nama, Tevai, Manevai, Vanou, Nelo, Tangaloa, in a word all the chiefs [*sic*] whose names I had learnt on my previous voyage and who came to my mind. He seemed temporarily nonplussed by this long recital and I thought I had tamed him, but he finally told me he was going to fetch the *aligui* of Paiou, that the coconuts were at my disposal, but that I had to go and sleep on board the ships, whereupon he fled. It would have been cruel to try to hold this poor wretch who was trembling with fear, and I did not entertain the idea. Later Messrs. Dumoulin and Dumoutier saw another one running away through the taro fields, but in spite of their efforts they were unable to catch up with him. This was the sum total of our contact with the islanders.[1]

The weather was worsening. As d'Urville and Simonet returned to the beach a heavy shower fell, causing them to fear they might be stranded overnight among unfriendly natives and in an unhealthy island; but it cleared after a while and they returned to the *Astrolabe*. The ships sailed along the western reef very slowly and cautiously and left at dawn. The French had a brief glimpse of Tinakula, whose volcano was sending up a large column of smoke and glowed eerily in the warm night. At

---

[1] *Voyage au Pôle Sud*, vol. v, pp. 9–10.

midday on the 12th, the weather now being fine, they sighted the south coast of San Cristobal. They were to spend the next three and a half weeks in the Solomons. They sailed past the northern point of Santa Ana, making for Malaita, passing close enough to the coast to see the villages and huts, and often surrounded by canoes mounted by natives bringing coconuts or small lances. The westernmost point of Malaita, Nialahau, still retains the alternative name of Cape Zélée, a tribute to the team of officers working under Vincendon Dumoulin who drew a remarkable set of charts of the islands. The mountain peaks of Guadalcanal were sighted on the 17th, then ahead a long stretch of lower-lying islands, the Nggela group, of which the largest is Florida. The ships sailed along their north-westerly coast, sighted the southeast point of Santa Isabel, and anchored in Thousand Ships Bay, choosing a small cove which they named—and which remains—Astrolabe Bay, situated on San Jorge Island. They began to collect firewood and fill their water casks. The local islanders were persuaded to come aboard, but d'Urville, remembering their evil reputation, watched them closely and issued orders that no one was to venture out of the bay or inland. Yet, although this was still what the French knew as Arsacides country, there were no incidents. Dumoutier, the phrenologist, did have difficulty in exercising his talents. It was his practice to take casts of heads whenever he could, and one of the natives did not object to the back of his head being treated in the appropriate way, but when he felt plaster on his forehead he took fright and ran to break the cast against a tree. The sorrowful Frenchman then asked whether he might purchase a skull; the natives, thinking he wished to eat brains, of which they were fond, started to organize what Dumoutier realized to his horror was a head-hunting expedition against a nearby enemy village. In time the French felt confident enough to spend the night ashore, still remaining on their guard with, as Vincendon Dumoulin points out, little justification:

It was one o'clock in the morning. My watch was ending and I was about to ask for my chance to sleep, when suddenly burning torches are noticed moving in the depth of the forest, the speed at which they are moving makes them seem more numerous, they come closer and warn us of the arrival of new visitors. We are all up in a flash. It is four men, each bearing a lighted torch, bringing with them a woman for the camp, the wife or one of the wives of the chief's son, who, to carry out all the duties imposed on him by hospitality, thought he ought to send for her to offer her to the foreigners. In truth, had the latter been consulted they would not have selected the newcomer; fairly old and very ugly, she was short and fat and lacked nearly every feminine feature. But we had to take their good will into account.[1]

The French left on 25 November under a lowering sky. D'Urville's hopes of hauling close along the south coast of Santa Isabel and Choiseul faded. On 2 December he reckoned himself to be near 'the low islands which fill most of the area between Isabel and Choiseul'—in other words at the entrance to Manning Strait. He was fortunate enough to avoid all the dangers which lie along this route and which rain and mist concealed from sight. Next he sighted 'a high peak crowning the eastern point of Choiseul and, unless I am mistaken, this must be de Surville's Île de Première Vue'. He was not mistaken, although now too far from the coast to see any details on the rare occasions when the weather cleared. Two days later he reached Cape Alexander at the western end of Choiseul and sighted the mountains of Bougainville. As they neared Cape L'Averdy in northern Choiseul, a fleet of some twenty canoes came to meet them, bringing bows and arrows to barter for axes. 'They also brought coconuts and bananas, but it was not easy to trade because they seemed not to prize the necklaces, knives, and lengths of cloths we could offer them. After six or eight minutes the canoes left us suddenly and went to join those who were alongside the *Zélée*.' The rest of the day was spent sailing north along the east coast of Buka. The ships then turned west towards New Ireland. When they reached it, on the afternoon of 8 December, d'Urville altered course for the north, intending to make for the Carolines. His instructions required him to go to the Dutch East Indies either through Torres Strait or by northern New Guinea, but his supplies were running low and he felt it wiser to sail to Guam.

The French crossed the Equator for the second time on 12

[1] Quoted in *Voyage au Pôle Sud*, vol. v, p. 62.

December, beginning their survey of the southern Carolines a week later. They anchored for several days from the 22nd in the Hogoleus, 'an interesting group I wanted to visit'. Large numbers of canoes soon surrounded the two corvettes, bringing fruit and creating a deafening din. The officers went to survey the near-by islands, meeting a friendly reception at some, being attacked in others. It does not seem that the inhabitants, most of whom had never seen Europeans before, were unfriendly, but rather that the French found themselves entangled in tribal politics: islanders allied to those near whom they had first landed welcomed them, while enemies quite as naturally proved hostile. Nevertheless, the French, totally unable to tell friend from foe, remained on their guard, and left on the 28th. On 1 January 1839 they anchored in Umata Bay, Guam. D'Urville found the island much poorer. The Governor especially, although generous and hospitable, was less fortunate than his predecessors, in that the flourishing monopoly of imports and government trade which they had enjoyed had now been abolished. The island itself was suffering from the gradual disappearance of Spanish shipping in the Pacific, and the French saw buildings falling into disrepair and all too many cases of leprosy and elephantiasis. They did, however, buy food at fair prices and enjoyed the respite from shipboard duties. An official dinner and dance brought their stay to an end, d'Urville recording his surprise at seeing priests joining in: 'Although dancing is in no way reprehensible I must say that these white cassocks clashed strangely in the whirl of our young officers' uniforms.' He sailed on the 10th, leaving behind two deserters from the *Zélée*, 'good-for-nothings' he felt he could do without.

The corvettes sailed south-west towards Yap and the Palau group, where d'Urville found two Malays who had been shipwrecked a year earlier and to whom he gladly offered a passage, for their knowledge of the islands and of the local dialect would assist him in his study of Pacific languages. On the 16th he reached the position assigned in Arrowsmith's map to Johannes Island; since there was no land in sight he agreed with Horsburgh, who had eliminated it from his chart. Four days later he sighted Palmas Island, 'this pretty little island, true oasis in the middle of the ocean. It is low and well wooded, and its beaches are covered with coconut trees under which we can see a large population . . .', but the currents were bearing the ships rapidly away and they were unable to come any nearer. Soon after this they were in sight of Mindanao and almost immediately becalmed. For three days 'we waited in vain for the wind to come and move our motionless corvettes'. They were near enough to the shore for the naturalists to row over for an excursion. A light breeze then took them as far as Sanguir, but, at less than half a mile from its south-eastern extremity, it failed:

The south-east point of Sanguir ends there in six or seven little islets whose sharp and tall needles threatened our corvettes with instant and complete destruction. . . . The wind suddenly blew from the south-east; we had no sooner manœuvred to take advantage of it than it dropped, and then this false move brought us definitely to the rocks which were now scarcely thirty yards away. Our loss was almost inevitable; the *Zélée* could be saved only through some unlikely chance. The *Astrolabe* alone could hope to skim these rocks without touching them and to anchor before reaching the shore. . . . A few minutes more and we would witness the agony of our consort, to perish ourselves maybe a few moments later. The threatening sea struck the foot of those terrible pyramids, then the wave seemed to caress these columns it could not destroy, before falling back with a roar in great spurts of foam which splashed back even on to the decks of our ships. Suddenly the breeze started up from the north-east . . . the *Zélée*, which a moment ago was far closer to her ruin than we were, moved quickly away. . . . Finally the breakers were foaming astern of us . . . everyone had recognized that our corvettes had escaped from the greatest danger a ship can run.[1]

The expedition continued to be troubled by calms for several days. It sighted Gilolo on the 29th and Ternate later the same day. D'Urville was again suffering from gout, which he was used to by now. He sent Demas and the *commis* Ducorps to call on the Dutch Resident, who offered to buy supplies. The officers went on excursions: 'One caravan of naturalists wended its way towards the summit of the volcano, while our scientists set up their

---

[1] *Voyage au Pôle Sud*, vol. v, pp. 217–18.

observatories by the sea. Mr. Thanaron [the *Zélée*'s second officer] began a plan of the harbour; our sailors enjoy on board a complete rest.' The officers bought 400 birds of paradise which the local Malays had obtained from New Guinea; and d'Urville felt well enough to land and pay an official visit on the Resident and the Sultan. The French sailed on 2 February for Buru and Ceram, anchoring in Amboina harbour on the 5th. Once again the Dutch were helpful and there were trips ashore while the ships took in food and water. D'Urville then went on to Banda and back to Ceram and the coast of New Guinea. His intention was to explore Torres Strait from the west. It was now early March. 'The wind seemed to have set from the west and to be eminently suited for my plan to survey Torres Strait; I therefore hastened to leave the coast of New Guinea and turning south I made for Cape Valsch, which I wanted to sight before entering the strait.'[1] He reached his target on 10 February, but the winds became variable.

[This] seemed to mark the end of the monsoon on which I had to depend to negotiate the thousand reefs which obstruct Torres Strait; finally, the next day a strong swell from the east seemed to show that winds from this direction had been prevailing for some time in the strait, and in that case I could not hope to reach Port Jackson through a route which is dangerous enough with favourable winds. It was my duty not to expose my ships to almost certain destruction to satisfy a mad personal whim. On the other hand I had not abandoned my idea of returning to try my luck in the polar ice. As a new attempt towards the Pole to the south of Tasmania could be made only in January and February, I had nine long months left before going to Hobart, which I could usefully spend on surveys in the great Asian archipelago.[2]

Although the winds turned north-westerly shortly after, he kept to his decision. He sighted New Holland—a name he continued to use—to the south on the 27th and anchored in Raffles Bay. The aborigines of Arnhem Land were obviously suffering from famine. They continually pestered the French for food and scrambled to pick up a handful of rice which some Indonesians fishing for trepang had thrown them. Demas, stalking kangaroos,

[1] *Voyage au Pôle Sud*, vol. vi, p. 25.   [2] Ibid., vol. vi, p. 27.

had a different experience. Seeing something moving in the tall grass, he was about to fire when he saw two aborigines spring up and run, yelling, 'Waterloo, Wellington'. 'These were names the English had given them. . . . We certainly did not expect to have those two words thrown at our heads by two wretched savages in the middle of the Australian desert.'[1] After a few days the French sailed to nearby Port Essington to call on the local commander, Commodore Bremer, and left on 8 April for the Aru Islands, off West New Guinea. They spent a few days there, hampered by calms and tropical rainstorms, but it was time to leave, for scurvy was beginning to appear. D'Urville might well have succeeded in making his way through Torres Strait and down the east coast of Australia, but his men were in no real condition to stand a slow and painful navigation—quite apart from the more telling argument that he would have been too early to sail to the Antarctic. Even now he could not begin work in the Dutch Indies until his men had recovered. He sailed to nearby Dubus harbour in New Guinea, which he found largely deserted, the inhabitants being subject to raids from both Indonesians and New Guinea hill tribes. There had been, however, at some time, a Dutch settlement, which the luxuriant jungle was now invading, but numerous coconut and lemon trees 'literary covered with fruit', were still standing. Enough was now generally known about scurvy to ensure that large numbers were fed to the scurvy-threatened crew. The rain stopped for a few days, enabling the officers and men to go hunting and fishing, or exploring cautiously the edge of the dense forest. When the rain returned, they sailed away, slowly because the breeze was weak and variable. On 5 May they were back in Ceram.

The next five months were spent among the islands of Indonesia, gathering a valuable collection of charts, but the cost in lives was to be high. The traces of scurvy had disappeared, thanks to the lemons of Dubus. Ceram provided quantities of inexpensive pigs, for the Moslem inhabitants had such an aversion for pork that the animals roamed through the island in their wild state and the French had only to capture them—unaided, as the natives

[1] Ibid., vol. vi, p. 264.

were even unwilling to help load them in the boats. A week was spent charting the north coast of Ceram, then the route led by way of Buru and Butung to Makassar in the Celebes. It was 22 May; they stayed until the 28th, when they left for Batavia, arriving on 8 June. They were happy to find some countrymen there, traders from Bordeaux. They learnt of the battle of San Juan of Ulloa, but were despondent because there was no news from Paris for them, above all no promotions. 'I had left the Ministry in ignorance of none of our achievements among the ice. When I gave the names of the officers who had taken a share in our work I had insistently asked for the rewards I believed each of them deserved, but the *Astrolabe* and the *Zélée* had been completely forgotten.'[1] Local Dutch society provided no consolation. Shocked by officers dressed informally in old uniforms and plaited hats, and by the now unpainted appearance of the corvettes, the staid Dutch were cool and, to French eyes, over-formal. Leaving on 19 June, the expedition sailed along the Sumatran coast and through the Straits of Bangka, to reach Singapore on the 27th, spending six days in the thriving British port, and leaving by way of the northern Anambas for Borneo. They spent the first half of July exploring the north-west coast, reaching the northernmost cape on the 16th, and turned east towards the Sulu group and Mindanao. It was in these parts that Sonnerat had sailed, rather daringly, in 1772. It was also an area where piracy flourished— the Malays of Bewan, in the Sulus, were at first frightened of the French corvettes, which they mistook for a Dutch punitive expedition. The local sultan was kindly disposed and welcomed d'Urville, who for once put on his full-dress uniform to visit him, but his authority over his people was nominal and, although he would have been pleased to see French trading vessels in his dominions, he could not promise adequate protection. D'Urville succeeded in obtaining supplies of fruits and poultry—trade was not easy with people to whom piracy was a more normal way of earning a living. The district looked attractive enough, with 'numerous white huts perched on hillsides in the middle of carpets of greenery', but mutual suspicion remained until the time came

---

[1] *Voyage au Pôle Sud*, vol. vii, p. 2.

to leave 'this nest of pirates'. Three days later, on 28 July, the ships dropped anchor in Zamboanga at the western tip of Mindanao. The Spanish Governor was far more helpful than the Dutch of Batavia; he placed his house at d'Urville's disposal and provided the officers with cotton clothes to replace their heavy uniforms. They remained there until 6 August, enjoying the rest in spite of the heat and the almost total absence of a breeze. They then sailed south towards Makassar Strait. Calms and currents were to make the following six weeks some of the most painful in the entire voyage. They did not emerge from the strait until 18 September. 'Never were our corvettes held up by more tenacious calms, broken only by the weakest of breezes which were often contrary.' Mafi-Kelepi, the young Tongan, died during this navigation:

Our poor Mafi, who had left his pleasant homeland, Vavau, to come and share with us a rough sailor's life, was unable to bear any longer its vicissitudes; he died of [tuberculosis]. This unfortunate lad wanted to see France and his mind was so firmly made up on this point that nothing could persuade him to leave the Astrolabe to try to restore his health . . . he was much loved by us all and was sincerely regretted. His body was preserved in a barrel of brandy and he forms part of the collection deposited in the Museum of Natural History.[1]

In addition to the unhappy Tongan—who was granted in this peculiar fashion his wish to go to France—two men died, one of dysentery, the other of tetanus, and soon Java was once more to exact a heavy toll of lives.

As the corvettes, at last finding a steady breeze, made for Semarang, Jacquinot took over from d'Urville, who was suffering from one of his periodic attacks of gout. 'The small attention the commander pays to his health is no doubt why he is easily affected by abdominal gout-like pains. . . . His choice of food is rather strange', commented Hombron[2] as other doctors had done before him. 'He often prefers smoked or salt meat to fresh . . . Mr d'Urville lives essentially on his nerves; privations and mental and

[1] Ibid., vol. viii, pp. 13–14.
[2] The Astrolabe's chief surgeon, quoted in ibid., vol. viii, p. 265.

physical strains accentuate this.' A cause of strain was the feeling
that he had to get to Hobart and the Antarctic in early summer and
that time was now running short. He reached Semarang on 24 September and stayed only a week, in spite of the presence of fifteen
European ships, including the *Bombay* from Bordeaux,[1] which
could have provided some exchange of visits and relaxation for
his men. He had sent an order for wine ahead to Batavia; he
stopped only long enough to load it, entered Sunda Strait on
7 October, and after three days in Lampongs Bay, Sumatra, set
off for Hobart on the 11th.

He had spent the minimum of time in Java, and everyone's
health, including his own, was satisfactory when he sailed. But
there were a few cases of fever and dysentery, mainly in the *Zélée*,
when he entered the Indian Ocean. On 13 October there were
twenty sick, including eight in the *Astrolabe*, but none serious.
Ten days later, the number had risen to twenty-six, including
La Farge, an *enseigne* from the *Zélée*, and one man in the *Astrolabe*
was causing anxiety. On the 29th Marescot Duthilleul had fallen
ill and there were twenty-eight other cases, all of them of dysentery.

The beginning of November was the most disastrous period for our
expedition. It was then that the winds settled again, and definitely,
from SSE. We therefore had to give up hope of seeing the early
arrival of the westerlies which our two corvettes were waiting for so
impatiently. . . . From that time until Hobart Town, our navigation
was, so to speak, one long scene of mourning and death where I had
every day to record the name of new victims taken from the *Astrolabe*
and the *Zélée*.[2]

Fourteen men and three officers—Marescot Duthilleul, La Farge,
and Gourdin—died before the expedition reached Hobart and six
died soon after, while another four had to be left behind at the
city hospital. On 6 November, when five men had already died,
Le Guillou, the *Zélée*'s chief surgeon, came to urge d'Urville to
put in at Swan River in Western Australia or make for Mauritius.

---

[1] Captain Goubie. The *Bombay* completed a circumnavigation from 8 Jan. 1838
to 30 Jan. 1840.
[2] *Voyage au Pôle Sud*, vol. viii, p. 75.

He claimed that his view was supported by a number of officers. D'Urville was faced with a dilemma. The *Zélée*, according to his instructions, should have been sent home after his exploration of New Guinea; should he not now transfer the sick to her and send her to Mauritius, where the south-easterlies would take her within a week or so? On the other hand, his instructions mentioned a call at Swan River; would he not be justified in making for the British settlement there, not far away to the south-east? Hombron, his own surgeon, was ill, and he hesitated to consult him. He decided to go in person on board the *Zélée*. Jacquinot and his officers knew nothing of Le Guillou's request: the surgeon had acted without authority and overstated his case. Storming against this 'shameful intrigue', d'Urville returned to his ship and the expedition continued on its way to Tasmania. The sick were transferred to a makeshift hospital as soon as the corvettes reached Hobart; but it was already 12 December. If he were to sail for the Antarctic with any hope of success, d'Urville would have to leave in early January. The epidemic showed no sign of ending—seven more men had been transferred to the hospital by the 21st—and few of the sick were expected to have sufficiently recovered by the end of the year to resist the new hardships of a navigation along the ice shelf. D'Urville decided to go south alone with all the fit men he could muster, and leave the *Zélée* behind with the sick and the remainder of her crew; Jacquinot, after resting the men for two months, would sail to a rendezvous in the Auckland Islands or in New Zealand. 'This decision appeared to upset Mr. Jacquinot very considerably. His courage and zeal rebelled at the thought of not taking part in one of the most glorious, although most dangerous, parts of the mission . . . [He] insisted so much on not leaving the *Astrolabe* that I promised to let the *Zélée* follow us if when we sailed all the sick had left the hospital and the sailors we could recruit on the spot were enough to make up our crews.'[1] It was far from easy to find replacements in Hobart. There were a number of deserters about, mostly from French whalers, but they had gone into hiding when the corvettes appeared. A few British sailors came up, but 'most of them were vagabonds', or at

[1] Ibid., vol. viii, p. 98.

376 DUMONT D'URVILLE'S LAST VOYAGE

least wise enough not to risk their lives in the Antarctic. The *Astrolabe* in fact sailed with only four new crew members, but Jacquinot secured five times that number and thus earned the right to sail with d'Urville on his second attempt to explore the Antarctic. Admittedly d'Urville's plans were modest: 'My intention [was] simply to sail far to the south of Tasmania, determine the latitude where I met solid ice and then sail either to the Auckland Islands or to one of the ports of New Zealand, while the *Zélée*, making a detour, would return to Hobart-Town to pick up our sick and then join us in one of the places I had selected.'[1]

Even so, anxiety began to mount as dysentery reappeared. Within a week, there were sixteen men affected, and on 15 January one of them died. The sea by then was 'monstrous' and snow was falling: the expedition had reached 58° south. The first ice appeared the next day, soon followed by the first iceberg. 'On my first attempt we had seen the first drift ice in the 59th degree of latitude and had been unable to cross the 65th; today we had reached only the 60th degree and I naturally concluded that we would soon come to the same ice barrier.' The sea was becoming calm, confirming his fear that he was leaving open waters. Nevertheless by the evening of the 18th the expedition crossed the sixty-fourth degree. Gigantic icebergs were floating silently over an increasingly smooth sea. The snow stopped the next afternoon and the sky suddenly cleared. Vincendon Dumoulin went aloft and reported what he thought was land straight ahead. 'Mr. Dumoulin was the first one out of us all to sight land. But he had been so often deceived by illusions of this kind that he was far from believing in his discovery, and was even one of the last to admit its existence.' The French were now further south than they had ever been and the sailors organized a suitable ceremony to mark the crossing of the Antarctic Circle, comparable to the entertainments which accompany the crossing of the Equator. But, while Father Antarctic made his burlesque appearance on board, the belief that land was near began to spread—no one in the *Zélée* now had any doubts. It was still not easy, however, to approach it through the long labyrinth of icebergs.

[1] *Voyage au Pôle Sud*, vol. viii, p. 127.

At eight o'clock [on 21 January] we were so tightly surrounded by
these floating masses that I was constantly afraid of seeing our corvettes
crashing into them. This navigation was indeed not without danger,
for the sea swirled so much around them that it would not fail to drive
a ship to her destruction if she were sheltered for a moment from the
wind by these high cliffs of ice. . . . Their sheer walls were far higher
than our masts; they overhung our ships whose size seemed absurdly
reduced in proportion with these enormous masses. The spectacle
before us was both grandiose and frightening. One might have thought
oneself in the narrow streets of a city of giants. . . . For nearly an hour
we saw nothing around us but vertical walls of ice. Then we entered
a vast basin formed by the land on one side and on the other by the
chain of floating ice we had just crossed. By midday we were only
three or four miles from our new discovery . . . it stretched out as far
as the eye could see to the south-east and the north-west and we could
not see its limits in either of these directions. It was completely covered
with snow, and reached at a guess a height of 1,000 to 1,200 metres. . . .
Nowhere either did we see any stain which might indicate the presence
of ground and we might have thought that we had reached an icefield
even larger than the ones we had met before if we could have believed
that ice fields could ever reach such a prodigious height.[1]

It was necessary to prove that this was land by some more
tangible evidence than this admittedly logical deduction. The
French sailed slowly westwards, sighting capes and bays everywhere covered with ice or obstructed by icebergs. In time bare
rock became visible, and at once boats went out from both ships
with men armed with pickaxes and hammers who brought back
enough geological samples to silence any critic. The French
tricolour was raised 'over this land which no human being before
us had ever seen or set foot on', and 'we took possession of it in
the name of France . . . it seemed to us that we had added a province to the territory of France by this pacific conquest'.[2] D'Urville
named it Terre Adélie after his wife Adèle; the cape they had
first seen was called Cap de la Découverte, and the point near
which the samples of rocks were obtained received the appropriate
name of Pointe Géologie. Adélie Land, a comparatively thin
sliver of land which runs to the South Pole, has remained France's

[1] Ibid., vol. viii, pp. 142–4.   [2] Ibid., vol. viii, p. 150.

incontestable claim to a share of the Antarctic continent and a valuable base for French scientists. It was d'Urville's most spectacular achievement. It was also timely, for the Wilkes expedition was in the neighbourhood and the French actually met the *Porpoise* on 29 January—although through some misunderstanding they did not communicate.

D'Urville's crews were in no condition to extend their discoveries. They had already encountered a violent storm, the winds were variable, and snow continued to fall steadily. The men were beginning to show signs of exhaustion, while every new manœuvre required increasing effort. The ships sailed slowly along an enormous ice cliff which continued for miles—d'Urville named it Côte Clarie[1]—before fog hid it from view. On the evening of 1 February 1840, being then in 65° 20′ south and just past 131° east—that is, ten degrees west of their first landfall—the French altered course for Hobart, since d'Urville had decided that the two corvettes would together fetch the sick and fresh supplies of food. His men, he thought, deserved a brief respite, and in view of the presence of Wilkes's ships he was anxious to make his discovery known.

The return journey took seventeen days and the stay was as short as he could make it. The corvettes sailed for the Auckland Islands, to the south of New Zealand, on 25 February. The westerlies sped them on, and they reached the group on 7 March. D'Urville agreed to spend a week there, to enable Vincendon Dumoulin to carry out a number of necessary observations and correct his estimated reckoning of the magnetic pole. The islands were deserted but for a Portuguese whaler, but the *Porpoise* had passed by recently and left a record of her voyage to the Antarctic, to which d'Urville added one of his own. There were also traces of French whalers about: a useful cabin had been erected by the whaler *Nancy*, and a freshly dug grave contained the remains of a Captain Lefrançois who had committed suicide in a fit of depression. Stewart Island, the southernmost part of New Zealand, was sighted on 23 March, but it took another four days, against con-

---

[1] Nothing corresponding to his description of it has been seen, and it is likely that he sailed for some time alongside a large mass of floating ice.

trary winds, before the French could approach the South Island and three more before they anchored in what d'Urville called Otago Harbour, but which was really Hooper's Inlet on the eastern side of Otago Peninsula. There they found the *Le Havre*, a whaler commanded by Captain Privat, which they had already met in Concepción. Privat told them that French whalers were forsaking the Eastern Pacific in favour of New Zealand and Australian waters, where whales were still plentiful. D'Urville was struck by the contrast between the Maoris he had met ten years earlier and those he now saw in the South Island, dressed in rags, living in vermin-infested huts, and spending their days begging or stealing. A European settlement around the peninsula had helped degrade the local natives, without engendering any feeling of security among the settlers, several of whom asked d'Urville for a passage to some safer district. The expedition continued slowly north along the coast, calling in at Akaroa, where the *Astrolabe* was caught by currents and was fortunate to escape destruction; there were four French whalers in the neighbourhood, including the *Gange*, under Captain Grandsaigne, and the *Héva*, Captain Lelièvre, whose whaleboat hastened to the *Astrolabe*'s assistance. D'Urville was able to help them in return in various ways, and Grandsaigne, who was about to sail home, took the expedition's mail with him. But the bay itself seemed more valuable as a port than as a site for the French colony which was then being organized:

To sum up, Akaroa basin seems most unsuitable to maintain a population of any real size; by choosing this point to found later an establishment the French Government considered only the beauty of the port, how easy it would be to defend it, and finally the valuable resources it offers our whalers. If it were a question of setting up a colony on Tavaii-Pounamou [the South Island], with a view to it spreading, so as to create in New Zealand settlements which might rival those of the English in Australia, then without doubt Akaroa Bay would be a very poor choice for a first settlement.[1]

Once he left the South Island, d'Urville hurried towards the Bay of Islands, as he had no wish to waste time off a coast he had

[1] *Voyage au Pôle Sud*, vol. ix, p. 155.

surveyed during his first voyage. He merely stopped on the way for supplies, wisely guessing that he could buy them at a better price in a district not populated by Europeans. He arrived at Kororareka on 26 April to learn that Britain had taken possession of the North Island. This was not unexpected, but the French took good care to do nothing that might imply recognition—Wilkes had done the same thing when he had called a few days earlier on his way to Tonga. Accordingly, when Hobson, the new Governor, sent an offer of services, d'Urville replied that he could only meet him as a fellow officer and would only accept the kind of assistance he would receive from a casually encountered naval captain. Hobson signified that he appreciated d'Urville's position and, when the latter let it be known that he would pay him a courtesy call, took care to avoid embarrassment by being away on business. 'I was not in the least upset by this result; we deposited our cards, and then went to Mr. Williams's house. We found only that missionary's wife at home; her welcome was cool, but polite.'[1]

D'Urville, still suffering from severe stomach cramps, spent most of his time on board, talking to the few French residents of the bay. Bishop Pompallier was in the interior, having left Father Petit in charge. It was through the latter's intervention that d'Urville and Simonet finally parted. The deserter's behaviour on board had been exemplary and d'Urville realized that he had taken him away from his family: 'I personally had long ago forgiven him; he had often been of service to the expedition and could moreover be most useful to the mission.' Simonet was therefore landed at Kororareka and even paid for the time spent on board the *Astrolabe*. Another Frenchman had a request to make of d'Urville. This was the unfortunate Baron de Thierry, whose land purchases were now threatened by the arrival of the British and the setting-up of land courts. D'Urville in spite of Thierry's earlier behaviour felt that he had a case, but he could not intervene on his behalf with Hobson without implicitly recognizing British rights over the country; nor did he think that the French Government, in view of Thierry's ambiguous nationality and his earlier

[1] *Voyage au Pôle Sud*, vol. ix, p. 183.

self-proclamation as king, would be prepared to take up his case.[1] However, he gave him a letter in which he expressed his personal view that his title to the land was unimpeachable under New Zealand conditions and that he was 'entitled to invoke, if need be, the assistance and protection of the French government'. He hoped that Hobson would read between the lines and realize that, had it not been for the recognition issue, d'Urville would have pleaded the Baron's case. The letter ended on a note which sheds a peculiar light on d'Urville's vanity: 'I repeat that this is only one man's opinion; but probably of the one who, in the entire world, has for the last twenty years been most concerned with New Zealand.'[2]

The French were now nearing the last stage of their voyage. When he left New Zealand, on 4 May 1840, d'Urville made for Torres Strait, which he had earlier failed to reach. The route took him rapidly to the Loyalty Islands, sighted through rain on the 12th; then to the Louisiade archipelago. The group was seldom visited and the southern islands especially were little known. The exploration of this area was to be, through Vincendon Dumoulin's excellent charts, a major contribution to hydrography. The ships made their way safely to the south coast of New Guinea and entered Torres Strait through Bligh's Pass on 31 May; but the next day the *Astrolabe*, followed by the *Zélée*, struck the Great Reef. The corvettes sustained considerable damage to their keels— how serious was not realized until they were surveyed in France— and were in danger of breaking up as the waves lifted them and crashed them down against the coral. The next high tide caused the corvettes to drag their anchors, and the violent currents bore them towards the main reef, so that an even more perilous and certainly bizarre situation arose:

The *Zélée*, like ourselves, had remained suspended, as it were, against the sides of the coral rock. This was our new situation: coral reefs rise perpendicularly from the bottom of the sea, like the walls of our houses; however, instead of being smooth like our walls, these coral rocks have large rough edges. The *Astrolabe*, when it had come

[1] In fact, a few months earlier, the French Government had been considering making use of Thierry's claims as a basis for a French protectorate over New Zealand. See Jore, *Océan Pacifique*, vol. i, p. 189.

[2] *Voyage au Pôle Sud*, vol. ix, p. 202.

against these sides, had in some way remained caught by them. . . . As the tide fell the *Astrolabe* began to list more and more, so that we feared that she might capsize. . . . At six in the evening, night found us in our most critical situation. The corvette had a 32° list and the tide had not yet reached its lowest point. . . . At nine the oscillometer registered a 38° list. The water reached the deck and little more would be needed to cause it to fill the ship; the weather was dreadful; a south-easterly gale blew in wild gusts, bringing heavy rain with it. Nothing could describe the horror of our situation: we were afraid of seeing the *Astrolabe* crash into the sea at any moment after turning over, and drag down to their destruction all the brave men who had sailed in her.[1]

With the help of high tides, the two corvettes were freed on 4 June. Very carefully, with boats sounding ahead every inch of the way, they continued on their way and emerged on the 12th. A week later the French reached Dutch Timor. 'The long voyage of the *Astrolabe* and the *Zélée* was now truly completed.' All that lay ahead was the voyage to Bourbon, where they dropped anchor on 19 July, and the final passage through the Atlantic. Leaving behind several men still weak from the after-effects of dysentery, and taking on a number of soldiers due to return to France after completing their term of service, d'Urville sailed from Bourbon on 30 July.

The only stop was at St. Helena in early September, where the French made the customary visit to the tomb of 'the most extraordinary man of modern times'; but they were to be the last such callers, as the Prince de Joinville was due shortly to take Napoleon's remains back to France. Finally, on 6 November 1840, the two corvettes entered Toulon harbour after a circumnavigation which had lasted thirty-eight months.

On 31 December 1840 Dumont d'Urville was promoted to the rank of rear-admiral. It set the seal on a long and fruitful career, bringing him that prompt official recognition which he appreciated as his due. The Société de Géographie gave him its gold medal. Publication of the official account of the voyage was ordered without delay at the public expense.[2] Promotions and

---

[1] *Voyage au Pôle Sud*, vol. ix, pp. 224, 229.
[2] Begun by d'Urville, the *Voyage au Pôle Sud* was completed after his death by Vincendon Dumoulin and Jacquinot.

rewards were granted to other members of the expedition, notably Jacquinot, du Bouzet, and Vincendon Dumoulin. A few voices were heard denigrating their achievements—it was pointed out that twenty-five men had died and many more were left behind in various hospitals, some of whom would not recover, but this merely underlined the hardships all had had to endure, for d'Urville's seamanship was unquestioned and his concern for his crews especially evident; he had never sailed further south than the sixty-seventh degree of latitude, whereas Weddell had reached the seventy-fourth and Ross would soon go beyond this, but the discovery of Adélie Land was enough to silence any critic, and the jealous whispers were ignored. The fact was that d'Urville, although almost constantly ill, had twice sailed to the very edge of the southern continent, and had brought back a wealth of information, so accurate and so reliable that the charts compiled by the officers of the *Astrolabe* and the *Zélée* were still in use sixty years later. He had once more proved himself to be a methodical and conscientious sailor, austere and dedicated as Baudin had been, admittedly vain and quick to take offence, but kind and with a talent verging on genius. Without doubt the man who made the greatest single contribution to the perfecting of the map of the Pacific,[1] he brought to a noble and honourable close the great period of Pacific exploration.

France had just learnt to accept him with pride when tragedy, which was never far away in his life, nor, indeed, in the life of any French explorer, came to claim him. He was killed on 8 May 1842 near Paris in one of France's earliest and grimmest train disasters. With him died his wife and his only surviving son.

---

[1] Faivre, *Expansion française*, p. 243.

CONCLUSION

THE theme of Anglo-French rivalry remains constant during the great period of Pacific exploration. The confrontation did not lessen until the expansionist era was under way, by which time third parties had arrived on the scene, notably the United States, followed a little later by Germany. Up to and including Baudin, the aim had been to find anti-British bases in order to keep the traditional enemy out of the Pacific or defeat him in a future major conflict. The Bougainville expedition was born out of the aftermath of the Seven Years War. De Surville sailed hurriedly for a non-existent island which he feared Britain might occupy ahead of France. François Péron, a little amateurishly, brought the nationalistic fervour of the new revolution to the coast of New South Wales. But, once James Cook had returned from his first voyage, national prestige became far more important than vague strategic possibilities. Here, in a non-military sphere, was a new opponent, someone to emulate and overshadow for the honour of France. 'Haunted by Cook', as d'Urville himself put it, the French set off for the Pacific with a new and at times a desperate determination. One is reminded irresistibly of the space race between the United States and the Soviet Union, where success in a specifically scientific field is full of implications of prestige and, eventually, of military advantages.

But who could emulate 'the incomparable Cook'? With the Paris court uninterested in distant seas and continents, and too often on the verge of bankruptcy to have money to spare for Pacific exploration, with the Académie des Sciences less influential then the Royal Society, it was frequently left to amateurs to put plans forward. The French approach was, typically and inevitably, predominantly individualistic—a comment which is valid even for the early stages of missionary and expansionist activities. Making allowance for the obvious difference of scale, it is interesting to compare the sponsoring of the voyage of the

Endeavour with the French authorities' casting about for a volunteer to take Ahu-toru back to Tahiti. More valid is the picture of Kerguelen setting off on 'the finest [voyage] that has ever been undertaken', on a great circumnavigation which would include the exploration of Antarctic or near-Antarctic waters where Cook had never sailed. It would be ludicrous to speak of the expeditions of Cook and Kerguelen in the same breath were it not for the fact that the one motivated the other. The Kerguelen failure furthermore put an end to the purely individualist period, for it finally spurred the French Government to mount an official expedition on a large enough scale to rival the British ones, and place at its head a sailor worthy of James Cook—and one who, incidentally, had proved to be a dangerous enemy of Britain in wartime.

When La Pérouse received his instructions, there was no hint of Gonneville Land, that perennial myth which had haunted earlier French explorers. Cook's second voyage had swept great areas of mystery from the southern seas, finding no trace of temperate land; and Kerguelen's fairy-tale reports had ensured that no one would take the fable seriously again. La Pérouse was directed instead to regions which Cook had not visited, notably the northwest. The mystery of his disappearance obscured the extent of his achievements: in their emotional, but entirely justified, desire to rescue him and his companions, the French sometimes overlooked the fact that they had in him a figure in many respects as 'incomparable' as Cook—for what might he not have achieved if fate had spared him for a second and a third voyage? The tragic disappearance of his expedition led to the equally tragic voyage of d'Entrecasteaux, whose instructions were planned to complement the work done by La Pérouse; and it stilled for a time, in spite of a growing conflict in Europe, the bitter rivalry. But with Baudin, although the scientific purpose of the expedition is unchallenged, the age-old enmity reappeared.

From the beginning of the nineteenth century, anti-British sentiment was focused, inevitably, on Port Jackson and Australia. Unlike Spain, unlike Holland, Britain and France lacked bases in the Pacific. The reports of captains from both nations were eagerly scanned for some discovery which might include a harbour backed by a fertile hinterland where some foothold might be established. Armchair geographers put forward the most improbable solutions, and in some instances—the Bismarck archipelago is one—their suggestions, taken up by the incompetent or the unscrupulous, led to tragedy. The point was that there is no suitable centrally situated land in the Pacific where such bases could be set up; and accordingly no opportunity for any single nation to dominate this enormous ocean. As with the Atlantic, relative mastery of the sea could only be gained from ports and colonies set up along its periphery. When, therefore, Britain established its first settlement in New South Wales, and it began to flourish beyond all expectations, French visitors recorded their envy and their exasperation.

But there are wars which, if they do not end war, at least change the patterns of enmity. Bougainville had held the belief that France needed bases—or at least an absence of British bases—for the next stage in the endless series of wars between the two countries. Freycinet, who opens the post-Napoleonic period of exploration, held no such view; nor did Bougainville's son. The latter's concern was far more typical of his time: Sydney was growing into a metropolis; why had France not thought of such a settlement and why was she not preoccupied with founding one now? The refrain becomes more insistent as the years go by, so that one is tempted to comment that Sydney became for the French in the nineteenth century what James Cook had been in the eighteenth: an object of admiration, self-reproach, and envy. The two rival empires were becoming commercial competitors, and their view of bases was changing accordingly. Colonial settlements need a deeper motivation than a desire for mere bases—the failure of Port Famine, which had disappeared almost without trace in the Straits of Magellan, was proof enough of this. And there were few organized attempts at colonial implantations in the early stages. Britain had not sent settlers, but convicts, to Botany Bay; colonial growth had come later. And the other habitable regions of the Pacific were taken over, not by colonists, but by missionaries. There was little scope yet for traders, since, apart from seals, whales, and sandalwood, the Pacific would have nothing to export until Europeans had arrived in adequate numbers to till the soil; so that we find none of the commercial struggles which had opposed the Dutch to the Portuguese and the Portuguese to the Spanish in earlier centuries. What we do find is a bitter fight developing between the Protestants of Britain and the United States, on the one hand, and the Catholics of France on the other. The policy of exclusiveness carried out by the Dutch and the Spanish with such determination until the close of the eighteenth century was re-enacted in a different context and by different actors among the peaceful islands of the Pacific.

While the French Government hesitated and shelved one proposal for a penal settlement after another (it finally set one up in New Caledonia), the Marist and the Picpus Fathers sailed out to challenge Methodist and Anglican missionaries in the Pacific. The two governments stood back, or attempted to, as individuals and organizations again affronted each other, no longer in the name of science, but of religious doctrine. The conflict was resolved in favour of toleration—it could hardly be otherwise in view of the new attitudes in Europe which gave rise, *inter alia*, to the Emancipation Act—but the prize was smaller than some had expected. True, if the Protestant missionaries had been allowed to carve out their little kingdoms in the Society Islands, in Hawaii, in the Marquesas, and elsewhere, while French missionaries were excluded, it would have been only a matter of time before the Colonial Office took over, and in the end France would have had no real foothold among the myriad islands. The religious struggle which forms the background to the various expeditions sent out during the reigns of Charles X and Louis-Philippe was consequent upon a religious fervour and a concern which were genuine enough; but the political and nationalistic undercurrent is equally evident. It was yet another facet of the long-standing rivalry. What must be borne in mind is how little bearing it had on the subsequent sharing-out of the Pacific. History tends to avoid such neat endings. True, Tahiti fell to the French, but this was an isolated case. The Sandwich Islands slid into the American sphere in spite of the defeat sustained by the Revd. Hiram Bingham, and simply because their relative proximity to the United States made them a natural target for colonialist activities. French eyes were turned towards the Marquesas, which became French but were a poor prize, and towards New Zealand, which did not but would have been a real one. Annexation was usually the result of the fortuitous conjunction of events and it was often marked by a genuine reluctance. In a situation where Anglo-French enmity might so easily have erupted into an actual clash, we find Britain turning a deaf ear to the complaints of Pritchard and the two powers arriving at amicable, albeit unusual, compromises, of which the Franco-British condominium over the New Hebrides —Bougainville's Grandes Cyclades—is perhaps the strangest example.

Of all the islands of the Pacific, the New Zealand group exemplifies most vividly the long rivalry between Britain and France. Typically, it involves James Cook, who reached it just ahead of de Surville. It promised, had they then realized it, everything Europeans needed for a successful settlement: a temperate climate, a fertile soil, a relatively small native population. It is interesting to speculate on what would have happened if de Surville's visit had not been so brief and Marion du Fresne's so disastrous. New Zealand would then not have become known to the French as a land of unpredictable and untameable cannibals. La Pérouse might have dispelled these notions had he been allowed to sail there, as had been planned; but he was sent instead to Botany Bay—and, anyhow, the death of de Langle would have predisposed him in favour of the traditional view. From that time, French explorers called but briefly, and in the very north, until reports received mainly through Australia began to suggest that the country could be both peaceful and profitable. But by then New Zealand, which had once seemed Cook's preserve, had become that of New South Wales; and Samuel Marsden had sent missionaries over to establish the first inevitable foothold, while escaped convicts and runaway sailors, mostly British, had created a kind of no-man's-land which was more a Little Britain than an Alsatia. Yet France dispatched her missionaries there, as she did to Tahiti, to counteract the influence of the Church Missionary Society. Had they arrived earlier, had Marsden been as unreasonable as Pritchard and Bingham, France might have come to the defence of her nationals, and stayed to establish a protectorate which might have delayed Wakefield's colonists and given Lavaud's their chance. The cost might have been that head-on clash between the two countries which so many predicted and which never eventuated. A more likely solution might have been an uneasy condominium or, with greater realism, partition—an alternative the twentieth century would have seized upon—granting the north to Britain and the south to France. But the question never arose and the French consoled themselves with the Marquesas.

The truth was that the Pacific was large enough for prizes to be available for all, and that there was little in it so valuable that it warranted a clash. It was also that the two ancient enemies were learning to become allies and, gradually, in a setting of exploration and scientific research, had come to terms in waters which, for quite different reasons and with slight accuracy, but almost symbolically, Magellan had once called Pacific.

If this period of exploration shows us a pattern of rivalry, it also reflects the technical changes which transformed the science of navigation, and the co-operation between the navigators and scientists of many nations which made them possible. The great problem had been the accurate determination of a ship's longitude. The pitiful attempts to estimate a position by dead reckoning became so much a thing of the past in the nineteenth century that one requires a conscious effort to recapture the atmosphere of uncertainty, impatience, and despair of the first voyages. Each successive explorer was granted a more accurate method of finding his way across the ocean as chronometers became more dependable and more precise. The importance of the astronomer or the scientist on board diminished year by year, until he disappeared for good. Naval officers with some scientific training, including a knowledge of natural history, became the rule—and they were far more valuable because they would obey orders in a way no passenger, no guest, however bound by agreements or a sense of duty, ever would. Scurvy disappeared almost entirely, even from the worst-organized expedition, but not dramatically: it took

many years before captains and sailors could be persuaded that
'land air' was not really what defeated sickness. But hygiene
improved immeasurably, within the limits imposed by ships
which were still small and, by our standards, grossly overcrowded.
Biscuit and salt meat remained the staple foods, and worms and
rats attacked both with much the same regularity; yet we note in
voyage after voyage the attempts made by scientists, and by the
Navy, to discover new and more efficacious ways of preserving
meat.

Life at sea in the days of sailing ships could never be anything
but hard. The men, although not inured to it, expected it to be.
Their sufferings are recorded in the journals of almost every
officer, for the romantic haze which surrounds the image of the
'jolly tar' is equally inaccurate in hiding from us the naval captains'
real concern for their men. De Surville, La Pérouse, Dumont
d'Urville, to select at random, were constantly preoccupied with
their sailors' well-being. Those who were not were not true men
of the sea, but men too conscious of their rank or their advancement. The Revolution, in breaking down class barriers to entry
into the Navy and to promotion once inside it, did not alter this
difference, which was the result of attitudes rather than birth.
If we see the condition of the sailors slowly improving, it is
because of technical, not personal, changes: the Pacific became
better known and less dangerous, and exploration became, one
must admit it, easier and less burdensome. The process was of
course gradual, and a step forward was sometimes followed by
one backward. Errors of judgement, wrong interpretations, and
sheer stupidity are as much part of the process of exploration as
great courage, daring, and endurance. Another necessary element
is planning and co-operation, which the French learnt slowly at
first, because the impoverished State could seldom afford to provide it. Just as the first generations had called on the Government
to support and finance the explorers, so those who came later
called for help on behalf of missionaries, traders, and settlers;
until eventually the great Pacific, so remote and unknown, became
a mere extension of Europe. Once this had happened, a new series
of problems emerged, economic, social, and political, which none

but the most prophetic of the old explorers and geographers could have foreseen.

Thus the exploration of the Pacific Ocean spreads before us in a wide panorama all the hopes, failures, and achievements of humanity, and the slow uneven march of what, for want of a better word, we call civilization.

BIBLIOGRAPHY

(a) MANUSCRIPTS

Abbreviations

A.N.M.   Archives Nationales, Marine. Paris.
A.T.L.   Alexander Turnbull Library. Wellington.
B.N., N.A.F. Bibliothèque Nationale, Nouvelles Acquisitions Françaises. Paris.
M.H.N.   Muséum d'Histoire Naturelle. Paris.
M.L.   Mitchell Library. Sydney.
S.H.M.   Service Hydrographique de la Marine. Paris.

Note: Manuscript sources are listed under the commander's name. Full titles and sub-references have been given, where appropriate, in the text or in footnotes.

BAUDIN

Journals and papers. A.N.M. 5JJ 24–57; B.N., N.A.F. 9440–1.
Journal du capitaine Baudin. (Hélouis transcripts) M.L.
Baudin papers. B.N., N.A.F. 9439: 107.
Official papers. A.N.M. BB4 995.
Correspondence of Decrès. S.H.M. 102/26.

BOUGAINVILLE, H.

Journals and papers. A.N.M. 5JJ 88–98.
Instructions and correspondence. A.N.M. BB4 1001.

BOUGAINVILLE, L.

Journals of the *Boudeuse*. S.H.M. 123: 1; A.N.M. 4JJ 142: 17, BB4 1001: 4.
Journal of La Giraudais. M.H.N. 1B 1195.
Journal of Caro. A.N.M. 4JJ 1: 5.
Journal of Vivès. B.N., N.A.F. 9407: 76.
Journal of Fesche. M.H.N. 1896-8.
Journal of Commerson. M.H.N. 680.
Instructions and sundry papers. B.N., N.A.F. 9407; A.N.M. B4 112, 114.
Journals and papers of Doublet, Duquesnel, and Laurens Olivier. B.N., N.A.F. 9438.
'Découvertes des terres australes'. M.L.
Papers of Commerson. M.H.N. 301–2.

BOUVET

Journal of the *Marie* (extract). Photostat A.T.L.
'Extrait du voyage 1738–39'. Photostat A.T.L.
Route of the *Aigle*. Photostat A.T.L.
Miscellaneous papers. B.N., N.A.F. 9341, 9407, 9438–9.

CÉCILLE

Instructions and reports. A.N.M. BB4 1010: 6; 1011: 1; typescripts in A.T.L.

D'ENTRECASTEAUX

Journals. A.N.M. 5JJ 5–13; M.H.N. 1041.
Anonymous journals (incomplete). S.H.M. 105: 5.
Instructions and correspondence. M.H.N. 46; A.N.M. BB4 992–4.

DUMONT D'URVILLE

(a) *Astrolabe* (1826–9).
Journals and registers. A.N.M. 5JJ 99–102C.
Reports and correspondence. A.N.M. BB4 1002.
Sundry papers. M.H.N. 104–9.

(b) *Astrolabe* and *Zélée* (1837–40).
Journals of the *Astrolabe*. A.N.M. 5JJ 127 and 144.
Journals of the *Zélée*. A.N.M. 5JJ 128 and 145.
Reports and correspondence. A.N.M. BB4 1009.
Sundry papers. A.N.M. 5JJ 158.

DUPERREY

Journals of the *Coquille*. A.N.M. 5JJ 80.
Journals of Bérard, Blois, Blosseville, Jacquinot, and Lottin. A.N.M. 5JJ 82.
Journal of d'Urville. M.H.N. 1602.
Journal of Lesson (incomplete). M.H.N. 1793.
Journal of Lejeune. S.H.M. A4211.
Sundry reports and correspondence. A.N.M. BB4 1000; B.N., N.A.F.
6785: 20–9; 9445.

DUPETIT-THOUARS

Journals. A.N.M. 5JJ 111 and 126.
Reports and correspondence. A.N.M. BB4 1005.

FREYCINET

Journals. A.N.M. 5JJ 58–79.
Reports and correspondence. A.N.M. BB4 998.
Instructions. A.N.M. BB4 999; 5JJ 68.

KERGUELEN

Journals of the *Rolland* and the *Oiseau*. A.N.M. 4JJ 142: 20–1.
Journal of Rosily (extract). B.N., N.A.F. 9438: 79.
Journal of St. Allouarn (extract). A.N.M. 4JJ 143: 26.
Sundry reports and correspondence. B.N., N.A.F. 9341, 9431, 9438–9;
  A.N.M. B4 317.
Court-martial documents. Naval Library, Brest, MS 171.
Admiralty Board Minutes. Public Records Office ADM 3: 91.
Sundry correspondence. National Maritime Museum, Greenwich, A.D.M.
  FP/24, M/410, M/412.

LA PÉROUSE

Journals (incomplete) and reports. B.N., N.A.F. 9410–25.
Instructions and correspondence. Typescripts. A.T.L.
Correspondence to and from Latouche-Tréville and the Baron de Gonneville.
  B.N., N.A.F. 9439.

LAPLACE

(a) *Favorite* (1829–32).

  Reports and correspondence. A.N.M. BB4 1004.
  Registers and notes. A.N.M. 5JJ 103–9.

(b) *Artémise* (1837–40).

  Journals. A.N.M. 5JJ 167–9.
  Reports and correspondence. A.N.M. BB4 1008.
  Papers on Education 1804–68. M.L.

MARION DU FRESNE

Journals of the *Mascarin*. A.N.M. 4JJ 84: 114 and 128: 38.
Journals of Du Clesmeur. A.N.M. 4JJ 109: 29; B.N., N.A.F. 9437; S.H.M.
  A5708.
Journals of Jean Roux. A.N.M. 4JJ 142: 18–19; B.N., N.A.F. 9437.
Journal of Crozet (extract). Microfilm A.T.L.
Miscellaneous correspondence. B.N., N.A.F. 9439.
Sundry papers. Archives of Mauritius, JE/1, Na 18: 5–6.

MARCHAND

Journal of the *Solide*. Archives de Marseille.

SURVILLE

Journal of Surville. A.N.M. 4JJ 143: 24.
Journals of Labé. A.N.M. 4JJ 143: 22–3.
Journals of Monneron. A.N.M. B4 316; B.N., N.A.F. 9436: 1–87.
Journal of Pottier. A.N.M. 4JJ 143: 25.
Sundry correspondence. A.N.M. B4 316; B.N., N.A.F. 9438: 84.
Appeal by Bourgeois and Gallois. A.T.L.

VAILLANT

Journals of Vaillant. A.N.M. BB4 1007: 5.

Officers' journals. A.N.M. BB4 1006.

Sundry reports. A.N.M. 5JJ 159–66.

(b) PRINTED WORKS

AMHERST, W. A. T., and THOMSON, B. (eds.), *The discovery of the Solomon Islands by Alvaro de Mendaña in 1568*. 2 vols., London, 1901.

[Anon.] *An account of the visit of the French frigate* L'Artémise *to the Sandwich Islands*. Honolulu, 1839.

ARAGO, J., *Promenade autour du monde pendant les années 1817–1820 sur les corvettes* L'Uranie *et* La Physicienne. 2 vols., Paris, 1822.

—— *Souvenirs d'un aveugle. Voyage autour du monde*. 2 vols., Paris, 1835.

ARAGON, L. A. C. D', *Un Paladin au XVIIIᵉ siècle, le prince Charles de Nassau-Siegen*. Paris, 1893.

ARVENGAS, H., *L'Exploration et le mystérieux naufrage de Lapérouse*. Albi, 1941.

AUDIAT, L., *François Péron, sa vie, ses voyages et ses ouvrages*. Moulins, 1855.

AUSTIN, H. C. M., *Sea fights and corsairs of the Indian Ocean: being the naval history of Mauritius from 1715 to 1810*. Port-Louis, 1935.

Australian Encyclopedia, [A. H. Chisholm, ed.-in-chief] 10 vols., Sydney, 1958.

[Australian Government], *Historical records of Australia*. Series I, vols. x–xiii, xvi, Sydney, 1914–1923.

AVEZAC-MACAYA, A. D' (ed.), *Campagne du navire* L'Espoir *de Honfleur 1503–1505: relation authentique du voyage du capitaine de Gonneville ès nouvelles terres des Indes*. Paris, 1869.

BACHAUMONT, L. P. DE, *Mémoires secrets de Bachaumont* (ed. P. L. Jacob). Paris, 1859.

BADOUIN, A., *L'Aventure de Port-Breton*, Paris, 1883.

BALTEAU, J., *Dictionnaire de biographie française*, vols. i–x, 1933–65.

BASSETT, F. M., *Realms and islands: the world voyage of Rose de Freycinet in the corvette* Uranie *1817–20 from her journal and letters*. London, 1962.

BAYLY, G., *Sea life sixty years ago: a record of adventures which led to the discovery of the relics of the long-missing expedition commanded by the Comte de la Pérouse*. London, 1885.

BEAGLEHOLE, J. C., *The discovery of New Zealand*. Wellington, 1939.

—— *The exploration of the Pacific*. London, 1934.

—— *The journals of Captain James Cook on his voyages of discovery*. Vol. i: *The voyage of the* Endeavour *1768–1771*; vol. ii: *The voyage of the* Resolution *and* Adventure *1772–1775*. Cambridge, 1955, 1961.

BELLESORT, A., *La Pérouse*. Paris, 1926.

BENOIT-GUYOD, G., *Au temps de la marine en bois*. 2 vols., Paris, 1942–4.

BÉRIOT, A., *Grands Voiliers autour du monde: les voyages scientifiques 1760–1850*. Paris, 1962.

BESSON, M., *The scourge of the Indies: buccaneers, corsairs and filibusters.* New York, 1929.

BLOSSEVILLE, E. P. DE, *Jules de Blosseville.* Évreux, 1854.

BOISSAIS, E., *Binot Paulmier dit le capitaine de Gonneville, son voyage, sa descendance.* Caen, 1912.

BONNASSIEUX, L. J. P. M., *Les Grandes Compagnies de commerce: études pour servir à l'histoire de la colonisation.* Paris, 1892.

BOUGAINVILLE, H. Y. P. P. DE, *Journal de la navigation autour du globe de* La Thétis *et de* L'Espérance *pendant les années 1824, 1825 et 1826.* 2 vols., Paris, 1837.

BOUGAINVILLE, L. A. DE, *Voyage autour du monde par la frégate du Roi* La Boudeuse *et la flûte* L'Étoile *en 1766–1769.* Paris, 1771. Second edition in 2 vols., 1772. English translation by J. R. Forster, London, 1772.

BOUVIER, R., and MAYNIAL, E., *Une Aventure dans les mers australes: l'expédition du commandant Baudin (1800–1803).* Paris, 1947.

BOWDEN, K. M., *George Bass, 1771–1803.* Melbourne, 1952.

BRÉARD, C., *Notes sur la famille du capitaine Gonneville.* Rouen, 1885.

BROOKES, J. I., *International rivalry in the Pacific islands (1800–1875).* Los Angeles, 1941.

BROSSARD, M. R. DE, *Moana, océan cruel.* Paris, 1966.

—— *Rendez-vous avec Lapérouse à Vanikoro.* Paris, 1964.

BROSSES, C. DE, *Histoire des navigations aux terres australes.* 2 vols., Paris, 1756.

BROWN, J. MACMILLAN, *The riddle of the Pacific.* London, 1924.

BUICK, T. L., *The French at Akaroa.* Wellington, 1929.

BURNEY, J., *A chronological history of the discoveries in the South Sea or Pacific Ocean.* 5 vols., London, 1803–7.

C—[anon.] *Découvertes dans la Mer du Sud. Nouvelles de M. de la Peyrouse jusqu'en 1794. Traces de son passage trouvées en diverses isles et terres [de] l'Océan Pacifique.* Paris, 1796.

CADY, J. F., *The roots of French imperialism in Eastern Asia.* New York, 1954.

CALLANDER, J., *Terra Australis Cognita, or voyages to the Terra Australis or Southern Hemisphere during the sixteenth, seventeenth and eighteenth centuries.* 5 vols., London, 1766–8.

CAP, P. A., *Philibert Commerson, naturaliste voyageur.* Paris, 1861.

CARRINGTON, H. [See Robertson, G.]

CARRUTHERS, J. H., *Captain James Cook R.N. One hundred and fifty years after.* London, 1930.

CHAILLEY-BERT, J., *Les Compagnies de colonisation sous l'Ancien Régime.* Paris, 1898.

CHARPENTIER, F., *Relation de l'establissement de la compagnie française pour le commerce des Indes orientales.* Paris, 1666.

CHEVRIER, R., *Bougainville: voyage en Océanie.* Paris, 1946.

CLARK, T. B., *Omai, first Polynesian ambassador to England; the true story of his voyage there in 1774 with Captain Cook . . .* San Francisco, 1940.

CLAVEL, C., *Les Marquisiens*. Paris, 1885.

COLLINGRIDGE, G., *The discovery of Australia*. Sydney, 1895.

—— *Pacifika*. Sydney, n.d.

COOK, J., *A Voyage to the Pacific Ocean . . . performed under the direction of Captains Cook, Clerke and Gore in His Majesty's ships* Resolution *and* Discovery. 3 vols., London, 1784.

—— [See Beaglehole, J. C.]

COOPER, H. M., *French exploration in South Australia*. Adelaide, 1952.

CORNELL, C., *Questions relating to Nicolas Baudin's Australian expedition 1800–1804*. Adelaide, 1965.

CORNEY, B. G. (ed.), *The quest and occupation of Tahiti by the emissaries of Spain during the years 1772-6*. 3 vols., London, 1913–19.

—— (ed.), *The voyage of Captain Don Felipe Gonzalez . . . to Easter Island in 1770-1*. Cambridge, 1908.

COURTONNE [see Paulmier de Courtonne, J.].

CROZET, J. [see Rochon, A. M.].

CRUISE, R. A., *Journal of a ten months' residence in New Zealand*. London, 1823.

DAHLGREN, E. W., *Les Relations commerciales et maritimes entre la France et les côtes de l'océan Pacifique (commencement du XVIIIᵉ siècle)*. Paris, 1909.

DALRYMPLE, A., *An account of the discoveries made in the South Pacifick Ocean previous to 1764*. London, 1767.

DAMPIER, W., *A new voyage round the world*. London, 1697.

DANIELSSON, B., *Love in the South Seas*. London, 1956.

DAY, G., *Dumont d'Urville*. Paris, 1947.

DE BEER, G. R. (ed.), *The sciences were never at war*. London, 1960.

DELATTRE, M., *Rapport sur la recherche à faire de M. de la Pérouse, fait à l'Assemblée nationale*. Paris, 1791.

DELLON, G., *Relation d'un voyage aux Indes orientales*. 2 vols., Paris, 1685.

D'ENTRECASTEAUX, J. A. B. [see Rossel, E. P. E. de].

DIDEROT, D., *Supplément au voyage de Bougainville* (ed. G. Chinard). Paris, 1935.

DILLON, P., *Narrative and successful result of a voyage in the South Seas performed by order of the Government of British India, to ascertain the actual fate of La Pérouse's expedition*. 2 vols., London, 1829.

DIXON, G. [see Portlock, N.].

DORSENNE, J., *La Vie de Bougainville*. Paris, 1930.

DUHAUT-CILLY, A., *Voyage autour du monde principalement à la Californie et aux îles Sandwich . . .* 2 vols., Paris, 1834.

DUMONT D'URVILLE, J. S. C., *Mémoire sur les îles Loyalty*. Paris, 1829.

—— *Voyage au Pôle Sud et dans l'Océanie sur les corvettes* L'Astrolabe *et* La Zélée *exécuté par ordre du Roi pendant les années 1837–1840. Historique*. 10 vols., Paris, 1841-6.

—— *Voyage de découvertes autour du monde et à la recherche de la Pérouse . . . sur la corvette* L'Astrolabe *pendant les années 1826–1829*. 5 vols., Paris, 1832-4.

—— *Voyage pittoresque autour du monde*. 2 vols., Paris, 1834-5.

DUMONT D'URVILLE, J. S. C. [see Wright, O.].

DUPERREY, L. I., *Mémoire sur les opérations géographiques faites dans la campagne de la corvette de S. M. La Coquille*. Paris, n.d. [1827].

—— *Voyage autour du monde exécuté par ordre du Roi sur la corvette La Coquille pendant les années 1822...1825*. Paris, 1826.

DUPETIT-THOUARS, A. A., *Voyage autour du monde sur la frégate La Vénus pendant les années 1836–1839*. 4 vols., Paris, 1840–3.

DUPETIT-THOUARS, F., *Mémoire adressé par la famille Du Petit-Thouars aux actionnaires et à l'équipage du Diligent expédié . . . à la recherche de M. de la Peyrouse*. Paris, n.d.

DUPOUY, A., *Le Breton Yves de Kerguelen*. Paris, 1929.

EBERSTADT, E., *The northwest coast*. New York, 1941.

EMMANUEL, M., *La France et l'exploration polaire: de Verrazano à La Pérouse 1523–1788*. Paris, 1959.

FAIVRE, J. P., and others, *La Nouvelle-Calédonie: géographie et histoire*. Paris, 1955.

—— *Le Contre-amiral Hamelin et la marine française*. Paris, 1962.

—— *L'Expansion française dans le Pacifique de 1800 à 1842*. Paris, 1953.

FESCHE, C. F. P., *La Nouvelle Cythère (Tahiti), journal de navigation inédit* (ed. J. Dorsenne). Paris, 1929.

FEUILLET, L., *Journal des observations physiques, mathématiques et botaniques faites par l'ordre du Roy sur les côtes orientales de l'Amérique méridionale & dans les Indes occidentales depuis l'année 1707 jusques en 1712*. 3 vols., Paris, 1714–25.

FINDLAY, A. G., *A directory for the navigation of the South Pacific Ocean*. London, 1874.

FLEURIEU, A. DE, *La Nomenclature française en Australie et Tasmanie*. Paris, 1914.

FLEURIEU, C. P. C. DE, *Découvertes des François en 1768 et 1769 dans le sud-est de la Nouvelle-Guinée et reconnaissance postérieure des mêmes terres par des navigateurs anglois qui leur ont imposé de nouveaux noms*. Paris, 1790.

—— *Voyage autour du monde pendant les années 1790, 1791 et 1792 par Étienne Marchand*. 6 vols., Paris, 1798–1809.

FLEURIOT DE LANGLE, P., *La Tragique Expédition de Lapérouse et de Langle*. Paris, 1954.

FLINDERS, M., *A voyage to Terra Australis . . . in the ship* The Investigator. London, 1814.

FORSTER, J. G. A. (ed.), *Franska Capitainens och Riddarens Jean François de Survilles Upptäckts-Resa*. Nyköping, 1795.

FORSTER, J. R., *Observations made during a voyage round the world*. London, 1778.

—— *A voyage round the world . . .* [see Bougainville, L. A. de].

FREYCINET, L. C. D. DE, *Voyage de découvertes aux terres australes exécuté sur les corvettes Le Géographe, Le Naturaliste et la goélette La Casuarina . . . 1800–04*. 2 vols., Paris, 1815.

—— *Voyage autour du monde entrepris par ordre du Roi . . . exécuté sur les corvettes de S. M. L'Uranie et La Physicienne*. 5 vols., Paris, 1827–39.

—— [see Péron, F.].

FREYCINET, ROSE DE, *Journal du voyage autour du monde à bord de* L'Uranie (ed. C. Duplomb). Paris, 1927.

FRÉZIER, A. F., *A voyage to the South Sea and along the coasts of Chile and Peru in the years 1712, 1713 and 1714.* London, 1717.

FROGER, F., *Relation d'un voyage fait en 1695 . . . par une escadre de vaisseaux du Roy, commandée par M. de Gennes.* Paris, 1698.

FROMENT-GUIEYSSE, G., *La Pérouse.* Paris, 1947.

GAFFAREL, P., *La Politique coloniale en France de 1789 à 1830.* Paris, 1908.

GAZEL, A., *French navigators and the early history of New Zealand.* Wellington, 1946.

GOEBELS, J., *The struggle for the Falkland Islands.* New Haven, 1927.

GOSSE, P., *The pirates' Who's Who.* London, 1924.

Great Britain, Hydrographic Office. *Pacific islands pilot.* 3 vols., London, 1946.

GROOTE, P. DE, *Nouvelle-France: colonie libre de Port-Breton.* Paris, 1880.

HALDANE, C. F., *Tempest over Tahiti.* London, 1963.

HAPDÉ, A., *Expédition et naufrage de Lapérouse: recueil historique.* Paris, 1829.

HARLOW, V. T., *The founding of the second British Empire 1763–1793.* 2 vols. London, 1952–64.

HENRY, TEUIRA, *Ancient Tahiti.* Honolulu, 1928.

HEYERDAHL, T., *American Indians in the Pacific.* London, 1952.

HOEFER, DR. (ed.), *Nouvelle Biographie générale.* 46 vols., Paris, 1853–66.

HOWARD, J. E., *Letters and documents of Napoleon I.* London, 1961.

HULOT, E. G. T., *D'Entrecasteaux 1737–1793.* Paris, 1894.

HYDE, H. M., *John Law.* London, 1948.

JORE, L. A. N. H., *Essai de bibliographie du Pacifique.* Paris, 1931.

—— *L'Océan Pacifique 1815–1848.* 2 vols., Paris, 1959.

JULIEN, C. A., *La Politique coloniale de la France sous la Révolution, le Premier Empire et la Restauration.* Paris, 1949.

JURIEN DE LA GRAVIÈRE, J. P. E., *L'Amiral Baudin.* Paris, 1888.

—— *Les Marins du XVe et XVIe siècle.* Paris, 1879.

—— *Souvenirs d'un amiral.* 2 vols., Paris, 1860.

KELLY, L. G., *Marion Dufresne at the Bay of Islands.* Wellington, 1951.

KERALLAIN, R. DE, *La Jeunesse de Bougainville.* Paris, 1896.

KERGARIOU, A. DE, *La Mission de* La Cybèle *en Extrême-Orient (1817–1818)* (ed. P. de Joinville). Paris, 1914.

KERGUELEN-TRÉMAREC, Y. J. DE, *Histoire des événements des guerres maritimes entre la France et l'Angleterre depuis 1778 jusqu'en 1796.* 3 vols., Paris, 1796.

—— *Relation de deux voyages dans les mers australes et des Indes faits en 1771–1774.* Paris, 1782.

KEYS, L. G., *The life and times of Bishop Pompallier.* Christchurch, 1957.

KIMBLE, G. H. T., *Geography in the Middle Ages.* London, 1938.

KOSKINEN, A. A., *Missionary influence as a political factor in the Pacific islands.* Helsinki, 1953.

KOTZEBUE, O. VON, *A new voyage round the world during the years 1823–1826.* 2 vols., London, 1830.

KUYKENDHALL, R. S., *The Hawaiian kingdom (1778–1854).* Honolulu, 1948.

LA BILLARDIÈRE, J. J. H. DE, *Relation du voyage à la recherche de la Pérouse.* 2 vols., Paris, 1799.

LA BORDE, J. B. DE, *Histoire abrégée de la mer du Sud.* 3 vols., Paris, 1791.

—— *Mémoire sur la prétendue découverte faite en 1788 par des Anglois . . . suivi d'un projet de souscription pour un armement destiné à la recherche de M. de la Pérouse.* Paris, 1790.

LACROIX, L., *Les Derniers Baleiniers français.* Nantes, 1947.

LAMBERT, S. M., *A doctor in paradise.* London, 1942.

LA PÉROUSE, J. F. G. DE [see Milet-Mureau, N. L. A.].

LAPEYROUSE-BONFILS, C. DE, *Histoire de la marine française.* Paris, 1845.

LAPLACE, C. P. T., *Voyage autour du monde par les mers de l'Inde et de la Chine exécuté sur la corvette de l'État La Favorite.* 5 vols., Paris, 1833–9.

—— *Campagne de circumnavigation de la frégate* L'Artémise *pendant les années 1837–1840.* 6 vols., Paris, 1841–54.

LA RONCIÈRE, C. G. M. B. DE, *Bougainville,* Paris, 1942.

—— *Histoire de la marine française.* 5 vols., Paris, 1899.

LA SALLE, J. A. A. DE [see Vaillant].

LE DRU, A. P., *Voyage aux îles Ténérife, la Trinité, Saint-Thomas, Sainte-Croix et Porto Rico . . . sous la direction du capitaine Baudin.* 2 vols., Paris, 1810.

LEFRANC, G., *Bougainville et ses compagnons.* Paris, 1929.

LE GENTIL DE LA GALAISIÈRE, G. J. H. J. B., *Voyage dans les mers de l'Inde, fait par ordre du Roy, à l'occasion du passage de Vénus sur le disque du soleil le 6 juin 1761 et le 3 du même mois 1769.* 2 vols., Paris, 1779–81.

LESSEPS, J. B. B. DE, *Journal historique du voyage de M. de Lesseps . . . depuis . . . Kamchatka jusqu'à son arrivée en France.* Paris, 1790.

LESSON, P., *Voyage autour du monde entrepris par ordre du gouvernement sur la corvette* La Coquille. 2 vols., Paris, 1838–9.

—— *Voyage médical autour du monde.* Paris, 1829.

LESSON, P. A., *Voyage aux îles Mangareva . . . publié par M. R. P. Lesson.* Rochefort, 1845.

LESSON, R. P., *Notice historique sur l'amiral Dumont d'Urville.* Rochefort, 1846.

LEWIS, W. H., *The splendid century, some aspects of French life in the reign of Louis XIV.* London, 1953.

LUSSAN, R. DE, *Journal du voyage fait à la Mer du Sud avec les flibustiers de l'Amérique en 1684 et années suivantes.* Paris, 1689.

McNAB, R., *From Tasman to Marsden.* Dunedin, 1914.

—— (ed.), *Historical records of New Zealand.* 2 vols., Wellington, 1908–14.

MAHAN, A. T., *The influence of sea power upon the French Revolution and Empire 1793–1812.* 2 vols., Boston, 1892.

MAINE, R., *La Pérouse.* Paris, 1946.

MAJOR, R. H. (ed.), *Early voyages to Terra Australis.* London, 1859.

MARCEAU, A., *Les Missions catholiques dans l'Océanie*. Lyons, 1845.

MARCEL, G., *La Pérouse*. Paris, 1881.

—— *Une expédition oubliée à la recherche de la Pérouse*. Paris, 1888.

MARCHAND, E., *Découvertes des îles de la Révolution*. Marseilles, 1792.

—— [see Fleurieu, C. P. C. de].

MARGRY, P., *Les Navigations françaises et la révolution maritime du XIVᵉ au XVIᵉ siècle*. Paris, 1867.

MARGUET, F., *Histoire générale de la navigation du XVᵉ au XXᵉ siècle*. Paris, 1931.

MARTIN-ALLANIC, J. E., *Bougainville, navigateur et les découvertes de son temps*. Paris, 1964.

MAUPERTUIS, P. L. DE, *Lettre sur le progrès des sciences*. Paris, 1752.

MILET-MUREAU, N. L. A. (ed.), *Voyage autour du monde . . . de la Pérouse*. 3 vols., Paris, 1797.

MOERENHOUT, J. A., *Voyage aux îles du Grand Océan*. 2 vols., Paris, 1837.

MONTESSUS, F. B. DE, *Martyrologe et biographie de Commerson*. Chalon-sur-Saône, 1889.

MORRELL, W. P., *Britain in the Pacific islands*. Oxford, 1960.

OEXMELIN, A., *Histoire des aventuriers qui se sont signalés dans les Indes*. 2 vols., Paris, 1688.

O'REILLY, P., and TEISSIER, R., *Tahitiens, répertoire bio-bibliographique de la Polynésie française*. Paris, 1962.

Pacific Islands Year Book. 8th edition. Sydney, 1959.

PAGÈS, P. M. F. DE, *Voyages autour du monde et vers les deux pôles, par terre et par mer pendant les années 1767–1776*. 2 vols., Paris, 1782.

PAULMIER DE COURTONNE, J., *Mémoires touchant l'établissement d'une mission chrestienne dans le troisième monde, autrement appelé la terre australe, méridionale, antarctique et inconnuë*. Paris, 1663.

PERNETTY, A. J., *Histoire d'un voyage aux îles Malouines fait en 1763 et 1764*. 2 vols., Paris, 1770.

PÉRON, CAPT., *Mémoires du capitaine Péron sur ses voyages* (ed. Brissot-Thivars). 2 vols., Paris, 1824.

PÉRON, F., *Voyage de découvertes aux terres australes . . . sur Le Géographe, Le Naturaliste et La Casuarina pendant les années 1800–1804*. Paris, 1807.

PÉRON, F., and FREYCINET, L. C. D. DE, *Voyage de découvertes aux terres australes exécuté par ordre de Sa Majesté l'Empereur et Roi . . . pendant les années 1800–1804* [completed by Freycinet]. 2 vols., Paris, 1807–16.

PERSON, Y., *La Nouvelle-Calédonie et l'Europe 1774–1854*. Paris, 1954.

PIGAFETTA, A., *Magellan's voyage around the world* (transl. and ed. J. A. Robertson). 2 vols., Cleveland, 1906.

PINGRÉ, A. G., *Mémoire sur le choix et l'état des lieux où le passage de Vénus du 3 juin 1769 pourra être observé*. Paris, 1767.

—— *Mémoire sur les découvertes faites dans la Mer du Sud avant les derniers voyages des Anglois et des François autour du monde*. Paris, 1778.

PORTLOCK, N., *A voyage round the world, but more particularly to the north-west coast of America, performed in 1785–1788 by Captains Portlock and Dixon.* London, 1789.

Prévost, A. F., *Histoire générale des voyages.* 19 vols., Paris, 1746–70.

Price, A. G., *The western invasions of the Pacific and its continents.* Oxford, 1963.

Priestley, H. I., *France overseas through the old regime: a study of European expansion.* New York, 1939.

Rainaud, A., *Le Continent austral.* Paris, 1893.

Raulin, G. de, *Dupetit-Thouars.* Paris, 1943.

—— *Rose de Freycinet, exploratrice maritime.* Paris, 1944.

Renaudet, A., *Études sur l'histoire intérieure de la France (Les finances).* Paris, 1946.

Robertson, J. A. [see Pigafetta, A.].

Robertson, G., *The discovery of Tahiti: a journal of the second voyage of* H.M.S. Dolphin (ed. H. Carrington). London, 1948.

Rochon, A. M. (ed.), [Crozet's] *Nouveau Voyage à la Mer du Sud commencé sous les ordres de M. Marion . . . On a joint à ce voyage un extrait de celui de M. de Surville.* Paris, 1783.

—— *Voyages à Madagascar et aux Indes orientales.* Paris, 1791.

—— *Voyages aux Indes orientales et en Afrique pour l'observation des longitudes en mer.* Paris, 1807.

Rollin, L., *Les Îles Marquises.* Paris, 1929.

Roquefeuil, C. de, *A voyage round the world between the years 1816–1819.* London, 1823 (French edition, Paris, 1823).

Rossel, E. P. E. de (ed.), *Voyage de Dentrecasteaux envoyé à la recherche de La Pérouse.* 2 vols., Paris, 1808.

Roth, H. L. (transl.), *Crozet's voyage to Tasmania, New Zealand, the Ladrones islands and the Philippines 1771–72.* London, 1891.

Roy, B., *Dans le sillage de la Pérouse.* Paris, 1946.

Russier, H., *Le Partage de l'Océanie.* Paris, 1905.

Saint-Yves, G., *Le Voyage autour du monde du capitaine Étienne Marchand.* Paris, 1897.

Schurz, W. L., *The Manila galleon.* New York, 1939.

Scott, E., *Australian discovery.* London, 1929.

—— *Lapérouse.* Sydney, 1912.

—— *Terre Napoléon, a history of French exploration and projects in Australia.* London, 1910.

Seixas y Lovera, F. de, *Théâtre naval hydrographique.* Paris, 1704.

Sharp, C. A., *The discovery of Australia.* Oxford, 1963.

—— *The discovery of the Pacific islands.* Oxford, 1960.

Skelton, R. A., *Explorers' maps.* London, 1958.

Smith, B., *European vision and the south Pacific 1768–1850.* Oxford, 1960.

Société de Géographie, *Bulletin,* 'Édition du centenaire de la mort de Lapérouse'. Paris, 1888.

Sonnerat, P., *An account of a voyage to the Spice islands and New Guinea.* London, 1781 (French edition, Paris, 1776).

SOTHEBY & Co., *Catalogue of the highly-important papers of Louis de Bougainville F.R.S. (1729–1811).* London, 1957.

SOULIER-VALBERT, F., *L'Expansion française dans le Pacifique-Sud: Tahiti et dépendances 1768–1908.* Paris, 1908.

SOUTH PACIFIC COMMISSION, *Venereal diseases: technical information circular No. 2.* Noumea, 1952.

SPARKS, J. P. (ed.), *Memoirs of the life and travels of John Ledyard.* London, 1828.

STEVENS, J. K., *American expansion in Hawaii.* Harrisburg, 1955.

Tasmanian Almanack. Hobart, 1827.

TAYLOR, A. C., *Le Président de Brosses et l'Australie.* Paris, 1938.

THIÉRY, M., *Bougainville, soldier and sailor.* London, 1932.

TRIEBEL, L. A., and BATT, J. C., *The French exploration of Australia, with special reference to Tasmania.* Hobart, 1957.

VANCOUVER, G., *A voyage of discovery to the north Pacific ocean and round the world.* 3 vols., London, 1798.

VAILLANT, A. N., *Voyage autour du monde exécuté pendant les années 1836 et 1837 sur la corvette La Bonite. Relation du voyage par A. de la Salle.* 3 vols., Paris, 1845–52.

VERGNIOL, C., *Dumont d'Urville.* Paris, 1931.

WAFER, L., *A new voyage and description of the Isthmus of America* (ed. L. E. Elliott-Joyce). Oxford, 1934.

WALKER, J. B., *Early Tasmania.* Hobart, 1902.

WARD, J., *British policy in the south Pacific.* Sydney, 1948.

WEBER, H., *La Compagnie française des Indes 1605–1875.* Paris, 1904.

WHIPPLE, A., *Yankee whalers in the south seas.* New York, 1954.

WOOD, G. A., *The discovery of Australia.* London, 1922.

WOOLF, H., *The transits of Venus: a study of eighteenth century science.* Princeton, 1959.

WRIGHT, O. (transl.), *New Zealand 1826–1827* [extracts from Dumont d'Urville's *Voyage de découvertes*]. Wellington, 1950.

—— *The voyage of the* Astrolabe, *1840* [extracts from Dumont d'Urville's *Voyage au Pôle Sud*]. Wellington, 1955.

WROTH, L. C., *The early cartography of the Pacific.* New York, 1944.

YZENDOORN, R., *History of the Catholic Mission in the Hawaiian islands.* Honolulu, 1927.

(c) ARTICLES AND CONTRIBUTIONS

Abbreviations

B.S.E.O.	*Bulletin de la Société des études océaniennes*
M.S.H.A.B.	*Mémoires de la Société d'histoire et d'archéologie de Bretagne*
J.P.S.	*Journal of the Polynesian Society*
J.S.O.	*Journal de la Société des Océanistes*
R.H.C.F.	*Revue d'histoire des colonies françaises*

BALDWIN, B. S., 'Flinders and the French', *Royal geographical society of Australasia proceedings*, vol. 65, 1964, pp. 53–67.

BLUE, G. W., 'The policy of France towards the Hawaiian islands'. *Pacific Historical Review*, Mar. 1933, pp. 61–3.

—— 'The project for a French settlement in the Hawaiian islands'. *Pacific Historical Review*, vol. ii, pp. 94–7.

BUFFET, H. F., 'L'explorateur malouin Marion du Fresne', *M.S.H.A.B.* Rennes, 1959.

—— 'L'explorateur port-louisien Julien Crozet, éponyme des îles Crozet dans la mer des Indes 1728–1780', *M.S.H.A.B.* Rennes, 1943.

—— 'Voyage à la découverte du port-louisien Surville', *M.S.H.A.B.* Rennes, 1950.

BUSSON, J. P. (ed.), 'Des Gambiers à Upolu avec Dumont d'Urville. Souvenirs d'un quartier-maître de *L'Astrolabe* 1838', *Revue historique de l'armée*, vol. 21, no. 3, 1965, pp. 49–61.

DAHLGREN, E. W., 'L'expédition de Martinez et la fin du commerce français dans la Mer du Sud', *R.H.C.F.*, 1913, pp. 257–332.

—— 'Voyages français à destination de la Mer du Sud avant Bougainville (1695–1749)', *Nouvelles Archives des missions scientifiques*, vol. xiv, 1907, pp. 423–568.

DE BEER, G. R., 'The relations between fellows of the Royal Society and French men of science when Britain and France were at war', *Notes and records of the Royal Society of London*, vol. 9, no. 2, 1952, pp. 244–99.

FAIVRE, J. P., 'La France découvre l'Australie: l'expédition du *Géographe* et du *Naturaliste* 1801–1803', *Australian Journal of French Studies*, vol. 2, no. 1, 1963, pp. 45–58.

—— 'Les idéologues de l'An VIII et le voyage de Nicolas Baudin en Australie 1800–1804', *Australian journal of French studies*, vol. 3, no. 1, 1966, pp. 3–15.

FORSYTH, J., 'Latouche-Tréville and his proposal to explore the south coast of New Holland', *The Mariner's Mirror*, vol. 45, no. 2, 1959, pp. 115–29.

GAUTIER, J. M., 'Apogée et déclin du mirage tahitien en Angleterre et en France (1766–1802)', *J.S.O.*, no. 6, Dec. 1951, pp. 270–3.

—— 'Tahiti dans la littérature française à la fin du XVIIIᵉ siècle: quelques ouvrages oubliés', *J.S.O.*, no. 3, 1947, pp. 43–56.

HAMY, E. T., 'James Cook et Latouche-Tréville', *Bulletin géographique, historique et descriptif*, 1904, pp. 206–22.

HERVÉ, R., 'Australia in French documents of the Renaissance', *Proceedings of the Royal Australian Historical Society*, vol. xli, 1955, pp. 23–55.

HORNELL, J., 'Sea trade in early times', *Antiquity*, Sept. 1941, pp. 223–56.

—— 'Was there pre-Columbian contact between the people of Oceania and America?' *J.P.S.*, vol. 54, pp. 167–91.

HOWAY, F. W., 'Authorship of the anonymous account of Cook's last voyage', *Washington Historical Quarterly*, 1921, pp. 51–8.

INGRAHAM, J., 'An account of a recent discovery of seven islands in the south Pacific ocean by Joseph Ingraham, citizen of Boston and commander of the brigantine *Hope* of 70 tons', *Collections of the Massachusetts Historical Society for the Year 1794*, pp. 20–4.

JACQUEMONT, S., 'Le mythe du Pacifique dans la littérature', in Rousseau, M., *L'Art océanien*. Paris, 1951.

JACQUIER, H., 'Jeanne Baret, la première femme autour du monde', *B.S.E.O.*, vol. 12, no. 141, 1962, pp. 150–6.

—— 'Le mirage et l'exotisme tahitiens dans la littérature', *B.S.E.O.*, vol. 7, 1944–5, pp. 3–7, 50–76, 91–114.

JORE, L., 'Le Capitaine irlandais Thomas Ebrill, sauveteur de la frégate française *L'Artémise*', *B.S.E.O.*, vol. 11, no. 135, 1961, pp. 261–80.

—— 'Le voyage du trois-mâts bordelais *La Comète* de Bordeaux à Honolulu (1826–1828)', *Revue maritime*, Sept. 1954, pp. 1183–96.

JUTEAU, R., 'Journal de bord du capitaine Étienne Marchand, commandant *Le Solide*', *B.S.E.O.*, vol. 11, no. 135, 1961, pp. 247–60.

KEYS, A. C., 'Zorai ou les insulaires de la Nouvelle-Zélande', *Journal of the Australasian Universities Language and Literature Ass.*, No. 9, Nov. 1958, pp. 36–47.

LA RONCIÈRE, C. G. M. B. DE, 'Le premier voyage français autour du monde', *Revue hebdomadaire*, Sept. 1907, pp. 22–36.

—— 'Les Antilles', in *Histoire des colonies françaises et de l'expansion de la France dans le monde* (eds. Hanoteaux and Martineau), vol. i, Paris, 1929.

—— 'Routier inédit d'un compagnon de Bougainville', *La Géographie*, vol. xxxv, no. 3, Mar. 1921, pp. 217–50.

LEPAUTE D'AGELET, 'Lettre à Condorcet', *La Géographie*, vol. lxix, 1939, pp. 112–14.

LESORT, A., 'Les transactions d'un négociant malouin avec l'Amérique espagnole (1719–1721)', *R.H.C.F.*, 1921, pp. 239–68.

LEVOT, P. [Biographical articles in *Nouvelle Biographie générale*, q.v. under Hoefer in section 'Printed Works'].

MARCHAND, L. R., 'The French discovery and settlement of New Zealand 1769–1840. A bibliographical essay on naval records in Paris', *Historical Studies*, Melbourne, vol. 10, May 1963, pp. 511–18.

MARTIN, J. E., 'Essai sur Bougainville circumnavigateur: la genèse de sa carrière maritime', *La Géographie*, Nov.–Dec. 1929, pp. 321–45.

MILLIGAN, R. R. D., 'Ranginui, captive chief of Doubtless Bay 1769', *J.P.S.*, vol. 67, Sept. 1958, pp. 181–203.

MILLIGAN, R. R. D., and DUNMORE, J., 'The Misnaming of North Cape', *New Zealand Geographer*, Oct. 1963, pp. 178–81.

NEWBURY, C. W., 'La conception du Pacifique au XVIIIe siècle', in *Le Monde non-chrétien*, vol. 27, July–Sept. 1953, pp. 305–12.

NORRIS, J. M., 'The policy of the British cabinet in the Nootka crisis', *English Historical Review*, vol. lxx, 1955, pp. 562–80.

O'REILLY, P., 'Le Chanoine Paulmier de Courtonne et son projet d'évangélisation des terres australes', *Revue d'histoire des missions*, Sept. 1932, pp. 322–39.

ROUSSIER, P., 'Un projet de colonie française dans le Pacifique à la fin du XVIIIe siècle', *Revue du Pacifique*, Dec. 1927, pp. 726–33.

SCOTT, E., 'Baudin's voyage of exploration to Australia', *English Historical Review*, Apr. 1913, pp. 341–46.

SELKIRK, H., 'La Pérouse and the French monuments at Botany Bay', *Royal Australian Historical Society Journal*, vol. iv, 1918, pp. 329–61.

SOCIÉTÉ FRANÇAISE D'HISTOIRE DE MÉDECINE, 'Le mal vénérien à Tahiti est-il français ou anglais?', *J.S.O.*, no. 1, Dec. 1945, p. 137.

SPATE, O. H. K., 'Terra Australis. Cognita?', *Historical Studies*, Melbourne, vol. 8, no. 29, Nov. 1957, pp. 1–19.

—— 'De Lozier Bouvet and mercantilist expansion in the Pacific in 1740', in *Merchants and scholars: essays in the history of exploration and trade*. Minneapolis, 1965, pp. 221–37.

TAILLEMITE, E., 'Le lieutenant Caro et sa relation inédite du séjour de Bougainville à Tahiti', *J.S.O.*, vol. xviii, Dec. 1962, pp. 11–19.

TAYLOR, N. M., 'French navigators in the Pacific', in *The Pacific: ocean of islands* (ed. C. L. Barrett). Melbourne, 1950.

TRIEBEL, L. A., 'Péron in Tasmania', *Australian Quarterly*, vol. xxi, Mar. 1949, pp. 100–7.

INDEX

PRINTED IN GREAT BRITAIN
AT THE UNIVERSITY PRESS, OXFORD
BY VIVIAN RIDLER
PRINTER TO THE UNIVERSITY